The Mid-Atlantic's Best Bed & Breakfasts

4th Edition

Delightful Places to Stay
Wonderful Things to Do
When You Get There

Fodor's Travel Publications, Inc.
New York • Toronto • London • Sydney • Auckland
www.fodors.com/

Copyright © 1998 by Fodor's Travel Publications, Inc.

Fourth Edition

ISBN 0–679–03434–X

The Mid-Atlantic's Best Bed & Breakfasts

Editor: Paula Consolo
Editorial Production: Janet Foley, Melissa Klurman
Maps: David Lindroth, *cartographer*; Bob Blake, *map editor*
Illustrator: Alida Beck
Design: Fabrizio La Rocca, *creative director*; Guido Caroti, *cover design*
Production/Manufacturing: Mike Costa
Cover Photograph: Francis Hammond

Special Sales

Contributors

Therese Cox, *a West Virginia native who updated the chapter on her state, writes about health for the* Charleston Daily Mail. *She also produces a monthly feature on traveling about the state.*

Alan Hines, *who wrote the chapter on Pennsylvania, is a novelist and screenwriter living in Bucks County, Pennsylvania.*

Bill Kent, *a novelist in Philadelphia, wrote the chapter on New Jersey. He is also the author of* Fodor's Vacations on the Jersey Shore.

Andrea Lehman *traveled from the mountains to the shore of her home state while working on this revision of the New Jersey chapter. Now living in Trenton, she edits many Fodor's travel guides.*

Sandra Manning, *a freelance writer living in Trenton, New Jersey, explored numerous country roads and small towns while updating sections of the New Jersey chapter.*

Rebecca Miller, *a former staff editor at Fodor's, began her love affair with the Empire State when she left her Manhattan office to explore the tall peaks and verdant forests of the Adirondacks. To revise the New York chapter, she investigated B&Bs from the mountains of the north to the sandy beaches of Long Island and the shores of the Hudson River.*

Mike Radigan, *updater of the Virginia chapter, is a native of the state and a seasoned hotel evaluator. He rated thousands of lodgings and restaurants for AAA for nearly a decade. Now president of a hospitality consulting firm, he recently purchased an Italianate Victorian in historic Petersburg, Virginia. He has no plans to convert it to an inn, however.*

Deborah K. Shepherd, *author of the New York chapter, is a social worker and freelance journalist.*

Susan Spano, *who lives in New York City's West Village, contributed the original chapters on Delaware, Maryland, Virginia, and West Virginia. She has written about travel for the* New York Times, New Woman, *and* British Heritage.

Janet Bukovinsky Teacher, updater of the Pennsylvania chapter, was a senior writer at *Philadelphia* magazine for many years before she decided to begin a freelance career.

Bruce Walker, *who updated the chapters on Maryland and Delaware, also contributes to several other Fodor's publications, including* Fodor's Washington, D.C. *He works for the* Washington Post's *weekly entertainment section,* Weekends.

Contents

Foreword

While every care has been taken to ensure the accuracy of the information in this guide, the passage of time will always bring change and, consequently, Fodor's cannot accept responsibility for errors that may occur.

All prices and listings are based on information supplied to us at press time. Details may change, however, and the prudent traveler will avoid inconvenience by calling ahead.

Fodor's wants to hear about your travel experiences, both pleasant and unpleasant. When an inn or B&B fails to live up to its billing, let us know and we will investigate the complaint and revise our entries where the facts warrant it.

Send your letters to the Mid-Atlantic B&B editor of Fodor's Travel Publications, 201 East 50th Street, New York, NY 10022, or e-mail us at editors@fodors.com (specifying the name of the book on the subject line).

Introduction

You'll find bed-and-breakfasts in big houses with turrets and little houses with decks, in mansions by the water and cabins in the forest, not to mention structures of many sizes and shapes in between. B&Bs are run by people who were once lawyers and writers, homemakers and artists, nurses and architects, singers and businesspeople. Some B&Bs are just a room or two in a hospitable local's home; others are more like small inns. So there's an element of serendipity to every B&B stay.

But while that's part of the pleasure of the experience, it's also an excellent reason to plan your travels with a good B&B guide. The one you hold in your hands serves the purpose neatly.

To create it, we've handpicked a team of professional writers who are also confirmed B&B lovers: people who adore the many manifestations of the Victorian era; who go wild over wicker and brass beds, four-posters and fireplaces; and who know a well-run operation when they see it and are only too eager to communicate their knowledge to you. We've instructed them to inspect the premises and check out every corner of the premier inns and B&Bs in the areas they cover, and to report critically on only the best in every price range.

They've returned from their travels with comprehensive reports on the pleasure of B&B travel, which may well become your pleasure as you read their reports in the pages that follow. These are establishments that promise a unique experience, a distinctive sense of time and place. All are destinations in themselves, not just spots to rest your head at night, but an integral part of a weekend escape. You'll learn what's good, what's bad, and what could be better; what our writers liked and what you might not like.

At the same time, Fodor's reviewers tell you what's up in the area and what you should and shouldn't miss—everything from historic sites and parks to antiques shops, boutiques, and the area's niftiest restaurants and nightspots. We also include names and addresses of B&B reservation services, just in case you're inspired to seek out additional properties on your own. Reviews are organized by state, and, within each state, by region.

In the italicized service information that ends every review, a second address in parentheses is a mailing address. A double room is for two people, regardless of the size or type of its beds. Unless otherwise noted, rooms don't have phones or TVs. Note that even the most stunning homes, farmhouses and mansions alike, may not provide a private bathroom for each individual. Rates are for two, excluding tax, in the high season and include breakfast unless otherwise noted; ask about special packages and midweek or off-season discounts.

What we call a restaurant serves meals other than breakfast and is usually open to the general public. At inns listed as operating on the Modified American Plan (MAP), rates include two meals, generally breakfast and dinner.

The following credit card abbreviations are used throughout this guide: AE, American Express; D, Discover; DC, Diners Club; MC, MasterCard; V, Visa.

Where applicable, we note seasonal and other restrictions. Although we abhor discrimination, we have conveyed information about innkeepers' restrictive practices so that you will be aware of the prevailing attitudes. Such discriminatory practices are most often applied to parents who are traveling with small children and who may not, in any case, feel comfortable having their offspring toddle amid breakable bric-a-brac and near precipitous stairways.

When traveling the B&B way, always call ahead; and if you have mobility problems or are traveling with children, if you prefer a private bath or a certain type of bed, or if you have specific dietary needs or any other concerns, discuss them with the innkeeper. At the same time, if you're traveling to an inn because of a specific feature, make sure that it will be available when you get there and not closed for renovation. The same goes if you're making a detour to take advantage of specific sights or attractions.

It's a sad commentary on other B&B guides today that we feel obliged to tell you that our writers did, in fact, visit every property in person, and that it is they, not the innkeepers, who wrote the reviews. No one paid a fee or promised to sell or promote the book in order to be included in it. (In fact, one of the most challenging parts of the work of a Fodor's writer is to persuade innkeepers and B&B owners that he or she wants nothing more than a tour of the premises and the answers to a few questions!) Fodor's has no stake in anything but the truth. If a room is dark, with peeling wallpaper, we don't call it quaint or atmospheric—we call it run-down, and then steer you to a more appealing section of the property.

So trust us, the way you'd trust a knowledgeable, well-traveled friend. Let us hear from you about your travels, whether you found that the B&Bs you visited surpassed their descriptions or the other way around. And have a wonderful trip!

Karen Cure
Editorial Director

CANADA

Georgian Bay

Lake Ontario

Lake Erie

St. Lawrence River

VERMONT

Lake Champlain

Lake George

ADIRONDACK MOUNTAINS

NEW YORK

CATSKILL MOUNTAINS

Hudson River

MASSACHUSETTS

CONNECTICUT

LONG ISLAND

Long Island Sound

Rutland

Saratoga Springs

Utica

Syracuse

Rochester

Niagara Falls

Buffalo

Jamestown

Warren

Bath

Binghamton

Williamsport

Scranton

Stroudsburg

Paterson

New York

Albany

Poughkeepsie

Northampton

Springfield

Hartford

Waterbury

Worcester

Bridgeport

Montauk

Southampton

Youngstown

90

91

91

87

88

90

80

80

80

x

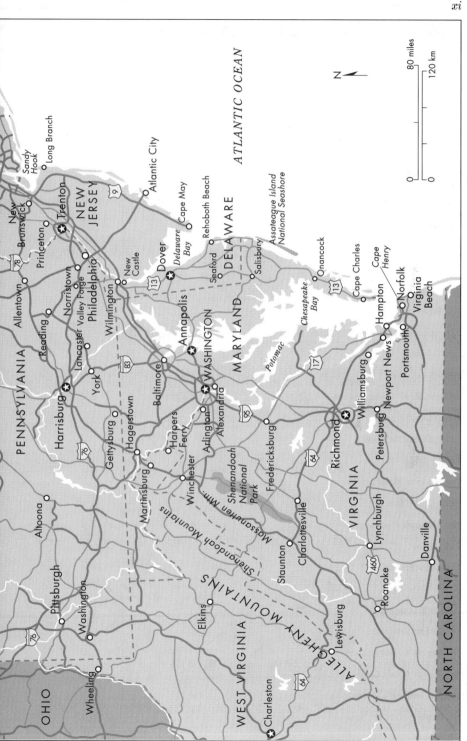

Special Features at a Glance

Name of Property	Accessible to Guests with Disabilities	On the Water	Good Value	Car Not Necessary	Full Meal Service	Historic Building	Romantic Hideaway
DELAWARE							
The Boulevard Bed & Breakfast			✓	✓			
Cantwell House			✓			✓	
Eli's Country Inn	✓		✓		✓		
The Inn at Canal Square	✓		✓				✓
The New Devon Inn	✓						✓
The Pleasant Inn							
Spring Garden Bed & Breakfast Inn			✓			✓	✓
The Towers						✓	✓
Wild Swan Inn				✓		✓	✓
William Penn Guest House			✓			✓	
MARYLAND							
The Admiral Fell Inn	✓	✓		✓	✓	✓	✓
Ashby 1663		✓				✓	✓
The Atlantic Hotel	✓				✓	✓	✓
Back Creek Inn	✓	✓					✓
The Bishop's House			✓	✓		✓	✓
Brampton	✓					✓	✓
The Catoctin Inn	✓				✓	✓	✓
Chanceford Hall						✓	✓
Gibson's Lodgings	✓					✓	
The Inn at Antietam							✓
The Inn at Buckeystown					✓	✓	✓
The Inn at Perry Cabin	✓	✓			✓	✓	✓
John S. McDaniel House			✓			✓	✓
Mr. Mole				✓		✓	✓

Luxurious	Pets Allowed	No Smoking Indoors	Good Place for Families	Near Arts Festivals	Beach Nearby	Cross-Country Ski Trail	Golf Nearby	Fitness Facilities	Good Biking Terrain	Skiing	Horseback Riding	Tennis	Swimming on Premises	Conference Facilities
		✓		✓			✓					✓		
		✓	✓						✓			✓		
	✓	✓	✓	✓	✓				✓		✓	✓		✓
✓				✓	✓		✓		✓		✓	✓		✓
✓				✓	✓		✓		✓					✓
		✓		✓	✓		✓		✓		✓	✓		
		✓							✓					
		✓			✓				✓				✓	
		✓		✓	✓		✓		✓			✓	✓	
									✓					
✓														✓
✓		✓					✓	✓	✓			✓	✓	✓
		✓		✓	✓		✓		✓		✓	✓		✓
		✓		✓			✓		✓			✓		✓
✓		✓	✓	✓			✓		✓			✓		
✓		✓					✓		✓		✓			
✓		✓	✓	✓			✓	✓	✓		✓	✓		✓
✓		✓					✓		✓			✓	✓	
		✓		✓	✓		✓		✓			✓		✓
✓		✓	✓	✓		✓	✓		✓					
		✓		✓			✓		✓					✓
✓							✓	✓	✓			✓	✓	✓
		✓		✓			✓		✓			✓		
✓		✓		✓			✓		✓					

Special Features at a Glance

Name of Property	Accessible to Guests with Disabilities	On the Water	Good Value	Car Not Necessary	Full Meal Service	Historic Building	Romantic Hideaway
The National Pike						✓	
The Robert Morris Inn		✓			✓	✓	✓
St. Michael's Manor		✓	✓			✓	✓
Spring Bank						✓	
The Tavern House		✓	✓			✓	✓
Tyler-Spite House			✓	✓		✓	✓
Wades Point Inn	✓		✓			✓	✓
The White Swan Tavern	✓					✓	✓
Widow's Walk Inn						✓	
The William Page Inn							
NEW JERSEY							
The Abbey			✓			✓	✓
The Albert Stevens Inn			✓			✓	✓
Amber Street Inn						✓	✓
Ashling Cottage			✓	✓		✓	✓
BarnaGate Bed & Breakfast			✓	✓		✓	
Barnard-Good House				✓		✓	✓
The Bayberry Barque						✓	✓
The Cabbage Rose Inn						✓	✓
Candlelight Inn						✓	✓
Captain Mey's Inn				✓		✓	✓
Carroll Villa			✓	✓	✓	✓	
Cashelmara		✓		✓		✓	
The Chateau	✓			✓		✓	
Chestnut Hill on the Delaware		✓		✓		✓	✓
Chimney Hill Bed and Breakfast						✓	✓

Luxurious	Pets Allowed	No Smoking Indoors	Good Place for Families	Near Arts Festivals	Beach Nearby	Cross-Country Ski Trail	Golf Nearby	Fitness Facilities	Good Biking Terrain	Skiing	Horseback Riding	Tennis	Swimming on Premises	Conference Facilities
		✓		✓			✓		✓			✓		
✓		✓			✓		✓		✓			✓		✓
		✓	✓		✓				✓			✓	✓	
		✓		✓			✓		✓			✓		
									✓			✓		
✓		✓		✓			✓		✓	✓	✓	✓	✓	✓
		✓		✓	✓		✓		✓			✓		
✓		✓		✓			✓		✓	✓	✓	✓		
		✓		✓			✓		✓			✓		
✓		✓		✓			✓		✓			✓		
		✓		✓	✓		✓		✓					✓
		✓		✓	✓		✓		✓					
		✓		✓	✓				✓					
		✓		✓	✓		✓		✓					✓
		✓		✓	✓		✓		✓					
		✓		✓	✓		✓		✓					
		✓		✓			✓		✓					✓
		✓		✓	✓		✓		✓					
✓		✓		✓	✓		✓		✓					
		✓	✓	✓	✓		✓		✓					✓
		✓	✓	✓	✓		✓		✓					✓
			✓	✓	✓		✓		✓					✓
		✓		✓										✓
✓		✓		✓			✓							

Special Features at a Glance

Name of Property	Accessible to Guests with Disabilities	On the Water	Good Value	Car Not Necessary	Full Meal Service	Historic Building	Romantic Hideaway
Conover's Bay Head Inn				✓		✓	
The Green Gables Inn					✓	✓	✓
The Henry Ludlam Inn		✓	✓			✓	✓
Hollycroft				✓		✓	✓
Holly House			✓	✓		✓	
Holly Thorn House			✓				
Hunterdon House				✓		✓	✓
The Inn at Millrace Pond					✓	✓	✓
Inn at 22 Jackson				✓		✓	✓
Isaac Hilliard House						✓	
Jerica Hill						✓	✓
The John F. Craig House				✓		✓	✓
La Maison				✓		✓	✓
The Mainstay Inn	✓			✓		✓	✓
The Manor House				✓		✓	✓
Normandy Inn				✓		✓	
Peacock Inn					✓	✓	
Pierrót by the Sea						✓	✓
The Queen Victoria	✓			✓		✓	
Sea Crest by the Sea				✓		✓	✓
The Seaflower			✓	✓		✓	
SeaScape Manor			✓	✓		✓	✓
The Southern Mansion	✓			✓		✓	
Springside			✓	✓		✓	
Stewart Inn						✓	✓
The Stockton Inn					✓	✓	

Luxurious	Pets Allowed	No Smoking Indoors	Good Place for Families	Near Arts Festivals	Beach Nearby	Cross-Country Ski Trail	Golf Nearby	Fitness Facilities	Good Biking Terrain	Skiing	Horseback Riding	Tennis	Swimming on Premises	Conference Facilities
		✓		✓	✓		✓		✓					✓
		✓		✓	✓		✓							
		✓		✓			✓		✓					
	✓			✓	✓		✓		✓					✓
		✓	✓	✓	✓		✓		✓					
				✓			✓						✓	✓
✓		✓		✓			✓							✓
✓	✓			✓			✓							✓
		✓		✓	✓		✓		✓					
		✓		✓					✓				✓	
		✓		✓			✓							✓
		✓		✓	✓		✓		✓					
	✓	✓		✓	✓		✓		✓					
✓		✓		✓	✓		✓		✓					
		✓		✓	✓		✓		✓					
✓		✓	✓	✓	✓		✓		✓					✓
	✓		✓	✓			✓		✓					✓
		✓		✓	✓				✓					✓
✓		✓	✓	✓	✓		✓		✓					✓
		✓		✓	✓		✓		✓					
		✓		✓	✓		✓		✓					✓
	✓	✓		✓	✓		✓		✓					
✓		✓		✓	✓		✓		✓					✓
		✓		✓	✓		✓		✓					
		✓		✓			✓						✓	
				✓			✓							✓

Special Features at a Glance

Name of Property	Accessible to Guests with Disabilities	On the Water	Good Value	Car Not Necessary	Full Meal Service	Historic Building	Romantic Hideaway
The Studio				✓		✓	
The Victorian Rose				✓		✓	✓
The Virginia Hotel				✓		✓	
The Whistling Swan Inn						✓	✓
The Wooden Duck							
The Wooden Rabbit				✓		✓	
NEW YORK							
The Adelphi Hotel						✓	✓
Albergo Allegria			✓				
Anthony Dobbins Stagecoach Inn						✓	
Aubergine						✓	✓
Audrey's Farmhouse			✓			✓	
The Bark Eater Inn						✓	
Beaverkill Valley Inn	✓	✓			✓		✓
The Bird and Bottle Inn					✓	✓	✓
Captain Schoonmaker's B & B		✓	✓			✓	✓
The Chester Inn			✓			✓	
Chestnut Tree Inn							✓
Country Road Lodge		✓	✓				
Crislip's Bed and Breakfast	✓		✓			✓	
Deer Mountain Inn					✓		✓
The Friends Lake Inn		✓	✓		✓		✓
Greenville Arms 1889 Inn			✓		✓	✓	
Hedges' Inn				✓	✓		✓
The Hill Guest House			✓				
Hilltop Cottage Bed and Breakfast			✓				

	Luxurious	Pets Allowed	No Smoking Indoors	Good Place for Families	Near Arts Festivals	Beach Nearby	Cross-Country Ski Trail	Golf Nearby	Fitness Facilities	Good Biking Terrain	Skiing	Horseback Riding	Tennis	Swimming on Premises	Conference Facilities
		✓		✓	✓	✓		✓		✓					
					✓	✓		✓		✓					
	✓			✓	✓	✓		✓		✓					✓
			✓		✓			✓							✓
			✓		✓		✓	✓						✓	
			✓	✓	✓	✓		✓		✓					
	✓				✓									✓	
				✓	✓		✓	✓			✓			✓	
							✓						✓		
		✓		✓				✓		✓				✓	
			✓	✓				✓		✓	✓	✓			
	✓		✓	✓		✓		✓	✓	✓			✓	✓	✓
	✓														
							✓			✓				✓	
				✓			✓					✓			
	✓		✓		✓			✓							
							✓				✓				
		✓	✓	✓											
	✓					✓									
			✓			✓	✓			✓	✓			✓	✓
			✓	✓	✓		✓	✓		✓	✓			✓	✓
						✓		✓		✓					
						✓		✓		✓					
			✓			✓									

Special Features at a Glance

Name of Property	Accessible to Guests with Disabilities	On the Water	Good Value	Car Not Necessary	Full Meal Service	Historic Building	Romantic Hideaway
The House on the Hill							
Hudson House		✓		✓	✓	✓	
The Huntting Inn				✓	✓	✓	
The Inn at Shaker Mill			✓		✓	✓	✓
The Interlaken Inn						✓	
J. Harper Poor Cottage			✓	✓		✓	✓
Lake Placid Lodge	✓				✓	✓	✓
The Lamplight Inn							✓
Le Chambord					✓	✓	
The Maidstone Arms				✓	✓	✓	✓
The Mansion						✓	✓
Mansion Hill Inn					✓	✓	
The Martindale Bed and Breakfast Inn			✓				✓
The Merrill Magee House	✓		✓		✓	✓	
Mill House Inn				✓		✓	
Mountainview Inn of Shandelee			✓		✓		
The Old Chatham Sheepherding Company Inn					✓	✓	✓
Old Drover's Inn					✓	✓	✓
Pig Hill Inn				✓			✓
Plumbush Inn					✓	✓	
Point Lookout Mountain Inn			✓		✓		
Ram's Head Inn		✓			✓		✓
The Redcoat's Return			✓		✓		✓
Sanford's Ridge Bed & Breakfast			✓			✓	
Saratoga Bed and Breakfast							
Saratoga Rose			✓		✓	✓	✓

Luxurious	Pets Allowed	No Smoking Indoors	Good Place for Families	Near Arts Festivals	Beach Nearby	Cross-Country Ski Trail	Golf Nearby	Fitness Facilities	Good Biking Terrain	Skiing	Horseback Riding	Tennis	Swimming on Premises	Conference Facilities
		✓				✓			✓					
			✓											
✓						✓	✓		✓			✓		✓
	✓		✓	✓		✓			✓	✓			✓	✓
		✓												
✓		✓			✓									
✓						✓	✓		✓	✓		✓	✓	✓
✓					✓	✓			✓	✓	✓			
								✓						✓
				✓	✓		✓		✓					
✓		✓		✓					✓				✓	
	✓													
		✓								✓	✓			
			✓										✓	✓
				✓	✓		✓		✓					
						✓			✓					
✓		✓				✓				✓				
✓	✓													
✓		✓							✓					
✓									✓					
	✓		✓	✓		✓			✓	✓				✓
✓	✓		✓		✓				✓			✓	✓	✓
			✓	✓		✓			✓	✓				
		✓					✓						✓	
			✓	✓		✓			✓					
						✓			✓					

Special Features at a Glance

Name of Property	Accessible to Guests with Disabilities	On the Water	Good Value	Car Not Necessary	Full Meal Service	Historic Building	Romantic Hideaway
The Sedgwick Inn			✓		✓	✓	✓
The 1770 House				✓	✓	✓	✓
Simmons Way Village Inn					✓	✓	✓
The Six Sisters							
The State House			✓			✓	✓
Troutbeck					✓	✓	✓
The Veranda House			✓			✓	
The Village Latch Inn						✓	✓
The Westchester House						✓	✓
PENNSYLVANIA							
Adamstown Inn			✓				
Ash Mill Farm			✓			✓	✓
The Bankhouse Bed and Breakfast			✓			✓	
Barley Sheaf Farm						✓	✓
The Bechtel Victorian Mansion Inn			✓			✓	
Bed and Breakfast at Walnut Hill			✓			✓	✓
Beechmont Inn			✓				✓
The Brafferton Inn			✓			✓	✓
Bridgeton House		✓				✓	✓
Brookview Manor			✓				
Bucksville House	✓					✓	
The Cameron Estate Inn	✓				✓	✓	✓
Century Inn	✓		✓		✓	✓	✓
Churchtown Inn			✓		✓	✓	✓
Clearview Farm Bed and Breakfast			✓			✓	✓
Cliff Park Inn					✓	✓	

Luxurious	Pets Allowed	No Smoking Indoors	Good Place for Families	Near Arts Festivals	Beach Nearby	Cross-Country Ski Trail	Golf Nearby	Fitness Facilities	Good Biking Terrain	Skiing	Horseback Riding	Tennis	Swimming on Premises	Conference Facilities
	✓		✓			✓			✓	✓				✓
✓				✓	✓		✓		✓					
✓							✓		✓					✓
		✓		✓		✓	✓		✓					
✓		✓												
✓						✓	✓		✓			✓	✓	✓
		✓												
✓	✓		✓		✓		✓		✓			✓	✓	✓
✓		✓		✓		✓	✓		✓					
				✓						✓				
		✓	✓	✓										
		✓	✓	✓										
✓		✓		✓									✓	✓
✓		✓												
				✓			✓		✓					
		✓	✓	✓					✓					
		✓	✓	✓		✓	✓		✓					
✓		✓		✓					✓					
		✓							✓					
		✓	✓	✓					✓		✓			
✓						✓	✓		✓	✓	✓	✓		✓
✓		✓					✓				✓	✓		
✓		✓	✓	✓		✓			✓					
		✓	✓			✓	✓		✓					
			✓			✓	✓		✓	✓				✓

Special Features at a Glance

Name of Property	Accessible to Guests with Disabilities	On the Water	Good Value	Car Not Necessary	Full Meal Service	Historic Building	Romantic Hideaway
The Doubleday Inn			✓				✓
Duling-Kurtz House & Country Inn			✓		✓	✓	
Emig Mansion						✓	✓
Evermay-on-the-Delaware		✓	✓		✓	✓	✓
Fairfield Inn					✓	✓	
Fairville Inn			✓			✓	✓
The French Manor					✓		✓
General Sutter Inn			✓		✓	✓	
Glasbern					✓		✓
Glendorn					✓		✓
Hamanassett						✓	✓
Highland Farms			✓			✓	✓
The Historic Farnsworth House Inn			✓		✓	✓	✓
The Inn at Fordhook Farm						✓	✓
The Inn at Meadowbrook			✓		✓	✓	✓
Inn at Phillips Mill		✓	✓		✓	✓	✓
The Inn at Starlight Lake		✓	✓		✓	✓	✓
The Inns at Doneckers	✓		✓		✓	✓	
The King's Cottage							
Lenape Springs Farm			✓				✓
Limestone Inn			✓			✓	
The Logan Inn		✓	✓	✓	✓	✓	
Longswamp Bed and Breakfast			✓			✓	✓
The Mansion Inn						✓	✓
Meadow Spring Farm			✓				
The Mercersburg Inn						✓	✓

Pennsylvania

Luxurious	Pets Allowed	No Smoking Indoors	Good Place for Families	Near Arts Festivals	Beach Nearby	Cross-Country Ski Trail	Golf Nearby	Fitness Facilities	Good Biking Terrain	Skiing	Horseback Riding	Tennis	Swimming on Premises	Conference Facilities
✓		✓		✓		✓			✓					
			✓	✓			✓		✓					✓
✓		✓												✓
✓				✓					✓					
			✓	✓		✓			✓					
✓		✓	✓	✓					✓					
✓						✓	✓		✓		✓			
			✓	✓										✓
✓			✓			✓			✓				✓	✓
✓						✓	✓	✓	✓	✓		✓	✓	✓
		✓												
			✓	✓					✓			✓	✓	
			✓	✓										
✓		✓		✓			✓		✓					✓
			✓	✓		✓			✓	✓	✓	✓	✓	
✓				✓		✓			✓					
			✓	✓	✓	✓			✓	✓		✓	✓	✓
			✓	✓					✓					
		✓		✓										
									✓					
			✓	✓					✓					
			✓	✓										✓
✓		✓	✓			✓	✓		✓					
✓		✓		✓					✓				✓	
			✓						✓				✓	
✓		✓	✓	✓		✓	✓		✓	✓				✓

Special Features at a Glance

Name of Property	Accessible to Guests with Disabilities	On the Water	Good Value	Car Not Necessary	Full Meal Service	Historic Building	Romantic Hideaway
The Old Appleford Inn			✓			✓	✓
The Overlook Inn					✓	✓	✓
Pace One					✓	✓	
Pinetree Farm						✓	✓
The Priory	✓					✓	
Scarlett House						✓	
The Settlers Inn					✓	✓	
1740 House		✓				✓	✓
Smithton Country Inn			✓			✓	✓
The Sterling Inn					✓	✓	✓
Sweetwater Farm						✓	✓
Swiss Woods	✓		✓				
The Tannery Bed and Breakfast			✓	✓			
The Wedgwood Collection of Inns	✓						✓
The Whitehall Inn	✓		✓			✓	✓
VIRGINIA							
Applewood			✓				
The Ashby Inn and Restaurant						✓	✓
Ashton Country House			✓			✓	
The Bailiwick Inn	✓				✓	✓	✓
Belle Grae Inn	✓				✓	✓	
Bleu Rock Inn					✓		✓
Cape Charles House						✓	
The Channel Bass Inn							✓
Chester House			✓			✓	
Clifton	✓	✓				✓	✓

Luxurious	Pets Allowed	No Smoking Indoors	Good Place for Families	Near Arts Festivals	Beach Nearby	Cross-Country Ski Trail	Golf Nearby	Fitness Facilities	Good Biking Terrain	Skiing	Horseback Riding	Tennis	Swimming on Premises	Conference Facilities
		✓	✓	✓			✓		✓					
			✓	✓		✓	✓		✓	✓			✓	✓
							✓		✓		✓	✓		✓
✓		✓				✓	✓		✓				✓	
				✓										✓
		✓					✓							
	✓		✓		✓	✓	✓		✓	✓				✓
				✓									✓	
✓	✓	✓		✓										
✓			✓			✓	✓		✓	✓			✓	
✓	✓			✓		✓	✓		✓				✓	✓
	✓	✓	✓		✓	✓			✓	✓				
		✓		✓										
✓		✓		✓										
✓		✓		✓		✓			✓					
		✓	✓	✓			✓		✓					
✓		✓	✓						✓		✓			✓
		✓				✓	✓		✓					
✓		✓	✓				✓		✓					✓
			✓				✓							
		✓							✓					✓
✓		✓	✓	✓			✓		✓					✓
				✓					✓					
							✓		✓					✓
✓		✓		✓			✓		✓			✓	✓	✓

Special Features at a Glance

Name of Property	Accessible to Guests with Disabilities	On the Water	Good Value	Car Not Necessary	Full Meal Service	Historic Building	Romantic Hideaway	
Colonial Capital								
Edgewood						✓	✓	
1817 Historic Bed & Breakfast						✓		
Fassifern						✓		
Fort Lewis Lodge		✓	✓		✓			
The Garden and the Sea Inn						✓	✓	
High Meadows and Mountain Sunset	✓					✓	✓	
The Holladay House						✓		
The Inn at Gristmill Square						✓		
The Inn at Little Washington					✓		✓	
The Inn at Meander Plantation						✓	✓	
The Inn at Monticello						✓		
The Inn at Narrow Passage		✓	✓			✓	✓	
The Inn at Poplar Corner and The Watson House								
Island Manor House								
Jordan Hollow Farm Inn					✓	✓	✓	
Joshua Wilton House					✓	✓		
Keswick Hall					✓		✓	
L'Auberge Provençale					✓	✓		
Lavender Hill Farm		✓	✓					
Liberty Rose							✓	
Miss Molly's Inn		✓				✓		
The Morrison House	✓			✓	✓		✓	
Newport House								
The Norris House Inn						✓		
North Bend Plantation		✓	✓			✓		

Luxurious	Pets Allowed	No Smoking Indoors	Good Place for Families	Near Arts Festivals	Beach Nearby	Cross-Country Ski Trail	Golf Nearby	Fitness Facilities	Good Biking Terrain	Skiing	Horseback Riding	Tennis	Swimming on Premises	Conference Facilities
			✓	✓			✓		✓			✓	✓	
							✓		✓				✓	✓
				✓			✓		✓					
		✓							✓					
			✓						✓				✓	✓
✓				✓	✓				✓					
✓	✓	✓							✓					✓
									✓					
			✓	✓			✓		✓	✓		✓	✓	✓
✓									✓					✓
		✓					✓		✓					✓
		✓		✓					✓				✓	
			✓			✓			✓	✓				
		✓			✓				✓					
		✓		✓	✓				✓					✓
			✓			✓			✓	✓	✓			✓
				✓		✓	✓		✓	✓				✓
✓				✓			✓	✓	✓			✓	✓	✓
✓		✓				✓					✓			
		✓							✓		✓			
		✓		✓			✓		✓					
		✓			✓				✓					
✓				✓			✓		✓					✓
		✓	✓	✓			✓		✓					
		✓		✓			✓		✓					✓
		✓	✓						✓				✓	

Special Features at a Glance

Name of Property	Accessible to Guests with Disabilities	On the Water	Good Value	Car Not Necessary	Full Meal Service	Historic Building	Romantic Hideaway	
Nottingham Ridge		✓	✓					
Pickett's Harbor		✓						
Prospect Hill	✓					✓	✓	
The Red Fox Inn					✓	✓		
The Richard Johnston Inn			✓	✓		✓		
Sampson Eagon Inn			✓	✓		✓		
Seven Hills Inn								
The Shadows						✓	✓	
The Silver Thatch Inn						✓	✓	
Sleepy Hollow Farm			✓			✓		
The Spinning Wheel Bed and Breakfast			✓			✓		
Sycamore Hill								
Thornrose House			✓					
Tivoli						✓		
Trillium House	✓							
200 South Street	✓					✓		
War Hill Inn			✓					
WEST VIRGINIA								
Aspen Hall						✓	✓	
Bavarian Inn and Restaurant	✓	✓			✓	✓		
Boydville						✓	✓	
The Cardinal Inn			✓			✓		
The Carriage Inn						✓	✓	
Cheat Mountain Club		✓	✓		✓	✓		
The Cottonwood Inn						✓		
The Country Inn	✓		✓		✓	✓	✓	

Luxurious	Pets Allowed	No Smoking Indoors	Good Place for Families	Near Arts Festivals	Beach Nearby	Cross-Country Ski Trail	Golf Nearby	Fitness Facilities	Good Biking Terrain	Skiing	Horseback Riding	Tennis	Swimming on Premises	Conference Facilities
		✓	✓		✓				✓					
		✓			✓				✓				✓	
✓								✓	✓				✓	✓
			✓											
			✓	✓			✓							
		✓	✓	✓			✓		✓					
			✓						✓					✓
		✓	✓	✓					✓					✓
			✓	✓			✓					✓		
			✓						✓					
		✓		✓	✓		✓		✓					
		✓	✓											
		✓		✓			✓		✓			✓		
			✓						✓					✓
	✓					✓	✓	✓		✓	✓	✓	✓	✓
✓			✓				✓		✓					✓
		✓	✓	✓			✓		✓					
		✓		✓			✓							
✓			✓	✓		✓	✓		✓			✓	✓	✓
		✓		✓			✓		✓				✓	
		✓				✓			✓	✓	✓			✓
		✓					✓		✓		✓			
		✓				✓			✓	✓	✓			
		✓	✓				✓		✓					
				✓		✓	✓			✓	✓			✓

Special Features at a Glance

Name of Property	Accessible to Guests with Disabilities	On the Water	Good Value	Car Not Necessary	Full Meal Service	Historic Building	Romantic Hideaway
The Current		✓	✓			✓	
Edgewood Manor						✓	
The General Lewis Inn	✓				✓	✓	✓
Gerrardstown's Prospect Hill						✓	✓
Graceland Inn	✓				✓	✓	✓
Hampshire House 1884							
Henderson House and A Governor's Inn			✓			✓	✓
Highlawn						✓	✓
Hillbrook						✓	✓
Hutton House			✓			✓	
The Inn at Elk River		✓	✓		✓		
Lynn's Inn			✓				✓
Thomas Shepherd Inn						✓	✓
The Warfield House			✓			✓	
Washington House Inn						✓	
Woodcrest			✓				

Luxurious	Pets Allowed	No Smoking Indoors	Good Place for Families	Near Arts Festivals	Beach Nearby	Cross-Country Ski Trail	Golf Nearby	Fitness Facilities	Good Biking Terrain	Skiing	Horseback Riding	Tennis	Swimming on Premises	Conference Facilities
	✓	✓	✓			✓			✓	✓	✓			
		✓												
	✓	✓	✓	✓			✓		✓		✓	✓		
		✓				✓			✓					
✓		✓		✓					✓	✓		✓		✓
		✓		✓										
		✓		✓								✓		
✓				✓		✓	✓		✓	✓	✓			
✓									✓					
		✓		✓		✓			✓	✓	✓			
		✓	✓			✓	✓		✓	✓	✓			
		✓		✓		✓	✓				✓			✓
		✓				✓	✓		✓					✓
		✓		✓		✓						✓		
		✓												
		✓	✓			✓			✓				✓	

New York

New York

Ogdensburg

Potsdam

Canton

30

Newton Falls

Tupper Lake

La Pl

37

11

3

Kingston

81

Watertown

Carthage

Adirondack

30

Adams

Lowville

28

Lake Ontario

Old Forge

Oswego

104

81

Remsen

12

Camden

Ohio

30

Fulton

Cleveland

Rome

104

Clyde

Syracuse

90

Utica

Northville

Oneida

Mohawk

Rock

River

Cazenovia

Geneva

Auburn

20

Sche

Penn Yan

Finger Lakes

Hamilton

Cobleskill

Interlaken

Cooperstown

Dryden

81

12

Oneonta

88

Gre

Watkins Glen

Ithaca

Whitney Point

Windham

27

Walton

Tannersville

28

Corning

Binghamton

17

Elmira

Lew Beach

Catskill Pa

38

37

Ki

Livingston Manor

17

209

Monticello

New

Forestburg

Wa

Scranton

Middletown

Ne

Goshen

Wilkes-Barre

N E W

J E R S E Y

Ne

0   60 miles

0   90 km

Allentown

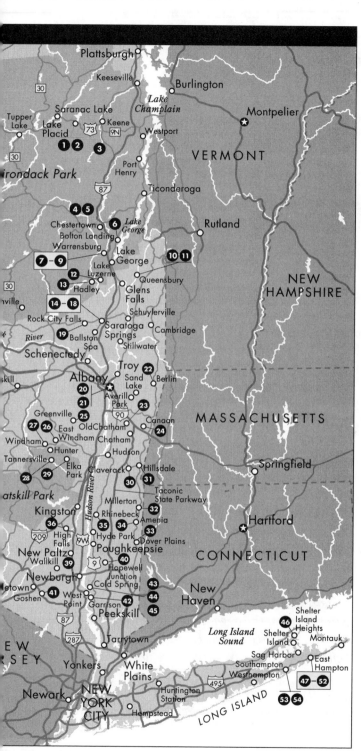

The Redcoat's Return, **29**

Sanford's Ridge Bed & Breakfast, **11**

Saratoga Bed and Breakfast, **16**

Saratoga Rose, **13**

The Sedgwick Inn, **22**

The 1770 House, **52**

Simmons Way Village Inn, **32**

The Six Sisters, **17**

The State House, **20**

Troutbeck, **34**

The Veranda House, **35**

The Village Latch Inn, **53**

The Westchester House, **18**

The Adirondacks Region: Lake George to the High Peaks

In the Adirondack Mountain range, the 6-million-acre forest preserve known as Adirondack Park encompasses 1,000 miles of rivers and more than 2,500 lakes and ponds. The southern sections are more developed, while the High Peaks region, in the north-central sector, offers the greatest variety of wilderness activities.

At the gateway to the Adirondack Park lies 32-mile-long Lake George, a four-season nirvana for those who like to vacation outdoors amid pine groves and pristine lakes. To be honest, not all of this "Queen of American Lakes" is pristine. There are plenty of ersatz Indian tepees, neon motel signs, and cheap-souvenir emporiums—in Lake George Village and at other lakeside outposts. Yet the lake itself, although not immune to 20th-century evils of acid rain and other pollutants, is probably as lovely as it was when it was discovered, in 1646. Other beautiful waterways in the area, most notably Lake Luzerne, Friends Lake, the Sacandaga River, and the northernmost reaches of the Hudson River, are worth visiting.

All this water naturally encourages water sports, including canoeing, swimming, fishing for record-breaking bass, and white-water rafting. Lakeside beaches are also super spots for sunning. At times other than the peak summer season, travelers come to the region for hiking, mountain climbing, and bird-watching; in winter they're drawn to the many cross-country ski trails and the excellent downhill slopes of Gore Mountain and Hickory Ski Center, where skiers at all levels will find reasonable lift rates and no long lines.

The area near Lake Luzerne is, surprisingly, dude-ranch country and the home of the oldest rodeo in the United States. Horses are available for trail rides. Warrensburg, an old lumber-mill town with more than 40 antiques shops, is a mecca for those seeking the perfect Adirondack chair, twig settee, or Victorian washstand. The region also has a variety of restaurants from which to choose. You'll find everything from exceptional hamburgers (at a roadside shack in Lake Luzerne called the Brass Bucket, where there's sometimes a two-hour wait) to haute cuisine, in places where you might expect more modest fare.

Lake Placid, the hub of the northern Adirondacks, has a main street lined with shops and restaurants, two lakes in its backyard, and the 1932 and 1980 winter Olympics facilities. The Ice Arena and speed-skating oval are in the center of town; the ski jump is a few miles out; Whiteface Mountain (scene of the downhill competitions) is a 10-minute drive away on Route 86; and the bobsled run at Mt. Van Hoevenberg, on Route 73, is 15 minutes away. All of these sites are open to the public.

Places to Go, Sights to See

Fort William Henry (Lake George Village, tel. 518/668–5471). If you're a fan of James Fenimore Cooper, you'll want to stop at this site, which figured so prominently in *The Last of the Mohicans*. The British constructed the fort in 1755; it was burned by the French in 1757. The restored complex presents visitors with a picture of life during the French and Indian War, and history tours, with demonstrations of military skills, are given in July and August. Closed Sept.–Apr.

Great Escape Fun Park (Lake George, tel. 518/792–6568). This is the North Country's largest amusement park.

Hyde House (Glens Falls, tel. 518/792–1761). A 1912 Italian Renaissance–style mansion, Hyde House is filled with French 18th-century and Italian Renaissance antiques. It also houses the Hyde Collection of Old Masters and American art, from the late-Gothic period to the 20th century.

Lake George Steamboat Cruises (tel. 518/668–5777) and **Lake George Shoreline Cruises** (tel. 518/668–4644) offer brunch, lunch, dinner, and moonlight cruises on an authentic Mississippi paddle wheeler, the *Minne-Ha-Ha*.

Outdoors Exploration. In the High Peaks region, if you're not headed up a mountain, you're headed out—across the water. Contact the Lake Placid Visitors Bureau (tel. 518/523–2445) for brochures on trailheads and canoe routes. **Jones Outfitters** (37 Main St., Lake Placid, tel. 518/523–3468) will rent you anything you need: canoes, kayaks, fishing gear, and more.

Shops. If you're looking for Adirondack kitsch—birch-bark lampshades, pine-cone-covered picture frames, twig furniture—check out **The Adirondack Store** (109 Saranac Ave, Lake Placid, tel. 518/523–2646) and **George Jaques Antiques** (Rte. 73, Keene Valley, tel. 518/576–2214).

World's Largest Garage Sale. Each fall in Warrensburg more than 500 dealers and private sellers gather to purvey a mixed bag that might contain anything from priceless antiques to tomorrow's collectibles. For exact dates, call the Warrensburg Chamber of Commerce (tel. 518/623–2161).

Restaurants

The **Shoreline Restaurant and Marina** (Kurosaka La., Lake George, tel. 518/668–2875) specializes in prime rib, veal, and fresh seafood dishes. For hearty Italian fare, try **Ciro's Restaurant** (Rte. 9N, Lake Luzerne, tel. 518/668–2665). The **Cottage Cafe** (Mirror Lake Dr., Lake Placid, tel. 518/523–9845) has an open-air deck that overlooks Mirror Lake. **Nicola's Over Main** (90 Main St., Lake Placid, tel. 518/523–4430) serves sophisticated Italian and Mediterranean dishes.

Tourist Information

Lake George Chamber of Commerce (Box 272, Lake George 12845, tel. 518/668–5755). **Lake Luzerne Chamber of Commerce** (Bridge St., Box 222, Lake Luzerne 12846, tel. 518/696–3500). **Lake Placid Visitors Bureau** (Olympic Center, Lake Placid 12946, tel. 800/447–5224). **North Warren Chamber of Commerce** (Box 490, Chestertown 12817, tel. 518/494–2722). **Warren County Department of Tourism** (Municipal Center, Lake George 12845, tel. 800/365–1050).

Reservation Services

Adirondack B&Bs Reservation Service (10 Park Place, Saranac Lake, NY 12983, tel. 518/891–1632 or 800/552–2627). **American Country Collection** (1353 Union St., Schenectady, NY 12308, tel. 518/370–4948 or 800/810–4948).

The Bark Eater Inn

Alstead Hill Rd., Box 139, Keene, NY 12942, tel. 518/576–2221, fax 518/576–2071

In the 1800s, this farmhouse with a spectacular view of the High Peaks was a stagecoach stop on a line that ran between Lake Placid and Lake Champlain. Since then, the house has been expanded and altered; today it's a delightful inn with horse stable. There are seven rooms in the main house and four in the newer Carriage House. In a hand-hewn log cottage a five-minute walk away, there are two additional three-room suites (individual rooms of the suites can be booked as well). Guest rooms have plain furniture, but that's okay: There's so much to do outside the inn, you probably won't spend much time in your room. When you do come indoors, you can get comfortable in front of the large stone fireplaces in the sitting and dining rooms.

Owner Joe-Pete Wilson is an avid rider and has more than 50 horses available for English- and Western-style riding; polo matches are often played in the neighboring field. Joe-Pete, a former Olympic bobsledder, is also an expert skier and will lead you to cross-country ski trails that connect with the extensive Jackrabbit Trail network. Right outside the inn's front door, these trails are also great for hiking.

Large and delicious breakfasts include a choice of several hot entrées. The inn's homemade granola is especially tasty. Dinner is available to both the inn's guests and outside diners if space permits.

▥ *4 rooms with baths, 7 rooms share 2 baths, cottage with 2 suites. TV in sitting room, cross-country skiing, hiking, horseback riding, mountain biking. $98–136; full breakfast; MAP available. AE, MC, V.*

The Chester Inn

Main St., Box 163, Chestertown, NY 12817, tel. 518/494–4148

The Chester Inn bed-and-breakfast sits right on Chestertown's Main Street, but there are 13 acres of meadows out back. Originally the home of Charles Fowler, a wealthy merchant, the Greek Revival mansion has been occupied by only three families since it was built in 1837.

A love of history and fond memories of European B&B stays persuaded Bruce and Suzanne Robbins to open an inn. Bruce, who had worked in construction, and Sue, who was in retail sales, carefully researched the house's past and attended to every detail in its restoration (they even had an original shade of paint reproduced by computer). Guests are pampered with candlelit gourmet breakfasts served on Federal-style china with sterling and crystal. Three guest rooms are furnished with Victorian antiques; a fourth, the Library Suite, is decorated in a spare, Shaker-like manner. While in Chestertown, don't miss the Robbinses' restored, turn-of-the-century ice-cream parlor and museum, one block from the inn.

▥ *2 double rooms with baths, 2 suites. Air-conditioning. $95–$110; full breakfast. MC, V. No smoking, no pets, 2-night minimum July–Aug. and holiday weekends.*

Country Road Lodge

HCR 1, No. 227 Hickory Hill Rd., Warrensburg, NY 12885, tel. 518/623–2207, fax 518/623–4363

You'll find nothing fancy at the Country Road Lodge, which is far off the beaten path: This was once a small, rustic camp cottage at the end of a long, winding dirt road, and, with some additions and improvements, it still is. "What we have is *setting,*" brag the owners, Steve and Sandi Parisi. Perched close enough to the churning Hudson River to practically fall in, and surrounded by mountain vistas, the small house is totally secluded. The hiking and cross-country ski trails go on for miles through the forests.

The Parisis keep the small guest rooms clean and snug; the unpretentious decor is "early garage sale," with some nice patchwork quilts. Steve worked on Madison Avenue before opening the lodge to skiers in 1974 (the Hickory Ski Center—Mogul Madness—is just down the way). Hearty breakfasts are provided for hikers, skiers, birders, and those who wish to just sit on the riverbank and commune with nature. Good conversation abounds: The meal sometimes lasts for hours.

▥ *2 double rooms with baths, 2 doubles share bath. Air-conditioning. $62; full breakfast. Lunch and dinner offered on winter weekends for extra cost. No credit cards. No smoking, no pets.*

Crislip's Bed and Breakfast

693 Ridge Rd., Queensbury, NY 12804, tel. 518/793-6869

You can see the Green Mountains of Vermont from the Italianate veranda of the Crislip's Bed and Breakfast. The Federal house, built in 1805 and remodeled in 1848 in the popular Greek Revival style, was owned by Queensbury's first doctor, who later became town supervisor. Queensbury is about halfway between Saratoga Springs and Lake George—near but just far enough off the beaten track.

Joyce Crislip is a former teacher, and her husband, Ned, teaches music. The hosts' musical interests are in evidence throughout the house: A Steinway grand piano is the focal point of the living room; the framed, 15th-century score of a Gregorian chant hangs on the wall of the studio. The Blue Room, with its canopied, carved mahogany bed and mahogany highboy, is favored by honeymooners; the first-floor studio (with a kitchenette) is often the choice of older couples. The Green Room has a king-size four-poster bed. Ned will gladly give you the tour and tell you the details of the period antiques that fill the house.

▥ *3 double rooms with baths. Air-conditioning, TV in family room and 2 bedrooms. $55–$75; full breakfast. D, MC, V. No smoking, small pets permitted by arrangement.*

The Friends Lake Inn

Friends Lake Rd., Chestertown, NY 12817, tel. 518/494-4751

The New York State record small-mouth bass was caught in Friends Lake, but you don't have to be an angler to enjoy the Friends Lake Inn and all it has to offer. This traditional Adirondack lodge was built in stages. The original building was a farmhouse constructed around 1850; a later addition served as a boardinghouse for workers in local tanneries. Innkeepers Greg and Sharon Taylor are avid skiers, and at the inn they have established a cross-country ski touring center with trails; they also offer special packages for alpine skiing.

After a day spent skiing (or fishing, rafting, canoeing, or hiking), guests gather at the inn's restaurant, which has received culinary accolades. With its pressed-tin ceiling and original chestnut woodwork, it is a romantic spot for lingering. Guest rooms are small and cozy and are furnished with antique beds and oak dressers. The most popular rooms are the ones with a view of the lake and those with whirlpool baths.

▥ *16 rooms with baths. Restaurant, whirlpool tubs in 8 rooms, wine bar, hot tub, beach, cross-country skiing. $105–$250; full breakfast; MAP available. AE, MC, V. Smoking in bar and lounge only, no pets.*

Hilltop Cottage Bed and Breakfast

Rte. 9N, Box 186, Bolton Landing, NY 12814, tel. 518/644–2492

Hilltop Cottage is an easygoing, reasonably priced alternative to the ersatz log cabins and tacky motels that proliferate in this popular resort area. Running a bed-and-breakfast comes naturally to retired educators Anita and Charlie Richards. Anita's parents lived in the 11-room house, and her mother rented rooms to tourists. During the 1920s and early '30s the building housed students of the legendary Metropolitan Opera diva Marcella Sembrich, who is honored in the Opera Museum just a short walk from the house.

The moldings, floors, and banister in this vine-covered house are made of Adirondack fir, and all the antique beds are covered with printed quilts from the 1940s and '50s. The Richardses' German heritage is evident throughout the house, from the art on the walls to Anita's German apple pancakes at breakfast. Those with allergies please take note: Although the Richardses don't accept pets, they have two cats and a dog.

🏠 *1 double room with bath, 2 doubles share bath, 1-room cabin with kitchenette and TV. Piano and wood-burning stove in living room. $50–$80; full breakfast. MC, V. No smoking indoors, no pets, 2-night minimum on holiday weekends.*

The House on the Hill

Rte. 28, Box 248, Warrensburg, NY 12885, tel. 518/623–9390 or 800/221–9390

In 1990 Joe and Lynn Rubino moved from New Jersey and made their vacation home of 20 years a full-time labor of love—and between the setting, the house, and the hosts, it is a B&B experience you won't soon forget. The white, wooden, circa-1750 house sits on a hill surrounded by 176 acres of meadows and forest, five minutes outside of Warrensburg. The common rooms are busy with all manner of antiques and knickknacks. Art and graphics fight for space on the crowded walls. Guest rooms are small but distinctive, combining a country decor with artistic touches; all have coffeemakers and café tables.

The Rubinos are active in local civic organizations—they know whom to contact for any area interest you want to pursue, from an airplane ride to exploring historical sites. Joe takes two Polaroids of every guest before they depart, one as a momento to take home and one for the inn's photo album.

🏠 *3 double rooms with baths, 1 double shares bath with owner. Air-conditioning. $89–$109; full breakfast. D, DC, MC, V. No smoking, no pets.*

The Interlaken Inn

15 Interlaken Ave., Lake Placid, NY 12946, tel. 518/523–3180 or 800/428–4369

You won't have to look hard to find this fully restored 1906 Victorian inn, which stands high on a hill overlooking Mirror Lake. The Interlaken is three stories high, and its clapboard exterior is painted colonial blue with cream trim. At night, tiny white lights outline the screened-in porch and roofline.

The large entryway is decorated with dried flowers, stuffed teddy bears, and an antique stroller filled with dolls. Also on the spacious first floor is a parlor room, breakfast porch, and dining room, which is popular with locals as well as guests. On weekends, a five-course dinner is included with the price of your room. Dinner may start with lobster crepes and asparagus soup, followed by Caesar salad and sorbet, and that's only the halfway point—a breast of duck *au poivre* may be next, and to end, mocha tiramisu.

Each bedroom is a trove of antiques or reproductions: bird's-eye maple dressers, Lincoln rockers, and handmade quilts. Some rooms have four-poster canopy or brass beds; all except those on the third floor have ceiling fans. The inn is within walking distance of downtown Lake Placid.

🏠 *11 rooms with baths. Restaurant. $120–$180; full breakfast, dinner included on weekends (dinner served Thurs.–Mon.). AE, MC, V.*

Lake Placid Lodge

Whiteface Inn Rd., Box 550, Lake Placid, NY 12946, tel. 518/523–2573, fax 518/523–1124

True Adirondack style permeates this property, from the twig and birch-bark furniture to the wood decks and stone fireplaces. Originally a rustic lodge built before the turn of the century, Lake Placid Lodge embodies the spirit of Lake Placid's past, but it cossets guests with the comforts of modern-day, luxurious amenities. Kathryn Kincannon, managing director, and her ever-accommodating staff do everything possible to ensure that your stay is a memorable one.

Guest rooms, which are named for the region's high peaks and lakes, are in three buildings: the main lodge, Lakeside Lodge, and Cedar Lodge. There are also 16 studio and one- and two-bedroom lakefront cabins. Although they vary in size, all the guest rooms are exquisite. Hearthside, one of the most popular, has wood paneling, log-beam trim, a large stone fireplace, a king-size bed, and a large soaking tub for two. Feather beds, terry-cloth robes, Crabtree & Evelyn toiletries, fresh fruit, and warm cookies left at your bedside complete the experience.

If seclusion is what you're after, don't overlook the cabins, which were built in the 1930s and are only a short walk from the main lodge. They sit right on the shores of Lake Placid and have big pic-ture windows and loads of privacy. All the cabins were renovated in 1997, and the attention paid to detail is remarkable, right down to the teas, coffees, and electric kettle placed in the room for early morning refreshment.

If you decide to pull yourself from your room or cabin (which can be difficult), you can walk down to the lake for a swim or canoe trip. A barge departs from the dock nightly for a sightseeing cruise on Lake Placid. If it's winter, you can head out on one of the many nearby cross-country ski trails. There's also a game room with puzzles, a billiards table, and an upright piano. And, if you decide to stay in your room after all, room service is available.

The restaurant serves new American cuisine, which is as good as—if not better than—many big-deal city restaurants. The innovative kitchen changes the menu seasonally; it may include grilled quail on rosemary branches with shiitake mushroom fritters or scallops with hickory-smoked mashed potatoes, grilled green onion, and oyster-spice vinaigrette. It's here in the dining room you'll also enjoy hearty Adirondack breakfasts, which include a cold buffet and hot entrée.

🏠 *22 rooms with baths, 16 cabins with baths. Restaurant, bar, phones in rooms, minirefrigerators in cabins, beach, bicycles, tennis, hiking, boating, golf. $200–$625; full breakfast. AE, D, DC, MC, V.*

The Lamplight Inn

231 Lake Ave., Box 70, Lake Luzerne, NY 12846, tel. 518/696–5294 or 800/262–4668

In 1890 the Lamplight Inn, a grand Victorian Gothic in the village of Lake Luzerne, was built by a wealthy bachelor lumberman as his summer playhouse. One can only guess at the romantic trysts of this 19th-century playboy, but adjoining doors (no longer used) to two other bedrooms from the master bedroom hint at the possibilities.

Today, the Lamplight is a romantic bed-and-breakfast for 20th-century guests, thanks to innkeepers Gene and Linda Merlino. In 1984 they were still dating when they bought this mansion on a whim. Within a year they were husband and wife; they spent their honeymoon painting the front porch. There have been quite a few proposals uttered on bended knee under this romantic roof, and honeymooning guests and other couples love the Lamplight, as room-diary accolades attest: "Our privacy was respected and our newness as a couple treated with gentleness and humor," one newlywed wrote.

The decor helps considerably. The downstairs sitting room has its original chestnut molding, wainscoting, and unusual keyhold staircase. On cool evenings the room is lit by two fireplaces. Wicker chairs beckon visitors to the front porch, and the airy dining room provides the perfect backdrop for Linda's granola and muffins and Gene's peach crepes and three-egg omelets.

Guest rooms are Victorian in the romantic sense of the word—they are flowery and lacy. One of the nicest places to stay is the Canopy Room, with an original carved-oak mantel, hearth tiles, and a gas fireplace. In a newly constructed wing is a unique room that perfectly matches the rest of the house: The Skylight Room has a carved-oak, high-back Victorian bed covered in an antique patchwork quilt, with a skylight overhead. It's hard to choose a room here, because so much love and attention to detail have gone into each one.

A guest entry in the Canopy Room diary probably sums up the Lamplight experience best: "Your rocking chairs, soft quilts, and warm hospitality have transformed us back into human beings."

And isn't that the purpose of getting away from it all?

🛏 *17 double rooms with baths. Air-conditioning, 7 rooms with TV, 12 rooms with fireplaces, 4 rooms with whirlpool tub, beach across street. $89–$165; full breakfast. AE, MC, V. No smoking in bedrooms, no pipes or cigars, no pets, 2-night minimum on weekends, 3-night minimum on holidays and during special events.*

The Merrill Magee House

2 Hudson St., Warrensburg, NY 12885, tel. 518/623-2449

In a grove of trees adjacent to a 19th-century bandstand sits the Merrill McGee House, a Greek Revival mansion built around 1840. The great-grandfather of Grace Merrill Magee, for whom the inn is named, fought in the American Revolution. Innkeepers Florence and Ken Carrington owned housekeeping cottages on Lake George for 30 years. A brief, unhappy retirement led to a new career as proprietors of this irresistible country inn.

The house overlooks a pretty yard where weddings are often held, and a field of wildflowers lies in back. Most of the guest rooms are located in a newer (but architecturally compatible) building behind the inn. All the new rooms have fireplaces and are decorated country style, with antique beds, patchwork quilts, and folk art. The inn features what may be the oldest (circa 1928) private swimming pool in New York State—it's a beauty. There's also a hot tub in the newer annex, which all guests can use.

🛏 *10 double rooms with baths. Restaurant, tavern, air-conditioning, pool, hot tub. $95–$115; full breakfast. AE, D, MC, V. No smoking in dining room, no pets, 2-night minimum on summer and holiday weekends, closed Mar.*

Sanford's Ridge Bed & Breakfast

749 Ridge Rd., Queensbury, NY 12804, tel. 518/793–4923

Sanford's Ridge is just a five-minute drive from the commercial stretch of Route 9, and yet it has a removed, bucolic feeling. In 1990 owners Carolyn and Bob Rudolph restored the 1797 Federal-style house, with its 14-foot ceilings, wide-plank pine floors, and fireplaces.

The three guest rooms are furnished with an eclectic collection of antiques. The spacious Webster Room has a queen-size canopied four-poster, a fireplace, a bath with a claw-foot tub, and a view of the Adirondacks. The Sanford Room has a fireplace and a four-poster queen-size bed decked with a patchwork quilt handmade by Carolyn.

▥ *3 double rooms with baths. Air-conditioning, TV in common room, pool. $75–$95; full breakfast. MC, V. No smoking, no pets, 2-night minimum on holiday weekends.*

Saratoga Rose

4274 Rockwell St., Box 238, Hadley, NY 12835, tel. 518/696–2861 or 800/942–5025

The Victorian mansion now housing this bed-and-breakfast inn was built in 1885 as a wedding gift for the daughter of one of the founding fathers of Hadley, a tiny Adirondack village between the Sacandaga and Hudson rivers. "I guess that's why it works so well for us," says innkeeper Nancy Merlino. "We're on an extended honeymoon here."

Nancy and her husband and co-owner, Anthony (he's also the chef for the inn's restaurant), married and in 1988 found the inn. The couple is proud of the acclaimed restaurant, which serves American regional and Italian cuisine. Candlelit dinners are served in the romantic, Victorian dining room with burgundy curtains and a fireplace, or on what is probably the only bright-pink veranda in the Adirondacks. In back are Victorian-style gardens with two ponds and a waterfall. The guest rooms have Victorian furnishings and decor; two rooms have oak highback beds, and one has a fireplace. The Victorian Room even has a pink fainting couch, and the Garden Room has a private deck.

▥ *6 double rooms with baths. Restaurant, bar, fireplaces, air-conditioning, and whirlpool tubs in 3 rooms, fireplace only in 1 room. $85–$175; full breakfast. D, MC, V. Smoking downstairs only, no pets, 2-night minimum on weekends.*

The Capital and Saratoga Region

Reminders of America's past—political, commercial, and social—abound in New York's capital and Saratoga region. A favorite of visitors seeking both history and 20th-century diversions, the area encompasses the city of Albany, the nation's sixth largest port, at the northernmost point of the navigable Hudson. Once on the decline—as described in Ironweed and other works of William Kennedy, a local favorite son—Albany is currently enjoying the revitalization of its downtown area. The additions to the city of the Nelson A. Rockefeller Empire State Plaza (completed in 1978) and the Pepsi Arena have inspired the restoration of surrounding neighborhoods. A tour of the city often includes the governor's mansion and the State Capitol—one of the few such buildings without a dome. You won't want to miss the Performing Arts Center, nicknamed "The Egg" for obvious reasons. It makes the Albany skyline unlike any other in the world.

Landlocked though Saratoga is, it boasts a natural asset: a prehistoric sea, trapped under limestone and capped with a layer of shale. The mineral waters that bubble through the cracks in the shale have made Saratoga Springs and the neighboring Ballston Spa a noted resort for two centuries.

Here visitors still "take the cure," sampling mineral waters from various fountains strategically located around town. Bring a drinking cup, and don't expect the water to taste like Evian or Perrier. Each spring reputedly possesses different elements conducive to health. The cure may include a trip to one of the area's mineral baths (several of which are located in Saratoga Spa State Park) and a massage.

"The August Place to Be," as Saratoga Springs advertises itself, attracts crowds the last two weeks in July and all of August, when the six-week thoroughbred-racing season is the centerpiece of a series of festive events. Lodging and seats at the city's excellent restaurants are hard to come by during this time; and hotel, inn, and bed-and-breakfast rates often shoot up to nearly twice the normal prices. To really enjoy this lovely city we recommend a visit at other times of the year.

Saratoga is a great place for strolling, with its superb Victorian architecture, especially along Union Avenue, North Broadway, Lake Avenue, and Circular Street. And don't miss the scene of the 1777 Battle of Saratoga, the "turning point of the Revolution," now a national historic park (tel. 518/664–9821) between the nearby towns of Stillwater and Schuylerville.

Places to Go, Sights to See

Historic Cherry Hill (Albany, tel. 518/434–4791). This Georgian home, built in 1787 by Philip Van Rensselaer, was inhabited by five generations of his family, until 1963. The furnishings range from 18th-century artifacts and 19th-century Chinese exports to early 20th-century kitchen appliances.

Lyrical Ballad Bookstore (7 Phila St., Saratoga Springs, tel. 518/584–8779). There are many first editions among the 60,000 books at this antiquarian bookseller; new remainders are also sold here.

New York State Capitol (Albany, tel. 518/474–2418). Built between 1867 and 1899, the seat of New York State government incorporates several styles of architecture. The interior features elaborate carvings and an impressive staircase.

New York State Museum (Albany, tel. 518/474–5877). Lifelike dioramas of New York State's past (including some depicting immigrant life in New York City in the late 19th and early 20th centuries) and a reproduction of an Iroquois village, including a full-size longhouse, make this museum one of Albany's most popular attractions. Also featured are changing art exhibits, films, lectures, demonstrations, and hands-on displays. The museum is an absorbing adventure for children.

Saratoga Race Course (Saratoga Springs, tel. 518/584–6200). The nation's oldest thoroughbred track, in operation since 1863, is the focus of Saratoga's August social scene. Post time is 1 PM. Early risers may breakfast at the trackside café and watch morning workouts. The **National Museum of Racing and Hall of Fame** (tel. 518/584–0400), right by the track, includes a reconstructed training barn and portraits of champions.

Saratoga Spa State Park (between Rtes. 9 and 50, tel. 518/584–2535). The land that now makes up this 2,000-acre park was reserved in 1909 to protect the area's unique mineral springs. Mineral baths (some of which still operate) were opened in the 1920s, and in the '30s the Works Progress Administration completed the spa buildings. The park has an Olympic-size swimming pool, golf courses, tennis courts, and ice-skating rinks. It is also the home of the **Saratoga Performing Arts Center** (tel. 518/584–9330), summer host of the New York City Opera, the New York City Ballet, the Philadelphia Orchestra, and the Newport Jazz Festival–Saratoga.

Yaddo (Saratoga Springs, tel. 518/584–0746). This 19th-century estate was the summer home of Katrina and Spencer Trask, wealthy patrons of the arts. Yaddo is their permanent legacy to creative work, an enclave where artists, writers, and musicians may work without disruption. Since 1926 more than 4,000 artists have resided here, including John Cheever, Langston Hughes, Katherine Anne Porter, Aaron Copland, and Milton Avery. Yaddo's gardens are open to the public.

Restaurants

In Albany, you can get generous servings of seafood at **Jack's Oyster House** (42 State St., tel. 518/465–8854). For tasty French bistro fare, try **Nicole's Bistro** (Clinton and Broadway, tel. 518/465–1111) in the Quackenbush House, an 18th-century Dutch structure.

In Saratoga Springs, try **Eartha's Kitchen** (60 Court St., tel. 518/583–0602), which has an eclectic menu including mesquite-grilled seafood dishes. **Hattie's** (45 Phila St., tel. 518/584–4790) serves up delicious Southern home cooking. The creative dinners at **43 Phila Bistro** (43 Phila St., tel. 518/584–2720) has made this spot a big hit on the Saratoga dining scene. Adirondack specialties—venison, trout, and duck with raspberry demi-glaze—are featured at the **Springwater Inn** (139 Union Ave., tel. 518/584–6440).

Tourist Information

Albany County Convention and Visitors Bureau (52 S. Pearl St., Albany 12207, tel. 518/434–1217 or 800/258–3582). **Rensselaer County Regional Chamber of Commerce** (31 2nd St., Troy 12180, tel. 518/274–7020). **Saratoga County Chamber of Commerce** (28 Clinton St., Saratoga Springs 12866, tel. 518/584–3255).

Reservation Service

The American Country Collection (1353 Union St., Schenectady, NY 12308, tel. 518/370–4948).

The Adelphi Hotel

365 Broadway, Saratoga Springs, NY 12866, tel. 518/587–4688

If Kublai Khan had decreed that his stately pleasure dome be built in late-19th-century Saratoga instead of in Xanadu, he might have come up with the Adelphi Hotel. This lodging is nothing like home, unless home is an Italianate-style palazzo, with the requisite piazza and ornamented by a maze of colorful fretwork. The opulent lobby with slowly rotating fans is done in a style so reminiscent of La Belle Epoque that one could picture the Divine Sarah Bernhardt holding court amid its splendor. It's hard to believe that not too long ago the Adelphi stood empty, evidence of fortune gone sour.

Saratogans shook their heads and laughed at what they took to be the foolhardiness of Gregg Siefker and Sheila Parkert when they bought the place in 1988, but no one's laughing anymore: The hotel is one of Saratoga's showpieces, its lobby bar and café a gathering place for natives and visitors alike (in July it's a favorite hangout of members of the New York City Ballet). Guests at the Adelphi have access to a parlor on the second floor, which has a grand porch overlooking Broadway. This is a great place for afternoon cocktails, especially during racing season, when it's fun to watch the buzz of activity on the street below. For a more quiet respite, the back courtyard has lots of flowering plants, Adirondack chairs, and an interestingly shaped pool that was designed by the owner.

No two rooms are the same: All the furnishings are eclectic—and recherché. If you seek accommodations that hark back to the Adirondack camps enjoyed by some of America's wealthiest families, ask for Room 16, the Adirondack Suite, with Mission-style furniture manufactured in upstate New York, a twig settee, Papago Indian baskets on the wall, and a wood-paneled bathroom. If you yearn for the south of France but can't afford to go there, the Riviera Suite (Room 12) may lessen the pangs somewhat. Its sitting area, furnished with rattan, is graced with a Mediterranean mural; an amusing Casbah painting hangs on the bedroom wall; and the bathroom is decorated in apricot tones. Other rooms are furnished with Tiffany lampshades, brass-and-iron beds with crocheted bedspreads, wicker settees, and Victoriana.

▥ *20 double rooms with baths, 18 suites. Restaurant (open July and Aug.), café, air-conditioning, cable TV in all rooms, phones in rooms, room service, pool. $90–$320; Continental breakfast. AE, MC, V. No pets, 2-night minimum on weekends in June–July, 3-night minimum in Aug., closed Nov.–Apr.*

Chestnut Tree Inn

9 Whitney Pl., Saratoga Springs, NY 12866, tel. 518/587–8681

This 1860 Empire-style bed-and-breakfast with a Mansard roof is on a side street near the center of Saratoga Springs and is in easy walking distance of Broadway, Congress Park, and the track. The house has a somewhat colorful history: It was a notorious rooming house. Bruce DeLuke, a retired firefighter, and his wife, Cathleen, both antiques dealers, have turned the place into an alluring, romantic retreat. Wicker furnishings and old-lace decor prevail, and the exterior color scheme of pink, mauve, and gray is repeated in the bedrooms and common areas.

The inn offers a first-floor double room, with a queen-size pencil post bed and pink Victorian lamp (which imparts an appropriate rosy glow). There is a tiny but charming bungalow in the backyard, which has a loft bed for children. The atmosphere here is easy and undemanding. Guests are free to mingle or not, and breakfast is laid out on a leisurely basis; you can serve yourself anytime of the morning.

▦ *7 double rooms with baths, 3 doubles share 2 baths. Cable TV in parlor, off-street parking. $55–$200; Continental breakfast. MC, V. No smoking, no pets, 3-night minimum on special-event weekends, closed Nov.–mid-Apr.*

The Mansion

Rte. 29, Box 77, Rock City Falls, NY 12863, tel. 518/885–1607

Rock City Falls, a 19th-century mill town 7 miles west of Saratoga Springs, seems an unlikely destination for travelers. The Kayaderosseras Creek still flows, but the mills and factories are quiet. Aside from a few antiques shops, there doesn't seem to be much that would draw visitors to this sleepy village . . . not much, that is, until one spots the Mansion, one of the most elegant and romantic bed-and-breakfasts you'll encounter anywhere. The Venetian villa-style residence was built in 1866 as a summer home for George West, a prominent industrialist and inventor of the folding paper bag. No expense was spared in the construction of the 23-room mansion; it has 12-foot etched-glass doors, marble fireplaces with inlaid mantels, copper and brass lighting fixtures, and Tiffany chandeliers.

It is a credit to proprietor Tom Clark and innkeeper Alan Churchill, who restored the mansion, that this bed-and-breakfast is both sumptuous and friendly. The art books stacked invitingly in the library are for browsing, perhaps while sipping iced tea or Saratoga water on the side porch on a lazy summer afternoon. Classical music—anything from Bach to Berlioz—wafts through the house. The art, which Tom collects on his travels, invites close inspection. The antique parlor organ is there for playing. All the guest rooms are enticing, but the Four-Poster Room, with its queen-size carved bed, and the Queen Room, with garden views, are particularly handsome.

And there are the flowers. Baskets of fuchsia hang from the porches; roses, peonies, and delphiniums fill the gardens; and bouquets of fragrant Casablanca lilies and foxglove may greet you in the front hall or parlors. Throughout the year floral arrangements brighten every guest room. Alan of the green thumb even grows orchids: In one guest room the mauve of an orchid plant picks up the colors of the bedspread.

Alan nurtures his guests the way he nurtures his flowers—you are made to feel like a treasured friend in this hospitable house. Everything here—from the Victorian furnishings to the homemade fruit breads served with breakfast—is in excellent taste. As Alan says, "The house demands it. It's so special."

▦ *4 double rooms with baths, 1 suite, 2-bedroom carriage house. Air-conditioning, pool. $95–$185; full breakfast. No credit cards. No smoking indoors, no pets, 2-night minimum in Aug. and on holiday weekends, closed Thanksgiving and Dec. 25.*

Mansion Hill Inn

115 Philip St., Albany, NY 12202, tel. 518/465–2038

Albany's only downtown inn, Mansion Hill, stands around the corner from the governor's mansion and occupies several adjacent restored Victorian-era buildings, one of which was once the neighborhood saloon. Owners Maryellen and Steve Stofelano (she's a former bank vice-president and he once taught high school) bought the buildings in 1984 and finished their first renovation project the following year. The inn's attractive restaurant soon became the neighborhood's hub—and Steve its unofficial mayor.

Accommodations range from double rooms with queen-size beds to two huge suites, each with a living room, den, full kitchen, bedroom, bath, and balcony. Furnishings are undistinguished but comfortable. The standard-issue rooms are eclipsed by the real draw here: the intimate dozen-table restaurant, which is open to the public but doesn't serve lunch. The dinner menu has an imaginative new American flair. Breakfast for guests of the inn might include blueberry pancakes or frittatas. Those who wish to explore Albany will find the State Capitol, the Empire State Plaza, and numerous historic sights easily accessible.

🏠 *8 double rooms with baths. Restaurant, air-conditioning, cable TV in rooms. $105–$155; full breakfast, dinner. AE, D, DC, MC, V.*

Saratoga Bed and Breakfast

Church St., Saratoga Springs, NY 12866, tel. 518/584–0920

This property on the outskirts of town boasts "the very last address" in Saratoga proper. Kathleen and Noel Smith opened their home to guests nearly 15 years ago, using just four rooms of their 1860 wood frame farmhouse. Today, they also manage a small separate motel, and the B&B includes rooms in a neighboring 1850 Federal-style brick house.

The rooms in the farmhouse are more country than high Victorian. They are named for the city's gracious old hotels. Handmade, signed quilts adorn the antique beds. The largest room, Union Hall, has a carved-oak bed, wicker furnishings, and a view of pine trees from every window. There's also a whimsical Adirondack-style room with trout on the walls and clouds painted on the ceiling.

The 1850 House, which has four exquisite suites, is a grand addition to the property. The elegant Grant Suite on the first floor has high ceilings and an en suite living room decorated with rich green and burgundy fabrics; a grandfather clock sits in the corner. If you like cozy, request the popular Irish Cottage attic suite; the slanted walls are covered

with purple-violet paper, the fireplace is white-painted brick, there's a lilac clawfoot tub, and the wood floors are painted green.

Noel is a former restaurateur, and his full Irish breakfasts are the high point of a stay here. If you can manage to move after breakfast, Kathleen, an amiable ambassador for her native city, will set up an itinerary for you. The operation is a family affair—even Bates Motel, the dog, gets into the act: He's the official welcoming committee.

🏠 *8 double rooms with baths in farmhouse and 1850 House. Air-conditioning, TV in farmhouse common room, TVs in 1850 House rooms, fireplaces in 4 bedrooms. $65–$225; full breakfast. AE, D, MC, V. No smoking, no pets, 2-night minimum on Aug. weekends.*

The Sedgwick Inn

Rte. 22, Berlin, NY 12022, tel. 518/658–2334

The Sedgwick Inn, a rambling New England farmhouse with Victorian additions, was built in 1791 as a stagecoach stop. It sits on 12 verdant acres at the foot of the Berkshires, in Berlin; it was once a favorite getaway of New York politicos and their cronies and later became a popular tavern. It is said that Cole Porter once performed here. Today the inn combines all three of its earlier incarnations: It's a way station, where vacationers and second-home owners stop to refresh themselves on their journeys to points north; New York City residents come to get away from it all; and the inn's renowned restaurant (with live piano music on Friday and Saturday nights) draws visitors and locals alike.

Another major draw is innkeeper Edie Evans, a former psychiatric social worker. Sixteen years ago Edie and her late husband, Bob, bought the then-defunct inn and spent a year restoring it. You can sense her presence throughout the establishment, from her original sculptures in the living room to her blueberry muffins at breakfast.

Although the restaurant dominates a large part of the first floor, including a large screened porch with a brick floor and ceiling fans, you can be assured that there's still plenty of private space for the inn's guests, from the blue and white living room and more formal parlor to the spacious and homey bedrooms. The decor of each room varies: Room 9 has a four-poster bed and Oriental rug, Room 7 has a king-size brass bed, and Room 11 has an American Renaissance–style bed and book-lined shelves.

Edie is particularly proud of the inn's restaurant, which has an eclectic menu that changes weekly. It's not just the food and drink that soothe the soul here but also the innkeeper's attitude: "We only have one sitting a night for each table," she notes. "We don't want our guests to feel rushed."

Behind the inn there's a six-unit motel annex. The rooms there, decorated with Cushman Colonial furnishings, are less expensive than those in the main house. Edie has transformed an old carriage house behind the inn into a gift shop; there you can find antique jewelry, crafts, and one-of-a-kind items.

🏠 *10 double rooms with baths, 1 suite (6 of these are in motel annex). Restaurant, TV with VCR in common room and in suite, limited room service, gift and gourmet shops. $65–$120; full breakfast. AE, D, DC, MC, V. Smoking in motel only, pets in motel with advance arrangements, 2-night minimum on holiday and summer weekends.*

The Six Sisters

149 Union Ave., Saratoga Springs, NY 12866, tel. 518/583–1173, fax 518/587–2470

On busy Union Avenue, just across the street from Saratoga's thoroughbred racetrack, stands this 1880 Victorian

home with a scallop-edge roof and basket-weave porches shaded by green-and-white stripe awnings. Owned by Kate Benton and Steve Ramirez, the inn is named in honor of Kate and her five sisters (each room is named after a different sister). Kate is a former high school guidance counselor from a native Saratoga family of 12, but the name Six Sisters and Six Brothers was a bit unwieldy.

While the house is not the "high Victorian" of some Saratoga properties, it's not without its touches: natural hardwoods, tiger oak door and mantle, stained glass, and some antiques. One of the most inviting of the guest rooms is Agatha Rosemarie, which has a whirlpool tub with separate shower and a spacious balcony; it is pleasingly decorated with rose-patterned wallpaper in shades of greens, tans, and pinks. Another coveted room, Bernice Irene, has a second-story balcony with its own table and sitting area. Steve is a terrific cook, so breakfast—which includes what may be the best corn bread north of the Mason-Dixon Line and delightful conversation with the hosts—is a real drawing card.

🏠 *5 double rooms with baths. Air-conditioning, whirlpools in 2 rooms, TV, minirefrigerators. $70–$275; full breakfast. AE, MC, V. No smoking, no pets, 2-night minimum on weekends Apr.–Nov., 4-night minimum in Aug.*

The State House

393 State St., Albany, NY 12210, tel. 518/427–6063, fax 518/465–8079

During the day, sunlight pours through the windows of this late-19th-century town house facing Albany's Washington Park. Dark mahogany architectural accents complement the hand-glazed walls of the interior, where high ceilings, fireplaces, and interesting antiques make you feel as if you're sitting in the pages of *Architectural Digest*. Don't worry though; this place isn't stiff. The charms of innkeeper Charles Kuhtic are apparent throughout the house, from the abundance of fresh flowers to the classical music that plays quietly in the sitting room.

The light and airy bedrooms are decorated in shades of white and cream, complemented by dark-wood moldings. Tall palms further add to the sense that you have been carried back to French Indochina. All the rooms are large and have sitting areas with either overstuffed chairs or small sofas, and the beds, which have down comforters and luxurious cotton sheets, are downright decadent.

🏠 *4 double rooms with baths. Phones and modem lines in rooms, library. $150–$185; Continental-plus breakfast. D, MC, V.*

The Westchester House

102 Lincoln Ave., Box 944, Saratoga Springs, NY 12866, tel. 518/587–7613 or 800/581–7613

This Queen Anne Victorian structure—a true painted lady—was built in 1885 by a master carpenter in Saratoga to house his own family. The elaborately carved fireplaces, fluted columns, handcrafted chestnut moldings, and other details make this bed-and-breakfast especially impressive. Innkeepers Stephanie and Bob Melvin furnished the house with antiques and works of art, but there is no air of the museum here. The Melvins—he worked in government and she sang opera in Washington, D.C. (you may be able to convince her to sing an aria)—are outgoing and happy to converse on subjects ranging from the Eastlake influence on their house to the culture and history of their adopted city. Their diverse interests are represented by the variety of books in the living room. An open doorway connects that room to the two-room breakfast area, which has arched windows overlooking an outdoor garden.

The guest rooms are tastefully furnished with such antique treasures as Louis XVI bedroom sets, oak washstands, Empire chests, and an art-nouveau cheval mirror. The hosts point out that the Victorians were the most eclectic of collectors and believe that they and the Westchester House "embody the true Victorian spirit."

🏠 *7 double rooms with baths. Air-conditioning. $75–$250; Continental-plus breakfast. AE, MC, V. Smoking on porch only, no pets, 4-night minimum in Aug., closed Jan.*

The Catskills

The Catskills are the stuff of legends both old and new. Several hundred years ago, Washington Irving's Rip Van Winkle took a 20-year nap in these mountains. In more modern times, such popular performers as Milton Berle, Eddie Fisher, Sid Caesar, and Jackie Mason got their starts at Catskills resorts.

The region's tradition of hospitality and fine dining dates back about 100 years. Originally the area attracted a number of wealthy New Yorkers who built their summer residences here, but it wasn't until such resorts as Grossinger's and the Nevele arrived on the scene during the 1920s that the Catskills became known across the country. Famous for the prodigious amounts of food they served, these establishments once catered to a primarily Jewish clientele, but today the major resorts attract a more diverse group of vacationers.

The Catskills still have their ethnic enclaves—East Durham and Leeds draw a great number of Irish-Americans, Round Top and Purling reflect a German influence, Haines Falls and Tannersville promote a number of Italian attractions, and a Ukrainian festival is held each year near Lexington and Jewett. The mountains everywhere, however, are the main lure for those who want a country vacation just a few hours' drive from Manhattan.

The area offers a variety of outdoor and seasonal pleasures, not the least of which is the region's natural beauty, which can be enjoyed whether you're fishing from one of the many Catskills lakes or streams or sitting on a front porch with a mountain view. Golfers have a choice of more than 40 courses. Alpine skiers can schuss down various slopes, including Belleayre Mountain, Bobcat, Cortina Valley, Holiday Mountain, Hunter Mountain, Scotch Valley, and Ski Windham. Miles of pristine cross-country ski trails are also accessible, both at a number of the larger resorts and at Eldred Preserve, Frost Valley, Hyer Meadows, and White Birches. Ski the Catskills (tel. 914/586–1944) has information on all area slopes and trails.

The Catskills attract a good number of anglers because the waters here teem with fish. One of the most famous trout-fishing streams in the United States—the Beaverkill—lies in the southern part of the area. Mountain-climbing enthusiasts find some of the East Coast's most challenging treks among the Catskills peaks. In addition, biking and hiking trails are plentiful.

Antiques, art, and crafts aficionados continue to find treasures in small towns and along back roads. The Woodstock Art Colony is noted for its galleries, boutiques, and restaurants. It was not, however, the location of the major celebration of the 1960s peace-and-love generation—that landmark cultural event occurred in a field on Max Yasgur's farm, in Bethel, about 45 minutes from Woodstock.

Places to Go, Sights to See

Bronck Museum (Pieter Bronck Rd., off Rte. 9W, Coxsackie, tel. 518/731–8862). Listed on the National Register of Historic Places, this complex of Dutch Colonial houses (one dating from 1663) and 19th-century barns has been a working farm for eight generations of the Bronck family. Exhibits include 18th- and 19th-century furnishings and art.

Catskill Game Farm (Catskill, tel. 518/678–9595). Rare and exotic animals from around the world can be seen here, and children will be well entertained at the petting zoo. Kids (the two-legged kind) bottle-feeding kids (the four-legged kind) makes for interesting photos.

Hunter Mountain Festivals (Hunter Mountain, tel. 518/263–3800). Each summer, this ski area hosts major ethnic and music festivals, attracting visitors from all over the country. Events include the German Alps Festival, with oompah bands and a Hummel-figurine look-alike contest; two country music festivals; the Celtic Festival; and the Mountain Eagle Indian Festival, which draws 400 tribes from throughout North America.

Opus 40 and **Quarryman's Museum** (Saugerties, tel. 914/246–3400). Professor Harvey Fite spent 37 years creating this 6½-acre sculpture garden—ramps, terraces, fountains, and a monolith—in an abandoned quarry. Sunset concerts are given in the summer.

Tubing the Esopus (Phoenicia). A 5-mile stretch of the Esopus Creek, between Shandaken and Mt. Pleasant, is the place to be on hot summer days in the Catskills. Visitors enjoy taking an inner tube to drift with the current and ride the rapids. The **Town Tinker** (Bridge St., tel. 914/688–5553) rents tubes and will show you how and where to tube; it offers beginner and advanced courses.

Restaurants

Fine northern Italian dishes are featured at **La Griglia** (Windham, tel. 518/734–4499). Innovative menus and antique tavern decor are draws at the **DePuy Canal House** (Rte. 213, High Falls, tel. 914/687–7777). The romantic **Locust Tree Inn** (215 Huguenot St., New Paltz, tel. 914/255–7888) serves American-Continental cuisine.

Tourist Information

Delaware County Chamber of Commerce (97 Main St., Delhi 13753, tel. 607/746–2281 or 800/642–4443). **Greene County Promotion Department** (Box 527, Catskill 12414, tel. 518/943–3223; 800/355–2287 outside NY). **Sullivan County Office of Public Information** (100 North St., Box 5012, Monticello 12701, tel. 914/794–3000, ext. 5010, or 800/882–2287). **Ulster County Public Information Office** (Box 1800, Kingston 12401, tel. 914/340–3000; 800/342–5826 outside NY).

Albergo Allegria

Rte. 296, Windham, NY 12496, tel. 518/734-5560

This gingerbread Victorian mansion in the northern Catskills—midway between Ski Windham and the White Birches cross-country trails—was originally two cottages that were part of a 19th-century summer boardinghouse colony. Owners Lenore and Vito Radelich had the two structures joined in 1985: The new middle section is indistinguishable from those sections built in 1867.

The bed-and-breakfast is noted for its stunning oak floors, original chestnut moldings, and keyhole windows. Guest rooms take their names from the seasons and months of the year: June has a stained-glass window, a cathedral ceiling, and a terrific view of Ski Windham; and Summer, the honeymoon suite, has a king-size bed, a skylight, and a double whirlpool bath. All rooms have down comforters. In January 1997, a new Carriage House annex with five rooms opened behind the main house. The rooms are more like spacious suites; each has a private entrance, a gaslit fireplace, a high cathedral ceiling with skylight, and a two-person whirlpool bath with a shuttered window that opens to the bedroom.

You'll find many thoughtful touches here. Beverages, such as raspberry iced tea in summer or hot cocoa in winter, are always available, and there's a large video library on the second floor of the main house with over 250 tapes from which to choose. The high quality of the food reflects the Radeliches' 25 years in the restaurant business. Breakfast is extensive, with items such as cashew-crusted banana pancakes or stuffed French toast. And if you're wondering whether the swimming hole by the waterfall out back is deep enough for diving—it was back when Johnny Weissmuller filmed his first *Tarzan* movie there.

▦ *21 double rooms with baths. Air-conditioning in 7 rooms, TVs and VCRs in all rooms, fireplaces in 8 rooms, whirlpool baths in 7 rooms, swimming hole, gift shop. $65–$195; full breakfast. D, DC, MC, V. No smoking in public areas, no pets, 2-night minimum on weekends, 3-night minimum on holiday weekends.*

Anthony Dobbins Stagecoach Inn

268 Main St., Maplewood Terrace, Goshen, NY 10924, tel. 914/294-5526

Since 1740, only three families have owned the Anthony Dobbins Stagecoach Inn. The present proprietor, Margo Hickock, takes pleasure in imagining what the original inn—complete with common room and bundling boards—must have been like. In its present incarnation as a bed-and-breakfast, the inn is no doubt a great deal more comfortable than its 18th-century predecessor. It even has an elevator.

The house is charmingly furnished with English antiques, some of which are family heirlooms. "Nothing matches, but everything fits," says Margo, whose family is descended from both Wild Bill Hickok and William Penn.

The William Penn room, with flowered wallpaper and Williamsburg-blue trim, has an antique four-poster bed, fireplace, sundeck, and private bath; it can be transformed into a double suite with the Roosevelt room next door. The Hickok Room has an antique brass bed and a fainting couch, and the Guggenheim Room has a small couch and two twin beds with high canopies.

You can breakfast on the terrace by the reflecting pool, in the sunroom by the fountain, with a pink flamingo, or at the Heplewhite table with Windsor chairs in the formal dining room. A collection of Currier and Ives prints and paintings of horses adorns the inn's spacious entry hall, but for the real thing, visitors need only walk half a block to the racetrack.

Goshen is known as the Cradle of the Trotters, and the harness track here is the nation's oldest. Tennis courts are also a short walk away, and hot-air-balloon rides can be arranged at a nearby airport.

🏨 *4 double rooms with baths. Air-conditioning, cable TV in public room. $85–$150; Continental breakfast, afternoon tea. AE, MC, V. Smoking in sunroom only, no pets, 2-night minimum on weekends.*

Audrey's Farmhouse

2188 Brunswick Rd., Walkill, NY 12589, tel. 914/895–3440, fax 914/895–8114

The Shawangunk mountain range rises dramatically behind this cedar-shingle farmhouse set on 135 acres of meadows in Walkill, a small hamlet about 20 minutes from New Paltz. With the "gunks" in its backyard, the activity quotient here is high. Owners Audrey and Don Leff have been hosting rock climbers, hikers, bikers, and cross-country skiers in their home for more than nine years. But if you're interested in less challenging feats, you can take a dip in the pool or hot tub. In summer, the yard is a great spot for lounging (try and snag the hammock if you can). There's also plenty of antiquing in nearby New Paltz.

The interior of the farmhouse is warm and inviting, with thickly plastered walls and dried flowers and baskets hanging from hand-hewn beams that cross the ceiling. In the smaller sitting room, you can see remnants of the original light blue milk paint that once decorated the floor.

The downstairs guest room has a magnificent view and a massive log bed (which dominates the small room) facing a window—it's just you, the bed, and the mountains. There's a private bath across the hall. The rooms upstairs are larger, especially the lofty Cathedral room, which has an angular beamed ceiling. Each room has a comfy down comforter, which is tied with ribbon and placed at the end of the bed.

A generous gourmet breakfast is served at a long rustic table in the larger sitting room. The menu might include potatoes, a fruit parfait, bacon or sausage, and California eggs with avocado, tomatoes, and string beans. Guests are welcome to use the kitchen throughout the day.

🏨 *3 rooms with baths, 2 rooms share bath. Pool, hot tub, hiking trails. $90–$120; full breakfast. AE, MC, V.*

Beaverkill Valley Inn

Lew Beach, NY 12753, tel. 914/439–4844

"I have laid aside business, and gone a-fishing," wrote Izaak Walton in *The Compleat Angler;* Walton would probably have loved the Beaverkill, America's most famous fly-fishing stream. Although the Beaverkill Valley Inn, built in 1893 as a boardinghouse at Lew Beach, never played host to Walton, Jimmy Carter, Robert Redford, Sigourney Weaver, Gary Trudeau, Jane Pauley, and assorted Kennedys have all been guests here. Owned and developed by Laurance Rockefeller and managed by able innkeeper Christina Jurgens, the inn caters to those who cherish privacy. Its surrounding forests and nearby fields, preserved as "forever wild," are protected from development.

This is not to say that accommodations are rustic at this wilderness retreat. The large house, which is on the National Register of Historic Places, sits proudly on an expanse of lawn that's met by the Catskill Mountains. The grounds, with an herb garden and pond, are immaculate, and a stretch of the Beaverkill River runs right through the property. Even the croquet court is outlined by small patches of flowers. White-painted rocking chairs line the wide porch, a welcoming fire warms the living room on frosty days, and the dining-room windows offer a panoramic view of the grounds. The card and billiard rooms, with their green-shade lamps, have a clubby, masculine atmosphere. Instead of card playing, however, you may see someone giving a lesson on how to tie a fly for tomorrow's catch. Fishing is definitely the draw here (the inn has a package arrangement with the Wulff Fly Fishing School nearby).

Guest rooms are simply furnished with brass-and-iron beds, comfortable chairs, handmade quilts, and good reading lamps. Many of the rooms have twin beds.

Dinner may include such offerings as poached Norwegian salmon with watercress sauce, and fillet of beef with blue-cheese sauce. All baked goods are made on the premises, and the inn uses home-grown herbs and salad greens.

For those not hooked on angling, there's certainly plenty else to do. A converted barn with a cathedral ceiling houses a heated swimming pool, a help-yourself ice-cream parlor, a theater, and a children's playroom. Sports enthusiasts also have access to tennis courts, hiking, and cross-country ski trails and skating in winter.

▥ *13 double rooms with baths, 8 doubles share 5 baths. Restaurant, bar, conference facilities, game rooms, pool, stocked pond, Beaverkill fishing. $260–$330; breakfast, lunch, afternoon tea, dinner. AE, MC, V. No smoking indoors, no pets, 2-night minimum on weekends, 3-night minimum on holiday weekends.*

Captain Schoonmaker's Bed-and-Breakfast

913 State Rte. 213, Box 37, High Falls, NY 12440, tel. 914/687–7946

You'll find it easy to lose yourself in the past in the meticulously restored 1760 Hudson Valley stone house where this inn's living room, dining room (where breakfast is served), library, solarium, and canopied decks are located. Americana is everywhere. The place at High Falls even claims its own Early American ghost, friendly Captain Fred.

And the new hosts, Judy and Bill Klock, are friendly, too. The inn's guest rooms are in the 1820 Carriage House, which is in front of the main stone house. The romantic rooms upstairs were once a hayloft, and the original beams have been left exposed. One downstairs room has a brass bed and a tree growing through the middle of a private deck. The upstairs rooms have private balconies.

Only the delicious breakfasts could tear guests away from their waterfall rooms: It's hard to ignore such culinary delights as lemon poppy-seed cake, poached pears in raspberry sauce, cheese soufflé, and blueberry strudel, served at an antique black-walnut table by the dining-room fireplace. Wines and cheeses are served in the afternoons as well. Nearby is the De Puy Canal House, a highly touted restaurant with a creative menu.

▥ *4 double rooms share 2 baths. Cable TV in library-den, fireplaces in 3 public rooms, swimming and trout fishing in stream. $80–$90; full breakfast, afternoon snacks. No credit cards. No pets, closed Christmas wk.*

Deer Mountain Inn

Rte. 25, Box 443, Tannersville, NY 12485, tel. 518/589–6268

If Deer Mountain Inn in Tannersville resembles a lodge designed for European nobility, it's no accident. Owner Danielle Gortel and her husband come from the mountains of Poland: It was only natural that these two avid skiers settle in Catskills ski country and that they keep an inn that resembles Spala, the ancient hunting seat of Polish kings.

Built as a private residence, the circa-1900 mansion stands in a 15-acre wooded enclave. This place is lushly packed with mountain ambience—moose heads, boar heads, bearskin rugs, ram's horn candleholders, paintings of European mountain villages, and heavy, overstuffed furniture. It is said that the house was once owned by the notorious gangster Legs Diamond.

Today the focus of the gracious cherry-paneled living room is a huge stone fireplace. In winter an après-ski snack of cheese, sausages, and wine is served by a bone-warming fire. The inn has a bright, airy breakfast room, and glass doors lead to the deck, a romantic spot for a summer evening. Some guest rooms have fireplaces, pine wainscoting, and diamond-pane windows.

▥ *7 double rooms with baths or showers. Restaurant, TVs in rooms. $95–$145; full breakfast. AE, MC, V. Smoking in public areas only, no pets.*

Greenville Arms 1889 Inn

R.D. 1, Box 2, Greenville, NY 12083, tel. 518/966–5219

Start with a turreted 1889 Queen Anne Victorian (built by William Vanderbilt as a private residence) on a tree-lined street in the center of the small town of Greenville. Add columned porches with the obligatory wicker rockers and gliders, croquet on the lawn, a brook, a carriage house, an intimate restaurant, and admirable antiques, and you have the Greenville Arms.

This delightful 6-acre property features a swimming pool and a lit shuffleboard court; golf and tennis facilities are nearby. It's an activity-filled retreat for families with older children and groups. The inn also offers 18 yearly painting workshops, with distinguished artist-instructors from all over the world, in the heart of Thomas Cole and Frederick Church country.

Eliot and Tish Dalton are the inn's owners. Eliot may be the only innkeeper in the state who was once a tugboat captain. Tish's background in the graphic arts has served her well in decorating the inn; she's also the inn's chef.

▥ *12 double rooms with baths, 1 suite. Restaurant, pool. $110–$145; full breakfast. MC, V. No smoking, no pets, 2-night minimum on holiday weekends.*

Mountainview Inn of Shandelee

913 Shandelee Rd., Livingston Manor, NY 12758, tel. 914/439–5070

This 1905 farmhouse in Livingston Manor has been a boardinghouse, a hotel, and even a bowling alley. But in 1994 when Bob and Maryann Witzak, two former bankers from New Jersey, bought it from owner Dick Lanza, it became their dream come true. "We've wanted to do something like this ever since our children were young," says Bob.

The inn sits in the heart of Sullivan County's trout haven, and anglers fly-fish on the nearby Beaverkill and Willowmec rivers. The property consists of 10 acres, complete with a beaver pond and herb and flower gardens. Guests may breakfast in the greenhouse dining room, surrounded by native pine and a variety of plants. A downstairs tap room has a fireplace, TV, and game machines, and pizza is served there. One room features an art deco–style bedroom set, and another has a high-back Victorian oak bed and an oak dresser (the same one advertised for $5.95 from the 1905 Sears Roebuck catalog).

▥ *8 double rooms with baths. Restaurant, tap room. $80–$87; full breakfast; MAP rates available. AE, D, DC, MC, V. No pets.*

Point Lookout Mountain Inn

The Mohican Trail, Rte. 23, East Windham, NY 12439, tel. 518/734–3381

On a clear day, you can see the mountain ranges of five states from Point Lookout Mountain Inn, a roadside lodge on the

Mohican Trail. The first Point Lookout tower, built as a tourist attraction, was used during World War II for spotting enemy aircraft. It was destroyed by fire in 1965, when the present structure was built.

In 1980 schoolteachers Rosemary Jensen, Mariana Di Toro, and her brother Lucio Di Torolieso bought what was then an abandoned discotheque and transformed it into this small hostelry. The nondescript rooms are decorated in pale tones, but there is plenty of color in the spectacular sunrises, sunsets, fall foliage, and rainbows that come free at Point Lookout. The inn's Bella Vista restaurant combines a variety of cuisines, including Italian and Mediterranean. The casual Rainbow Café serves soups, salads, sandwiches, and some Southwestern fare.

▥ *13 double rooms with baths. Restaurant, TV in rooms, recreation room with hot tub. $60–$115; Continental-plus breakfast. AE, DC, MC, V. Pets permitted with deposit, 2-night minimum on winter weekends.*

The Redcoat's Return

Platte Cove (Dale La.), Elka Park, NY 12427, tel. 518/589–9858

Up a twisting mountain road in the Catskill Game Preserve, you'll encounter a little bit of the spirit of England at the Redcoat's Return. Once the center of a potato-and-dairy farm, the 1860 home at Elka Park was later a summer boardinghouse. Now this lodging is known in the area for its English country hospitality.

Tom (the Redcoat) and Peg Wright have owned the inn since 1973; he was once a chef on the *Queen Mary* and she was an actress. The inn features extensive art and antiques collections that bring together mementos of trips abroad—and there's a moose head, named Basil, over the fireplace. Tom, who has a quirky sense of humor, says that he plays golf in his spare time and that "Peg is interested in metaphysics." Both are practiced conversationalists. Tom is full of stories about his objets d'art, which include a cricket bat and a framed antique scarf commemorating the first boxing match between an Englishman and an American, in 1860. Zoe, the Wrights' Bernese mountain dog, can also be a charming hostess.

The Wrights have chosen to preserve the atmosphere of the old boardinghouse, so rooms are small but pleasantly cozy. Antique iron beds and oak dressers are part of the original decor. Third-floor bedrooms have eaved ceilings, and one large room offers two double beds. Rooms are supplied with bathrobes for guests.

Hikers should enjoy the numerous trails that lead from the inn onto nearby Overlook, Indian Head, Twin, and Hunter mountains. There are cross-country trails and three alpine ski areas close by. Spring anglers have access to a trout stream on the property, and golfers will find several fine courses a short drive away.

▥ *7 double rooms with baths, 5 doubles share 3 baths. Restaurant. $70–$95; full breakfast. AE, MC, V. 2-night minimum July–Oct. and on Feb. weekends, 3-night minimum on holiday weekends.*

The Hudson River Valley

Few of America's waterways can compete with the Hudson River's combination of majestic grace and history. From the earliest explorations of the continent, in the 17th century, through the Revolutionary War, this 315-mile-long river has played an important part in the development of the nation.

Long a major thoroughfare of commerce, the Hudson was home to the first commercial steam-power boat, Fulton's Clermont; *several years later the opening of the Erie Canal clinched the river's claim as the nation's most important waterway; and in the mid-1800s the river port of Hudson even became a center of the whaling industry.*

The natural beauty of the river has attracted many prominent artists and writers. In the 19th century the Hudson River School of painters was formed, inspired by the noble river and by the works of Washington Irving, one of the first American writers to be recognized abroad. As we retreat up the Hudson from where it empties into the Atlantic Ocean at Manhattan, we behold the same beautiful vistas—the majestic hills and splendid palisades—that inspired those 19th-century artists.

Many old river towns, such as Tarrytown, Cold Spring, and Hudson, retain the atmosphere of the distant past, and some have even been restored to their 19th-century glory.

The valley merits careful exploration by the traveler. The largely unspoiled countryside includes prosperous farms and splendid estates once inhabited by some of America's most distinguished families: the Roosevelts, Vanderbilts, Harrimans, and Rockefellers. In addition to visiting those palatial estates, visitors can explore numerous historical sites, such as Philipsburg Manor (the residence of a 17th-century Dutch shipping magnate), Sunnyside (home of Washington Irving), Stony Point Battlefield, and Washington's Headquarters in Newburgh. Also, the valley is home to some of the nation's most prestigious institutes of higher learning: the U.S. Military Academy at West Point, Vassar College, Sarah Lawrence College, and Bard College. The Culinary Institute of America, which has schooled many prominent chefs, is in the area.

Travelers can reach the Hudson and its valley both on Hudson River cruises and on Amtrak. Driving through the valley, however, gives explorers more freedom to visit historic places and pursue antiquing, hiking, fishing, sailing, and hot-air ballooning as the mood strikes.

The valley's seasonal pleasures include cross-country skiing in state parks in winter, strolls through historic gardens in spring, summer picnics on river bluffs, and leaf watching and apple picking in fall. The many valley orchards make the region one of the country's chief apple producers: A perfect excursion could include a picnic in one of the pick-your-own orchards—with dessert right off the tree, of course. The Hudson Valley's vineyards are also starting to build a worldwide reputation, and many can be visited.

Places to Go, Sights to See

The Culinary Institute of America (Hyde Park, tel. 914/471–6608). Many of this country's leading chefs received their training at CIA, which was founded in New Haven in 1946. In 1972 the school moved to its present site, a former Jesuit seminary at Hyde Park, overlooking the Hudson River. More than 4,000 meals are prepared here every day, and visitors may dine at any of the institute's four restaurants: the award-winning American Bounty, the Escoffier, St. Andrew's Café, and the Caterina de Medici Dining Room. Reservations are essential.

Franklin Delano Roosevelt National Historic Site (Hyde Park, tel. 914/229–9115 for tour information). The Roosevelt family estate, retreat of our 32nd president, is in Hyde Park. Here visitors will find the setting of some of Roosevelt's "fireside chats," as well as many of his personal effects, including his wheelchair and books. The graves of the president and his wife, Eleanor, are in the Rose Garden, next to the house. The FDR Library and Museum are also on the grounds.

Hudson Valley Wineries. There are a number of notable wineries on both sides of the river. Most are open to the public—some by appointment—and offer tours, tastings, and restaurants. Among them are *Millbrook Vineyards*, on Wing and Shunpike roads in Millbrook (tel. 914/677–8383); *Brotherhood* (America's oldest winery), in Washingtonville (tel. 914/496–9101); and *Clinton Vineyards*, in Clinton Corners (tel. 914/266–5372).

Olana State Historic Site (Hudson, tel. 518/828–0135, reservations advised). The home of Hudson River School artist Frederick Edwin Church commands a stunning view of the river. The Persian-style mansion is surrounded by gardens and carriage trails. The house, designed by the artist and built between 1870 and 1891, is shown by guided tour only, mid-April through late October, but the grounds are open year-round for outdoor pursuits such as walking, running, and cross-country skiing. Olana is outside the city of Hudson, near the Rip Van Winkle Bridge.

The Shaker Museum (Old Chatham, tel. 518/794–9100). This off-the-beaten-track museum houses the largest collection of Shaker artifacts in the United States. More than 40,000 items, from baskets to wagons, are on display in the eight buildings that make up the exhibition.

The United States Military Academy (tel. 914/938–2638 for tour information). Known simply as West Point, the academy has been the training ground for U.S. Army officers since 1802. The site is also the country's oldest military base in continuous operation. Athletic events (especially the yearly contest between the Army and Navy football teams) draw many visitors to the post. There's also an outstanding military museum.

Restaurants

Larry Forgione's **Beekman 1766 Tavern** (Rhinebeck, tel. 914/871–1766) serves updated American colonial fare in a romantic inn setting. **Xaviar's** (Garrison, tel. 914/424–4228), open weekends only, offers a prix-fixe menu with some of the best cooking in the Hudson Valley. **Riverview** (45 Fair St., Cold Spring, tel. 914/265–4778) has a trattoria-style menu, which includes great pizzas from the wood-fired brick oven.

Tourist Information

Hudson Valley Tourism (tel. 800/232–4782).

Aubergine

Intersection of Rtes. 22 and 23, Hillsdale, NY 12529, tel. 518/325–3412

This 1783 Dutch redbrick Colonial sits on one of the four corners at the traffic light in Hillsdale, a quiet town just a few miles from the Massachusetts border. David and Stacy Lawson took over the inn in 1994. (It was formerly the well-known L'hostellerie Bressane, established by Jean Morel in 1971.) The new owners have made changes to the decor and to the menu, but one thing has stayed the same: It's still "a restaurant with rooms," says David, the chef-owner. A native Minnesotan who studied under Albert Roux in London, David was the executive chef at Blantyre, in Lenox, Massachusetts.

The French-inspired country cooking is the main draw here. For starters, try the restaurant's signature dish: Maine scallop cakes with shiitakes, scallions, and bean sprouts in a warm ponzu vinaigrette. For your main course, the Atlantic salmon au poivre served over a fondue of leeks with rich red wine sauce is delectable, as is the pan-roasted skate with spinach, Thai chile, and lemon sauce. One of the most popular desserts is the moist chocolate hazelnut cake with pistachio sauce.

This inn is the perfect place for a gourmet getaway: You can leisurely eat a scrumptious meal and then toddle upstairs to your room. The rooms are simply furnished, and the two on the second floor have private baths, although they are down the hall. The two rooms on the third floor have attached baths. David loves to chat with his guests at breakfast, which is served in the bar area. With its shuttered windows and French country chandelier, the bar works very well as a breakfast room.

🏨 *4 double rooms. Restaurant (closed Mon.–Tues., no lunch), air-conditioning. MC, V. $85–$110; breakfast not included. No smoking.*

The Bird and Bottle Inn

Old Albany Post Rd., Rte. 9 (R 2, Box 129), Garrison, NY 10524, tel. 914/424–3000, fax 914/424–3283

The Bird and Bottle Inn in Garrison predates the Revolutionary War and was once a way station on the old Albany–New York post road. Today it is a homey but sophisticated country inn and restaurant with a well-deserved international reputation—and it's only an hour from Manhattan. The inn's owner, Ira Boyar, has been in the hospitality industry for more than 25 years, and he applies his expertise to all aspects of the inn, from marketing to menu choices.

All the elegantly Colonial rooms have fireplaces. The Emily Warren Room offers a queen-size canopy bed draped in rose-color fabric. The John Warren Room boasts the original wainscoting and fireplace, and the suite has a private terrace. The cottage suite, 50 yards from the inn, appeals to couples seeking a secluded getaway. The wooded setting includes Indian Creek, babbling along the back of the inn, and hiking along miles of historic roads.

🏨 *2 double rooms with baths, 1 suite, 1 cottage. Restaurant, air-conditioning. $210–$240; breakfast and dinner. AE, DC, MC, V. No pets, 2-night minimum with Sat. reservation.*

Hudson House

2 Main St., Cold Spring, NY 10516, tel. 914/265–9355

From the foot of Main Street in the charming 19th-century village of Cold Spring, this 1832 inn (the second oldest inn in continuous operation in the state) takes in spectacular views of the Hudson River, West Point, and Storm King Mountain. Visitors here should request a room facing the river.

The entire inn, from the wood-paneled bar and sitting area downstairs to the 15 guest rooms, was renovated in 1981. Many rooms are furnished with old-fashioned painted-iron beds (quite a few have twin beds), and all feature country decor and accessories. River-view rooms on the second floor open onto a wraparound porch. One of the two suites, with twin beds in one room and a double in the other, has just one bathroom and is best suited for a family.

Guests without cars will find the Hudson House an ideal spot for a weekend of antiquing and exploring on foot—the railroad station is just 500 feet from the inn's door.

🏨 *12 double rooms with baths. Restaurant, air-conditioning. $105–$180; full breakfast. AE, MC, V. No smoking, no pets.*

The Inn at Shaker Mill

Cherry La., off Rte. 22, Canaan, NY 12029, tel. 518/794–9345 or 800/365–9345, fax 518/794–9344

The Inn at Shaker Mill, 10 miles from Tanglewood and from skiing at Jiminey Peak, is an unusual establishment for two reasons: its Shaker decor and its gregarious host, Ingram Paperny.

As befits a converted 1823 Shaker mill, the rooms are simply furnished in a comfortable but utilitarian style. Pegboards hang from the plaster walls, and in the Shaker tradition the common room has a barrel roof—though it also boasts a glass wall that looks out on the mill's picturesque brook and waterfalls.

After 25 years in the business, Mr. Paperny has been called the doyen of New England innkeepers. A stay at the inn is like spending time in the home of a fascinating new friend. As might be expected of a former consultant to the United Nations, Ingram is an internationalist; he speaks four languages and relishes playing host to an eclectic bunch of visitors. During summer he brings European hiking and cultural groups to the United States, acts as their tour leader and host, and encourages them to mix with the American guests at the inn. He is also a woodworker and is responsible for all the carpentry done in the building.

The inn is unique in another way: It charges per person, so singles who want to get away from the city can retreat to a place that doesn't put the emphasis on couples (which isn't to say that a room overlooking the waterfalls wouldn't serve as a romantic retreat for two). Also, several of the rooms are large enough to accommodate families: The stone-wall, wood-beam suites on the third floor can sleep six.

The inn's hospitality extends to meals as well. Breakfasts include juice, fresh fruit, cereals, yogurt, cheese, bagels, muffins, breads, and eggs. Dinners vary with the whim of the chef. On Saturday nights in summer there are outdoor barbecues.

🏨 *20 double rooms with baths. Restaurant, swimming pond, sauna. $80–$150; full breakfast and dinner. MC, V. No smoking in dining room.*

Le Chambord

2075 Rte. 52, Hopewell Junction, NY 12533, tel. 914/221–1941 or 800/274–1941, fax 914/221–1941

Although it is housed in an 1863 Georgian-style mansion one minute from the Taconic Parkway, Le Chambord could easily be the focal point of an antebellum Southern plantation. In fact, Scarlett O'Hara would feel right at home on its pillared veranda. The mansion's involvement with things Southern is more than skin-deep, however: The trap door under the inn's bar leads to a former stop on the Underground Railroad.

Miss O'Hara was not far from the mind of innkeeper Roy Benich when he named the latest additions to Le Chambord: Tara Hall, containing 16 rooms; and Butler Hall, which has corporate and banquet facilities. Both structures are in keeping with the genteel traditions of the opulent dining and banquet rooms and the nine handsome bedrooms in the main building.

Roy, a former art-and-antiques dealer, has designed Le Chambord for aesthetic appeal and treats it as his home. "It's my wife and children," he says. He lives on the premises and laments that he works up to 19 hours a day on the inn and the restaurant. (You'll know that he's a bachelor as soon as you see him in one of the outrageous neckties for which he is renowned.) He chooses all the art and antiques for the inn, from the dining room's Chinese breakfront to the sofas and wing chairs covered in imported floral tapestries. No expense has been spared in selecting furniture and accessories—or food and wine, for that matter.

The owner's focus on visual delights is shared by his chef, Leonard Mott, a Culinary Institute of America graduate. For more than 10 years the two have collaborated on an elegant menu that satisfies both the palate and the eye.

Despite such luxuries, the inn is quite affordable. True, the wine list offers a 1929 Château Lafite Rothschild for $1,500—but there are also good wines in the $15 range.

▥ *25 double rooms with baths. Restaurant, air-conditioning, cable TV in all rooms, facilities (including fax) for corporate meetings, fitness room. $115; Continental breakfast. AE, DC, MC, V. No pets.*

The Martindale Bed and Breakfast Inn

Rte. 23, Box 385, Claverack, NY 12513, tel. 518/851-5405

The Martindale Bed and Breakfast Inn is located in rural Columbia County. The 1852 building is a Hudson Valley "bracket house," a hybrid of Southern, Victorian, and Federal architecture. It was in the same family for 134 years before it began its new life as a bed-and-breakfast. It is now supervised by innkeepers Terry and Soll Berl—a retired teacher and a physician, respectively.

The Berls opened up a warren of small, dark spaces and turned it into an airy and elegant B&B. The wide-board floors found throughout are originals, and the chestnut molding was fashioned from trees growing on the property when the house was built.

Guest rooms have antique brass or four-poster oak beds and are graced with 19th-century prints and dried-flower wreaths. The antiques-furnished sitting room has a TV, VCR, and CD player, but guests often prefer to pass the time in the homey kitchen munching on Terry's muffins and scones.

▥ *2 double rooms with baths, 2 doubles share bath. TV with VCR in parlor, dinner available with 24 hrs' notice. $65–$75; full breakfast. No credit cards. Smoking on veranda only, 2-day minimum on weekends June–Labor Day and Oct.*

The Old Chatham Sheepherding Company Inn

99 Shaker Museum Rd., Old Chatham, NY 12136, tel. 518/794-9774, fax 518/794-9779

As you approach, you'll probably hear a faint "baaaa" coming from the pastoral fields of this working sheep farm. In 1993 Tom and Nancy Clark purchased the 500-acre farm, and in October 1995, they opened the property's 1790 Georgian Manor House as a restaurant and inn. In the time it's been open, the restaurant has become a favorite with folks in the surrounding area. Sunday brunch is an especially active time, posing a problem for overnight guests, who have to compete for living room couches with diners waiting to eat at the restaurant.

The guest rooms—spread throughout the main house and two neighboring buildings—are beautiful, and if you choose one with a private terrace, you may never want to leave it. Shrapshire, one of the smaller rooms in the main house, has a four-poster bed with down pillows and reading lamps on either side. The stunning bathroom has a sloping ceiling and large freestanding tub with wood banister handles. Amenities include terry bathrobes embroidered with a sheep, lots of fluffy towels, and Neutrogena products. A few steps from the main house, past the 19th-century stone smokehouse, is a cottage with two rooms: Hampshire and Cotswold (all the rooms are named after breeds of sheep). Shades of periwinkle and yellow decorate Hampshire, and whimsical Peter Rabbit tiles border the bathroom. The bedroom has a twig bed and quilted chair, and there are two small yellow chairs in the entry hall. Two more rooms share the Carriage House with the company store, where you can buy the farm's delicious cheeses—try the Sheep's Milk Camembert—baked goods, and other sheep paraphernalia.

The landscape—sweeping vistas of verdant sheep meadows dotted with large patches of woods—is remarkably reminiscent of the English countryside. Seemingly endless paths weave through the property for those interested in hiking or biking. There's a swimming hole for summer, and cross-country skiing in winter; golf, tennis, and horseback riding are nearby. Nancy and Tom don't live on the premises, but there's a full-time innkeeper.

▦ *5 rooms with baths in main house, 2 rooms with baths in Carriage House, 2 rooms with baths in cottage. Air-conditioning, phones in rooms, fireplaces in 4 rooms, meeting room. $185–$350; full breakfast. AE, MC, V. No smoking, no pets, 2-night minimum May–Nov. weekends, 3-night minimum holiday weekends.*

Old Drover's Inn

Off Rte. 22, Dover Plains, NY 12522, tel. 914/832–9311

Although there are only four guest rooms at this inn, you're pampered as if it were a luxury hotel. Not surprising, considering it has a staff of 22! Although these employees also run the award-winning restaurant, there is always someone to cosset you. Innkeepers Alice Pitcher and Kemper Peacock have undoubtedly created one of the state's most romantic hideaways. Old Drover's is one of only three Relais & Chateaux properties in Upstate New York.

One of the most wonderful things about the inn is its age: It's nearly 250 years old. It was opened by John and Ebenezer Preston in 1750 as the Clear Water Tavern, and it hosted many of the area's cattle drovers on their way to New York City. Since then, the deed has only changed hands three times, and the inn has always been open for business. You can absolutely *feel* the authenticity of the place. You may notice a slight rise and fall as you walk across the entryway's undulating floorboards, and if you're over 6-feet-1, you may have to duck when you're in the dining room.

The idiosyncratic charms of the house are matched by the great mix of furniture styles—a Louis XVI–style chair here, an American Chippendale there. There are plenty of places for lounging, from the library with down-filled couches and many, many books, to the sitting room, to the property's 12 acres.

Three of the guest rooms have working fireplaces, and all are stocked with terrycloth robes, soaps, bubble bath, shampoo, and conditioner. The largest room is the Meeting Room, with two double beds, a sitting area, and a high barrel-vault ceiling painted to look like parchment paper. It is also the only room with both a tub and shower (others have tubs only). Lovely botanical prints hang on the walls and built-in benches line the room, reflecting its original use as a hall for town meetings.

Everyone faces the center of the Federal dining room, which is lined with red banquettes. Murals, painted in 1941 by Edward Paine, cover three walls. The largest of the inn's nine working fireplaces is here. It's a dark, regal room where classical music quietly plays. Weekday Continental breakfasts include granolas, fruit, and homemade breads—the house specialty is an Amish Friendship bread. Weekend breakfasts are much more elaborate, with items such as Belgian malted waffles and Southern-style grits.

Downstairs, where lunch and dinner are served, bartender Charlie has been serving his infamous double cocktails for 33 years. Copper pots hang from the dark-beamed ceiling, and empty bottles of impressive wines fill the shelves that line the room. The menu will include the inn's signature dishes—a silky-smooth cheddar cheese soup and browned turkey hash—along with other, more sophisticated entrées, perhaps seared Mahi Mahi with ginger tomato sauce or roasted veal loin with shallot and truffle sauce. Don't pass up the lamb chops if they're offered.

At press time, there was talk of adding cabins to the property. If you're looking for the ultimate private getaway, call to see if they're available.

🏠 *4 double rooms with baths. Restaurant (no lunch Mon.–Thurs.), air-conditioning, fireplaces in 3 rooms and 6 public areas, hiking. $150–$395; full breakfast. D, MC, V. Pets permitted with prior arrangements, 2-night minimum on weekends.*

Pig Hill Inn

73 Main St., Cold Spring, NY 10516, tel. 914/265-9247

There aren't any real pigs in residence, and the Federal-style building wasn't built on a hill named for swine, but owner Wendy O'Brien's affection for porkers is evident throughout Pig Hill Inn: There's a painted-piggy floor cloth in the entryway, and folk-art pig carvings are set amid antiques throughout the inn's three floors. Guests enter the inn by way of an antiques store on the first floor.

Each guest room is unique. Room 1 imparts a rustic feeling, with Indian rugs, antlers hung above the fireplace, and a settee made from birch logs. Room 6 contains a full four-poster bed and inviting burgundy wing chairs, and Room 7 has its own wood-burning stove and a stunning antique pine armoire.

The downstairs sitting room has rag rugs, comfortable chairs, and a collection of classic children's books, including *Charlotte's Web*, whose main character is a pig named Wilbur. The fictional Wilbur had to settle for slops in the barn, but guests at Pig Hill are pampered with breakfast in bed of shirred eggs and freshly baked breads and a copy of the day's *New York Times*.

🏠 *4 double rooms with baths, 4 doubles share 2 baths. Air-conditioning, fireplaces in 6 rooms. $100–$150; full breakfast. AE, MC, V. No smoking, no pets.*

Plumbush Inn

Rte. 9D, Cold Spring, NY 10516, tel. 914/265-3904

Once the estate of American-born marquise Agnes Rizzo dei Ritii, Plumbush was transformed into an elegant Hudson Valley restaurant in 1976. Several years later, Swiss-born owners Giere Albin and Ans Benderer, who grew up in the hotel-and-restaurant business, decided to convert the Victorian mansion's unused second floor to overnight accommodations.

The grounds are fenced in and nicely landscaped; the buildings are painted—well, plum. Inside, the walls of the Marchesa Suite are covered with flowered paper; the room is furnished with a large iron-and-brass bed and Victorian settee and has a full bath. Two smaller rooms have similar Victorian appointments and private baths.

Breakfast includes homemade croissants, pastries, jams, juices, coffee, and tea and may be served in the guest rooms or on the small downstairs porch. Local attractions include lush golf courses, state parks for hiking and cycling, and the antiques shops in Cold Spring, five minutes away.

▦ *2 double rooms with baths, 1 suite. Restaurant (closed Mon. and Tues.), air-conditioning, cable TV in sitting room. $95–$125; Continental breakfast. AE, MC, V. Smoking in one section of the restaurant area only.*

Simmons Way Village Inn

33 Main St., Millerton, NY 12546, tel. 518/789–6235

Simmons Way Village Inn, set on a wide expanse of lawn in the middle of Millerton, was built by the village's first merchant in 1854 and was transformed into a handsome country inn in 1983.

Current owners Richard and Nancy Carter (he is a management consultant and educator, she is a bank vice-president) bought Simmons Way in 1987 with the idea of running an inn that combined "European civility and American comfort" and served the best in international cuisine. The Carters' son, Erich, works closely with his parents managing the daily activity of the inn.

There are two common rooms on the first floor, one of which opens onto the inviting front porch, where guests may eat breakfast in the warmer months. The second room is home to Max the parrot, who may say hello if he's feeling sociable. The main dining room was added in 1986 but is hard to distinguish from the original structure.

The bedrooms (six on the second floor and three on the third) are furnished with English and European country antiques. Each has its own charm; but Room 5, with its rose-floral wallpaper, queen-size antique iron bed, embroidered bedspread, wicker love seat, and 6-foot French bathtub with hand-held shower, is perhaps the most romantic. Room 2, the Bridal Suite, offers a private covered porch, marble fireplace, and queen-size crown-canopy bed; and Room 4 has peach walls, an English brass canopy bed, swag curtains, and a stripped-pine armoire.

If you can bear to leave these attractive rooms (where breakfast may be taken, if desired) and venture beyond the inviting front porch, the surrounding area is well worth exploring. A swimming pool is 3 miles away, golf courses are close by, and the inn offers special weekday packages that include tickets to the nearby Lime Rock (auto) Race Track—where you might just catch a glimpse of Paul Newman, who frequently races there. "We strive for a full country-inn ambience," says Richard, "—rooms, spirit, and cuisine."

▦ *9 double rooms with baths. Restaurant, air-conditioning, cable TV in common room, banquet facilities, complimentary sherry. $145–$260; Continental breakfast, afternoon tea or wine. AE, DC, MC, V. Smoking in designated areas only, no pets, 2-night minimum on weekends May 1–Nov. 1, 3-night minimum on holiday weekends.*

Troutbeck

Leedsville Rd., Amenia, NY 12501, tel. 914/373–9681, fax 914/373–7080

This Tudor-style manor house set amid 442 gracious acres outside the hamlet of Amenia figured prominently in American literary and political history. It was once home to Myron B. Benton, whose circle of friends included Emerson, Thoreau, and John Burroughs. The estate served as a gathering place for the likes of Sinclair Lewis, Teddy Roosevelt, and Lewis Mumford in the early 20th century, and black leaders formed the NAACP under its roof.

Today Troutbeck also serves the movers and shakers of the corporate world as a conference center during the week. On weekends, however, it is transformed into a country inn, the vision of genial innkeeper Jim Flaherty and his partner, Bob Skibsted. The atmosphere makes this a popular place for weddings, so beware, you may find yourself caught in the middle of someone else's romantic celebration.

The Troutbeck package includes three gourmet meals a day, an open bar, and access to all sorts of recreational activities, ranging from tennis, swimming (indoor and outdoor), fishing, and cross-country skiing to strolling through walled gardens and watching video movies or major sports events on cable TV.

Most of the guest rooms are charming, although the rooms in the main house seem more so. For the premium prices charged by Troutbeck, guests might prefer a room with a fireplace or sunporch in the manor house (with its leaded-glass windows, 12,000-book oak-panel library, and English country appointments) or the Garden House (overlooking the walled gardens) to the Americana offered in the neighboring Century Farmhouse rooms. Of course, guests in any of the buildings have access to all the inn's amenities.

If you can tear yourself away from the estate, the surrounding area is prime antiquing territory, and guests can take elegant prepared picnics with them on excursions. The inn will also arrange transportation to concerts at Tangle-wood, dance performances at Jacob's Pillow, and Shakespeare at the Mount.

🏨 *37 double rooms with private baths, 5 doubles share 3 baths. Restaurant, air-conditioning, fireplaces in 9 rooms, banquet facilities, indoor and outdoor pools, tennis courts, fitness center. $375–$600; 3 meals, wines, and spirits. AE, MC, V. No smoking in dining rooms, no pets, closed weekdays for conferences.*

The Veranda House

82 Montgomery St., Rhinebeck, NY 12572, tel. 914/876–4133

Linda and Ward Stanley, originally from Philadelphia, are the sixth owners of this late Federal house with drop-spindle decoration and green shutters. Unlike many B&B owners, the Stanleys live in the same building where guests stay. They share the TV-sitting room and the dining room with their guests (they close the pocket doors between the living and dining rooms when they are entertaining). The Stanleys also engage in friendly, interesting conversation with visitors.

The house has been immaculately restored, and the decor is very tasteful with a mix of antique furniture and modern abstract paintings by Linda. There is one guest room on the first floor and three upstairs. Rooms have ceiling fans and pencil-post spindle beds. Breakfast is served in the dining room or out on the porch if weather permits.

🏨 *4 rooms with baths. Air-conditioning, phones in rooms. $75–$120; full breakfast. No credit cards. No smoking in house, no pets.*

Eastern Long Island

The eastern end of Long Island first attracted English colonists in the 1640s. They fled the harsh New England winters for the ocean-tempered island and founded the towns of East Hampton and Southampton. The East Hampton area (called Maidstone by these settlers) was purchased from the Shinnecock tribe for 20 coats, 24 hatchets, 24 hoes, 24 looking glasses, and 100 tools the tribe would use for making wampum (beads of polished shell, often used as money). The vacation-time invasion of the farming communities on the island's bucolic eastern end began in the late 19th century and mushroomed when the Long Island Railroad started service to the region from Manhattan's Pennsylvania Station.

Today the ocean is the area's big draw. Those not lucky enough to own beachfront property "south of the highway" (the Montauk Highway) have access to miles of white, sandy public beaches. Although the beaches are free, passes are required for parking. A number of bed-and-breakfasts and inns offer free passes to guests. One pleasant way to avoid parking charges is to bike to the beach.

In summer the South Fork, from Southampton to Montauk, is one big—and somewhat crowded—playground for the tan and well heeled. The main thoroughfare to the eastern end of the island is Route 27, a two-lane nightmare on summer weekends. For those who don't want to drive, there's the Hampton Jitney bus and limousine service from Manhattan (tel. 516/283–4600) and a local airport, as well as numerous marinas for docking the family yacht. Be prepared to pay a premium for lodging.

Summer brings warm ocean breezes and roadside stands brimming with the bounty of Long Island's farms. Boutiques are open, as are many chic nightspots. It's a wonderful time here. Still, when planning a visit, consider that the beach is here all year—even when the crowds are not. The ocean sometimes remains warm enough for swimming into October, and restaurant reservations are certainly easier to come by out of season. Of course some places close for the winter, and those who like the summer scene will be disappointed with the quiet that begins around mid-September.

Not all of Eastern Long Island is trendy and developed. The North Fork is an agricultural area, with some of the state's most productive farms. Thanks to conservationists, more than 6,800 acres on the South Fork have been turned into nature preserves. Eastern Long Island's salt marshes, dunes, pine barrens, woodlands, and grasslands are home to many endangered species of flora and fauna, and preservationists are determined that at least part of the island will stay as it was in the 1600s, when the first big real-estate deal was completed.

Places to Go, Sights to See

Home Sweet Home Museum (East Hampton, tel. 516/324–0713). The childhood home of poet John Howard Payne, who wrote the song "Home Sweet Home" in the early 1800s, is now a museum in a simple 1680 rough-shingle house, which features a three-century collection of furnishings and a 19th-century windmill. It's open all year.

John Drew Theater of Guild Hall (East Hampton, tel. 516/324–4050). Events—held most nights during the summer and occasionally during other seasons—include theater; concerts; a film series; children's events; and lectures on the arts, the environment, and politics. Memberships, subscriptions, and single-event tickets are available.

Long Island Wineries. There are a dozen wineries in the area. The climate and soil here provide unique growing conditions, and the area is fast becoming a source of award-winning wines. The town of Cutchogue is home to several wineries, including *Hargrave Vineyard* (tel. 516/734–5158) and *Peconic Bay Vineyards* (tel. 516/734–7361). Peconic offers *Lenz Winery* (tel. 516/734–6010) and *Pindar Vineyards* (tel. 516/734–6200). *Duck Walk Vineyard* (Southampton, tel. 516/726–7555) is on the South Fork. Many vineyards offer tours and tastings.

Mashomack Preserve (Shelter Island, tel. 516/749–1001). The Nature Conservancy, a nonprofit organization that manages the world's largest privately held nature preserve, protects and maintains a pristine 2,039-acre habitat on Shelter Island. The salt marsh and wooded areas are home to a number of endangered species, including the osprey and the piping plover. Osprey nesting areas may be observed (and should be left undisturbed) all over the island. The preserve is open for hiking every day but Tuesday, and guided walks are offered.

Restaurants

There's always a crowd at **Babette's** (66 Newtown La., East Hampton, tel. 516/329–5377), a funky café that serves innovative dishes. The trendy **Nick & Toni's** (136 N. Main St., East Hampton, tel. 516/324–3550) offers tasty Tuscan fare. The **American Hotel Restaurant** (25 Main St., Sag Harbor, tel. 516/725–3535) is a French country restaurant, with more than 1,200 wines on the wine list. If you're looking for basic American cuisine at moderate prices, the **Driver's Seat** (62 Job's La., Southampton, tel. 516/283–6606) is the place.

Tourist Information

East Hampton Chamber of Commerce (37A Main St., East Hampton 11937, tel. 516/324–0362), for information on Wainscott, East Hampton Village, Springs, Amagansett, and Montauk). **Greater Westhampton Chamber of Commerce** (Box 1228, Westhampton Beach, 11978, tel. 516/288–3337). **Sag Harbor Chamber of Commerce** (Box 116, Sag Harbor 11936, tel. 516/725–0011). **Shelter Island Chamber of Commerce** (Box 598, Shelter Island 11964, tel. 516/749–0399). **Southampton Chamber of Commerce** (76 Main St., Southampton 11968, tel. 516/283–0402).

Hedges' Inn

74 James La., East Hampton, NY 11937,
tel. 516/324–7100

If you're up early enough, you might see pheasants searching out breakfast in the front yard of Hedges' Inn. The property sits across from a pond where cattle grazed in the mid-1600s, when the area was first settled. In winter, when skaters glide over the frozen pond, the vista is a Currier and Ives print brought to life.

The inn, now owned by the Palm Management Corporation, was built as a private residence in 1774. A varied selection of flowers in brilliant hues lines the brick path to the columned front porch, where visitors can ease themselves into green-cushioned wicker chairs and enjoy the passing scene. Guest rooms are attractively furnished with patchwork quilts, frilly shams, and throw pillows. You sit down to breakfast at English-pine tables adorned with baskets of blooms in a small, sunny dining room. A buffet is set on a carved-pine hutch. In warm weather, guests dine on the canopied flagstone patio.

▥ *11 double rooms with baths. Restaurant, air-conditioning. $165–$250; cold buffet breakfast. AE, DC, MC, V. No pets, 3-night minimum on July–Aug. weekends, 5-night minimum July 4 and Labor Day weekends.*

The Hill Guest House

535 Hill St., Southampton, NY 11968,
tel. 516/283–9889 or 718/461–0014 (Nov.–
Apr.)

Built around 1890, the Hill Guest House is the Hamptons without frills. Located a mile from the village of Southampton and a two-minute drive from the beach, the house offers clean and pleasant accommodations at low rates. Owners Mauro and Ronnie Salerno have been here since 1964, when they came for a two-week vacation at the guest house and ended up buying it. Mauro was in the

meat business ("Selling rooms is the same as selling sausages," he says with a laugh) and today spends his spare time swimming and serving as a hospital volunteer. Ronnie is a gourmet cook who "does the *New York Times* crossword puzzle in ink," boasts Mauro.

The rooms have twin beds (which can be pushed together); most beds are made of antique iron painted to match the decor. The front porch has painted wicker chairs, and on cool evenings the living-room fireplace is the cheery focal point of the inn.

▥ *1 double room with bath, 2 doubles share bath, 3 doubles share 2 hall baths. $70–$80; breakfast extra. No credit cards. No pets, 2-night minimum on weekends June and Sept., 3-night minimum on weekends July–Aug., closed Nov.–Apr.*

The Huntting Inn

94 Main St., East Hampton, NY 11937,
tel. 516/324–0410, fax 516/324–8751

Huge elms and maples surround the Huntting Inn, a pre-Revolutionary landmark set on 2½ acres in the midst of East Hampton Village. The 1699 house, originally a saltbox, was built by the Church of England for the Reverend Nathaniel Huntting. In 1751 Huntting's widow, probably short of cash, turned her home into a public house, and it's been an inn ever since. During the American Revolution it became the only neutral meeting ground in the area.

Innkeeper Linda Calder (who also manages Hedges' Inn, owned by the same corporation) has been here since 1980. Her warmth, boundless energy, and good humor are evident as she tends to the needs of guests in the two inns.

The inn's dining room will look familiar to Manhattan's restaurant cognoscenti—it's run by the Palm Restaurant and has similar decor, including a pressed-tin ceiling, oak wainscoting, wide-board floors, bentwood chairs, a brass-rail bar, and drawings of celebrities lining the walls. As at the Palm, steaks and lobsters come in colossal portions.

Guest rooms, many with floral-print wall coverings, are somewhat tired. One of the most pleasing rooms here is also the smallest, with a single brass-and-iron bed, a hand-crocheted bedcover, and lace curtains. The suite, done in a white-and-green scheme, has antique oak furnishings and lace curtains on the windows. It also offers a king-size bed and a queen-size pull-out couch to accommodate families.

Across the street you'll find public tennis courts, and there's a golf course nearby. The inn provides guests with town stickers for parking in beach areas. It lies within walking distance of all of East Hampton's shops, theaters, and museums.

▦ *17 double rooms with baths, 2 single rooms with baths, 1 suite. Restaurant, air-conditioning, TVs in rooms, phones in rooms. $165–$395; Continental breakfast. AE, DC, MC, V. No pets, 2-night minimum on weekends May–June and Sept.–Oct., 3-night minimum on weekends July–Aug., 5-night minimum July 4 and Labor Day weekends.*

J. Harper Poor Cottage

181 Main St., East Hampton, NY 11937, tel. 516/324–4081

Gary and Rita Reiswig have created the *definitive* East Hampton retreat, where you will be coddled as you should be in the Hamptons. More mansion than cottage, this inn dates back to the 1600s and has been expanded and renovated several times. It sits right on Main Street across from the village green.

In 1910 then-owner James Harper Poor hired architect Joseph Greenleaf Thorp to make renovations, mostly in the style of the English arts-and-crafts school. When the Reiswigs bought the property

in July 1996, they hired architect Eric Woodward and interior designer Gary Paul to revive the very tired house. Today, exquisite William Morris papers cover the walls, and plush, overstuffed furniture graces the sitting rooms, which are filled with fresh flowers and a good collection of books. The spacious, airy public spaces are ever-so-genteel. You truly feel as if you're in an English country manor.

As you head upstairs, notice the portrait of Mrs. Poor hanging in the stairwell—it's on loan from her grandchildren. (The late Mrs. Poor was married in the house in 1915.) The guest rooms are stunning, with high-quality fabrics, serene colors, and tasteful furnishings. Each is stocked with terry robes and Caswell Massey products. Feather duvets and ceiling fans add to the ambience.

Formal English gardens grace the back of the property, and a 200-year-old white wisteria vine climbs the side of the house. If you decide to leave the shelter of the gardens, beach towels and beach parking passes are available. Large, extravagant breakfasts include an entrée, which might be pancakes, waffles, or eggs, plus a buffet of fresh fruit, juices, cakes, and muffins.

▦ *5 double rooms with baths. Air-conditioning, 2 phones per room with voice-mail, TVs and VCRs in rooms, in-room safes. $275–395; full breakfast. No pets, 3-night minimum on summer weekends.*

The Maidstone Arms

207 Main St., East Hampton, NY 11937, tel. 516/324–5006, fax 516/324–5037

The original settlers of East Hampton called the village Maidstone, after their native area in England, so it's not surprising that the Maidstone Arms has the air of a British seaside resort. Owner Coke Anne Saunders has sacrificed most of that British influence as she transformed the Maidstone into what she calls "a year-round, classic American village inn." The Victorian inn, built in the 1830s, features porches with white-wicker furniture, blue-and-white-striped awnings, and an enclosed courtyard—the perfect spot for tea on a balmy afternoon.

Rooms are brightly decorated: Some walls are stenciled, and others have wallpaper with a flower motif. White dotted-Swiss curtains and lots of wicker complete the furnishings.

One suite has its own sunporch. Each of the three cottages (which are rented by the week during the summer) has a queen-size bed, a sitting room, and a fireplace.

▥ *12 double rooms with baths, 4 suites, 3 cottages. Restaurant, air-conditioning, cable TV in rooms, car service from jitney, train, and East Hampton airport. $165–$325; Continental breakfast. AE, MC, V. No pets, 4-night minimum on holiday weekends, 3-night minimum during peak weekends.*

Mill House Inn

33 N. Main St., East Hampton, NY 11937, tel. 516/324–9766

On the shadow of East Hampton's landmark Hook Windmill is the appropriately named Mill House Inn. This 1790 saltbox reminiscent of New England architecture was converted to a Dutch Colonial in 1890. In 1994 New Yorkers Katherine and Dan Hartnett gave up their careers in the city—he was a social worker, she a chef at the Pierre on Fifth Avenue—to pursue their dream of renovating and running an old B&B. "It combines our great interest in people and cooking with our desire to live in a wonderful place," says Dan.

Lush gardens surround the house, and you get a clear view of the historic windmill across the street from the front porch; both are wonderful places to sit and enjoy a cool drink in summer. The

fireplaces and whirlpool tubs in many of the guest rooms will help you wind down after a hard day at the beach. Mornings start with one of Katherine's distinctive gourmet breakfasts.

▥ *8 double rooms with baths. Cable TV in rooms, phones in rooms, gas fireplaces in 6 rooms, whirlpool tubs in 4 rooms, beach passes. $200–$300; full breakfast, afternoon beverages. AE, MC, V. No smoking, no pets, 3-night minimum on holiday weekends.*

Ram's Head Inn

108 Ram Island Dr., Shelter Island, NY 11964, tel. 516/749–0811, fax 516/749–0059

Ospreys nest atop the telephone poles by this inn on Shelter Island. A yellow-and-white awning shelters the patio, and a beached rowboat sits in a children's play area on the wide front lawn. The voice of Billie Holiday is often heard in the dining room. The 1929 center-hall Colonial-style building is all weathered shakes, white trim, and green shutters. Guests can walk to a gazebo by the tennis courts, and a grassy path leads down to 800 feet of beachfront on Coecles Harbor. Summer guests are cooled by bay breezes.

Owners James and Linda Ecklund and innkeeper Peter McCracken collaborate in running the place, and each fills in wherever necessary to make sure guests are taken care of. In 1980 the Ecklunds bought the inn in a rather "decayed state," as they put it, and they have spent the intervening years restoring it.

The common rooms are often flooded with natural light. The lounge, decorated in a nautical theme, features ships' lanterns and a model sloop on the mantel. Green wicker couches have flowered cushions, and the library is the perfect spot for a rainy-day read. Here framed sheet music lines the walls, and a piano occupies an honored place. Every Sunday in summer from 7 to 11 PM, a local jazz group livens up the atmosphere. The dining-room menu stresses New American cuisine and includes fresh seafood creatively prepared and presented. You might choose from such specialties as shellfish bisque garnished with caviar and lobster, and braised red snapper accompanied by oyster mushrooms and artichokes.

Guest rooms are simple, bright, and airy; some have porches. Those with a water view are often requested, but in summer the harbor can be glimpsed only through the leaves of majestic oak trees.

🏠 *5 double rooms with baths, 4 doubles share 2 baths, 4 suites. Restaurant, free use of tennis court and boats. $110–$230; Continental breakfast. AE, MC, V. Smoking in lounge only, no pets, 3-night minimum on holiday weekends, 2-night minimum other weekends.*

The 1770 House

143 Main St., East Hampton, NY 11937, tel. 516/324–1770

At various times in its history the 1770 House, actually a 1740 Colonial built for one of East Hampton's earliest families, has been a general store; a dining hall for students at the Clinton Academy next door; and, finally, an inn that had its heyday in the 1940s and '50s. The late parents of brother and sister Wendy and Adam Perle bought the house in 1977 in a state of decline. Undaunted by the formidable task, they restored it, and today Wendy and Adam have turned it into a successful inn.

Guest rooms are furnished with fine antiques of various periods and origins. One room has a fireplace and an English-style carved canopy bed. Another has an Early American highboy. The inn's elegant library features English-pine paneling and a fireplace. The dining room holds an extensive collection of clocks and apothecary jars.

Behind the house sits a converted carriage house fit for four people. Furnished with antiques, it has a master bedroom with queen-size, canopied bed and a combination living room and library. An elegant hand-carved staircase leads to an auxiliary loft bedroom with double bed.

🏠 *8 double rooms with baths. Air-conditioning, fireplaces in 2 rooms and 2 public areas. $150–$280; full breakfast. AE, MC, V. No smoking, no pets, 3-night minimum on summer weekends, 2-night minimum other weekends.*

The Village Latch Inn

101 Hill St., Box 3000, Southampton, NY 11968, tel. 516/283–2160 or 800/545–2824

The theatrical air to the 5-acre compound that makes up the Village Latch Inn is no accident. Owner Marta White spent her life in the theater, and she revels in setting a stage. Her husband and fellow innkeeper, Martin, is a photographer who used to work in commercial films. The main house is "old Southampton, turn-of-the-century, Gatsby-style," says Marta. The circa-1900 building, once the annex to Southampton's most opulent hotel, may have been a Sanford White design. Near the main house are what Marta refers to as the "outbuildings," which were part of the old Merrill Lynch estate. These include the Terry Cottage, which features a comfortable living room with flowered wallpaper and Victorian dining room; the Potting Shed, where the first American locomotive was built and which is now used for corporate meetings; six modern duplexes with private decks; and two other large houses connected by a Victorian greenhouse. One of these houses has a distinguished collection of Mexican folk art.

The living room in the main house could be the set of a movie—perhaps *Around the World in 80 Days with Auntie Mame.* Plush leopard-print cushions and gold- and silver-threaded pillows are tossed artfully on the couches. Balinese marionettes hang from the walls. It's all eccentric, eclectic, and artsy—and it works.

No guest room resembles another, and Marta is always changing things. "If I'm not creating space, then it's boring," she comments. The rooms are decorated with a collection of antiques from different periods. Despite its lavishness, the inn is cozy—the sort of place where guests can help themselves to coffee or a cold drink any time of the day, even if the sign says KITCHEN CLOSED.

A number of the buildings can be rented to groups, and the facilities have been used for everything from fashion shoots to family reunions. The greenhouse is the perfect setting for an intimate wedding. The inn is a five-minute walk from town and a mile from the beach.

🏠 *50 double rooms with baths, 11 suites, 6 duplexes. Lunch catering on request, air-conditioning, cable TV and phones in rooms on request, pool, tennis courts. $99–$350; Continental breakfast. AE, D, DC, MC, V. Pets by prior arrangement, 3-night minimum July–Aug. weekends, 2-night minimum other weekends.*

Pennsylvania

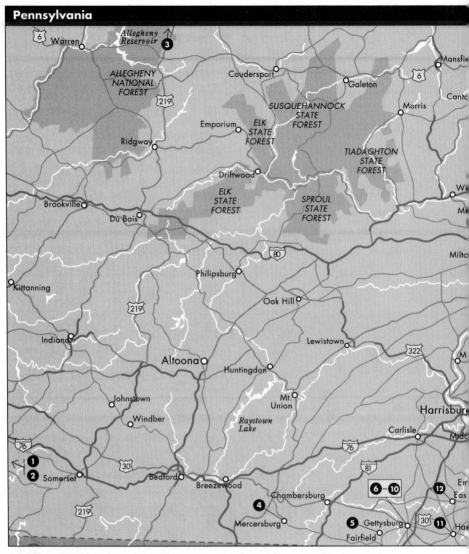

Pennsylvania

(Map labels)

Warren · 6 · Allegheny Reservoir · 3 · Coudersport · Galeton · 6 · Mansfi

ALLEGHENY NATIONAL FOREST · 219 · Morris · Cant

SUSQUEHANNOCK STATE FOREST · Emporium · ELK STATE FOREST

Ridgway · TIADAGHTON STATE FOREST

Driftwood

ELK STATE FOREST · SPROUL STATE FOREST · W

Brookville · Du Bois · M

80 · Milt

Philipsburg

Kittanning · 219 · Oak Hill

Indiana · Altoona · Lewistown · 322 · M

Huntingdon

Johnstown · Mt. Union · Harrisbur

Windber · Raystown Lake · Carlisle · Mid

76 · 30 · 76 · 81

1 · 2 · Somerset · Bedford · Breezewood · 6–10 · 12 · Er · Eas

219 · 4 · Chambersburg

Mercersburg · 5 · Gettysburg · 30 · 11 · Ha

Fairfield

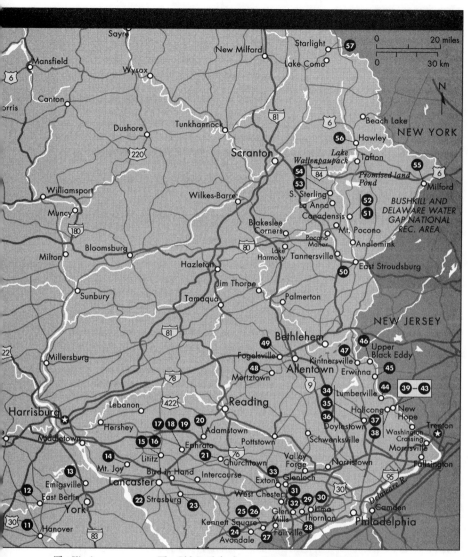

The King's Cottage, **22**	The Old Appleford Inn, **9**	Sweetwater Farm, **28**
Lenape Springs Farm, **31**	The Overlook Inn, **51**	Swiss Woods, **16**
Limestone Inn, **23**	Pace One, **29**	The Tannery Bed and Breakfast, **10**
The Logan Inn, **40**	Pinetree Farm, **36**	The Wedgwood Collection of Inns, **42**
Longswamp Bed and Breakfast, **48**	The Priory, **2**	
	Scarlett House, **26**	
The Mansion Inn, **41**	The Settlers Inn, **56**	The Whitehall Inn, **43**
Meadow Spring Farm, **25**	1740 House, **44**	
The Mercersburg Inn, **4**	Smithton Country Inn, **19**	
	The Sterling Inn, **53**	

The Poconos

Although the Poconos are best known as the Honeymoon Capital of the World—the land of the glitzy motel, with heart-shape beds, hot tubs, and bottomless champagne glasses—the "other" Poconos may be Pennsylvania's best-kept secret. The northeast corner of the state, bordering the Delaware River, encompasses 2,400 square miles of mountainous wilderness, with lakes, streams, waterfalls, woods, and enchanting country inns.

The region consists of four counties: Carbon, Monroe, Pike, and Wayne. The discovery of anthracite coal in Carbon County led to its development as a mining region, a railroad center, and a land of opportunity for European immigrants. The town of Mauch Chunk, founded in 1815 (now called Jim Thorpe, after the great Native American athlete), became home to a dozen coal and railroad millionaires. Monroe County, along the Delaware River, was first inhabited by the Delaware and Shawnee tribes, then settled by the Dutch in 1659, and by the English and Germans a century later. In the 1820s people began visiting the Poconos in summer for the crisp mountain air. Boardinghouses were built along the Delaware Water Gap, Monroe County developed a small resort industry, and by 1900 thousands were coming each summer from Philadelphia and New York City.

A back-roads drive through the woodlands and rolling hills will turn up dairy farms and quaint villages, country stores, and lots of antiques and crafts shops. In winter there are downhill and cross-country skiing, ice skating, snowmobiling, and sledding. In summer there are theater, golf and tennis, boating, swimming, horseback riding, and hiking. And any time after a full day, you'll find a good night's sleep in a country inn.

Places to Go, Sights to See

Bushkill Falls (Bushkill, tel. 717/588–6682). The Niagara of Pennsylvania, on 300 acres, has trails leading to eight waterfalls. There's an exhibit of Pennsylvania wildlife, and there are picnic grounds, fishing, paddleboats, and a silversmith shop.

Grey Towers (Milford, tel. 717/296–6401). You can tour the house and gardens of the stone ancestral home of Gifford Pinchot, first chief of the U.S. Forest Service and twice governor of Pennsylvania.

Jim Thorpe (Rte. 209). This late-Victorian mountain-resort town, once called Mauch Chunk (from the Native American *Machktschunk*, Mountain of the Sleeping Bear), has first-rate antiques shops and galleries, the Asa Packer Museum, St. Mark's Church, Flagstaff Park, the Overlook, and a restored railroad station.

Lake Wallenpaupack (between Greentown and Hawley). Year-round activities along the 52-mile shoreline of the largest recreational lake in the state include waterskiing, swimming, boating, fishing, snowmobiling, ice skating, cross-country skiing, and ice fishing. Hiking trails lead to scenic overlooks.

Pocono Indian Museum (Bushkill, tel. 717/588–9164). Exhibits of artifacts and crafts and a replica of a longhouse trace the history of the Delaware Indians.

Promised Land State Park (10 mi north of Canadensis, tel. 717/676–3428). This natural forest and recreational area of 11,010 acres, filled with deer, bear, and smaller game, has seasonal sports, picnic grounds, and 25 miles of marked hiking trails.

Quiet Valley Living Historical Farm (Stroudsburg, tel. 717/992–6161). Authentically costumed "family members" reenact farm life in a 1765 log house. Demonstrations include spinning, baking, gardening, and tending the animals.

Ski Areas and Resorts

You'll find beginner, intermediate, and expert trails in the region. All have ski schools, rentals, cross-country ski trails, ice skating, and night skiing. Many offer indoor swimming, tennis, racquetball, and entertainment. Inquire about midweek packages.

Alpine Mountain (Analomink, tel. 717/595–2150 in PA; 800/233–8240 outside PA). **Blue Mountain Ski Area** (Palmerton, tel. 610/826–7700). **Camelback** (Tannersville, tel. 717/629–1661). **Fernwood** (Bushkill, tel. 717/588–9500). **Jack Frost Mountain** (Blakeslee, tel. 717/443–8425). **Mount Airy Lodge** (Mt. Pocono, tel. 717/839–8811 in PA; 800/441–4410 outside PA). **Mount Tone** (Lake Como, tel. 717/798–2707). **Pocono Manor Inn and Golf Resort** (Pocono Manor, tel. 717/839–7111 in PA; 800/233–8150 outside PA). **Shawnee Mountain** (Shawnee-on-Delaware, tel. 717/421–7231). **Split Rock Resort** (Lake Harmony, tel. 717/722–9111 in PA; 800/255–7625 outside PA). **Tanglwood** (Tafton, tel. 717/226–9500).

Restaurants

Every single bed-and-breakfast or country inn that we mention in this section, with the exception of Brookview Manor, houses its own restaurant (you'll find MAP meal plans much more common here than in other areas of the state). You should reconsider an otherwise justifiable bias against in-hotel eating when you travel here, and sample the victuals at any one of our recommendations—the caliber of cuisine and service is outstanding and categorically outranks local dining options in presentation and performance. But if you still resist the notion or are looking for more variety, here's a handful of creditable restaurants within easy driving distance of our entries.

A young couple runs the small (maximum seating 30–35) but celebrated **Le Gorille** (tel. 717/296–8094) in Shahola, near Milford; contemporary American recipes predominate here. For nearly 20 years, the **Homestead Inn** (tel. 717/595–3171) in Cresco has been serving fine Continental cuisine in a cozy ambience, with entrées about $16. **Peppe's** (tel. 717/421–4460), in East Stroudsburg, does homemade pasta, seafood, and veal chops in the Northern Italian tradition. Mount Pocono's **B.J.'s Gathering** (tel. 717/839–8305) offers moderately priced American-style fare in a casual atmosphere.

Tourist Information

Pocono Mountains Vacation Bureau, Inc. (1004 Main St., Stroudsburg 18360, tel. 717/424–6050 or 717/421–5791; 717/421–5565 for 24-hr ski hot line).

Brookview Manor

Rte. 447 (R.R. 1, Box 365), Canadensis, PA 18325, tel. 717/595–2451 or 800/585–7974

Guests at Mary Anne Buckley's Brookview Manor often end the evening in the parlor that overlooks the wooded grounds, playing a game of Monopoly or chatting. Informality, idleness, and comfort are the bywords here.

Buckley, a former insurance agent, bought this cream-colored summer residence in 1996 from previous owners Lee and Nancie Cabana. She promptly refurbished the interior with new wallpaper, carpeting, and four-poster and sleigh beds.

The main structure—built in 1911 for a wealthy Scranton family—and adjacent carriage house have four working fireplaces, original stained-glass windows, and comfortable country furnishings. Two rooms have whirlpools and one has a fireplace. There are some views of Broadhead Creek (room 2 overlooks it). The property covers only 4 acres, but it is surrounded by 400 acres of privately owned forest. Guests are free to roam the long, wooded trail, which leads to a 50-foot waterfall. For dinner, the nearby Pine Knob Inn or the Homestead restaurant in Cresco is recommended.

🏠 *9 double rooms with baths, 1 suite. Whirlpool baths in 2 rooms, fireplace in 1 room, TV in den, pool table, Ping-Pong, game room. $100–$150; full breakfast, afternoon tea. AE, D, MC, V. No smoking indoors, no pets, 2-night minimum on holiday weekends.*

Cliff Park Inn

Cliff Park Rd. (R.R. 4, Box 7200), Milford, PA 18337, tel. 717/296–6491 or 800/225–6535, fax 717/296–3982

This historic country inn, built as a homestead in 1820, has been in inn-keeper Harry W. Buchanan's family for five generations. The three-story white-clapboard Colonial building with green trim is a mile west of Milford, and its 600 acres surround one of the country's first golf courses. In the main parlor you'll find a wealth of Victorian family heirlooms, Buchanan ancestral portraits, and a stone fireplace. Guest rooms are decorated with family antiques and reproductions; some have porches that overlook the golf course. Three nearby cottages, ideal for families or groups, have exposed beams, large fieldstone fireplaces, and eclectic furnishings. In the winter season, guests can make full use of the 7 miles of marked cross-country ski trails. During summer months, the inn's maple-shaded veranda is a favorite gathering place. There you can watch the golfers and the deer that come at dusk.

🏠 *19 double rooms with baths. Restaurant, air-conditioning, conference facilities, TV with VCR in meeting rooms, 9-hole golf course, pro shop, stable. $128–$205 (full breakfast and dinner); $110–$210 (breakfast only). AE, D, DC, MC, V. No pets, closed Dec. 24–25.*

The French Manor

Huckleberry Rd. (Box 39), off Rte. 191, South Sterling, PA 18460, tel. 717/676–3244 or 800/523–8200, fax 717/676–9786

The 40-acre setting of this inn is aristocratic and the views exquisite. Rolling hills and mountain ranges reveal themselves periodically as you drive up the winding, wooded road toward the crest of Huckleberry Mountain to the fieldstone manor house with its slate roof, cooper-mullioned windows, and arched oak door.

Built between 1932 and 1937 as a summer residence for mining tycoon and art collector Joseph Hirschorn, the house was modeled after Hirschorn's château in southern France. After changing hands several times, it became an inn in

1985, and in 1990 it was bought by Ron and Mary Kay Logan, who own and manage the nearby Sterling Inn.

The 40-foot-high Great Room, with a vaulted cherry-wood ceiling and a mammoth plastered-stone fireplace at each end, makes a spectacular restaurant. French doors with leaded glass open onto a slate terrace that has a sweeping view of the countryside. The guest rooms, named after European cities, have cypress and cedar walls and ceilings and are decorated in a mix of contemporary style and French antique reproductions. "Venice" has an ornate headboard on its king-size bed. Baths have old-fashioned tile with pedestal sinks. The carriage house has two suites each with fireplace and whirlpool bath and two rooms; it is furnished like the manor house but the rooms are smaller. Although it is secluded, the carriage house feels new, which makes it not nearly as nice as the larger house.

A full-service, no-smoking dining room with a full liquor license treats guests to an à la carte menu that changes about every two months and features highly touted French cuisine. A recent selection included grilled beef tenderloin nestled on a roasted garlic and tomato *concassée* cream; and fresh salmon baked in a sauce of champagne, white peppercorn, and asparagus.

With panoramic views as a backdrop, you can take peaceful walks or go cross-country skiing. Golf, horseback riding, and other recreations are nearby. The medieval atmosphere of the house creates a feeling of timelessness, and the thoughtful service of the Logans and their staff allows you to put your worries away.

🏠 *6 double rooms with baths, 3 suites. Restaurant open, in season, daily for breakfast and dinner, air-conditioning in bedrooms, TV in lounge, croquet. $120–$225; full breakfast. AE, D, MC, V. No smoking, no pets.*

The Inn at Meadowbrook

Cherry Lane Rd. E (R.D. 7, Box 7651), East Stroudsburg, PA 18301, tel. 717/629–0296 or 800/249–6861, fax 717/620–1754

Guests who arrive at The Inn at Meadowbrook after dark are often relieved to find they aren't lost. On the long and winding 4½ wooded miles from Tannersville you may begin to think you've missed it, but suddenly, around a corner, there it is, blanketed by soft light and trees and chirping night sounds: a white clapboard manor house with green trim. And just across the road is a white mill house that's part of the inn. If you're going to get pleasantly lost anywhere in the Poconos, this is the place to do it.

For many years the 1867 house and its 43 acres were a horse farm, and in 1985 Kathy and Bob Overman bought the estate and turned it into a bed-and-breakfast. Kathy, an artist who loves to garden, has given each of the guest rooms a distinctive decor. Bob, the resident gourmet chef, has mastered the celebrated raspberry-cinnamon-raisin pudding recipe you may be lucky enough to sample for breakfast.

You can curl up with a book on the leather sofa in the light-flooded parlor or in wing chairs that face the fireplace, or you can simply gaze out the windows at the pond, gazebo, and mill house. The spacious hunter-green dining room, added in the '20s, is a setting out of *The Great Gatsby*, with 15-foot ceilings, arched columns, and tall Palladian windows on three sides framing the gardens, the rushing brook with footbridge, and a pond. French doors open onto the terrace for dining in warm months.

The guest rooms are furnished with English and American antiques and country pieces. There are patchwork quilts, lots of books, wicker chairs, and convenient reading lamps. Room 9, a favorite of guests, has rich burgundy paisley draperies, hunter-green walls, an antique brass bed, and a view of the stables. Room 10 overlooks the pond and has a white birch four-poster bed that Bob built.

On the inn's grounds you can swim, fish, play tennis, ice-skate, and take leisurely walks with a picnic lunch. Bob and Kathy can arrange horseback riding and carriage and sleigh rides. The area also has its share of antiques shops and flea markets.

⊞ *10 double rooms with baths, 6 doubles share 2 baths. Restaurant, TV with VCR in recreation room, pool, 2 tennis courts, shuffleboard, pond. $60–$95; full breakfast. AE, D, DC, MC, V. Smoking in common rooms only, no pets, 2-day minimum on weekends.*

The Inn at Starlight Lake

Starlight (Box 27), PA 18461, tel. 717/798–2519 or 800/248–2519, fax 717/798–2672

The hamlet of Starlight, nestled in the foothills of the Moosic range, was once a railroad stop, and in 1909 this Adirondack-style lodge was built on the lake nearby to serve passengers. Today the sprawling white-and-green clapboard inn looks much as it did around the turn of the century, and it's just as peaceful. Jack and Judy McMahon have been innkeepers here since 1974. Before that they lived in New York City and worked in the theater, where they met while performing.

The rambling parlor, with its wood-burning stove, stone fireplace, and baby-grand piano, sets the homey, lodgelike mood. There's a comfortable mixture of antiques, Mission oak furniture, and well-lived-in pieces, with numerous Tiffany-style lamps for reading. In winter you might expect Bing Crosby to step out and warble "White Christmas."

Guest rooms on the second and third floors are simple and unpretentious, with framed prints on floral-papered walls, crocheted doilies, and lots of magazines.

You'll find iron beds and marble-top dressers, but mostly a hodgepodge of old and not-so-old furniture. A row of recently renovated cottages is furnished with antique reproductions. The suite has a king-size bed and a whirlpool bath for two; above it is another charming room with an iron bed and a fieldstone fireplace.

Chef David Giles presides in the dining room. Everything served is made on the premises, including breads, pastas, ice cream, and pastries. You can work off a little of David's duck with orange sauce with a game of pool, Ping-Pong, or tabletop shuffleboard in the inn's game room.

No motors are allowed on the 45-acre lake, so it's quiet and crystal clean for swimming and fishing. On occasional murder-mystery weekends, whodunits are performed by the Starlight Players. In winter there's ice-skating, and the McMahons's son, a certified ski instructor, can take you down the property's slopes or show you the best trails for cross-country skiing. On crisp autumn mornings you are likely to see deer or flocks of wild turkeys through the early mist.

⊞ *20 double rooms with baths, 2 doubles share bath, 1 suite, 3-bedroom family house. Restaurant, bar, TV with VCR in sunroom, baby-sitting arranged, bicycles, tennis court, canoes. $115–$200; full breakfast, dinner. MC, V. No smoking in dining room, no pets, 2-day minimum in season, 3-day minimum on holidays, closed 1st 2 wks in Apr.*

The Overlook Inn

Dutch Hill Rd. (Box 680), Canadensis, PA 18325-9755, tel. 717/595–7519 or 800/590–3845

The porch around this yellow three-story inn just outside Canadensis is so high that when you're on it you feel as though you're up in the pines. In early 1994, Peter and Hannele Wawra, natives of Austria, took over the reins of the inn from previous owners Debbie and

Arthur Bolger. Peter has spent his career in the hospitality business; he managed the New York Yacht Club and, before that, Donald Trump's Grand Hyatt Hotel in Manhattan. Guest rooms in this 1870 Victorian farmhouse are furnished in a mix of Early American reproductions and Victorian antiques. The rooms downstairs are warm and intimate. On cool evenings, a fire crackles in the stone fireplace in the living room, and from the window seat in the library you might see deer grazing on the lawn. Nothing's fussy here, yet gourmet dinners in the dining room do attract a well-dressed following. The Bolgers will gladly point you to the trails for cross-country skiing on the inn's 20 wooded acres or help you plan a drive down scenic back roads. Next door to the inn is the Flying Dollar, a single-engine airport where you can take off, in season, on a thrilling ride and air tour for as little as $25.

🏨 *18 double rooms with baths, 2 suites. Restaurant, air-conditioning available, phones in rooms, TV in library, conference facilities, pool. $95–$115; breakfast, afternoon tea, dinner. AE, MC, V. No smoking in dining room or guest rooms, no pets.*

The Settlers Inn

4 Main Ave., Hawley, PA 18428, tel. 717/226–2993 or 800/833–8527, fax 717/226–1874

This rambling Tudor-style grand hotel built in 1927 has been restored as a country inn. It's on a well-traveled bend of Route 6, five minutes from Lake Wallenpaupack, but once you enter the high-ceilinged living room, with its chestnut beams and massive stone fireplace, you'll forget about the location. Antique marble-top tables and Victorian chairs and sofas evoke the atmosphere of an English country hotel. The rooms, furnished with "early attic" antiques, also have Early American memorabilia.

The popular dining room is the domain of Grant Genzlinger, who's not only chef-innkeeper but also a student of ancient Chinese languages. He and his wife, Jeanne, share innkeeping duties with their partner, Marcia Dunsmore, and distinguish themselves mightily in the kitchen arts. The flavorful, amply portioned dinners testify to the proprietors' assiduous search for locally grown ingredients as well as to their loyalty to regional specialties. Dishes reflect the joy of a year-round pursuit of the best and brightest in the Pennsylvania agricultural community. Witness the cheddar pasta supper dish, composed of fettuccine, leeks, and spinach tossed in a sauce of Up Country Pennsylvania sharp cheddar and Forest Home Dairy fresh cream; or the chicken schnitzel, a scallop of chicken dipped in a light lemon and thyme batter, scented with nutmeg, sautéed, and served with fettuccine and roasted zucchini, peppers, yellow squash, onions, and tomatoes. You'll dine sitting in one of the more than 100 Gothic, church-school chairs brought from the Bryn Athyn Cathedral near Philadelphia.

If you detect a sometimes whimsical, sometimes earnest voice in the menu descriptions, trust it for its very contradictions. The trio in charge does it all with a winning combination of dead seriousness and an insouciant aptitude for gustatory lucky strikes. Where else would you find garlic additions to an entrée honored on the menu as the "errant lily"?

The location is ideal for getting to winter or summer sports, and the town has enough antiques shops to keep you browsing for days.

🏨 *16 double rooms with baths, 2 suites. Restaurant, air-conditioning, TV in sitting room, 2 meeting rooms, large banquet room, gift shop. $83–$143; full breakfast. AE, D, MC, V. Smoking in lounge and bar only, no pets.*

The Sterling Inn

South Sterling, PA 18460, tel. 717/676–3311, 717/676–3338, or 800/523–8200

Ron Logan, owner of the Sterling Inn, has put together a 10-page document tracing the site's history, from its occupation by the Nini subtribe (a branch of the Leni–Lenape) all the way up to his and his wife's proprietorship. "There is little wonder why the Indians would choose this particular site for their village," he observes. "Mountains on either side, the Wallenpaupack Creek with an abundance of trout, level fertile land, bubbling springs, and plenty of deer, bear, and other game."

It's still lovely here today, and this in itself is testimony to Ron and Mary Kay Logan's talent, energy, and restraint. The inn consists of an inviting white clapboard main house with hunter-green rooftop, built in 1857, and a cluster of cottages. It all sits on the road, nestled in a forested valley traversed by nature trails and winding waterways. The couple provides once-a-week lectures and guided nature walks, conducted by local author John Serrao, so that guests can absorb more than a glimpse of the 105 surrounding acres of birch, hemlock, and American beech, not to mention the wildflowers and bird life.

A fresh, countrified air prevails inside the inn, notwithstanding a few modern embellishments—a heated indoor pool, a poolside bar, and a spa. The dining room, open to guests and nonguests alike, is dominated by a large stone fireplace and decorated with a delicate floral-patterned wallpaper, pink tablecloths and woodwork, and bright blue cotton curtains over broad window valances. Resident chef George Pelepko Filak, a graduate of the Culinary Institute of America, is happy to accommodate special diets, but each standard menu is lavished with entrées like medallions of veal lombardi; scampi with scallops, garlic, and wine; and steamed red snapper.

The rooms, accented by playful ruffles and flounces, echo the clean, bright-eyed ingenuousness of the downstairs dining room. They all have phones and private baths; fireplace suites and cottages are available. The Logans offer several discount package rates. Romance and privacy give visitors here a true escape. Winter delights include horse-drawn sleigh rides and cross-country skiing; in the summer diversions such as swimming, hiking, horseback riding, and fishing abound.

▦ *38 double rooms with baths, 16 suites. Phones in rooms, indoor pool, spa, restaurant; 9-hole putting course, cross-country ski trails, nature trails. $140–$220; full breakfast, dinner. AE, D, MC, V. No smoking in dining room, no pets.*

New Hope, Bucks County, and Beyond

Since the 1930s, when Bucks County was discovered by Broadway's smart set, the area has been a popular retreat from the hectic urban pace. The rolling hills, stone barns, and quaint covered bridges that once attracted George S. Kaufman, Dorothy Parker, and Oscar Hammerstein II can still be found here in abundance. But easy access from Philadelphia (one hour) and New York (two hours) has brought crowds and traffic jams on summer weekends.

Despite its rapid growth, much of Bucks County's 625 square miles remains bucolic. The sleepy, sylvan beauty of the 18th- and 19th-century villages and the lush banks of the Delaware River make it an enchanting place to explore. You'll see many of Pennsylvania's famous "bank barns" (built against a bank or hill, so wagons could roll right into the loft). Stray off the beaten path and you will discover ageless scenic roads that centuries ago were the forest trails of the Leni-Lenape Indians. George Washington's Continental Army later used these roads to reach the Delaware River, which it crossed on an icy Christmas Eve in 1776.

New Hope, settled in the early 1700s, is the heart of Bucks County. This idyllic village on the Delaware River is a tapestry of stone houses, narrow streets and alleys, hidden courtyards, and charming restaurants. Doylestown, the county seat, an important coach stop in the 18th century, is today a showcase of American architecture and fine museums of Americana.

Places to Go, Sights to See

Bucks County Carriages (tel. 215/862–3582) offers 30-minute tours of New Hope in horse-drawn carriages, daily in summer and weekends only in spring and fall.

Bucks County Playhouse (New Hope, tel. 215/862–2041), housed in a mid-18th-century mill, presents Broadway drama and musical hits. The season runs from May through Christmas.

Farley's Bookshop (New Hope, tel. 215/862–2452) is a booklover's boon, an independent operation that houses well-stocked, gloriously disheveled, and eminently perusable stacks.

Fonthill (Doylestown, tel. 215/348–9461) was designed and constructed by Henry Chapman Mercer, a leader in the Arts and Crafts movement, a noted antiquarian and archaeologist, and a pioneer ceramicist. Built with all the grandeur of a medieval castle, the house contains collections of decorative tiles, prints, prehistoric pottery, and memorabilia.

Ghost Tours of New Hope (tel. 215/957–9988) consist of one-hour walks by lantern lights to explore the haunted spots of the area.

Historic Fallsington (Fallsington, tel. 215/295–6567) is the 300-year-old village where William Penn attended Quaker meetings. The restored buildings span three centuries.

The James A. Michener Art Museum of Bucks County (Doylestown, tel. 215/340–9800) opened in 1988. The renowned author grew up in Doylestown. Twentieth-century American art is the focus; rotating exhibits showcase everything from quilt making to photography to the performing arts.

Mercer Museum (Doylestown, tel. 215/345–0210) contains a collection of early Americana, tools, and implements of trades and crafts before mass production. There are antique vehicles, a log house, and a 14,000-volume library.

Moravian Pottery and Tile Works (Doylestown, tel. 215/345–6722) is now restored as a living-history museum; here you can watch decorative Arts and Crafts–era tiles being made in original molds.

New Hope Mule Barge Co. (tel. 215/862–2842) offers one-hour excursions on the Delaware Canal, through the countryside, and past 18th-century cottages and artists' workshops, with a historian and a folksinger on board.

Parry Mansion (New Hope, tel. 215/862–5652), a restored stone house built in 1784 by Benjamin Parry, a prosperous merchant and mill owner, is furnished in period antiques that date from the late-18th to the early 20th century.

Pearl S. Buck House (Hilltown, tel. 215/249–0100), the home of the Pulitzer- and Nobel Prize–winning author, has its original furnishings, including many Chinese artifacts.

Peddler's Village (Lahaska, tel. 215/794–4000) is a re-created 18th-century village of 62 old-fashioned country shops and "Early American" restaurants. There's a new outlet mall across the street.

Pennsbury Manor (Morrisville, tel. 215/946–0400) is William Penn's reconstructed 17th-century country estate. The estate's 43 acres contain the manor house (with period furnishings), outbuildings, livestock, and gardens.

Rice's Sale and Country Market (Solebury, tel. 215/297–5993) offers bargains in clothing, antiques, linens, shoes, and plants Tuesday from dawn to 1 PM.

Washington Crossing Historic Park (tel. 215/493–4076) has the old McConkey's Ferry Inn, replicas of Durham boats (the type George Washington used), a restored gristmill, and a wildflower preserve with displays, lectures, and trails.

Restaurants

In Doylestown, you can walk from the Mercer Museum to **B. Maxwell's Restaurant and Victorian Pub** (tel. 215/348–1027). Entrées run $12–$20. **Russell's 96 West** (tel. 215/345–8746) is a little pricier (entrées $18–$22), but there's a $16.95 early-bird special.

For a *very* casual evening of English "pub grub" and 24 beers on tap, try the Australian-run **Wookey Hole Pub** (tel. 215/794–7784), in Buckingham, between Doylestown and New Hope. New Hope proprietors recommend the cuisine at the **Inn at Phillips Mill** (*see below*) and at **Martine's** (tel. 215/862–2966), which offers simple Continental dinners for $8–$20 in its downstairs pub and second-story dining room. **Odette's Restaurant** (tel. 215/862–2432) is famous for the cabaret performers it attracts from all over the world.

From New Hope, it's a quick jaunt across the bridge to New Jersey and **Meils Bakery and Restaurant** (tel. 609/397–8033) in Stockton. Everything's homemade and portions are large; you can pick up a bottle of wine across the street before dinner. Farther north, **Chef Tell's Harrowe Inne** (tel. 610/847–2464) in Ottsville specializes in Continental dining and fine wines. Or take Route 32 upriver from New Hope to the small town of Kintnersville and check out the down-home

Great American Grill and Food Store (tel. 215/847–2023) for ribs, chicken, and onion rings.

Tourist Information

Bucks County Tourist Commission (152 Swamp Rd., Doylestown 18901, tel. 215/345–4552). **New Hope Borough Information Center** (1 W. Mechanic St., New Hope 18938, tel. 215/862–5880 or 215/862–5030).

Ash Mill Farm

Rte. 202 (Box 202), Holicong, PA 18928, tel. 215/794–5373

Ash Mill Farm, on 11 pastoral acres, is 10 minutes by car from both New Hope and Doylestown. As you turn up the drive off Route 202, you will pass sheep grazing in the meadows and then come to the charming buff plaster-over-stone 1790 Federal manor house with the large veranda. When Jim and Patricia Auslander moved from New York City and became innkeepers in 1989, Jim traded in legal briefs for cookbooks and Patricia called upon her corporate managerial skills. They refurbished Ash Mill with eclectic treasures collected from Ireland and England, American antiques, and Shaker reproductions. The downstairs rooms have high ceilings, random-width floors, and deep-set windows; the bedrooms have tranquil views, rag rugs, canopy beds, and antique Irish armoires. Several magazines and sales catalogues have organized fashion shoots here because of Ash Mill's exterior and interior charms. If an outing is in order, antiques shops and Peddler's Village are only minutes away.

🛏 *3 double rooms with baths, 2 suites. Air-conditioning in bedrooms. $90–$145; full breakfast, afternoon tea, complimentary brandy. No credit cards. Smoking on veranda only, no pets, 2-day minimum with Sat. reservation, 3-day minimum on holiday weekends.*

Barley Sheaf Farm

Rte. 202 (Box 10), Holicong, PA 18928, tel. 215/794–5104, fax 215/794–5332

Turn off well-traveled Route 202 10 minutes from New Hope, and you'll see sheep grazing in the pastures on either side of a sycamore-flanked lane. At the end is Barley Sheaf Farm, the 1740 mansard-roofed fieldstone house that in the '30s was the hideaway of playwright George S. Kaufman. Today this charming 30-acre farm, though just around the bend from the bustling antiques shops of Peddler's Village, manages to retain the quiet gentility that prevailed when Lillian Hellman, Alexander Woollcott, and Moss Hart visited here.

The swimming pool, a duck pond, and the bank barn add texture and a relaxed appeal to the house and grounds, which have been designated a National Historic Site. On a visit to the States in 1994, Peter and Veronika Suess, two businesspeople from Switzerland, saw Barley Sheaf and fell in love with it. They quit their jobs, bought the property via international fax, and arrived the first night to a full house of guests.

The house and adjacent cottage are furnished in a mixture of English and American antiques, with rich Oriental rugs scattered over the wide-plank floors. Guests gather in the common room by the fire for chess, checkers, and conversation.

The bedrooms on the second and third floors have elegant views. The rooms are decorated with floral prints and brass-and-iron beds. Peter and Veronika have brought with them from Switzerland furniture, antiques, and traditions, including breakfast *grittibaenz* (little men made of bread with raisin eyes).

The separate cottage is cozy, and in winter months there's always a crackling fire. The three bedrooms here are decorated with American folk art, both antique and reproduction. Each room has sloping eaves, hooked rugs, and antique pine furniture. Though the rooms are small, the cottage is perfect for families.

You should expect to hear noises in this rural setting—the noises of a working farm: the baaing of sheep, the buzzing of bees (which manufacture 300 pounds of honey annually), and the occasional rumble of a tractor. But that means you can count on the abundant breakfasts (which include eggs, bread, jams, and honey) to be farm fresh.

🏨 *7 double rooms with baths, 5 suites. Air-conditioning in bedrooms, TV in study, pool, badminton, croquet, meeting room in barn. $110–$235; full breakfast, afternoon tea. AE, MC, V. No smoking, no pets, 2-day minimum on weekends, 3-day minimum on holidays.*

Bridgeton House

River Rd. (Box 167), Upper Black Eddy, PA 18972, tel. 610/982–5856

At the foot of the bridge to Milford, New Jersey, is a three-story 1836 Federal brick building that has been a residence and a general store. In 1982, with a dozen years of inn experience behind them, Beatrice and Charles Briggs completely transformed it into a terra-cotta-colored bed-and-breakfast. You will find American country antiques, reproductions, and contemporary furnishings. Five rooms on the riverside have four-posters, country quilts, and screened-in private porches with breathtaking views of the morning mist. A spiral staircase leads to a huge third-floor penthouse suite so ultra-high-tech you might think you were in Manhattan. But the view—as though you're suspended over the Delaware—tells you otherwise. In winter, the cozy sitting room is a perfect place to gaze out at the snow falling on the river. In summer, you can watch people paddle canoes and float lazily along in inner tubes—or you might indulge.

🏨 *6 double rooms with baths, 2 suites, garret, penthouse. Air-conditioning in bedrooms, fireplaces in dining room and suites. $89–$225; full breakfast. MC, V. No smoking indoors, no pets, 2-day minimum on weekends, 3-day minimum on holiday weekends, closed Dec. 24–25.*

Bucksville House

4501 Durham Rd. and Buck Dr., Kintnersville, PA 18930, tel. 610/847–8948

This bed-and-breakfast, which sits on the edge of 5½ acres in northern Bucks

County, was once a stagecoach stop. Innkeepers Barbara and Joe Szallosi restored the 1795 Colonial fieldstone-and-stucco house while she wasn't teaching and he wasn't doing carpentry.

The living room is decorated in English and American antiques, and in the den (once the tavern), you will find a coal stove to curl up in front of. The dining room, once the old wheelwright shop, has a walk-in fireplace, a Mercer tile floor, and a long country table. Dried herbs and antique baskets hang from the beams of the low ceiling. In the bedrooms, antiques blend nicely with reproductions hand-crafted by Joe—cupboards and pencil-post beds. In 1992 Joe bought 12,000 bricks and built a courtyard terrace and herb garden. And a new, spacious unit equipped for visitors with disabilities was christened the same year. Grapes grow on an arbor near the gazebo, and Joe makes his own wine. Chances are, he will bring a bottle up from the cellar for you to sample.

🏨 *4 double rooms with baths, 1 suite. Air-conditioning in bedrooms, cable TV in den, fireplaces in 3 bedrooms, water garden with waterfall, gazebo. $100–$130; full breakfast. AE, D, MC, V. No smoking, no pets.*

Evermay-on-the-Delaware

889 River Rd. (Box 60), Erwinna, PA 18920, tel. 610/294–9100, fax 610/294–8249

Thirteen miles north of New Hope is Evermay-on-the-Delaware, a romantic country hotel with a carriage house and cottage set on 25 parklike acres between the river and the canal. Here Victorian elegance is still very much in fashion.

The mansion, which is on the National Register of Historic Places, was built in 1790 and had a third floor added in 1870. From 1871 through the early 1930s, it was a popular country hotel. It was the Stover family home for many years and was opened as an inn in 1982. Current innkeepers William and Danielle Moffly purchased the inn in 1996.

In the stately double parlor you can meet for afternoon tea or for an aperitif in the evening. The fireplace is inset with Mercer tiles, and there are crystal chandeliers, tapestry rugs, a Victorian grandfather clock, and brocade camel-back settees. Breakfast is served in a conservatory off the back parlor. The bedrooms, carefully decorated with Victorian antiques and named after Bucks County notables, have wide-plank squeaky floors; some retain their original fireplaces. Carved walnut beds, massive headboards, marble-top dressers, Victorian wallpaper, and fresh fruit and flowers are everywhere. Ask for one of the six bedrooms in the main house that face the river. The carriage house may be preferable for groups traveling together. It has a two-bedroom suite with sitting room and bath on the second floor and two double rooms on the ground floor.

The inn's restaurant is open Friday, Saturday, and Sunday nights for one seating at 7:30 (6:30 on Sunday in winter). A six-course, fixed-price meal is served, starting with a glass of champagne and hors d'oeuvres. There are two choices of entrée, which might include roast loin of venison.

Evermay is ideally located for enjoying the countryside in any season. If you venture out back into the meadows or into the old barn, you will run across sheep, chickens, and pheasants.

▦ *16 rooms with baths. Restaurant, air-conditioning and phones in bedrooms, hookups for modem. $95–$180; Continental-plus breakfast, afternoon tea. MC, V. No smoking, no pets, 2-day minimum with Sat. reservation, 3-day minimum on holidays, closed Dec. 24.*

Glasbern

2141 Pack House Rd., Fogelsville, PA 18051-9743, tel. 610/285–4723, fax 610/285–2862

You will understand why Al and Beth Granger chose this name (which means "glass barn" in Old English) when you see their country inn. Glasbern is a 19th-century German bank barn, tucked into a quiet valley 10 miles west of Allentown, and the Grangers have reconstructed it of stone, wood, and lots of glass. The Great Room resembles a lofty stone sanctuary, with a fireplace and hand-hewn beams that crisscross through the high, open spaces. Guest rooms are decorated traditionally, with standard antique reproductions, and in contemporary style with glass tables and wicker. Brick walkways lead to a farmhouse and a carriage house, both renovated and similarly decorated—there's a certain sameness about the decor. All suites have whirlpool baths, and some have kitchenettes and private entrances. Nine rooms have fireplaces. Skiing, hiking, and antiquing are close by, but you may find you're content with just being on these 113 peaceful acres in the middle of nowhere.

▦ *14 double rooms with baths, 10 suites. Restaurant, air-conditioning in bedrooms, TV with VCR and phones in bedrooms, conference facilities, pool, bicycles. $115–$300; full breakfast. MC, V. No pets, 2-night minimum on fall weekends in suites.*

Highland Farms

70 East Rd., Doylestown, PA 18901, tel. 215/340–1354

Bordering the Doylestown Country Club golf course is the 1740 fieldstone country manor that was once home to lyricist Oscar Hammerstein II. Innkeeper Mary Schnitzer bought the estate and opened it as a bed-and-breakfast on Valentine's Day, 1988. The elegant, high-ceilinged rooms are furnished in American and English antiques. Flanking a foyer with a grandfather clock and a Victorian pier glass are a spacious parlor and a formal dining room. Wicker and ferns fill a sunroom that overlooks a white carriage house, bank barn, and a 60-foot pool. The library is richly decorated with green velvet sofas and chairs and a collection of Hammerstein memorabilia. You can spend cozy evenings by the fire here watching a musical from the video collection. Each bedroom is named and thematically decorated after one of Hammerstein's musicals. You will wake to the aroma of fresh hazelnut coffee and, in late summer, the sight of corn growing "as high as an elephant's eye."

🏠 *2 double rooms with baths, 2 doubles share bath. Air-conditioning in bedrooms, cable TV with VCR in library, phone in library, pool, tennis court. $135–$195; full breakfast. AE, MC, V. No smoking, 2-day minimum on weekends, 3-day minimum on holidays.*

The Inn at Fordhook Farm

105 New Britain Rd., Doylestown, PA 18901, tel. 215/345–1766, fax 215/345–1791

The Inn at Fordhook Farm, set on 60 acres a mile and a half from the center of Doylestown, is the Burpee family estate. There's a bank barn and a carriage house, surrounded by the fields and meadows where W. Atlee Burpee first tested seeds for his company before the turn of the century. The oldest part of the fieldstone-and-plaster house with a mansard roof dates from 1740. Through the years, additions were carefully made to blend architecturally with the original structure. Burpee's grandchild, Jonathan Burpee, grew up here. Thinking that a bed-and-breakfast would be a good way to preserve the family home, Jonathan and his wife, Carole, opened it to guests in 1985.

The house is furnished with English and American family antiques and photographs, grandfather clocks, and other Americana. In the dining room, the mantel is inlaid with Mercer tiles, and the long mahogany table is set with heirloom china each morning for breakfast. French doors open to a large terrace shaded by a 200-year-old linden tree, with a view of the broad, sweeping lawn. In the bedrooms, you will find floral prints, quilts, 19th-century four-poster beds, window seats, and family photographs and portraits.

The carriage house is a spacious two-bedroom suite not quite as carefully decorated as the main house, but ideal for a family or for two couples. The chestnut-paneled Great Room there, once a study, has a vaulted ceiling and Palladian windows, and children's books, photographs, and other Burpee memorabilia everywhere.

The style at Fordhook Farm is a quiet, casual elegance. Carole serves an elaborate Saturday tea—by the fire during the winter, outdoors on the generous terrace in warm months.

🏠 *5 double rooms with baths, 2 doubles share bath. Air-conditioning in bedrooms, conference room. $100–$300; full breakfast. AE, MC, V. No smoking, no pets, 2-day minimum on weekends, 3-day minimum on holidays.*

Inn at Phillips Mill

2590 N. River Rd., New Hope, PA 18938, tel. 215/862–2984

Perched at a bend in the road, in a tiny hamlet on the Delaware Canal near New Hope, is a 1750 stone inn that looks like an illustration from Grimm's Fairy Tales. There may be no country inn with a setting more romantic than the Inn at Phillips Mill. Built as a barn and a gristmill, it once stood next to the village piggery—a copper pig with a wreath around its neck now welcomes you from just above the deep-blue door.

For 70 years the gristmill has been the September home of the Phillips Mill Community Art Show. In the early 1970s, the main building and its walled garden caught the imagination of Brooks and Joyce Kaufman. Thinking it had the look of a European village, they bought it; Brooks, an architect, started the renovation, and Joyce began doing the interior. They opened in 1977.

The guest rooms are small, but they will enchant you. Some are tucked imaginatively into nooks and under eaves, and each is whimsically furnished. There are brass and iron and late-19th-century four-poster beds, and an eclectic mix of antiques, wicker, quilts, dried bouquets, hand-painted trays, embroidered cloths on night tables, Provençal fabrics, floral wallpapers, and oil paintings. The cottage, also decorated in a mix of French country and American antiques, has a bedroom, a bath, and a living room with a stone fireplace. If you wish, breakfast will be delivered to your bedroom door in a big basket. When you lift the blue-and-white checkered cloth, you will find muffins and a pot of coffee or tea.

Phillips Mill is famous for its restaurant, and rightly so. The candlelit tables in the three dining rooms are intimately nestled into nooks and crannies under low, rough-beamed ceilings. The menu is French and may feature garlic-encrusted swordfish in a beurre blanc sauce, or smoked breast of moulard duck with herbed lentils. Two pastry chefs, Roz Schwartz and Thomas Millburn, prepare *les délices de la maison* (house delights).

The winding back roads are perfect for hiking, bicycling, or driving to see the fall foliage.

🏠 *4 double rooms with baths, 1 suite, 1 cottage. Restaurant, air-conditioning in bedrooms; pool. $80–$125; Continental breakfast extra. No credit cards. No pets, BYOB, 3-night minimum on holiday weekends, closed early Jan.–early Feb.*

The Logan Inn

10 W. Ferry St., New Hope, PA 18938, tel. 215/862-2300

This Colonial tavern and shuttered fieldstone inn in the heart of New Hope was established in 1722. Gwen Davis has been the innkeeper here for more than 10 years. Wide hallways lead into spacious bedrooms with four-posters and Victorian and Colonial reproductions. Lace curtains and baskets of flowers fill the deep-set window embrasures that overlook the village's main thoroughfare. The tavern has a Colonial fireplace, a dartboard, and restored 18th-century murals of theatrical scenes. A wall of stained glass gives a Victorian elegance to the Garden Dining Room. A huge canopied patio encourages a booming summer business. High chairs, booster seats, and special children's menus make this a good place for families. The Logan is within easy walking distance of all area sights. Gwen, a longtime resident who has worked with the historical preservation society, will fill you in on local lore and nearby attractions.

🏠 *18 double rooms with baths. Restaurant, tavern, air-conditioning in bedrooms, cable TV and phones in bedrooms, meeting room, free off-street parking. $95–$145; Continental-plus breakfast. AE, D, DC, MC, V. No pets, 2-day minimum on weekends May–Dec., 3-day minimum on holiday weekends.*

Longswamp Bed and Breakfast

1605 State St., Mertztown, PA 19539, tel. 610/682-6197

This white clapboard Federal manor house is in a rural village about 15 minutes southwest of Allentown. Elsa and Dean Dimick restored the house, which was built in 1789, and opened it as a bed-and-breakfast in 1983. When they're not innkeeping, he's chief of medicine at the Lehigh Valley Hospital, and she's a professional chef. In the parlor, with its wood-pegged floors, deeply set windows, and settees before the fireplace, you can sit and enjoy the Dimicks' vast collection of books and music. The large, sunny guest rooms are decorated in a mix of Pennsylvania and Victorian antiques, with Amish quilts and one-of-a-kind antique iron beds. The cottage at the side, used by the Underground Railroad, is much more haphazardly decorated, with antiques and family hand-me-downs. Golf, tennis, and horseback riding are nearby, and the Dimicks can help you map out drives down scenic back roads through farmland or to antiques shops for browsing.

⚏ *4 double rooms with baths, 4 doubles share 2 baths, 2 suites. Air-conditioning in bedrooms, TV in summer kitchen and suites, hiking trails on 40 adjoining acres. $78–$83; full breakfast, afternoon tea. AE, MC, V. No smoking, no pets, children welcome.*

The Mansion Inn

9 S. Main St., New Hope, PA 18938, tel. 215/862–1231, fax 215/862–0277

An atmosphere of romantic luxury and calm fills the Mansion Inn, just steps off bustling Main Street in New Hope. The pale yellow, 1865 Second Empire–style Victorian building, with a mansard roof and arched front door, is owned by Dr. Elio Filippo Bracco and Keith David, who opened the inn in 1995. They restored what had been a doctor's office, adding modern baths, some with whirlpool tubs. Innkeeper Diana Smith is on hand to offer suggestions for touring, shopping, and dining, but she also respects guests' privacy.

The two high-ceilinged sitting areas are formal yet comfortably inviting. The buttery yellow drawing room is filled with floral-print furniture, some works by local artists, and Depression glass. The smaller drawing room, done in soothing beige tones, has books and games for adults. Besides the seven rooms in the house, the inn has two in a garden cottage. Each has a different color scheme, from the blue toile de Jouy print in Ashby to the rose chintz of Windsor. All rooms have antiques, such as settees, armoires, or trunks; some have four-poster canopy beds or fireplaces. Egyptian cotton towels, starched and ironed sheets, and toiletries add luxurious touches, and many rooms have TVs and blow dryers. Nightly turndown includes home-baked cookies and bottled spring water. You may hear some street noise on busy weekends in rooms facing Main Street.

Breakfast is served at white wicker tables and chairs in the green-and-white-wallpapered breakfast room. Early birds can have coffee and a newspaper delivered to their rooms. The hearty buffet of fresh-baked muffins, breads, fresh fruit, and granola is followed by a choice of a special French toast or an egg dish.

The English-style garden has a gazebo. A fenced-in swimming pool is just off the guests' parking area yet feels delightfully private—much like the inn itself.

⚏ *5 rooms with baths, 4 suites. Air-conditioning, TVs in most rooms, phones with data port jacks, swimming pool. $160–$265; full breakfast. AE, MC, V. No smoking, no pets, 2-night minimum on weekends, 3-night minimum on holiday weekends.*

Pinetree Farm

2155 Lower State Rd., Doylestown, PA 18901, tel. 215/348–0632

One mile south of Doylestown is a white stucco-and-fieldstone 1730 Quaker farmhouse that has been carefully restored by innkeepers Joy and Ron Feigles. Joy jokes that she majored in hotel administration "and then 29 years later we bought an inn." The interior is white, light, and airy, and it's decorated with American Colonial antiques and reproductions. A solarium overlooks the swimming pool and 16 acres of pine trees. The bedrooms have stenciling, Oriental rugs, marble fireplaces, writing desks, four-poster beds, iron beds, and in the Pink Room, a canopied white twig bed that's a masterpiece. Stuffed toy lambs are perched on each bed; the deep window seats have mounds of pillows to curl up into while you admire the view. The Feigles, lifelong residents of Doylestown, have plenty of suggestions if you should want to explore nearby villages or shop for antiques.

🏠 *2 double rooms with baths, 2 doubles share bath. Air-conditioning in bedrooms, cable TV in study, pool. $145–$165; full breakfast. No credit cards. No smoking, no pets, 2-day minimum on weekends, 3-day minimum on holiday weekends.*

1740 House

River Rd., Lumberville, PA 18933, tel. 215/297-5661

Travel 6½ miles north from New Hope on Route 32, one of the most scenic roads in Pennsylvania, and you will come to the 1740 House, an inn that takes full advantage of its picturesque location. The original 1740 two-story clapboard farmhouse, and its more recent attached additions, sit just off River Road and just a few feet from the Delaware Canal and the Delaware River. The guest rooms are decorated in beige and Wedgwood blue, many with wicker furniture and exposed beams. All have a balcony or terrace with an impressive view of the river. The suite has large windows on three sides and a four-poster bed. You'll have breakfast in the candlelit dining room, lined with plants and paintings and overlooking the river.

Innkeeper Robert John Vris has been connected to the inn since his grandfather Harry Nessler bought it in 1966; Bob took over in 1994 when Harry died. He will describe the walks you can take—up to 15 miles in either direction along the towpath, or across the river on a footbridge to a small state park.

🏠 *23 double rooms with baths, 1 suite. Pool. $75–$125; Continental-plus breakfast. No credit cards. No smoking in dining room, no pets, 2-day minimum on weekends in season.*

The Wedgwood Collection of Inns

111 W. Bridge St., New Hope, PA 18938, tel. 215/862-2570

You can't miss the Wedgwood Inn. This hip-gabled 1870 Victorian clapboard house on a tree-lined street is only two blocks from the center of New Hope, and it's painted bright Wedgwood blue. It has a large veranda loaded with pots of flowers and hanging ferns, a portecochere, and garden walks that wind around to a gazebo. The companion property next door, called Umplebey House, was built of plaster and stone about 1830 in the Classic Revival tradition. It has walls that are 26 inches thick, brick walkways through flowering gardens, and a carriage house in back. Across the street is another companion property, the Aaron Burr House, a six-bedroom Victorian with a maximum capacity of 18 guests, popular for business conferences.

Innkeeping seems a logical profession for owners Nadine Silnutzer and Carl Glassman, 14-year veterans of the B&B game. They like gardening, and they delight in finding antiques at auctions and flea markets. Carl, with his colleague Ripley Hotch, has published a book, *How to Start and Run Your Own Bed & Breakfast Inn* (Stackpole Books). He teaches innkeeping at New York University.

Wedgwood pottery, oil paintings, handmade quilts, and fresh flowers are everywhere in the sunny interior. The parlors in each house have coal-fed fireplaces and plush Victorian sofas and chairs. The windows are covered with lace swag curtains. Persian rugs lie on hardwood floors. Each house has bedrooms with bay windows, brass and four-poster beds, and Victorian antiques. The circa-1890 carriage house has a small sitting room, a glass-enclosed porch, a kitchenette, and a four-poster bed in a loft overlooking a small deck. It's a private retreat that's ideal for reading a novel, or maybe writing one.

Days begin casually with a "Continental-plus" breakfast, served in the sunporch, the gazebo, or if you prefer, in bed. If you ask, Carl and Dinie will get you theater tickets, make dinner reservations, and arrange picnics, dinner in the gazebo, or a moonlight carriage ride.

🏨 *16 double rooms with baths, 2 suites. Air-conditioning in bedrooms, TV in parlors, concierge services, swimming and tennis privileges for nominal fee at nearby club. $75–$205; Continental-plus breakfast, afternoon tea. AE, MC, V. No smoking indoors, 2-day minimum on weekends, 3-day minimum on holiday weekends.*

The Whitehall Inn

1370 Pineville Rd., New Hope, PA 18938, tel. 215/598–7945 or 888/379–4483

Ten minutes southwest of New Hope and five minutes from Peddler's Village is the Whitehall Inn, a white plaster-over-stone manor house, circa 1794, set on 12 rolling acres, with a huge white barn and stables at the side. It is one of the most peaceful and secluded inns in Bucks County.

Two transplanted Oklahomans, Mike and Suella Wass, are responsible for elevating the business of innkeeping to a fine art. No guest will feel neglected here; from the moment you cross the threshold, the Wasses convince you that your visit is important to them. They encourage your interest in the area, engage you

in conversation, and ultimately earn your compliments. After years in their niche, the Wasses continue to stand above the rest.

Inside the house, past the sunroom, are high ceilings, Oriental rugs on wide-plank floors, and windows with deep sills. The parlor has a fireplace, a late-19th-century pedal organ, comfortable contemporary sofas with lots of Victorian lamps, and the soothing sounds of antique clocks ticking everywhere. The bedrooms (four with fireplaces) are furnished in a mixture of late Victorian and American country antiques. You will find a basket of apples, a bottle of mineral water, and Crabtree and Evelyn soaps, colognes, and shampoos. The linens are imported, and in winter you sleep between flannel sheets.

Heirloom china and ornate Victorian sterling flatware are used for breakfast, a sybaritic and beautifully orchestrated four-course feast, with lighted tapers on the table and sideboards. The Wasses keep your menu on file, so you'll never get a repeat unless you make a special request.

High tea is served at 4 each afternoon with crystal, china, and silver. In summer, you can relax by the pool, play tennis, or go horseback riding nearby. In October, you can walk in the gardens or fields, enjoy the foliage, and spend evenings by the fire in the candlelit parlor. Lovers of chocolate and/or chamber music should inquire about special-event weekends in the spring.

🏨 *4 double rooms with baths, 2 doubles share bath. Air-conditioning in bedrooms, pool. $130–$180; full breakfast, afternoon tea. AE, D, MC, V. No smoking, no pets.*

The Brandywine River Valley

About an hour from Philadelphia, where southeastern Pennsylvania meets northern Delaware, the Brandywine River flows lazily from West Chester to Wilmington, amid rolling hills where streams wind through dense woodlands. The pastoral valley has sheltered artists and millionaires, Revolutionary War soldiers, and slaves on the Underground Railroad. While development has taken its toll, much of the region looks as it did 250 years ago.

Beginning in 1623 the Dutch, the Swedes, and the English moved in successively, coexisting with the Leni-Lenape Indians, the region's earliest residents. But it was not until 1682 that William Penn and the English finally stabilized the region. Quaker millers and farmers began to settle here in the early 1700s. Powder mills supplied munitions for George Washington's army, and in the fall of 1777 more than 30,000 soldiers fought the Battle of Brandywine. After a resounding defeat Washington's army camped that winter at nearby Valley Forge until the famous Christmas crossing over the Delaware River.

Early in this century the illustrator Howard Pyle and other artists began building the reputation of the Brandywine School, dominated today by three generations of Wyeths— N.C., Andrew, and James. A century before the Wyeths began capturing the local landscape on canvas, the du Pont family was ornamenting it with grand mansions and gardens. Pierre-Samuel du Pont, the patriarch, escaped with his family from post-Revolutionary France and settled in northern Delaware. His son Eleuthère Irénée (E.I.) founded the Du Pont Company in 1802 and made the family fortune, first in gunpowder and iron, later in chemicals and textiles (see Delaware, The Wilmington area).

Log cabins, 18th-century stone farmhouses, and the ornate estates of the du Ponts are all reminders of the past. Today you can visit world-famous formal gardens and museums of the decorative arts. You can explore backcountry roads and antiques shops (without the crowds that you find in Bucks County), then check into a restful country inn.

Places to Go, Sights to See

Brandywine Battlefield State Park (Chadds Ford, tel. 610/459–3342). British troops defeated the Continental Army nearby in the fall of 1777. On the site are two restored farmhouses that once sheltered Washington and Lafayette.

Brandywine River Museum (Chadds Ford, tel. 610/388–2700). This restored Civil War–era gristmill, on the banks of the Brandywine River, now houses a collection of landscape paintings, American illustrations, and works by three generations of Wyeths. Outside are gardens and nature trails.

Franklin Mint Museum (Franklin Center, tel. 610/459–6120). The world's largest private mint creates collectibles—books, records, jewelry, furniture, porcelain, bronzes, and crystal.

Longwood Gardens (Kennett Square, tel. 610/388–1000). The grounds boast some 350 acres of magnolias and azaleas in spring; roses and water lilies in summer; fall foliage; and winter camellias, orchids, and palms in a 19th-century arboretum.

Valley Forge National Historical Park (Valley Forge, tel. 610/783–1000). On these 3,500 serene acres, George Washington's army endured the winter of 1777–1778. There are picnic areas and 6 miles of paved trails.

Restaurants

In Dilworthtown, just south of West Chester off Route 202, you'll find the **Dilworthtown Inn** (tel. 610/399–1390), a French Continental dining room in a 1785 Colonial edifice. Entrées cost $18–$20, and the lobster is renowned. **La Cocotte** (tel. 610/436–6722), in the heart of West Chester on West Gay Street, specializes in French country cuisine: light lunches and elegant dinners.

In the Kennett Square area, **The Unicorn** (tel. 610/444–3328) offers traditional English-style cuisine, including fish-and-chips and Cornish pastie. An 18th-century barn set on 20 landscaped acres houses the **Stone Barn** (tel. 610/347–2414), an all-American establishment serving up beef and shrimp dishes until Sunday afternoon, when it goes Scandinavian with a smorgasbord. The **Terrace Restaurant** (tel. 610/388–6771), on Route 1, occupies a wonderful site overlooking the landscaped grounds of Longwood Gardens. The presentation and service are graceful, and the clientele is international. For breakfast, visit **Hank's Place** (tel. 610/388–7061), an original 1940s diner with great home-style food near the Brandywine Museum. For lunch downtown, head over to the **Kennett Square Inn** (tel. 610/444–5688).

One mile north of the Brandywine River Museum you'll find **Chadds Ford Cafe** (tel. 610/558–3960), a casual, moderately priced spot for sandwiches and soups or unpretentious dinner fare. For rich country cooking and a creditable wine list, try **Pace One** (tel. 610/459–9784) in Thornton. Prices for the lamb, seafood, and pasta dishes are medium to medium-high.

Tourist Information

Brandywine Valley Tourist Information Center (Rte. 1, Kennett Square 19348, tel. 610/388–2900 or 800/228–9933). **Valley Forge Convention & Visitors Bureau** (Box 311, Norristown 19404, tel. 610/278–3558).

Reservation Services

A Bed & Breakfast Connection/Bed & Breakfast of Philadelphia (Box 21, Devon 19333, tel. 610/687–3565 or 800/448–3619, fax 610/995–9524). **Association of B&Bs in Philadelphia, Valley Forge, and Brandywine** (Box 562, Valley Forge 19481-0562, tel. 610/783–7838 or 800/344–0123, fax 610/783–7783). **B&B of Chester County** (Box 825, Kennett Square 19348, tel. 610/444–1367).

The Bankhouse Bed and Breakfast

875 Hillsdale Rd., West Chester, PA 19382, tel. 610/344-7388

Just outside West Chester, this 18th-century stucco-over-stone house is built into the bank of a hill. It once housed the servants of a large estate. Innkeepers Diana and Michael Bové, who both worked in media services at a nearby university, opened their home to travelers in 1988, and Diana now manages the bed-and-breakfast full-time.

You enter the second-floor guest rooms by an outside staircase. (The two double rooms can be rented as a single suite, with private bath, on request.) The homey upstairs sitting room has an extensive collection of books, games, and brochures. Bedrooms are decorated with 19th-century oak antiques, stenciling, and fresh roses from Diana's English gardens. The quilts she makes are displayed and are also for sale. Guests often linger in the narrow dining room over a hearty country breakfast; Diana specializes in apple soufflé pancakes and baked lemon crepes. You can look down through one deeply recessed window out to the pond and the split-rail fence that borders a meadow across the road. You can gaze at the scenery; or you can explore the shops in West Chester, canoe the Brandywine, or bike down country lanes.

🏠 *2 double rooms share bath. Air-conditioning. $70–$90; full breakfast. No credit cards. No smoking, no pets.*

Bed and Breakfast at Walnut Hill

541 Chandler's Mill Rd., Avondale, PA 19311, tel. 610/444-3703

This white clapboard-and-fieldstone Pennsylvania mill house just outside Kennett Square was built before 1840. Proprietors Tom and Sandy Mills, who

have lived here for three decades, opened it as a bed-and-breakfast in 1985. Across the crooked little road, beyond horses grazing in the meadow, is a creek where it's so quiet you can hear every trickle as you watch for Canada geese, deer, or the occasional red fox to meander across the meadow. The house is warmly decorated with early 19th-century country antiques and reproductions; you'll find bunches of dried herbs and flowers, pie safes, and a New England whaler's lamp over the table. The bedrooms are furnished with writing desks, Victorian wicker, and pencil-post beds. The paneling throughout is made from old barn siding. Sandy—a trained social worker, gourmet cook, and morning person par excellence—and Tom are glad to offer tips on the best routes for biking, hiking, or touring. This amiable couple likes to think that their guests arrive as strangers but leave as friends.

🏠 *2 double rooms (1 with TV) share bath. Air-conditioning, 2 fireplaces, and cable TV/VCR in family room, hot tub. $65–$80; full breakfast. No credit cards. Smoking in common room only, no pets.*

Duling-Kurtz House & Country Inn

146 S. Whitford Rd., Exton, PA 19341, tel. 610/524-1830, fax 610/524-6258

On a country road midway between Valley Forge and the Brandywine Battlefields is the Duling-Kurtz House & Country Inn. The driveway is lined with converted gas street lamps, and there are formal gardens, a Victorian-style gazebo, and a footbridge that crosses a stone-lined brook. The 1830s farmhouse and the adjacent barn, both white plaster over fieldstone, were elegantly restored and opened in 1983. Raymond Carr and David Knauer, who did the restoration, named the property after their mothers. The current owner, Michael Person—who hails from Vienna, Austria, and has a background in hotel management—has orchestrated a massive upgrading since taking over in 1992, and he is a decidedly hands-on operator. He staunchly defends the concept of fine dining and lodging at affordable prices, and he runs an intimate, service-oriented inn.

The guest rooms (in the barn) have been restored and furnished in Williamsburg period reproductions. You will find marble-top sinks; Oriental rugs; writing desks; and canopied, brass, and four-poster beds. One suite has its own courtyard. Rooms are named for historic figures: Honeymooners often request the George Washington Room, with its king-size, cherry-wood canopy bed and step-down bathroom with claw-foot tub. A Continental breakfast is served on china in the parlor.

A sheltered brick walkway connects the barn and the farmhouse restaurant, which is also furnished with Colonial reproductions. Near the entrance you'll discover an unusual 18th-century beehive bread oven. Four of the dining rooms have stone fireplaces, and richly mullioned windows detail the dining areas. Under the direction of chef Michael Favacchio, the dinner menu features hickory smoked buffalo filet, duck confit with sweet potato ravioli, and a rich crepe stuffed with lobster and draped in brie sauce. The steaming, freshly baked popovers, served with tangy lemon curd, are legendary. Dinner entrées range from $18 to $30.

You can stroll through peaceful wooded areas adjoining the inn, and when it's warm you can enjoy tea in the gazebo. Museums and battlefields are not far away, and Michael and his staff will point you to the best antiquing and shopping.

🏠 *15 double rooms with baths, 3 suites. Restaurant open 7 days a week, air-conditioning in bedrooms, cable TV and phones in bedrooms, room service, 3 conference rooms with catering. $55–$120; Continental breakfast. AE, D, DC, MC, V. No pets; call for additional restrictions.*

Fairville Inn

Rte. 52 (Box 219), Fairville, PA 19357, tel. 610/388–5900, fax 610/388–5902

In the heart of Andrew Wyeth country, on the road between Winterthur Museum and Longwood Gardens, this country-house inn is set on 5½ acres behind a split-rail fence. It is surrounded by estates, beautiful gardens, and miles of country roads. The hub of the inn is a pale yellow–colored 1826 Federal plaster-over-double-brick house with dark green shutters. There's a Victorian-style veranda across the front. In back are the Spring House and Carriage House, buildings that were constructed about 10 years ago but designed to match the character of the main house.

Swedish-born Ole Retlev and his wife, Patricia, both former ski instructors, owned two different inns in Mt. Snow, Vermont. But, as Ole explains, "There's more to draw travelers here on a year-round basis." So, in 1986, they moved to the Brandywine River valley and opened the Fairville Inn.

The rooms are bright and airy, appealingly furnished with Queen Anne and Chippendale reproductions. Before the fireplace in the living room are two blue settees, with a large copper-top coffee table between them. The flowered draperies and potted plants give the room an understated "relaxed formal feel," as Ole calls it. The bedrooms in the main house, all of quirky size and shape, are done in light, elegant country colors and are carpeted. You will also find four-poster beds, canopy beds, settees, writing desks, floral wallpapers—and fresh flowers. The four rooms in the Spring House are somewhat larger, and all have working gas fireplaces. Siding from the old barn has been used for mantels and paneling, and some of the sinks have copper drain boards.

Private terraces, balconies that overlook a pond and rolling farmland, and gas fireplaces make the Carriage House rooms most appealing. They are at the back of the property and away from traffic noise. With cathedral ceilings and old barn timbers for beams and mantels, two suites in the Carriage House are the most architecturally interesting.

Canoeing, hiking, antiquing, and museum-browsing are only some of the area's pastimes. Why not attend a polo match during one of the warmer months?

🏠 *13 double rooms with baths, 2 suites. Air-conditioning, cable TV, and phones in bedrooms. $140–$195; Continental breakfast, afternoon tea. AE, D, MC, V. No smoking, no pets.*

Hamanassett

Rte. 1 (Box 129), Lima, PA 19037, tel. 610/459-3000

Meet Evelene Dohan, the proprietor of Hamanassett: She has taught English literature, run a catering business, and gone home a multiple champion from the Philadelphia Flower Show. Her gifts are evident both on the grounds and in the decor of this secluded estate.

The hilltop residence overlooks 48 acres of woods and meadow, shaded garden pathways, and stone-walled ponds. In April and May, approaching guests travel on a ½-mile driveway lined with ancient rhododendrons and well-established azaleas, blossoming in profusion all the way up to the ellipse that fronts the main house. Inside, the innkeeper's cut-flower arrangements grace each room; potted plants and hanging ferns flood the light-filled solarium. Mrs. Dohan, who came as a bride in 1950 and raised her children here, has appointed the rooms with four-poster canopied beds, Oriental rugs, and handsome antiques. And she single-handedly serves up delectable country breakfasts with homemade jams, compotes, and freshly baked confections.

Hamanassett was built in 1856 for Dr. Charles Meigs, a Philadelphia pioneer in obstetrics, but what you see today bears little resemblance to the doctor's summer retreat. As Mrs. Dohan will tell you, the little farmhouse then consisted of just "three rooms down, and three rooms up." But in 1870 her late husband's grandfather purchased the estate. His son—her father-in-law—didn't like the sensation of enclosure, and so he added onto and redefined the original structure (including the pumpkin pine flooring). He installed arched passageways instead of doors between rooms on the first floor, so the main body of the house feels united, allowing fluid movement from room to room and a less obstructed flow of light. Before ascending the main staircase, note the blue-and-white delft tile depiction of human history encased in the broad white arch to your right: The story begins with the expulsion from the Garden of Eden.

You may find yourself so seduced by the beauty this proficient innkeeper has created that you won't want to venture outside it. But if you do, all the most popular points of interest are only minutes away. Hamanassett sits just off well-traveled Route 1, but its acreage makes an ample buffer between the estate and the roadway.

🏠 *7 rooms with private baths, 1 suite. Air-conditioning in some rooms, TV in all, solarium. $90–$125; full breakfast. No credit cards. No smoking, no pets, 2-night minimum year-round.*

Lenape Springs Farm

580 W. Creek Rd. (Box 176, Pocopson), West Chester, PA 19366, tel. 610/793-2266 or 800/793-2234

You'll need directions to get to this out-of-the-way location in the Brandywine River Valley, but that's what makes it so wonderful. Though only 4 miles north of Chadds Ford, Sharon and Bob Currie's 32-acre farm is down a dead-end country road that runs along a secluded section of the Brandywine River, and is, as Bob says, "nicely isolated."

The three-story stone, Federal-style farmhouse was built in 1847 and is surrounded by hills, fields, arbors, gazebos, cows, and deer. The Curries bought the property in 1977 and spent 12 years renovating before opening their B&B.

Every view is a good one. From the glassed-in porch you can see the early 1800s, three-tiered bank barn. You can watch the horses from the windowed alcove while you eat breakfast or admire the sweeping lawn down to the Brandywine River as you unwind in the hot tub on the outdoor deck.

The house and its five bedrooms are filled with fun touches. The Bow Room has a collection of old bottles that were found on the property; the Doll Room has more than 60 dolls, many from Sharon's childhood; the quilt hanging on the wall was made by Sharon's great grandmother.

There are plenty of leisurely things to do, including a walk along the Brandywine that may turn up an artifact or easily twisting Bob's arm for a game of pool.

▥ *5 double rooms with baths. Air-conditioning, pool table. $70–$94; full breakfast. MC, V. Smoking in designated areas only, no pets, children welcome.*

Meadow Spring Farm

201 E. Street Rd. (Rte. 926), Kennett Square, PA 19348, tel. 610/444-3903

Just minutes north of Kennett Square and Longwood Gardens, up a country lane past grazing cows, is the brick Colonial 1836 house of this 120-acre working farm. Anne Hicks arrived here as a bride more than 45 years ago. She raised five children in this house, and in 1984 she opened it as a bed-and-breakfast. She's an accomplished cook, craftswoman, and collector of dolls and family antiques. You'll find big, sunny farmhouse bed-

rooms, including one with a fireplace, Amish quilts, family photographs, a Chippendale bed with a crocheted canopy, and a carved sleigh bed with a headboard 7 feet tall. There are also three rooms over the garage, but these lack the character of those in the main house. Breakfast is served on the long mahogany table in the dining room, or in the solarium, a glassed-in porch overlooking the flower gardens. Anne's 150-plus cow collection, scattered throughout the house, is replaced in winter by more than 200 Santas. With Temba, the farm dog, you can stroll with your children through the meadows or visit the pigs and chickens in the barns.

▥ *5 double rooms with baths. Air-conditioning and TV in bedrooms, game room with pool table and table tennis, hot tub, kitchen privileges, pool, carriage rides. $75–$85; full breakfast, afternoon tea. No credit cards. No pets.*

Pace One

Thornton and Glen Mills Rds. (Box 108), Thornton, PA 19373, tel. 610/459-3702, fax 610/558-0825

Set in a secluded hamlet, Pace One makes a charming base from which to explore the nearby museums and countryside. Innkeeper Ted Pace, who comes from a family of restaurateurs, bought the four-story 1740 fieldstone barn more than a decade ago and transformed it into a country inn. You'll find the original hand-hewn poplar beams and walls that are 2 feet thick, hung with the work of local artists. Dormer windows make the six guest rooms cozy; they're furnished with Shaker-style oak beds, dressers, and small writing tables, handmade by a local craftsman. Downstairs, the heart of Pace One, is an excellent restaurant and a taproom that has the feel of an authentic Colonial tavern. In a labyrinth of intimate dining areas, Ted serves what he calls "country imaginative" cooking. Pace One maintains the highest standards of service and cuisine, yet Ted and his staff are not stuffy—the atmosphere is warm and casual.

🏨 *6 double rooms with baths. Restaurant, air-conditioning and phones in bedrooms, 3 conference rooms with catering, free use of nearby tennis and racquetball courts. $75–$95; Continental breakfast. AE, DC, MC, V. No pets, children welcome, closed Dec. 25.*

Scarlett House

503 W. State St., Kennett Square, PA 19348, tel. 610/444–9592 or 800/820–9592

It's been around only since October 1990, but Scarlett House has risen quickly to the top with its comfort, beauty, and professionalism. The house sits right in the heart of Kennett Square's historic district. While the rough granite exterior may not seduce you, the minute you walk into the front door (flanked by leaded glass panes and twin inglenooks) you'll pledge allegiance to this residence. It was built in 1910 by a prominent Quaker businessman for his son, Robert Scarlett, who lived here until the 1960s.

Innkeepers Sam and Jane Snyder are aficionados of adventure travel who have trekked the Himalayas and explored other exotic locations. He is a retired interior designer, she a former teacher. They have embellished the house with an eclectic collection of music boxes, spice canisters, miniatures, and teapots. Many of the furnishings were procured from house sales and auctions by the previous proprietor, Susan Lalli Ascosi, who had enough knowledge and decorative sense to take some license with Victorian tradition by manipulating color schemes. Where Victorians would have stayed with darker tones, Susan splashed pastels on the wooden walls of the bedchambers.

The second-floor master suite is decorated in high Victoriana. Its walls are pink, trimmed at the top with a light floral border. The ornate walnut bed is the room's decided cynosure. It's a stunner, with a huge Renaissance headboard looking down on all-cotton, hand-ironed sheets. Walnut reappears in a more ornately carved dresser with a framed full-length mirror; an exquisite plain-faced corner cupboard of the same wood, crafted by an Amish man in 1820, sits directly opposite.

Business travelers have closed deals in this place; women have completed theses; amorous young couples have basked in its charms. All guests eventually gravitate to the sitting room on the second floor: It faces south, so it's engulfed by light. This is a perfect place to leaf through all the local literature (including restaurant listings, with current menus) that the Snyders keep.

🏨 *1 double room with bath, 2 doubles share bath, 1 suite. Air-conditioning, cable TV, fireplace and newspapers in downstairs parlor. $75–$125; full breakfast. AE, D, MC, V. No smoking indoors, no pets, 2-night minimum on some weekends, children welcome during the wk.*

Sweetwater Farm

50 Sweetwater Rd., Glen Mills, PA 19342, tel. 610/459–4711, fax 610/358–4945

Fifteen minutes east of Chadds Ford, at the end of a circular driveway, is a stately 1734 Georgian fieldstone manor house with shutters the color of lemon custard. Sweetwater Farm once sheltered wounded Revolutionary War soldiers and the Marquis de Lafayette and was a refuge for slaves on the Underground Railroad.

In the fields around the 16-room house, thoroughbreds and goats graze amid wildflowers. From each window there are views of majestic maples on the 15 lush acres, and of the 50 undeveloped acres beyond. Proprietors Grace Le Vine and Richard Hovespian were drawn to this bucolic charm. Le Vine, a niece of the late Princess Grace of Monaco, has filled the living room with a marvelous display of vintage photos of her famous aunt.

Inside you will find tall, deep-set windows and a sweeping center-hall staircase. Almost every room has a wood-burning fireplace, random-width floors of oak and pine, and original paintings. Rustic Pennsylvania primitive pieces are mixed with 18th- and 19th-century antique furnishings and reproductions. The guest rooms have canopy beds and four-posters, with handmade quilts and fine linens, embroidered spreads, dried-flower wreaths, and hidden nooks containing odd collectibles.

There are a library with a fireplace and wall of books, a living room with a well-stocked humidor for cigar aficionados, and a sunroom with TV, which becomes a "boardroom" for small business meetings and luncheons. In warm weather, the broad back veranda overlooking the fields and the swimming pool is a favorite spot. With more than 20 horses residing on the property, guests can easily arrange for a ride through the countryside.

Breakfast, served in the dining room in front of the fireplace, features everything from sweet-potato waffles or puff pancakes with brown-sugar syrup to home-fried potatoes with sausage and bacon. Five cottages, also furnished in American antiques, are the ultimate romantic hideaways, with fireplaces, kitchens, and four-poster canopied beds. Museums, historic houses, and antiques shops are all nearby.

▦ *7 doubles with baths, 5 cottages. Air-conditioning, conference room, pool. $180–$275; full breakfast. AE, MC, V. No smoking, children and pets welcome.*

Lancaster County/Amish Country

*Lancaster County, Pennsylvania Dutch country, lies 65 miles
west of Philadelphia. In the early 18th century, this vast,
rolling farmland became home to the so-called Plain People—
the Amish, Mennonites, Dunkards, and Brethren—German
and Swiss immigrants escaping religious persecution. The
Pennsylvania Dutch population consists of about 20 sects,
and they aren't Dutch at all; the name comes from "Deutsch,"
or German. They came to Pennsylvania to live, work, and
worship in harmony. Today, in clinging to traditional dress
and a centuries-old way of life, some of their descendants have
turned their backs on the modern world—and have attracted
the world's attention. In this patchwork quilt of cultures many
small farms are still worked with horses and mules, and
buggies are a frequently seen mode of transportation. Few
power lines disturb the tranquil countryside.*

*The Amish are a prime attraction of, though not the only lure
to, the area. Lancaster (which the English named after the city
in Lancashire) is an intriguing town of restored Colonial
homes, taverns, shops, and churches. It is the nation's oldest
inland city, dating from 1710, and it was the nation's capital*

*for one day during the Revolution, when Congress fled
Philadelphia after the Battle of Brandywine.*

*The region can be hectic, especially on summer weekends.
Busloads of tourists on their way to souvenir and crafts shops
and outlet stores often jam Routes 30 and 340, the main
thoroughfares. But there is still charm here if you take the
back roads. On country lanes you will find general stores, one-
room schoolhouses, and hand-painted signs advertising quilts,
produce, and eggs for sale at Amish farms.*

Places to Go, Sights to See

Abe's Buggy Rides (Bird-in-Hand, no phone). Abe will give you background
information on the Amish during a 2-mile spin down country roads in an Amish
family carriage.

Amish Country Tours (between Bird-in-Hand and Intercourse, tel. 717/392–
8622). Of the variety of tours conducted in large buses or minivans, the most
popular are the two- and four-hour Amish farmland trips.

The Amish Farm and House (Lancaster, tel. 717/394–6185). Take a guided tour
of an Amish house with its working farm, and sample the fare in the food pavilion.

Central Market (Lancaster, tel. 717/291–4723). One of the oldest covered
markets in the country is located in Lancaster. This is where the locals shop for
fresh produce, meats, and baked goods.

Ephrata Cloister (Ephrata, tel. 717/733–6600). Here you can get a look at a
religious communal society of the 1700s best known for its publishing center, a
cappella singing, Fraktur (ornate decorative calligraphy), and medieval-style
German architecture.

Green Dragon Farmers Market and Auction (Ephrata, tel. 717/738–1117). In
this traditional agricultural market, Amish and Mennonite farmers sell meats,
fruits, vegetables, fresh-baked pies, and dry goods at 450 indoor and outdoor
stalls. Open Fridays only, year-round.

Landis Valley Museum (Lancaster, tel. 717/569–0401). Displays on Pennsylvania
Dutch life and folk culture before 1900.

Lititz. This town was founded by Moravians who settled in Pennsylvania to do
missionary work. Along a tree-shaded main street are 18th-century cottages and
shops selling antiques, crafts, and clothing. Nearby are the *Julius Sturgis Pretzel
House* (tel. 717/626–4354), the nation's oldest pretzel bakery, and the Wilbur
Chocolate Company's *Candy Americana Museum Outlet* (tel. 717/626–1131).

People's Place (Intercourse, tel. 717/768–7171). This excellent introduction to the Amish, Mennonites, and Hutterites includes hands-on exhibits on transportation, dress, and schools and on the effects of growing old and mutual aid in these communities.

Strasburg Rail Road (Strasburg, tel. 717/687–7522). Wooden coaches are pulled by a steam locomotive on this scenic 9-mile excursion.

Wheatland (1½ mi west of Lancaster, tel. 717/392–8721). This is the restored 1828 Federal mansion of James Buchanan, the only U.S. president from Pennsylvania.

Restaurants

Family-style is big in Lancaster County, and so is reasonably priced food—which is not to say you can't find sophisticated cuisine here. Less expensive options in Lancaster include the casual **D & S Brasserie** (tel. 717/299–1694); the **Family Style Restaurant** (tel. 717/393–2323); and **Plain 'N Fancy** (tel. 717/768–8281), which heaps huge portions on your plate and is part of a complex of gift shops, museums, and outlet stores. **Isaac's Deli, Inc.** (tel. 717/393–6067), is good for sandwiches, soups, and desserts.

The **Restaurant at Doneckers** (tel. 717/738–9501), in Ephrata, is a gem of a place with both low-cost, low-cholesterol selections and sophisticated French cuisine—for which you pay a few dollars more. The honest-to-goodness Pennsylvania Dutch cooking at **Groff's Farm Restaurant** (tel. 717/653–2048) in Mount Joy, a small town west of Lancaster, has become world-renowned. **Log Cabin** (tel. 717/626–1181) in Leola and **Market Fare Restaurant** (tel. 717/299–7090) in Lancaster are dependable and moderately priced. The casual **Historic Revere Tavern** (tel. 717/687–8602), on Route 30 outside of Lancaster in Paradise, is a bit pricier, but the 18th-century building is warm and inviting.

Last but not least, consider an option many inns offer their guests: Make dinner reservations at the home of a local Amish couple via your innkeeper and sample authentic Pennsylvania Dutch cuisine in a traditional Amish setting.

Tourist Information

Mennonite Information Center (2209 Millstream Rd., Lancaster 17602, tel. 717/299–0954). **Pennsylvania Dutch Convention & Visitors Bureau** (Dept. 2064, 501 Greenfield Rd., exit off Rte. 30, Lancaster 17601, tel. 717/299–8901 or 800/735–2629).

Reservation Services

Hershey Bed & Breakfast Reservation Service (Box 208, Hershey 17033, tel. 717/533–2928).

Adamstown Inn

62 W. Main St., Adamstown, PA 19501,
tel. 717/484–0800 or 800/594–4808, fax
717/484–1384

Adamstown, the antiques capital of
Pennsylvania, is 20 minutes northeast
of Lancaster. This three-story yellow-
brick Victorian house is on a residential
street in the heart of the antiques district. It was built in 1838 and rebuilt in
1925. Tom and Wanda Berman, both avid
antiques collectors, left Baltimore and
their banking careers to open a bed-and-
breakfast in April 1989. You'll find
leaded-glass windows and doors, mag-
nificently refinished chestnut woodwork,
and wallpaper in Victorian motifs. Each
guest room is decorated with family heirlooms, handmade quilts, lace curtains,
Oriental rugs, and fresh flowers. Baskets of towels and soaps sit on Victorian
beds. Two rooms have a two-person
whirlpool bath. On summer weekends
more than 3,000 antiques dealers exhibit
their wares in Adamstown. You can
browse through stalls, or, if you're looking for something specific, the Bermans
can direct you. They'll also point you to
nature trails and biking paths.

🛏 *4 double rooms with baths. Air-*
conditioning in rooms, cable TV in 3
bedrooms, off-street parking. $70–$115;
Continental-plus breakfast. MC, V. No
smoking, no pets, 2-night minimum on
weekends Apr.–Dec.

The Cameron Estate Inn

1855 Mansion La., Mount Joy, PA
17552, tel. 717/653–1773 or 888/722–6376,
fax 717/653–1773

On 5 wooded acres 15 miles west of Lancaster stands this redbrick Federal mansion built in 1805 and listed on the
National Register of Historic Places. A
trout-stocked stream flows beneath an
arched stone bridge nearby, and the veranda overlooks a sweeping lawn. Between towering oaks you can see an
18th-century church and Amish farms.

Wide hallways and a central staircase
lead to guest rooms furnished with
Williamsburg reproductions. Eight of
the bedrooms have working fireplaces; in
all of them you'll find quilts, four-posters,
sitting areas, and writing desks.

David and Becky Vogt bought the inn in
January 1997 and operate it as a bed-and-
breakfast with a separate conference center. Dinner is no longer served, but guests
enjoy a full breakfast on the glass-
enclosed sunporch overlooking the woods
and stream or in the main dining room.
The Vogts have developed a master plan
to turn the grounds into a historically accurate example of 19th-century horticul-
tural practices. An herb and culinary
garden is complete; a formal rose garden
will be planted in spring 1998; and antique irises, peonies, French lilacs, and
heirloom vegetables are to come.

🛏 *16 double rooms with baths, 1 suite,*
conference center (up to 35 people). Air-
conditioning in rooms, fireplaces in
8 rooms, TV with VCR in sitting area.
$125–$200; full breakfast. AE, D, DC,
MC, V. No smoking, no pets, closed
Thanksgiving and Dec. 24–25.

Churchtown Inn

Rte. 23, Churchtown (2100 Main St.,
Narvon, PA 17555), tel. 717/445–7794

Across from the historic church in this
tiny Pennsylvania Dutch village is the
Churchtown Inn, a circa-1735 Georgian
fieldstone inn and carriage house that
are listed on the National Register of
Historic Places. From 1804 to 1853 the
inn was the home of Edward Davies, a
member of the 25th Congress and a state
legislator. Once you enter the restored
mansion you will know it was built for
the gentry.

To the right of the entryway are two
parlors with Victorian antiques and original ornate mantels. Here each evening,
innkeepers Jim Kent and Stuart and
Hermine Smith entertain guests with
music and conversation. Before opening

their bed-and-breakfast in April 1987, the three stayed at 150 B&Bs in six states to pick up ideas. Back in New Jersey, Hermine was a health-food retailer, Stuart was a choral director whose choirs appeared at Lincoln Center and Carnegie Hall, and Jim was an accountant and ballroom-dancing teacher. (He'll gladly give you a quick lesson.) Stuart is known to delight guests with a concert on the grand piano, or he might wind up an antique music box from the inn's fine collection.

The 15-room center-hall mansion is decorated throughout with European and American antiques. The glassed-in garden room, where breakfast is served, overlooks farmland and a distant mountain range. A onetime summer kitchen with a walk-in fireplace has been converted into a den with a TV with VCR. Guest rooms have antique marble sinks, and brass, iron, sleigh, carved, or four-poster canopy beds. You'll find wardrobes, washstands, and TV cabinets handmade by an Amish craftsman. Each room has a sitting area. The dormer rooms on the third floor are comfortable but have low ceilings.

On many weekends special packages are offered that include scheduled events. These vary from Victorian balls, carriage rides, and murder mysteries to authentic Amish wedding feasts, barbecues with music, cabaret, classical string quartets, and festive holiday dinners. The inn is close to antiques and crafts markets, the Reading outlets, and Amish farms. You can bike, hike, fish, or cross-country ski in nearby French Creek State Park.

▥ *6 double rooms with baths, 2 doubles share bath, 1 suite in carriage house. Air-conditioning and TV in rooms. $55–$135; 5-course breakfast. MC, V. No smoking, no pets, 2-night minimum on weekends, 3-night minimum on holiday weekends.*

Clearview Farm Bed and Breakfast

355 Clearview Rd., Ephrata, PA 17522, tel. 717/733–6333

Up a winding road along the base of a mountain ridge in northern Lancaster County is a beautifully restored three-story limestone farmhouse built in 1814. It sits on 200 acres of peaceful Pennsylvania farmland, and there's a huge bank barn nearby. There's also a pond out front that's the domain of two swans. The setting of Clearview Farm is elegantly pastoral; it's the kind of place you want to keep secret. Mildred and Glenn Wissler bought the house when they married nearly 40 years ago. Glenn is a farmer who also has a good eye for color, and Mildred is a talented decorator who grew up learning about her father's antiques business. After working together to choose the right furnishings and decorations, they opened the bed-and-breakfast in 1989.

Country antiques and collectibles are mixed with exquisite Victorian furnishings throughout. You'll find a fireplace in the den, and there are hooked rugs on the original random-width floors. Exposed beams and limestone walls give the kitchen a homey feel. Guest rooms are lushly textured with lots of colors and patterns. The Royal Room has an ornately carved walnut Victorian bed, a Victorian mirrored étagère displaying turn-of-the-century knickknacks, Victorian chairs, and marble-top tables. The Princess Room is lavished with lace and fitted with a canopy bed, a Victorian marble-top dresser, and a washstand. The French Room has a highly carved antique bed in a curtained alcove, a matching armoire, and French upholstered chairs. In the rooms on the third floor, hand-pegged rafters and limestone walls are exposed. Here you'll find homemade quilts, country antiques, and a doll collection.

Breakfast is served in the formal dining room that overlooks the fields. The dining room has elegant draperies and Victorian-print wallpaper. Every morning Mildred prepares a full country breakfast.

The mountain ridge behind the house is great for hiking or quiet walks. In autumn, you can enjoy the fall foliage by car or by bike—just follow Clearview Road; it's one of those scenic back roads you always hear about. Nearby are Wahtney's Inn (an excellent restaurant), farmers' markets, and five antiques malls.

🏠 *5 double rooms with baths. Air-conditioning in rooms, TV in family room. $95–$130; full breakfast. D, MC, V. No smoking indoors, no pets.*

The Inns at Doneckers

318–324 N. State St., Ephrata, PA 17522, tel. 717/738–9502, fax 717/738–9554

The Inns at Doneckers is a group of four turn-of-the-century brick Victorian houses that are part of the "town within a town" tourist attraction developed by Bill Donecker. The complex includes a department store, a noted French restaurant, and a warehouse mall of artists, craftspeople, and art galleries called Artworks. The inns are furnished with French and American antiques, and antique hooked rugs hang on the stenciled walls. In the bedrooms you will find sinks in reproduction Victorian vanities, upholstered headboards, and fresh fruit. Some suites have fireplaces and/or whirlpool baths. Doneckers is neatly packaged; you never have to get in your car. But if you should venture forth, the authentic Amish countryside is only minutes away.

🏠 *40 double rooms with baths, 12 suites. Restaurant (open Thurs.–Tues.), air-conditioning in rooms, cable TV in common room. $69–$185; Continental breakfast. AE, D, DC, MC, V. No pets, closed Dec. 24–25.*

General Sutter Inn

14 E. Main St., Lititz, PA 17543, tel. 717/626–2115, fax 717/626–0992

This three-story, redbrick inn, built in 1764 in Georgian style, overlooks the Lititz village square. It's said to be the oldest Pennsylvania inn in continuous operation. Originally known as Zum Anker, the name was changed in 1930 to honor John Augustus Sutter, the gold-rush pioneer who retired to Lititz. Richard Vetter was an Episcopal priest and then an assistant headmaster before becoming innkeeper here with his wife, Joan, in 1980. Inside, the decor is decidedly Victorian. In the parlor, there are medallion-backed sofas before the fireplace, marble-top tables, a pump organ, and crystal parlor lamps. Lovebirds and finches twitter in Victorian wire cages. Guest rooms are decorated with antique country and Victorian furnishings. The General Sutter is frayed around the edges just enough to add to its authenticity. There's a spacious tree-shaded terrace out front, where you can relax and watch the passing parade of villagers, and it's only a short walk to the Wilbur Chocolate Factory (the maker of Godiva chocolates) and the town's lovely Moravian Square.

🏠 *8 double rooms with baths, 2 suites. Restaurant, coffee shop, air-conditioning in rooms, TV and phones in rooms, library, 2 conference rooms can be combined. $75–$100. AE, D, MC, V.*

The King's Cottage

1049 E. King St., Lancaster, PA 17602, tel. 717/397–1017 or 800/747–8717, fax 717/397–3447

Perched on a residential corner of Lancaster is a Spanish Mission Revival house, built in 1913, that's listed on the National Register of Historic Places. Hosts Jim and Karen Owens opened their bed-and-breakfast in 1987. He's an engineering consultant and she's a former educator. The interior is a successful blend of many different architectural styles: The living room has an Art Deco fireplace, the elegant library is Georgian-influenced, the bright and cheerful Florida Room has rattan furniture and ceiling fans, and the dining room has a crystal chandelier and fine Chippendale reproductions. The guest rooms are furnished in 18th-century reproductions with some antiques. Inside antique wardrobes, you'll find fluffy terry-cloth robes. The Princess Room has three walls of windows and a private balcony that overlooks the water garden. Karen and Jim will be glad to make arrangements for you to have dinner with an Amish family. The Honeymoon Cottage out back has a fireplace and a whirlpool bath.

▥ *9 double rooms with baths, 1 carriage house suite. Air-conditioning in rooms, cable TV in library, off-street parking. $100–$175; full breakfast, afternoon tea. D, DC, MC, V. No smoking, no pets, 2-night minimum on weekends, 3-night minimum on holiday weekends.*

Limestone Inn

33 E. Main St., Strasburg, PA 17579, tel. 717/687–8392 or 800/278–8392

In the very heart of the Amish country, in Strasburg's historic district, is the Limestone Inn. This elegant bed-and-breakfast, listed on the National Register of Historic Places, was built about 1786 as a merchant's residence. From 1839 to 1860 the principal of the noted Strasburg Academy boarded about 50 boys here. After the Civil War, the house served as an orphanage.

The 16-room house, based on a symmetrical five-bay Georgian plan, has a central hallway and some Germanic overtones. Details like the pent roof and decorative stonework (called tumbling) between the second-floor windows give the inn a distinctive architectural sense.

Innkeepers Jan and Dick Kennell are both natives of New Hampshire. Friends who ran a B&B gave them the idea of establishing their own, and they opened the Limestone in May 1985. Dick was with the Department of Agriculture and Forestry in Washington, D.C., for 30 years; and Jan, who is versed in Colonial history, was a tour guide in Annapolis.

Although antique clocks in the elegant rooms tick away, time stands still. The inn is furnished with Colonial and primitive family antiques and reproductions, and you'll find whitewashed walls, wide-planked wavy floors, and Williamsburg colors in every room. In the keeping room there are woven woolen rugs, lots of books and folk art, and settees in front of the fireplace. A spinning wheel stands in the corner. There are old family photographs and a player piano in the living room. Up the steep, narrow stairs you'll find the guest rooms, with old pegged doors, quilts, trunks, and complimentary chocolates. On the third floor, the original numbers on the doors indicate where boys from the academy once slept.

For the multicourse breakfast, served in the dining room at a long table set with a lace cloth, Dick, an excellent chef, may whip up his French toast or sourdough pancakes. He and Jan often serve their guests in period costumes.

The Limestone Inn is quiet and homey, and it's close to antiquing facilities. The Kennells have Amish friends nearby who have quilts for sale for less than you'd pay in commercial centers. With advance notice, they will set you up for dinner at an Amish home.

▥ *6 double rooms with baths. Air-conditioning. $75–$110; full breakfast. AE, V. No smoking, no pets, 2-night minimum on holidays and weekends, no children.*

Smithton Country Inn

900 W. Main St., Ephrata, PA 17522, tel. 717/733–6094

Twelve miles north of Lancaster is one of the best inns in all of Pennsylvania

Dutch country: the Smithton Country Inn, which began taking in lodgers in 1763. It was built by Henry and Susana Miller, who were householders of the Ephrata Community, an 18th-century Protestant monastic sect. Stone walls and flower gardens surround the fieldstone building on a hill overlooking the Ephrata Cloister. Innkeeper Dorothy Graybill is Pennsylvania Dutch. She bought Smithton in 1979, attentively restored it down to the most minute detail, and reopened it in 1982.

At dusk, lamps are lit in each window. The first floor has a Great Room and library to the right, and a dining room, where breakfast is served, to the left. Upstairs, guest rooms are individually decorated, but in each you'll find a working fireplace, antique or handmade reproduction furniture, handmade quilts, reading lamps, stenciling, minirefrigerators, and chamber music. Feather beds are kept in trunks for guests who request them. Flannel nightshirts, coordinated to the color scheme of the room, hang on wooden pegs behind the doors. Many rooms have canopy beds; some have whirlpool baths.

The attached duplex suite has its own entrance. Inside there are a living room, a snack area, a queen-size bed, a twin cupboard bed, and a whirlpool bath. In 1992 Dorothy added a new unit, the Purple Room, on the second floor facing the back gardens. It includes hand-planed cherry woodwork and floors, an exposed-stone wall, a fireplace, a king-size canopied bed, an all-ceramic bathroom, and a whirlpool.

Numerous decorative influences come from the nearby Ephrata Cloister. The hand-hewn doors are pegged and have wooden hardware. Dorothy's partner, Allan Smith, hand-planed the old floorboards and made the clay tiles for the bathrooms and a Cloister-inspired buffet for the dining room.

Guests enjoy Smithton's breakfast, served by candlelight—usually a plate of fresh fruit, juice, Pennsylvania Dutch waffles, and pastry. Afterward, Dorothy gives tips on the proper etiquette when meeting the Plain People of Lancaster County. This is the place to find out how to avoid the tourist traps and spend your time at authentic preserves of the area's heritage.

🏠 *7 double rooms with baths, 1 suite. Air-conditioning in bedrooms. $75–$170; full breakfast. AE, MC, V. No smoking, inquire about pets, 2-night minimum with Sat. reservation and on holidays.*

Swiss Woods

500 Blantz Rd., Lititz, PA 17543, tel. 717/627–3358 or 800/594–8018, fax 717/627–3483

In northern Lancaster County, nestled in rolling, wooded hills that overlook a lake, is Swiss Woods. When you enter the white brick modified Swiss chalet, Debrah Mosimann will greet you with a glass of chilled Swiss-made sparkling cider. She's a Lancaster County native who met her husband, Werner, in Austria while working with an interdenominational mission. They built their bed-and-breakfast on 30 acres of family-owned land and opened it in 1986. Swiss Woods is bright and airy, with natural woodwork, and it's decorated in country contemporary style. In the common room, there's a large sandstone fireplace to curl up in front of; in the bedrooms, you'll find handmade Swiss rugs, goosedown covers, and Swiss chocolates. Two rooms have whirlpool baths, and every room has either a balcony or a patio from which you can enjoy a spectacular view. The Mosimanns keep a canoe for guests, and they'll direct you to the best trails for hiking or biking.

🏠 *6 double rooms with baths, 1 suite. Air-conditioning in bedrooms, TV in suite and in common room, Jacuzzi whirlpools, kitchenette for guest use. $88–$128; full breakfast. D, MC, V. No smoking, no pets, 2-night minimum on weekends, 3-night minimum on holidays.*

Gettysburg and York

Gettysburg and York are in the middle of Pennsylvania's east-west axis, near the Maryland state line. The Susquehanna River is the region's eastern border, and to the west is the Allegheny National Forest. Thousands of visitors are drawn each year to these two relatively small places that have been the sites of significant events in U.S. history.

Gettysburg dates from the early 1700s, when Samuel Gettys acquired 381 acres from the descendants of William Penn. Gettys's son James eventually had town lots drawn up and gave the area his family name. Every schoolchild knows that Gettysburg was the site of the bloodiest Civil War battle. The three-day encounter, in July 1863, claimed 51,000 casualties and was a turning point in the war. Five months later President Abraham Lincoln dedicated the cemetery at Gettysburg and gave his famous address.

Thirty miles from Gettysburg is York, first settled in 1736 and named after the city of York, England. In Colonial days, its fields were so fertile that it was known as the Breadbasket of America. Between September 30, 1777, and June 28, 1778, York was the site of the nation's capital. During that period the

Continental Congress met at the York Courthouse and adopted the Articles of Confederation, the first document to describe the Colonies as the United States of America.

A visit to Gettysburg and York today gives a unique insight into 18th- and 19th-century life. Gettysburg remains a small town of about 7,000 people, in the midst of apple orchards and rolling hills. Visitors can tour the historic battlefield and see the battle reenacted through various media. York, with a population of about 42,000, has preserved and restored much of its Federal and Victorian architecture. In both towns you will discover brick walkways, carved doors, stained-glass windows, and houses with cast-iron trim. You will find relatively unspoiled the surrounding gently sloping farmlands, where cannons once roared, rifles cracked, and drums rolled. Passing through villages you will see taverns, quaint shops, and inns with candlelit windows, one of which may be your lodging for the night.

Places to Go, Sights to See

Battlefield Bus Tours (Gettysburg, tel. 717/334–6296). This two-hour, 23-mile tour with taped commentary narrated by Hollywood personalities creates a "you are there" experience.

Eisenhower National Historic Site (tel. 717/334–1124). At the Gettysburg Visitor Center you can purchase tickets and board shuttle buses to visit the farm home of President and Mrs. Dwight D. Eisenhower. The 495-acre estate includes a 15-room Georgian-style home, an 1887 bank barn, and lots of memorabilia.

General Lee's Headquarters (Gettysburg, tel. 717/334–3141). Lee and his staff made their battle plans in this fieldstone house in Gettysburg, which now contains a fine collection of Civil War uniforms and relics.

Gettysburg National Military Park (tel. 717/334–1124) consists of the historic 3,500 acres where the Battle of Gettysburg was fought. The best way to see it is from your car, following a step-by-step narrated tour. Licensed battlefield guides can be engaged at the visitor center, which is a good place to begin your tour.

Golden Plough Tavern (York, tel. 717/845–2951). This Germanic half-timber building dating from 1741 contains a fine collection of furnishings from the early 18th century.

Jennie Wade House & Olde Town (Gettysburg, tel. 717/334–4100; 800/447–8788 outside PA). The home of Gettysburg's heroine, the battle's only civilian casualty, has been carefully restored. Behind the house is a re-created village courtyard with shops of the era.

Lincoln Room Museum (Gettysburg, tel. 717/334–8188). The house and bedroom where Lincoln finished the final draft of his Gettysburg Address have been preserved, with many original furnishings.

York County Colonial Courthouse (York, tel. 717/845–2951). Artifacts and memorabilia are displayed in this reconstruction of the building where the Continental Congress adopted the Articles of Confederation in 1777.

Restaurants

East of Gettysburg, look for **Altland House** (Abbottstown, tel. 717/259–9535), whose dining room and pub both boast a creative menu with entrées under $20, and **Hofbrauhaus** (Abbottstown, tel. 717/259–9641), which features German specialties. **Patty and John's** (Hanover, tel. 717/637–2200) sits right on the edge of a golf course; American-cuisine entrées run $12–$19.

In Gettysburg, service at the casual **Blue Parrot Bistro** (tel. 717/337–3739) is exemplary; the menu lists an array of $7–$12 entrées such as pasta, stew, ribs, and tenderloin. At the **Historic Farnsworth House Inn** (tel. 717/334–8838) patrons have a choice of $12–$18 entrées ranging from scallops to Yankee pot roast, and young guests may order from their own children's menu. **Herr Tavern** (tel. 717/334–4332), featuring classical American and European cuisine, is pricier but offers a freebie wildly popular with out-of-town clientele: chauffeured limousine service to and from the restaurant. Go to **Dobbin House Tavern** (tel. 717/334–2100) for "general amusements and merrymaking," or to the attached **Alexander Dobbin Dining Room** for something more elegant and sedate (and more expensive: entrées run $15–$19).

For family dining west of Gettysburg near Mercerburg, try the nearby **Foot of the Mountain Restaurant** (Cove Gap, tel. 717/328–2960); its two dining areas make both formally and informally dressed visitors completely at home.

Tourist Information

Gettysburg Convention and Visitors Bureau (35 Carlisle St., Gettysburg 17325, tel. 717/334–6274). **York County Chamber of Commerce and Visitors Bureau** (1 Market Way E, Box 1229, York 17405, tel. 717/848–4000 or 800/673–2429). **York County Visitor Information Center** (1618 Toronita St., York 17402, tel. 717/843–6660).

The Bechtel Victorian Mansion Inn

400 W. King St., East Berlin, PA 17316, tel. 717/259-7760

In 1897 the leading local businessman built this 28-room Queen Anne mansion in the center of East Berlin as a residence for his family. It's such a fanciful, through-the-looking-glass place that you'll know it at once. The yellow-brick-and-white-trim building has a high pointed turret, a long curved porch, and Victorian gardens.

Owners Charles and Mariam Bechtel live in Fairfax, Virginia, but every weekend they are resident hosts. Charles grew up on a nearby farm and will give you inside tips on touring the countryside. Innkeeper Ruth Spangler, who is always on hand, is knowledgeable about local history and customs.

The Bechtel, which became an inn in 1983, is furnished with American and European 19th-century antiques. It's on the National Register of Historic Places. Although some guests may find it a bit worn, those with a love of art and architecture will appreciate the intricate artisanship that went into the building and restoration of the house. The Victorian parlor has vertical shutters, sliding pocket doors, and a handsome mantel—all in elegant cherry wood. The dining room has etched-glass windows and a large window seat. The breakfast room was the original kitchen, and you'll find French windows in the chimney corner. Many rooms have original brass chandeliers, and handmade furniture, pottery, and paintings by local artists are distributed throughout the house.

Each bedroom is furnished in antiques, with handmade Pennsylvania quilts, lace curtains, and a brass chandelier. In many you will find built-in wardrobes with full-length mirrors, and two have private balconies. Bathrooms retain their ornate Victorian decor (though the plumbing is new). One of the most popular guest rooms is the Sara Leas Room, with its turret-shaped bay window and view of East Berlin's National Historic District.

You can easily spend a weekend exploring the Bechtel's nooks and crannies. Its location—almost equidistant from York, Gettysburg, and Hershey—makes it an ideal base for touring the area.

🏠 *8 double rooms with baths, 1 suite. Air-conditioning in bedrooms, TV with VCR in common areas, gift shop in carriage house. $85–$150; full breakfast. AE, D, DC, MC, V. No smoking indoors, no pets, 2-night minimum on holiday weekends and Oct. weekends.*

Beechmont Inn

315 Broadway, Hanover, PA 17331, tel. 717/632-3013 or 800/553-7009

This 1834 Federal redbrick town house, with black shutters and window boxes overflowing with flowers, is on a tree-lined street in Hanover, about 13 miles south of Gettysburg and York. In 1994 William and Susan Day bought the Beechmont, after having worked here for three years. Bill was the handyman and Susan served the breakfast; now they live in the carriage house out back. The inn is furnished with elegant Federal-period antiques and replicas. In the library are 18th-century books and a collection of Civil War memorabilia. One suite has a marble fireplace, and one has a whirlpool. Up the winding staircase, guest rooms have four-poster beds, writing desks, and lace curtains. During warmer months you can relax in the old-fashioned glider in the landscaped courtyard.

🏠 *4 double rooms with baths, 3 suites. Air-conditioning and phones in bedrooms, off-street parking. $80–$135; full breakfast, afternoon tea. AE, D, MC, V. No smoking, no pets, 2-night minimum on weekends for suites.*

The Brafferton Inn

44 York St., Gettysburg, PA 17325, tel. 717/337–3423

A stay at the Brafferton Inn may be the most pleasant way to get a full sense of Gettysburg's historical richness. The 10-room stone house built in 1786, the first residence in town, faces a mid-19th-century street and has an adjacent six-room pre–Civil War clapboard addition. On the first day of the battle, a bullet shattered an upstairs window. It lodged in the mantel and is still there today. During the war, services were held here while the church was being used as a hospital. And just down the street is the house where Lincoln completed his Gettysburg Address.

In 1993 Jane and Sam Back purchased the inn, which is listed on the National Register of Historic Places. Sam has a master's degree in history and was interested in the Civil War, and Jane worked in the admissions office of a boarding school in Connecticut. Both were ready for a midlife change.

The inn has high ceilings, oversize doors, and odd nooks, turns, steps up and steps down that will constantly surprise you. It glows with Colonial colors. In the living room is the original fireplace and an 18th-century grandfather clock bracketed by portraits of Sam's ancestors dating from before the Civil War. Here you'll also find a pre–Revolutionary War mirror hanging over an 18th-century lowboy. Guests breakfast in the dining room encircled by a folksy mural on four walls that depicts the area's historic buildings.

An atrium connects the stone house to the carriage house. This area, with brick floors and walls, is decorated with primitive pieces and pottery. Farm implements are displayed on the walls, and opened antique cupboards are filled with antique toys. Down a wooden walkway is a deck and small garden, where dahlias, zinnias, petunias, and marigolds grow.

The guest rooms, with 18th-century stenciling on whitewashed walls, are furnished with country antiques and family pieces. You'll also find oil paintings, prints, and drawings. A local potter made the basins for washstands and dressers that have been transformed into sinks.

After a candlelight breakfast set to classical music, you can relax in the atrium while you plan the day. The inn is an easy walk from the battlefield, shops, and restaurants.

🏠 *11 double rooms with baths, 5 doubles share 2 baths, 2 suites. Air-conditioning in bedrooms, off-street parking. $90–$125; full breakfast. MC, V. Smoking in atrium only, no pets.*

The Doubleday Inn

104 Doubleday Ave., Gettysburg, PA 17325, tel. 717/334–9119

You don't have to be a Gettysburg Battle buff to enjoy a stay at the Doubleday Inn, but if you are, you can't get any more "battlefieldy" than this. The Doubleday is the only B&B that is actually *on* the Gettysburg Battlefield. Situated upon Oak Ridge, with a view of the town of Gettysburg a half mile away, the inn nestles in a grove of trees on a monument-lined road, with the Railroad Cut, the Peace Light Memorial, and an observation platform all just a few steps from the door.

In 1994 Charles Wilcox, a financier in the futures industry, and his wife, Ruth Anne, a registered nurse, gave up their jobs and moved from Illinois to pursue their dream of owning and operating an inn. They bought the Doubleday, named after Abner Doubleday, the man who "invented" baseball and who also, as Brigadier General, commanded the Union forces the first day of the battle on what is now the site of the inn.

Charles and Ruth Anne brought with them loads of Colonial country furniture and scoured Pennsylvania and Ohio for suitable period antiques. The recently redecorated bedrooms are a mix of four-posters, brass beds, iron beds, and an oak pineapple bed. Two rooms are what Ruth Anne calls "Grandma's rooms," with thick quilts and old-fashioned fabric prints. Another room has a Laura Ashley look. The third-floor attic room is more masculine, with dark greens and reds, bookcases, and both a double and a twin bed.

Every morning a full, hot breakfast is served by candlelight, on china and crystal. Civil War literature is available to read, and every Saturday night throughout the year and Wednesday nights during the busy season, a licensed battlefield guide comes to lecture and answer questions about the battle. Breakfast discussions the following mornings are especially spirited.

▥ *5 double rooms with baths, 4 doubles share 2 baths. Air-conditioning. $84–$104; full breakfast, afternoon tea. D, MC, V. No smoking, no pets, 2-night minimum on holiday weekends.*

Emig Mansion

3342 N. George St. (Box 486), Emigsville, PA 17318, tel. 717/764–2226

This elegant Victorian Greek Revival mansion, 10 minutes north of York, is a treat to the senses. It has gorgeous leaded and stained-glass windows, intricate inlaid flooring, ornate molding, and Victorian antiques throughout. Breakfast is served in a formal dining room at a walnut dining table that's long enough to seat 30. In guest rooms you will find brass, iron, and massively carved beds. Three rooms have fireplaces. This house was built in 1850 by John Emig, Jr., who made his fortune producing the commercial wagons that hauled goods along 19th-century roads. Innkeeper Linda Bailey recently took over the inn from her mother, Jane Llewellyn, who extensively restored the mansion, then opened it as a bed-and-

breakfast in June 1984. There are antiques shops and factory outlets nearby. Or you can just relax on the expansive porch and gaze across the road at the old wagonworks, just as the Emig family did 100 years ago.

▥ *3 double rooms with baths, 4 doubles share 2 baths. Air-conditioning in rooms, off-street parking. $85–$110; full breakfast. MC, V. Smoking on balconies only, no pets.*

Fairfield Inn

Main St., Fairfield, PA 17320, tel. 717/642–5410

This fieldstone structure with its two-story open gallery is in a sleepy little village 8 miles west of Gettysburg. Built as a plantation home in 1757, it became a hotel and stagecoach stop in 1823. David Thomas managed a hotel in Washington, D.C., before he bought the inn in 1976. Throughout you will find random-width floors, low ceilings, original brass hardware, crystal chandeliers, lace curtains, and a Williamsburg-influenced mix of antiques and reproductions.

The inn is well known for its classic country fare. (In fact, Mrs. Dwight Eisenhower frequently chose to entertain here.) Fall-foliage spectators should ease their way up to Arendtsville from here for the National Apple Harvest Festival in October—it's as close to a state fair as some city folk will ever get, and children will glory in it. The Gettysburg battle sites are also nearby.

▥ *2 double rooms share bath. Restaurant, air-conditioning in common areas and bedrooms, meeting room. $50–$75; Continental breakfast. AE, MC, V. No smoking in dining room, no pets, closed Sun., Mon., 1st wk of Feb., and 1st wk of Sept.*

The Historic Farnsworth House Inn

401 Baltimore St., Gettysburg, PA 17325, tel. 717/334–8838, fax 717/334–5862

Confederate sharpshooters once occupied this 1810 redbrick Federal house near the National Cemetery, and you can still see lots of bullet holes. Loring H. Shultz sells Civil War prints and books in a shop next door, and he and his family opened the bed-and-breakfast in 1989. The lushly Victorian guest rooms have antique marbletop dressers, beds with fishnet canopies, and Oriental rugs scattered before the fireplaces. A wicker-filled sunroom is the perfect place to relax; it looks out on gardens where, in summer, you can dine in the open air, alongside a stone-lined stream that provided water for both armies. The restaurant specializes in mid-19th-century food, and an excellent house specialty is a game pie of pheasant, duck, and turkey. In the attic and basement, the Shultzes display their collection of artifacts from daily life in the Civil War period.

▥ *5 double rooms with baths. Restaurant, air-conditioning in bedrooms, TV in sunroom. All rooms $85; full breakfast. AE, D, MC, V. Smoking in sunroom only, no pets, 2-night minimum on some weekends.*

The Mercersburg Inn

405 S. Main St., Mercersburg, PA 17236, tel. 717/328–5231, fax 717/328–3403

Mercersburg, at the foot of the Blue Ridge Mountains, is a historic village off I–81, an hour and a half from Washington, D.C. This country inn, on the outskirts of town, is an impressive Classic Revival redbrick structure with white trim, adorned with numerous porticoes, porches, and terraces.

It's the kind of place where you expect something romantic has either already happened or will. In the entrance hall,

twin staircases wind dramatically to the second floor, and rose and green Scaglioli columns accent the chestnut wainscoting. The classic Arts and Crafts sunroom has a tiled floor and fireplace, high beamed ceilings, and a wall of broad windows. It's done in peach and blue, with flowered upholstery and curtains. You can sit back on the deep window-seat cushions and admire the stately grounds.

Restored antiques and locally handmade pieces fill the spacious guest rooms. You will find four-poster, canopy, and king-size beds. Some rooms have fireplaces; others have private balconies with views of the mountains. Three rooms have tiled, high-ceilinged bathrooms with antique needle showers, pedestal sinks, and freestanding tubs. Each bathroom has been meticulously restored to its turn-of-the-century grandeur.

In the formal mahogany-paneled dining room, there are a deep green marble fireplace, leaded-glass built-in cabinets, Tiffany stained-glass light fixtures, and parquet floors. Here the award-winning restaurant serves à la carte and five-course fixed-price dinners of regional new American cuisine.

A bit farther north is a pocket of Amish country that most tourists never hear about. Walter and Sandy Filkowski, who bought the property in June 1997 and took over as innkeepers, will fill you in on the area's touring, antiquing, fishing, and hiking opportunities.

▥ *15 double rooms with baths. Restaurant (open Thurs.–Sat.), air-conditioning and phones in bedrooms, whirlpool bath in 1 room, TV with VCR in game room, conference room. $115–$225; full breakfast. D, MC, V. No smoking indoors, no pets, 2-night minimum on fall-foliage and ski-season weekends and holidays.*

The Old Appleford Inn

*218 Carlisle St., Gettysburg, PA 17325,
tel. 717/337–1711 or 800/275–3373, fax
717/334–6228*

This bed-and-breakfast, a few blocks from Gettysburg's Lincoln Square, is a gray brick Italianate Victorian house built in 1867, with a carriage house in back. The house has a gabled roof and arched windows framed by black shutters. Frank and Maribeth Skradski, hosts since 1987, stayed here first as guests and fell in love with the place. Before starting a life of innkeeping, he was a research engineer in Illinois and she owned an antique-clothing shop. There's a gracious Victorian parlor with a baby-grand piano; a library with lots of books, Civil War memorabilia, and a wonderful collection of old Kodak cameras; and a plant-filled sunroom with a well-stocked refrigerator. Two of the guest rooms have ornamental fireplaces, and all are decorated with Victorian antiques and brass beds, sleigh beds, and iron beds—some so high you have to climb up into them.

🏨 *9 double rooms with baths, 1 suite. Air-conditioning in bedrooms, off-street parking. $80–$138; full breakfast, afternoon tea. AE, D, MC, V. No smoking, no pets, 2-night minimum on special-event weekends.*

The Tannery Bed and Breakfast

*449 Baltimore St., Gettysburg, PA 17325,
tel. 717/334–2454*

Two blocks from the National Cemetery and the visitor center is a tan, Gothic-structured house with chocolate-brown trim and a gabled roof. In 1868, when a Mr. Rupp built the clapboard house, his tannery business was right next door. Charlotte Swope's grandfather bought the house in 1920; she and her husband, Jule, turned it into a bed-and-breakfast in 1989 and named it after the tannery, which is no longer standing. Debbie and Charlie Raffenesberger bought the place in 1996 and have maintained its interesting blend of periods: Light, clean-lined modernism meets lofty Victoriana, and the charm still manages to shine through. Guest rooms are decorated with soothing Williamsburg colors and new carpeting. You will find traditional reproductions and a handful of family antiques. There's a wide, airy porch where you can sit and rock and watch a world of Civil War buffs go by.

🏨 *9 double rooms with baths, 1 suite. Air-conditioning in bedrooms, TV in sitting room, off-street parking. $85–$125; Continental-plus breakfast. MC, V. No smoking, no pets.*

Pittsburgh and Environs

The point where the Monongahela and Allegheny rivers meet to form the Ohio River commands a stunning natural position, one exploited by westward-bound settlers who established Ft. Pitt, later called Pittsburgh. Prosperity in coal, iron, and steel made the city a giant in the industrial age—and earned it its nickname of Smoky City. Today the smoke has cleared, and Pittsburgh—recently rated one of the "nation's most livable cities"—has been recast into an artful blend of turn-of-the-century architectural masterpieces and modern skyscrapers.

Downtown, an area framed by the three rivers and called the Golden Triangle, contains Point State Park and major hotels, restaurants, and theaters; several beautifully restored or maintained commercial and public buildings date from Pittsburgh's early boom days. East of downtown, Oakland is the headquarters of many of the city's cultural, educational, and medical landmarks.

Northeast of Pittsburgh the Laurel Highlands region has Revolutionary War–era forts and battlefields, restored inns and taverns, and lush mountain scenery. The region is noted for white-water rafting, hiking, and skiing.

Places to Go, Sights to See

Allegheny County Courthouse and Jail (5th Ave. and Grant St., tel. 412/355–5313). H. H. Richardson's courthouse, built in 1884, is one of the country's outstanding Romanesque buildings.

Andy Warhol Museum (117 Sandusky St., tel. 412/237–8300). The seven floors of this 1994 museum are devoted to the work of the native Pittsburgher and Pop Art icon.

The Carnegie (4400 Forbes Ave., tel. 412/622–3131 or 412/622–3289 for tours). This opulent cultural center houses the Museum of Art, the Museum of Natural History, the Music Hall, and the Carnegie Library, all under one Beaux Arts roof. Don't miss the 19th-century French and American paintings; the Hall of Architecture, which re-creates in plaster some of the world's architectural masterpieces; the dinosaur collection; and the extravagant Music Hall lobby.

Carnegie Science Center (Allegheny Center, tel. 412/237–3300). Explore a planetarium, aquarium, hands-on science exhibits, and a four-story Omnimax theater.

Fallingwater (Rte. 381, Mill Run, tel. 412/329–8501). Frank Lloyd Wright's residential masterwork—a stone, concrete, and glass house dramatically cantilevered over a waterfall—is located northeast of Pittsburgh in the Laurel Highlands region. Call for reservations to view the property.

Frick Art and Historical Center (7227 Reynolds St., tel. 412/371–0606 or 412/371–0600). Clayton, the turn-of-the-century home of Henry Clay Frick, preserves the home's original furnishings and art, while the Frick Art Museum possesses a small but choice collection of Old Master works.

Point State Park (tel. 412/471–0235). This 36-acre park contains the Ft. Pitt Blockhouse and Ft. Pitt Museum (tel. 412/281–9284).

Schenley Park. A lake, trails, golf, cross-country skiing, and Phipps Conservatory (Schenley Park, tel. 412/622–6914)—Henry Phipps's Victorian gardens—are the main attractions here.

Station Square (tel. 412/471–5808). On the Monongahela, across the Smithfield Bridge, is a restored turn-of-the-century rail station with boutiques, restaurants, and nightclubs.

Two Mellon Bank Center (5th Ave. and Grant St., tel. 412/234–5000). The interior of this Flemish-Gothic structure, formerly the Union Trust Building, has a glass rotunda.

Restaurants

Many of the city's lawyers and judges dine in the three dining rooms of the **Common Plea** (310 Ross St., tel. 412/281–5140)—one in dark wood; one with glass and mirrors; and a formal room with floor-to-ceiling wine cabinets and crystal chandeliers. Wraparound windows offer a majestic view from the Colonial-style dining rooms of the **Georgetowne Inn** (1230 Grandview Ave., tel. 412/481–4424); the American cuisine is exceptional, and the low-key atmosphere makes it a good place for family dining. Set in a dazzlingly restored Beaux Arts railroad terminal, the **Grand Concourse** (1 Station Sq., Carson and Smithfield Sts., tel. 412/261–1717) features seafood, homemade pastas, and gracious service. **Primanti Brothers** (46 18th St., tel. 412/263–2142; 11 Cherry Way, tel. 412/566–8051; Market Square, tel. 412/261–1599) started out 50 years ago as a working-class bar and is now a Pittsburgh favorite with six locations. The cheese steak comes with fries, coleslaw, and tomato—all *in* the sandwich.

Tourist Information

Greater Pittsburgh Convention and Visitors Bureau (4 Gateway Center, 15222, tel. 800/366–0093).

Century Inn

Rte. 40, Scenery Hill, PA 15360, tel. 412/945-6600

This hand-hewn stone building with a long porch and two large stone chimneys on either end is listed on the National Register of Historic Places. Since 1794, Century Inn has offered hospitality to travelers passing through this village 35 miles south of Pittsburgh. In 1945 Dr. and Mrs. Gordon Harrington restored the inn and furnished it with heirlooms and rare American antiques. Today, their daughter-in-law, Megin Harrington, continues the tradition. In the parlors are two identical fireplaces, a display of antique paperweights and glassware, and an original flag from the Whisky Rebellion hanging above one mantel. The guest rooms are as carefully furnished with antiques as the public areas. Superb meals are served in the five dining rooms. In the Keeping Room (the original kitchen), the massive fireplace has a hand-forged crane and curious cooking utensils. Megin will gladly direct you to the best places for antiquing, boating, and skiing—which are all within a short distance.

▦ *6 double rooms with baths, 4 suites. Restaurant (closed Dec. 23–Feb. 13) with conference facilities, air-conditioning in bedrooms, tennis court, croquet. $80–$140; full breakfast. AE, D, DC, MC, V. No pets.*

Glendorn

1032 W. Corydon St., Bradford, PA 16701, tel. 814/362–6511 or 800/843–8568, fax 814/368–9923

Tucked away on 1,280 acres in northwestern Pennsylvania near Allegheny National Forest, Glendorn was the summer retreat of the Dorns, who made their fortune in oil early in the century. Open to the public since 1995, it captures the spirit of rustic luxury. The lodge, a four-hour drive from Pittsburgh or Cleveland and 1½ hours from Buffalo, is for people who appreciate special places off the beaten path.

The magnificent all-redwood main lodge was begun in 1929. Up to 30 guests can stay in four rooms here and in nearby cabins. The Dorns (who still use some cabins) left many family items such as china and books, which enhance the feeling of being at the home of a wealthy friend. Managers Gene and Linda Spinner are unobtrusive hosts who care for guests' needs efficiently and pleasantly.

A two-story-high sandstone fireplace dominates the wood-beamed great hall where meals are served. You can relax on the sofas, have a snack from the butler's pantry, or try billiards in the game room. Lodge rooms include the Green Suite, with a tiled fireplace and chintz sofa. All six cabins have fireplaces. The one-bedroom Miller Cabin has chestnut paneling and overlooks a stream; the three-bedroom Roost has pecky cypress paneling and separate baths in the master bedroom.

The delicious meals (all included in the cost) are substantial. Fruit and a muffin or coffee cake precede eggs or pancakes. Dinner, for which men wear jackets and women wear dresses or nice pants, follows cocktails and appetizers. Chef Casey Fichte's American country cuisine includes seafood and game entreés.

Among the popular activities (included in the price) are skeet and trapshooting. Three small lakes are stocked with trout and bass, so bring your poles. Snowshoeing and cross-country skiing (use your own skis) are winter pleasures. For an extra cost, golf is nearby, and downhill skiing is a 45-minute drive away.

▦ *2 rooms with baths, 4 suites (2 in guest house), 5 1-bedroom cabins, 1 3-bedroom cabin. Air-conditioning in 2 suites, TVs in all rooms, phones, refrigerators and coffeemakers in cabins, terry-cloth robes and slippers, swimming pool, exercise room, hiking trails, bicycles, canoes, 3 tennis courts, conference facilities for 24. $373–$1,045 (for 3-*

bedroom cabin); all meals included. AE, MC, V. No pets, 2-night minimum stay on weekends, 2-night minimum stay in cabins. Closed Jan.

The Priory

614 Pressley St., Pittsburgh 15212, tel. 412/231-3338, fax 412/231-4838

It's appropriate that innkeeper Mary Ann Graf should purchase the flour and wheat berries for the breakfast bread she serves her guests from the Benedictines at St. Vincent's College; after all, the Priory was once a monastery. Mary Ann and Edward, her husband, purchased the building in 1984. They promptly embarked on a million-dollar renovation, transforming the brick, tin-ceilinged monks' residence into a 24-room inn complete with private baths and handsome public rooms for business and social events. What was monastic more than a century ago is now warmed by Victorian lace, oil lamps, wrought-iron beds, and armoires. As testimony that Mary Ann has done something right, the YWCA named her Pittsburgh's Entrepreneur of the Year in 1988.

Notwithstanding the modern amenities, you may still be affected by the structure's meditative past and have to pull yourself away from private contemplation for shopping or sight-seeing in downtown Pittsburgh, just across the river.

▦ *21 double rooms with baths, 3 suites. Air-conditioning, TV, and phones in rooms, weekday-morning transportation downtown. $98–$145; Continental-plus breakfast. AE, D, DC, MC, V. No pets, children welcome.*

New Jersey

The Abbey, **32**
The Albert
Stevens Inn, **33**
Amber Street Inn, **25**
Ashling Cottage, **16**
BarnaGate Bed &
Breakfast, **29**
Barnard–Good
House, **34**
The Bayberry
Barque, **26**
The Cabbage
Rose Inn, **6**
Candlelight Inn, **31**
Captain Mey's Inn, **35**
Carroll Villa, **36**
Cashelmara, **14**
The Chateau, **17**
Chestnut Hill on the
Delaware, **8**
Chimney Hill Bed and
Breakfast, **11**
Conover's Bay Head
Inn, **22**
The Green Gables
Inn, **27**
The Henry Ludlam
Inn, **30**
Holly House, **37**
Holly Thorn House, **5**
Hollycroft, **18**
Hunterdon House, **9**
The Inn at
Millrace Pond, **3**
Inn at 22 Jackson, **38**
Isaac Hilliard House, **24**
Jerica Hill, **7**
The John F. Craig
House, **39**
La Maison, **19**
The Mainstay Inn, **40**
Manor House, **41**
Normandy Inn, **20**
Peacock Inn, **12**
Pierrót by the Sea, **28**
The Queen Victoria, **42**
Sea Crest by the Sea, **21**
The Seaflower, **15**
SeaScape Manor, **13**
The Southern
Mansion, **43**
Springside, **44**
Stewart Inn, **4**
The Stockton Inn, **10**
The Studio, **23**
The Victorian Rose, **45**
The Virginia Hotel, **46**
The Whistling Swan
Inn, **2**
The Wooden Duck, **1**
The Wooden Rabbit, **47**

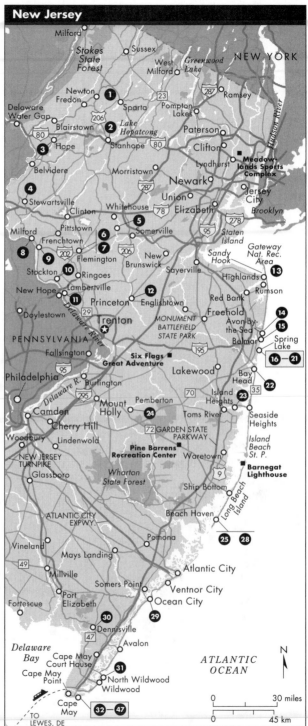

The Delaware and Its Surroundings

The Delaware River begins as a trickling brook in upstate New York and gathers momentum as it moves south, drawing the border between Pennsylvania and New Jersey before emptying into the broad basin of Delaware Bay. The sites most interesting to tourists are concentrated along the 80 miles of river between the New York border and Washington Crossing, where on Christmas night, 1776, Washington and the Continental Army crossed the river and surprised the Hessians in nearby Trenton. This stretch includes the Delaware Water Gap, in the state's northwest corner, well known to canoeists, kayakers, and white-water enthusiasts. The small towns of Lambertville, Stockton, Frenchtown, and Milford are good bases for antiquing and sightseeing in New Jersey and Pennsylvania. Lambertville, the largest, is home to many of the artists, craftspeople, and restaurateurs of its neighbor across the river, New Hope, but it also has galleries, antiques shops, and excellent eateries of its own.

Inland a bit, there are other places of note. The hilly terrain around highlands towns, such as Fredon, Hope, and Clinton, makes for great cycling if you have strong legs, and leisurely country drives or stunning hot-air balloon trips if you don't.

Flemington, about 10 miles east of Frenchtown, has a cluster of outlets, auctions, and antiques shops, while Princeton, to the south and east, is a pretty Ivy League town with a business district full of upscale shops.

Continuing south on "the other Jersey shore," the river gets wider and the towns get less quaint. Still, there's plenty to see and do. Trenton, the state capital, has its share of museums and, like many places in this part of the state, the requisite "George Washington fought here" site. It also has Chambersburg, a residential neighborhood crammed with dozens of Italian restaurants. Wending its way toward Philadelphia, the river passes suburban communities before reaching the aging industrial city of Camden, home to Walt Whitman, Campbell's Soup, and the state aquarium. By now a mighty, navigable waterway, the Delaware rolls past Salem and Cumberland counties, where flatland cradles farmland and old, Eastern Shore–like towns that time seems to have forgotten.

Places to Go, Sights to See

Ballooning. The generally still, windless mornings and tranquil twilight hours make this area perfect for hot-air ballooning, which costs approximately $165 per person for a three-hour trip, transportation usually included. (Be warned, though, that rainy or windy weather, most common in spring, can scuttle plans.) It's traditional to open a bottle of champagne at the finish; ask if your carrier supplies one. *Dekay Aviation* (Box 198, Baptistown, tel. 908/996–7760) and *Sky Promotions* (Sky Manor Airport, Pittstown, tel. 908/996–6638) operate year-round.

Brew Pubs. You can have a brewed-on-premises beer, often with a view of the process, at several area establishments. *The Ship Inn* (61 Bridge St., Milford, tel. 908/995–7007) has added beer making to its huge selection of English beers and pub fare. *Triumph Brewing Co.* (138 Nassau St., tel. 609/924–7855) is a multistory operation in Princeton, and *The Brew Cellar at Joe's Mill Hill Saloon* (300 S. Broad St., Trenton, tel. 609/394–7222) is in the basement of a popular Cajun/international restaurant.

Delaware & Raritan Canal State Park. Biking enthusiasts can tour the area on a towpath that stretches from Frenchtown to New Brunswick, with a few gaps in Trenton. North of Trenton, the towpath parallels the Delaware, passing through Washington Crossing State Park, Lambertville, and Stockton. Cyclists share the towpath with joggers, hikers, and, on occasion, horses. Bike rentals are available from *Freeman's Bicycle* (52 Bridge St., Frenchtown, tel. 908/996–7712).

McCarter Theatre Centre for the Performing Arts (91 University Pl., Princeton, tel. 609/683–8000). The Tony Award–winning theater presents memorable avant-garde and revival shows as well as music and dance performances and public lectures.

New Jersey State Museum (205 W. State St., Trenton, tel. 609/292–6308). A dinosaur exhibit, geology displays, Native American artifacts, a planetarium, and a changing fine-arts exhibit make the drive into Trenton worthwhile.

Princeton. *Orange Key Tours* (tel. 609/258–3603) employs undergraduates to show visitors around campus. Free tours leave daily from the Maclean House (73 Nassau St.), next to Nassau Hall. *The Historical Society of Princeton* (tel. 609/ 921–6748) gives tours of the town every Sunday at 2, starting from Bainbridge House (158 Nassau St.).

Thomas H. Kean New Jersey State Aquarium (1 Riverside Dr., Camden, tel. 609/365–3300). The focus of this indoor-outdoor facility is a 760,000-gallon open-ocean tank full of 40 different species, including sharks and rays, and a shipwreck. Other highlights are touch pools, performing seals, and displays of native New Jersey species. When you're tired of looking under the water, you can gaze out through the aquarium's wall of windows over the tugs and barges on the Delaware to the Philadelphia skyline.

USGA Golf House Museum (Rte. 512, Far Hills, tel. 908/234–2300). Housed in a Georgian Colonial–style mansion built in 1919, this museum and library is visited by golfers from all over the world.

Washington Crossing State Park (355 Washington Crossing–Pennington Rd., Titusville, tel. 609/737–0623). Washington crossed the Delaware here prior to surprising the British in the famous Battle of Trenton. You can visit a museum featuring Revolutionary War artifacts, hike the nature trails, or enjoy concerts and plays in the *Washington Crossing Open Air Theatre* (tel. 609/737–1826).

Waterloo Village (Waterloo Rd., Stanhope, tel. 201/347–0900). In this beautifully restored Revolutionary War–era canal town, you can watch resident craftspeople and buy samples of their works. There's also a Native American museum and a summer concert series, featuring all kinds of music.

Wineries. New Jersey's wineries offer daily tours that end with tastings for those 21 and older. Don't expect first-class Bordeaux, but do expect to be surprised at the reasonably good vintages produced at the *Four Sisters Winery* (Rte. 519, Belvidere, tel. 908/475–3671), *Alba Vineyard* (269 Rte. 627, Milford, tel. 908/995–7800), and *Amwell Valley Vineyard* (80 Old York Rd., Ringoes, tel. 908/ 788–5852). Ask your bed-and-breakfast hosts for other recommendations.

Restaurants

It's a good thing there are lots of sports in the region, because you'll need to exercise after eating so much good food. Starting from the north, the **Black**

Forest Inn (149 U.S. 206, Stanhope, tel. 973/347–3344) has a German and Continental menu. For a special occasion (a.k.a. *very* expensive), try chef Craig Sheldon's cuisine at the **Ryland Inn** (U.S. 22W, Whitehouse, tel. 908/534–4711). The **Olde Mill Ford Oyster House** (17 Bridge St., Milford, tel. 908/995–9411) offers fresh, not-strictly-seafood food in a simply furnished village home. Equally fresh but quite a bit fancier is the **Frenchtown Inn** (7 Bridge St., tel. 908/996–3300), a top-notch, modern, French restaurant. The casual **Meil's** (Bridge and Main Sts., Stockton, tel. 609/397–8033) is open for breakfast, lunch, and dinner and has a bakery, too. Lambertville's good wild-mushroom and sun-dried-tomato spots include the elegant **Ferry House** (21 Ferry St., tel. 609/397–9222), the tablecloth-free **Full Moon** (23 Bridge St., tel. 609/397–1096), and the intimate **New Orleans Cafe II** (9 Kline Ct., tel. 609/397–2322), which offers, what else, Cajun cuisine. Surprising for the button-down town of Princeton, **Mexican Village II** (42 Leigh Ave., tel. 609/924–5143) has great south-of-the-border fare, especially the *salsa cruda*. It's hard to go wrong in Trenton's Chambersburg (a.k.a. "the Burg"), but one of the best is **Diamond's** (132 Kent St., tel. 609/393–1000). Great Italian food can also be found north of town at **Antonio's Italian Restaurant** (71 W. Upper Ferry Rd., Trenton, tel. 609/882–4105), where the chicken with sun-dried tomatoes is a particular favorite.

Tourist Information

Hunterdon County Chamber of Commerce (2200 Rte. 31, Suite 15, Lebanon 08833, tel. 908/735–5955). **Princeton Area Convention and Visitors Bureau** (179A Nassau St., Princeton 08542, tel. 609/683–1760). **Trenton Convention & Visitors Bureau** (Lafayette at Barrack St., Trenton 08625, tel. 609/777–1771). **Warren County Department of Economic Development and Tourism** (Dumont Administration Bldg., Rte. 519, Belvidere 07823, tel. 908/475–6580).

Reservation Services

Amanda's Bed & Breakfast Reservation Service (21 S. Woodland Ave., East Brunswick 08816, tel. 732/249–4944, fax 732/246–1961). **Bed & Breakfast Adventures** (2310 Central Ave., Suite 132, North Wildwood 08260, tel. 609/522–4000 or 800/992–2632 for reservations, fax 609/522–6125). **Bed and Breakfast of Princeton** (Box 571, Princeton 08542, tel. 609/924–3189, fax 609/921–6271).

The Cabbage Rose Inn

162 Main St., Flemington, NJ 08822, tel. 908/788–0247

The romantic mood of this 1890 Queen Anne house has been preserved by new owners Debbie and Jerry Squitieri, who still offer the popular "Romance & Roses" package—including, what else, a bouquet of long-stemmed roses and handmade Victorian chocolates. The parlor's hand-carved mahogany fireplace and stairs are set off against cheery pinks and a cabbage-rose motif. The Primrose Pink room has a pink claw-foot tub right in the room. Another favorite has a four-poster bed and two wing chairs cozied up to a gas fireplace. Breakfast is served in rooms on request.

Set on Flemington's busy Main Street, the inn is within the city's historic district, close to plenty of outlet shopping, and about 15 minutes from Lambertville and New Hope.

🏠 *5 double rooms with baths. Air-conditioning, cable TV in parlor, phones in rooms, guest pantry, on-site parking. $85–$135; Continental-plus breakfast on weekdays, full breakfast on weekends. AE, D, MC, V. Smoking on porch only, no pets, 2-night minimum with Sat. reservation.*

Chestnut Hill on the Delaware

63 Church St., Milford, NJ 08848, tel. 908/995–9761, fax 908/995–9761

The only thing separating Chestnut Hill's rocker-lined veranda from the river is a sloping bank and a set of train tracks; once a day a train chugs slowly by. You can walk along the tracks to the cute little town of Milford or to cliffs where Native Americans once lived; go bicycling, canoeing, or tubing (rentals nearby); or do the obvious thing—sit and watch the traffic on the old metal bridge to Pennsylvania, the river, and the river's wildlife. Rumor has it that a bald eagle was recently spotted soaring over the Delaware.

Innkeepers Rob and Linda Castagna have returned the exterior of the house to its original colors, while inside they have tried to balance Victorian and other more comfortable furnishings. The antiques-laden formal drawing room has a 9½-foot-by-13-foot black-walnut apothecary unit and the wedding dress of a previous owner (only three families have lived in the house since it was built in 1860). In contrast, the two third-floor bedrooms, rented only to those traveling together, are littered with 150 teddy bears. A country cottage comes with tropical hues, carousel horses, a raft of modern conveniences, and absolute privacy.

🏠 *3 double rooms with baths, 2 doubles share bath, 1 housekeeping suite. Air-conditioning, cable TV in 4 rooms and parlor, phones in all rooms, fireplace in parlor, on-site parking, transportation to and from bus. $90–$140; full breakfast. No credit cards. No smoking, no pets, 2-night minimum on weekends and at all times for cottage.*

Chimney Hill Bed and Breakfast

207 Goat Hill Rd., Lambertville, NJ 08530, tel. 609/397–1516, fax 609/397–9353

Owners and innkeepers Terry and Richard Anderson continue to make changes at this inn on 8 landscaped acres on a ridge above the quaint town of Lambertville. The original 1820 fieldstone building was enlarged in 1927 by Margaret Spencer, one of the first female architects to graduate from MIT. Now the Andersons are planning the conversions of the carriage house and greenhouse with an eye to boosting corporate business.

It's hard not to want to curl up by the fire on one of the wicker chaises in the beamed sunroom, where windows on two sides bathe the stone room in light.

Breakfast is served at candlelit tables in the low-ceilinged dining room, lined with hunt prints, and the adjacent guest pantry stocks sherry and snacks for other hours. Echoing the landscaping outside, flora is the dominant motif in the bedrooms, from the rose-covered bed and ivy stenciling of the Ivy Room to the sunflowers of Vincent's Hideaway (named for Van Gogh).

🏠 *8 double rooms with baths. Air-conditioning in rooms, fireplaces in 5 rooms and 3 public areas, on-site parking, balloon trips from inn arranged. $75–$185; Continental breakfast on weekdays, full breakfast on weekends. AE, MC, V. No smoking indoors, no pets, 2-night minimum on weekends in season, 3-night minimum on holiday weekends.*

Holly Thorn House

143 Readington Rd., Whitehouse Station, NJ 08889, tel. 908/534–1616, fax 908/534–9017

When Anne and Joe Fosbre bought this house in the late '70s, it was a 35-year-old cinder-block cow barn. Joe and their three sons transformed it into an extremely long home, and when the kids were grown, the couple opened it as a B&B.

From the Hunt Room's dark four-poster and hunt print–covered walls to the paneled billiard room with game table, Holly Thorn feels like an English country manor house. The Fosbres go to England once a year and often bring furniture back with them. Anne's collection of monk mugs, statues, and chairs—which now includes a rabbi mug—fills a wall and corner in the dining area. The great room, big enough to have two fireplaces and two staircases stretching to the second-floor balcony, has different areas for sitting, eating, and playing the grand piano. Other fireplaces grace the suite and the upstairs gathering room, which has deep-red walls, parquet floors, antique wicker and other traditional furnishings, a TV with VCR, and plenty of books, games, and snacks to while away the time. Those visitors determined to work despite the availability of more pleasant pursuits can hunker down at desks provided in each bedroom.

🏠 *4 double rooms with baths, 1 suite. Air-conditioning in rooms, minirefrigerators in gathering and billiard rooms, pool, cabana, on-site parking. $115–$145; full breakfast. AE, D, MC, V. No smoking in rooms, no pets.*

Hunterdon House

12 Bridge St., Frenchtown, NJ 08825, tel. 908/996–3632 or 800/382–0942, fax 908/996–2921 (call first)

The exterior of this 1864 Italianate Victorian mansion is striking. Sitting in a beautifully landscaped garden, the taupe house with plum-and-beige trim is crowned with a belvedere, where guests can sit and look down on the river town. The interior is just as striking. High ceilings, tall shuttered windows, and period antiques make words like *formal* and *grand* seem insufficient when describing the blue parlor. Here guests can help themselves to cream sherry, coffee or tea, and baked goods. Guest rooms, named for members of the Apgar family, who lived here for 96 years, are dominated by huge, carved, mixed-wood Victorian bedroom sets.

Clark and Karen Johnson bought the bed-and-breakfast in 1992 and with the help of historic preservationists have restored it inside and out. The third-floor garret suite has slanting ceilings and a Leonardo da Vinci–design circular window—the Hunterdon House trademark.

The inn is half a block from the river, across the street from the highly rated Frenchtown Inn restaurant, and a short walk from the crafts, antiques, and specialty shops that line Bridge Street. Lambertville and New Hope are a 12-mile drive; public transportation is nearby.

🏠 *6 double rooms with baths, 1 suite. Air-conditioning in rooms, fireplaces in 1 room, parlor, and dining room, on-site parking. $85–$145; full breakfast. AE, MC, V. Smoking on porch only, no pets, 2-night minimum on weekends.*

The Inn at Millrace Pond

313 Johnsonburg Rd., Rte. 519, Box 359, Hope, NJ 07844, tel. 908/459–4884, fax 908/459–5276

In the historic Moravian village of Hope, an old millrace leaves a small millpond and flows through a chasm of slate toward a 1769 stone gristmill, which once supplied flour to Washington's troops and is now an inn. When you enter its gorgeous foyer, you can look down a story and a half at the skeleton of the old wheel and walk downstairs between stone walls to see where the millrace once ran (in summer, a little water still flows in the channel). The spot now serves as the inn's wine cellar. Though the inn complex also includes two other Colonial buildings used for lodging, as well as antiques and gift shops, the focus is on the gristmill with its guest rooms, tavern, and gourmet restaurant. The architecture is stunning, from the bottom-floor tavern, with its huge walk-in fireplace, cage bar, and flour chute, to the top floor's bedrooms, where cathedral ceilings reveal the enormous timbers of the roof. The building's beams and wide-board floors have been preserved throughout.

The gristmill bedrooms have Shaker reproductions; elsewhere there are regional antiques made in New York, Pennsylvania, and New Jersey. The six-bedroom Millrace House, a frame building that was the miller's dwelling, has more formal furnishings and a parlor with a fireplace. Its bedrooms and the two in the Stone Cottage have collections of Queen Anne, Chippendale, and Sheraton pieces. Each of the Stone Cottage bedrooms (one upstairs and one down) has its own entrance, and they are prized for romantic seclusion. Previous inn guests have included Nick Nolte, Barbra Streisand, Dustin Hoffman, and Michael Feinstein.

Innkeepers Cordie and Charles Puttkammer took over in 1994 and have been sprucing up the place since. She is a professor of childhood development, and he runs the inn from a table in the dining room—that is, when he isn't collecting things or out about the property. They are currently completing renovations to a building moved to the site to serve as a center for business meetings. It should open sometime in 1998.

🏠 *15 double rooms with baths, 1 suite. Restaurant; tavern; air-conditioning; cable TV in 10 rooms and parlor; phones in all rooms; fireplaces in 1 room, parlor, and tavern; tennis; on-site parking. $85–$165; Continental breakfast. AE, DC, MC, V. No smoking in rooms, pets allowed upon approval, 2-night minimum with Sat. reservation.*

Isaac Hilliard House

31 Hanover St., Pemberton, NJ 08068, tel. 609/894–0756 or 800/371–0756

On the edge of Ft. Dix, surrounded by farmland and cranberry bogs and not too far from Philadelphia and the Pine Barrens, is the old town of Pemberton, where you're considered a newcomer unless you've lived here for more than 30 years. The circa-1750 Isaac (pronounced I-*zay*-ic) Hilliard House was named for one of the town's most-beloved citizens of 150 years ago. He added much of the home's Victorian ornamentation.

Dan and Marian Michaels are the enthusiastic innkeepers who have adorned the house with Dan's handmade miniatures, Marian's plate and oil-lamp collections, an old Victrola and sewing machine, and antique baby furniture. Bedrooms contain a mix of antiques and reproductions. The former includes a courting bench perched in a bay window, while the latter encompasses repros of old-fashioned radios (and tapes of old programs) in each room. The romantic suite has a lace-draped Rice four-poster canopy bed; two wedding gowns, one of which Marian wore when she and Dan renewed their vows for their 25th anniversary; and a big bathroom with a garden tub.

🏠 *3 double rooms with baths, 1 suite. Air-conditioning, cable TV/VCR and fireplaces in suite and parlor, mini-refrigerators in suite, pool, bicycles, on-site parking. $55–$130; full breakfast, welcoming refreshments. AE, MC, V. No smoking indoors, no pets, 2-night minimum on holiday weekends.*

Jerica Hill

96 Broad St., Flemington, NJ 08822, tel. 908/782–8234

The first bed-and-breakfast established in Flemington, this completely restored, turn-of-the-century Queen Anne Victorian, set on a tree-lined street in the historic district, is painted in shades of gray with burgundy trim. The inn blends Victorian architecture with country hospitality and creature comforts and is outfitted not with Victorian furnishings but with cozier upholstered pieces, wicker, brass, oak, and mahogany. Visitors can savor complimentary sherry in the living room, beverages and a full cookie jar in the guest pantry, and chocolates, a small basket of fruit, and sparkling water in the bedrooms. Bay windows make several of the rooms especially appealing. Taller guests may appreciate a king-size bed in one room.

Balloon trips can be arranged, and those interested in a back-road driving tour of the countryside and area wineries can request directions and a picnic lunch, complete with Jerica Hill wineglasses.

🏠 *5 double rooms with baths. Air-conditioning, TV, and phones in rooms, fireplace in living room, on-site parking. $85–$110; Continental-plus breakfast. AE, MC, V. No smoking, no pets, 2-night minimum on most weekends.*

Peacock Inn

20 Bayard La., Princeton, NJ 08540, tel. 609/924–1707, fax 609/924–0788

In the center of Princeton, a two-minute walk from the university campus, this inn has hosted visitors for more than a century. Built as a private home in 1770, the structure was moved in 1875 from its original site on the Princeton campus to its current location. It's the town's only full-time bed-and-breakfast, so guests should book far in advance for the fall and spring, when visiting educators, alums, and parents fill its rooms. Albert Einstein, F. Scott Fitzgerald, and Bertrand Russell are listed among the inn's distinguished guests.

The rooms here vary in color scheme and decor, featuring French, Early American, and English antiques and reproductions. There is a unifying theme, however: the peacock. This showy bird appears on screens, in bedside lamps, and on mantels. The owners, animal lovers, even have six live peacocks (not on the premises), and pets are welcome. On most nights, guests can take advantage of a special $32 prix-fixe menu at Le Plumet Royal, the inn's ordinarily ultra-expensive French restaurant.

🏠 *14 double rooms with baths, 2 doubles share bath. Restaurant, bar, air-conditioning and phones in rooms, cable TV in 6 rooms and lounge, fireplaces in restaurant, on-site parking. $100–$135; Continental-plus breakfast. AE, MC, V.*

Stewart Inn

708 S. Main St., Box 6, Stewartsville, NJ 08886, tel. 908/479–6060, fax 908/479–4211

Owner and innkeeper Lynne McGarry, an antiques collector and needlework-kit manufacturer, presides over this rambling 1770 fieldstone manor house. It was originally built for the owner of Stewartsville's gristmill, which ground flour to feed George Washington's troops during the Revolutionary War. Between 1800 and 1967, countless additions were made and it passed between many owners, among them Broadway producer Harry Bannister and his wife, actress Ann Harding, whose friends in the entertainment industry—among them Clark Gable—used the house as a retreat. Although the stars left nothing behind, the inn has retained a dramatic atmosphere.

About a 25-minute drive from the many fine restaurants of Lambertville, Stewart Inn has 16 acres of lawns, formal perennial gardens, a stocked trout stream, and a meandering pasture that leads to a working farm with ducks, sheep, goats, and peacocks. The eggs served at breakfast are provided by the farm's chickens. Lynne has a wild-game license, and it's not unusual for there to be a wounded animal in residence that she's nursing back to health. More animals, in the form of knickknacks, make their home in the common areas downstairs.

The best times to visit the inn are summer, when the swimming pool offers a respite from the heat, and fall, when the maple and apple trees show off their bright colors. (Unfortunately, the hum from nearby I–78 mars the otherwise bucolic setting.) In the winter, the house is filled with plants brought in from the outside.

Inside, off-white walls bring out the richness of the dark cherry and mahogany furnishings and the colorful tapestries and rugs. Many rooms have antique jam cupboards, and all have brass oil lamps on night tables beside the beds. Needlework is displayed throughout the house, and Lynne sells kits for those who are inspired. Long-term guests, often businesspeople in transit, frequently stay at the inn, taking breakfast in the cozy kitchen. Short-term visitors eat at individual tables in the dining room and enjoy such standbys as Jack's Flaps, named for a former longtime guest who loved to cook pancakes.

🏠 *5 double rooms with baths, 2 suites. Air-conditioning, cable TV and phones in rooms, fireplaces in 2 rooms and 5 common areas, badminton, on-site parking. $95–$125; full breakfast. AE, D, MC, V. Smoking on porch only, no pets, 2-night minimum on weekends May– Oct.*

The Stockton Inn

1 Main St., Box C, Stockton, NJ 08559, tel. 609/397–1250, fax 609/397–8948

In 1934 Richard Rodgers and Lorenz Hart escaped from Manhattan to this inn, which inspired their 1936 musical, *On Your Toes,* and its song "There's a Small Hotel with a Wishing Well." Even today people call to ask if the wishing well is still there. It is, in the terraced garden with waterfalls and a trout pond.

Built as a private home in 1710, the inn became a stagecoach stop in 1796 and a hotel in 1832. Rooms are furnished with simple, tasteful Colonial-style reproductions and some antiques, and two suites share a balcony overlooking the small town of Stockton. Historic touches remain—eight bedrooms and the five dining rooms have working fireplaces— but the mood is more that of the famous "small hotel," with modern conveniences like cable TV and in-room phones scheduled to be added by 1998. The inn comprises four buildings: the inn itself, two carriage houses, and a house across the street. All have similar rooms. A good restaurant serving contemporary American and Continental food keeps the place bustling.

🏠 *3 double rooms with baths, 8 suites. Restaurant, air-conditioning and TV in rooms, minirefrigerators in some rooms, on-site parking. $60–$165; Continental-plus breakfast. AE, D, MC, V. No pets, 2-night minimum on weekends, 3-night minimum on holiday weekends.*

The Whistling Swan Inn

110 Main St., Stanhope, NJ 07874, tel. 973/347–6369, fax 973/347–3391

The Cabbage Rose Inn has cabbage roses, the Peacock Inn has peacocks, and the Whistling Swan Inn has swans. It also has innkeepers Paula Williams and Joe Mulay, who saw the potential in this 1904 house and renovated, restored, and reshaped it into a lovely Victorian B&B. They kept and enhanced what was beautiful—the tiger-oak woodwork, the octagonal tower room with conical ceiling—and added what was missing, most notably 11 bathrooms. The only original bath, now called Tubs for Two, has a pair of claw-foot soakers for double dipping.

Most of the inn's guest rooms contain country Victorian antiques and reproductions, but three have themes—Art Deco, 1940s, and Oriental.

In a tiny village in New Jersey's highlands, the Whistling Swan is close to winter skiing and ice skating, summer water sports on the lakes, and cultural activities in Waterloo Village. The Delaware River is a 25-minute drive away.

▥ *9 double rooms with baths, 1 suite. Air-conditioning, cable TV in rooms and parlor, phones in rooms, fireplaces in foyer and parlor, bicycles, on-site parking. $90–$135; full breakfast. AE, D, MC, V. Smoking on veranda only, no pets, 2-night minimum on holiday weekends.*

The Wooden Duck

140 Goodale Rd., Newton, NJ 07860, tel. 973/300–0395, fax 973/300–0395

Bob and Barbara Hadden just wanted a place in the country, but on their first visit to this 1978 luxury home on 17 acres surrounded by Kittatinny Valley State Park, they were persuaded not only to purchase it but also to turn it into a B&B. The Wooden Duck, named for the Haddens' prominently displayed collection of hand-carved ducks, has country in abundance. Deer wander across the property, and the bird feeder outside the dining room window hosts chipmunks and the occasional bluebird. You can hike or cross-country ski from the patio to the trails in the park or simply enjoy the view from the pool deck.

Those so inclined can remain indoors, snacking on cookies, playing bumper pool, or working puzzles downstairs in front of the double-hearth fireplace. Chocolates and terry-cloth robes are just some of the amenities provided in the large bedrooms in the main house and the more privately situated accommodations in the carriage house.

▥ *5 double rooms with baths. Air-conditioning, cable TV/VCR in rooms and game room, on-site parking. $100–$120; full breakfast. AE, D, MC, V. No smoking, no pets, 2-night minimum on holiday weekends.*

The Jersey Shore

Nowadays the 127-mile stretch of sandy beaches, bays, marshes, and inlets along the Jersey Shore is one of the busiest vacation destinations in the country. It has been discovered, colonized, divided, subdivided, developed, renovated, and restored so many times that few natural, get-away-from-it-all places remain.

Swimming and water sports predominate. Fishing, on the ocean or in the back bays, is convenient by party or charter boat. Murky visibility limits, but does not preclude, the joys of scuba. You're at most a short car trip away from golf, horseback riding, and tennis; bicycling on most boardwalks is permitted during early morning hours.

Proximity to the beaches or bays (for boaters) is desirable, although beach areas tend to be noisy and busy at the height of the season. Admission to all New Jersey beaches, with the exception of those in Atlantic City, the Wildwoods, and Cape May Point, requires a beach tag, which most bed-and-breakfasts provide free or for a small fee.

If you'd like to sidestep the crowds, visit during the off-season: September is the best month. The days then are shorter, the breezes cooler, the ocean warm and tranquil, and most restaurants and attractions are still open. May is also pleasant. The cold, quiet months of November and December are becoming popular for business retreats.

One final note about being "down the Shore": As you go from one town to another, the mood changes as quickly as the tides. Busy seaside resorts crammed with boardwalk amusements sit next to quiet, primarily residential communities with undeveloped waterfronts; aging cities; and quaint towns with restored Victorian districts. There's bound to be at least one place that's got just what you want, because after all, the area is—as those cutesy license plates declare—"Shore to Please."

Places to Go, Sights to See

Amusement parks. Boardwalk rides are most extensive in *Wildwood* and *Seaside Heights. Six Flags Great Adventure* (Rte. 537, Jackson, tel. 732/928–2000 or 732/928–1821 for recording) comprises a roller coaster–filled theme park and drive-through safari park.

Atlantic City. Synonymous with casino gambling and adult-oriented entertainment and extravagance, Atlantic City hasn't seen much benefit from its "new" industry (backroom gambling has existed here for more than 150 years), and the city remains pretty run-down overall.

Cape May County Park and Zoo (U.S. 9 and Crest Haven Rd., Cape May Court House, tel. 609/465–5271 or 609/465–9210). The pleasantly landscaped park area contains a picnic ground, playground, bike trail, gazebo, tennis courts, and a free 25-acre zoo with more than 300 species. It has facilities for persons with disabilities.

Concerts. *Albert Music Hall* (Rte. 532 and Wells Mills Rd., Waretown, tel. 609/971–1593) presents concerts of folk music, country, bluegrass, and old-time pinelands ballads every Saturday night at 8. New Jersey's largest enclosed auditorium, the *Great Auditorium* (Pilgrim Pathway, Ocean Grove, tel. 732/775–0035), hosts a variety of musical events in summer. Ethnic festivals and musical performances of all types are held at the open-air amphitheater of the *PNC Bank Arts Center* (Garden State Pkwy., Exit 116, Holmdel, tel. 732/335–0400) throughout the summer.

Flea markets. Monmouth County flea markets and auctions include *Basics Flea Market* (2301 U.S. 9, Howell, tel. 732/308–1105), *Collingwood Park Auction & Flea Market* (Rtes. 33 and 34, Farmingdale, tel. 732/938–7941), and the *Englishtown Auction* (90 Wilson Ave., Englishtown, tel. 732/446–9644).

Island Beach State Park (Rte. 35, tel. 732/793–0506). This 12-mile stretch of virtually pristine beach and overgrown dune has a new nature center. Admission is charged by the carload ($6 or $7 in season, $4 in off-season).

Leaming's Run Botanical Gardens (1845 U.S. 9, Swainton, tel. 609/465–5871). A delightful place for a leisurely walk, these 25 gardens on 20 acres in Cape May County also have a small Colonial farm.

Lighthouses. At the northern end of the shore is the *Sandy Hook Lighthouse* (Gateway National Recreation Area, tel. 732/872–0115), the oldest continuously operating lighthouse in the country, built in 1764. The *Twin Lights* (Lighthouse Rd., Highlands, tel. 732/872–1814), about 8 miles south, marks the entrance to New York Harbor. *Barnegat Lighthouse* (Broadway and the bay, Barnegat Light, tel. 609/494–2016), the famous red-and-white tower built in 1858 and known as Old Barney, is at the northernmost end of Long Beach Island, in Barnegat Lighthouse State Park. The *Hereford Inlet Lighthouse* (1st and Central Aves., North Wildwood, tel. 609/522–4520) has a small museum and information center.

Living history. Within a 3,000-acre state park of the same name, *Allaire Village* (Rte. 524, Farmingdale, tel. 732/938–2371 or 732/938–2253) is a re-created 18th-century iron-making village. *Longstreet Farm* (Holmdel Park, Holmdel, tel. 732/946–3758) is a working farm from the 1890s. An 1888 glass factory and glass-making demonstrations are the highlights at *Wheaton Village* (1501 Glasstown Rd., Millville, tel. 609/825–6800 or 800/998–4552).

Monmouth Battlefield State Park (Rte. 33, Freehold, tel. 732/462–9616). At this Revolutionary War battle site, Molly Pitcher earned her place in American history.

New Jersey Coastal Heritage Trail (Box 568, Newport 08345, tel. 609/447–0103, fax 609/447–0108). The trail, when finished, will connect significant natural and cultural resources along the shore, with five planned routes. The first two themes, maritime history and coastal habitat, have signs now in place; the wildlife migration route is under development; and historic settlements and relaxation and inspiration are still in the planning stage.

Noyes Museum (Lily Lake Rd., Oceanville, tel. 609/652–8848). This unusual museum has displays on contemporary American art and folk art.

Racetracks. Horse-racing fans can visit *Monmouth Park* (175 Oceanport Ave., Oceanport, tel. 732/222–5100) and *Atlantic City Race Course* (4501 Black Horse Pike, Mays Landing, tel. 609/641–2190) for summertime Thoroughbred racing or *Freehold Raceway* (U.S. 9 and Rte. 33, Freehold, tel. 732/462–3800) for harness racing the rest of the year.

Sandy Hook (tel. 732/872–0115). At this aptly named peninsula of barrier beach, part of the Gateway National Recreation Area, sandbar ecology and fortifications built to protect New York Harbor are preserved. You can glimpse the New York City skyline, splash in the gentle, shallow surf; and explore Ft. Hancock.

Theater. *South Jersey Regional Theater* (Gateway Playhouse, 738 Bay Ave., Somers Point, tel. 609/653–0553) presents revivals, classics, and new American drama in Atlantic County. *Surflight Theatre* (Beach and Engleside Aves., Beach Haven, tel. 609/492–9477) stages summer-stock plays and musicals on Long Beach Island.

Wineries. Worth visiting are *Balic Winery* (U.S. 40, Mays Landing, tel. 609/625–2166) and *Renault Winery* (72 N. Breman Ave., Egg Harbor City, tel. 609/965–2111).

Restaurants

In Highlands, options include **Bahrs Landing** (2 Bay Ave., tel. 732/872–1245), for seafood; gourmet **Cousin's Cafe** (123 Bay Ave., tel. 732/291–7667); and the Continental **Doris and Ed's** (348 Shore Dr., tel. 732/872–1565). Farther south in Monmouth County, **La Nonna Pianacone's Cafe** (Main and McCabe, Bradley Beach, tel. 732/775–0906) is one of the town's many good Italian eateries. **Ollie Klein's Waterside Cafe** (708 River Rd., Belmar, tel. 732/681–1177) is short on atmosphere but long on really good fresh seafood. **Whisper's** (Hewitt Wellington Hotel, 200 Monmouth Ave., Spring Lake, tel. 732/449–3330) is a small, quaint, but fancy restaurant with a changing menu. For a special occasion, the **Old Mill Inn** (Old Mill Rd., Spring Lake Heights, tel. 732/449–1800) serves fine Continental cuisine in dining rooms that overlook a mill pond. **Rod's Olde Irish Tavern** (507 Washington Blvd., Sea Girt, tel. 732/449–2020) is a friendly neighborhood tavern that got big, and so did the portions.

On Long Beach Island, **Roberto's Dolce Vita** (1 E. New Jersey Ave., Beach Haven, tel. 609/492–1001) has a very good northern Italian menu with a lot of seafood. **Tucker's** (101 West Ave., Beach Haven, tel. 609/492–2300) serves varied fare with indoor and outdoor dining overlooking the bay. For haute cuisine and haute prices to match, try the reservations-only, prix-fixe, five-course but no choice dinners at **The Green Gables Inn and Restaurant** (212 Centre St., Beach Haven, tel. 609/492–3553; also see inn listing).

In Cape May County, the **Deauville Inn** (Willard and Bay Drs., Strathmere, tel. 609/263–2080), a former speakeasy, has both dockside and inside dining and a good selection of seafood and steaks. **Ravioli House** (Bennett and New Jersey Aves., Wildwood, tel. 609/522–7894) is an inexpensive choice.

Tourist Information

Cape May County Chamber of Commerce (Box 74, Cape May Court House 08210, tel. 609/465–7181, fax 609/465–5017). **Greater Atlantic City Convention & Visitors Authority** (2314 Pacific Ave., Atlantic City 08401, tel. 609/348–7100 or

800/262–7395, fax 609/345–2200). **Monmouth County Dept. of Public Information & Tourism** (6 W. Main St., Freehold 07728, tel. 732/431–7476 or 800/523–2587, fax 732/866–3696). **New Jersey Division of Travel and Tourism** (CN 826, Trenton 08625-0826, tel. 609/292–2470 or 800/537–7397, fax 609/633–7418). **Ocean County Tourism Advisory Council** (Box 2191, Toms River 08754-2191, tel. 908/929–2138 or 800/365–6933, fax 908/506–5370). **Southern Ocean County Chamber of Commerce** (265 W. 9th St., Ship Bottom 08008, tel. 609/494–7211 or 800/292–6372, fax 609/494–5807).

Reservation Services

Amanda's Bed & Breakfast Reservation Service (21 S. Woodland Ave., East Brunswick 08816, tel. 732/249–4944, fax 732/246–1961). **Bed & Breakfast Adventures** (2310 Central Ave., Suite 132, North Wildwood 08260, tel. 609/522–4000 or 800/992–2632 for reservations, fax 609/522–6125).

Amber Street Inn

118 Amber St., Beach Haven, NJ 08008, tel. 609/492–1611

In 1991 RNs Joan and Michael Fitzsimmons took an old Victorian summer house, gave it some much needed nursing, and turned it into a new Victorian B&B. Built circa 1885 for one of the daughters of the Wilson family, "Rosalind Cottage" was named after a Shakespearean heroine, as were three other nearby Wilson homes.

Some original furnishings remain, including chestnut mantels on the fireplaces in the dining room and small entryway parlor, but Joan and Michael have added their own. The Veranda Room has a bed with tented oak headboard and a porch overlooking a small English garden; Portia's Suite (another Shakespearean lady) has an iron bed, pull-out love seat, and rooftop view; and Adrien's room, named for the Fitzsimmons' teenage daughter, is dressed in "her colors"—lavender and green—and graced with a delicate antique crocheted coverlet with pansies and a vase of peacock feathers.

Open weekends in the shoulder seasons but all week in summer, the inn is a block from the beach and across from Bicentennial Park, site of summer concerts on Wednesday evenings and art shows and other events on alternate Saturdays.

🏠 *6 double rooms with baths. Air-conditioning in 4 rooms, outbound-only phones in rooms, bicycles, outdoor shower, beach tags and chairs. $115–$160; Continental breakfast Mon.–Sat. and full breakfast Sun. No smoking indoors, no pets, 2-night minimum on weekdays mid-June–mid-Sept. and weekends mid-June–July, 3-night minimum on weekends in Aug., 3- or 4-night minimum on holiday weekends, closed mid-Nov.–mid-Feb.*

Ashling Cottage

106 Sussex Ave., Spring Lake, NJ 07762, tel. 732/449–3553 or 888/274–5464, fax 732/974–0831

Goodi Stewart calls the style of her 1877 cottage Carpenter Gothic "because, as far as we can tell, the carpenter made it up as he went along." Furnishings are a mix of antiques and reproductions, and utilitarian wood closets are built into many of the rooms. Flowers turn up everywhere in this intimate, unpretentious house—in the fabrics of spreads and drapes as well as in garlands hung on windows and wrapped around headboards. One room has an intriguing sunken bathroom, while another has an attractive iron four-poster.

Ashling's atmosphere is easygoing, and innkeepers Goodi and Jack Stewart are experts at down-to-earth informality. The most popular room is the solarium, where guests savor the buffet breakfasts and occasional impromptu afternoon refreshments while looking out at Spring Lake and the beach, both about a block away. The inn has an extensive collection of games and books for whiling away quiet hours.

🏠 *8 double rooms with baths, 2 doubles share bath. Air-conditioning in 7 rooms, cable TV/VCR and gas fireplace in parlor, minirefrigerator in solarium, bicycles, beach tags, towels, and chairs, on- and off-site parking, transportation to and from train and bus. $75–$170; full breakfast. No credit cards. Smoking on porch only, no pets, 2-night minimum on weekends, 3-night minimum on holiday weekends, closed mid-Nov.–Apr.*

BarnaGate Bed & Breakfast

637 Wesley Ave., Ocean City, NJ 08226, tel. 609/391–9366, fax 609/399–5048

Don't be confused by the name: It refers not to any of the Barnegats (located north of here), but to owners Frank and Lois Barna, who thought it conjured up images of the Jersey Shore. Called simply a "seashore cottage," this homey 1896 guest house in Ocean City's historic district has no definable architectural style. The exterior is vaguely Queen Anne, with a broad porch and burgundy awnings. Inside feels just like grandma's house. A Second Empire oak dining room is framed by Lois's collections of spoons, teapots, and bells. Frank collects John Wayne memorabilia and is happy to show the Duke's movies.

Three blocks from the beach and convenient to Ocean City's busy downtown shopping area, the inn is reasonably priced by shore standards. Rooms, named for flowers, are dressed with country Victorian antiques and handmade quilts and afghans and are stocked with Perrier water and candies. (Ocean City is a dry town, but you're welcome to bring a bottle of wine and chill it in the Barnas' refrigerator.) Under the eaves on the third floor, two bedrooms and an adjacent sitting area make a cozy family suite.

▥ *1 double room with bath, 1 double with ½ bath, 3 doubles share 2 baths. Cable TV in parlor, minirefrigerator in 3rd-floor sitting area, outdoor shower, beach tags, transportation to and from train and bus. $70–$120; Continental-plus breakfast in winter, Continental breakfast other times. AE, MC, V. Smoking on porch only, no pets, 2-night minimum on holiday weekends.*

The Bayberry Barque

117 Centre St., Beach Haven, NJ 08008, tel. 609/492–5216

This porch-wrapped house was built in 1888 for a member of the Philadelphia Orchestra. Barbara and Tom De Santo (she's a former nursery school teacher, he's an attorney) own it now and manage to operate the easygoing inn while continuing to live in Central Jersey for much of the year. Barbara stays at the B&B

full-time in summer; the rest of the season it's open only on weekends.

Guest rooms are painted in rich colors authentic to the period of the house and are filled with a blend of antiques, reproductions, bric-a-brac, wicker, and such country Victorian touches as straw hats trimmed with ribbons and lace. The striking 4-foot-by-8-foot stained-glass window on the staircase is part of the original structure.

The inn is within walking distance of restaurants, movies, a theater, nightclubs, and outdoor concerts, and it's just one short block from the beach.

▥ *5 double rooms with baths, 3 doubles share bath. Cable TV in living room, minirefrigerator in hall, outdoor shower, beach tags and chairs. $70–$135; Continental breakfast, Sat. afternoon wine-and-cheese parties in summer. MC, V. No smoking indoors, no pets, 2-night minimum on weekends and 3-night minimum on holiday weekends mid-June–mid-Sept., closed Nov.–Apr.*

Candlelight Inn

2310 Central Ave., North Wildwood, NJ 08260, tel. 609/522–6200, fax 609/522–6125

Three blocks from the beach and boardwalk, this 1905 Queen Anne Victorian sits just over the border from Wildwood and its amusements but light-years away in mood. Paul DiFilippo and Diane Buscham, inspired by blissful stays in bed-and-breakfasts, sold their motel to open North Wildwood's first B&B. Also the operators of a B&B reservation service, they are dedicated to providing the personal touches that make stays memorable.

Guests can relax by soaking in a private whirlpool (available in some rooms) or the house hot tub (on the sundeck). They can sip sherry in the foyer's fireplace nook or in their rooms, which have appropriate names like Oak, Pine, Walnut, Satin and

Lace, and Bay Window. In the main house, there's a vintage air. Period antiques, such as converted brass gaslight fixtures and the parlor's 1855 Empire sofa and 1890 Eastlake piano, adorn the second-floor common areas. Downstairs, two bedrooms can be rented as a suite with a private fireplace-warmed parlor. Out back in the newly converted, two-unit Surveyor's Cottage, fireplaces have gas logs instead of wood, but though the feeling is modern, it's just as romantic.

⊞ *8 double rooms with baths, 2 suites. Air-conditioning in 8 rooms, cable TV in 3 units and parlor, minirefrigerators in 3 units, beach towels and chairs, on-site parking. $115–$260; full breakfast, afternoon refreshments. AE, D, MC, V. Smoking on porches only, no pets, 3-night minimum on weekends July–Aug., closed Jan.*

Cashelmara

22 Lakeside Ave., Avon-by-the-Sea, NJ 07717, tel. 732/776–8727 or 800/821–2976, fax 732/988–5819

Sitting on the appropriately named Lakeside Avenue, just off the equally appropriately named Ocean Avenue, this 1901 house looks out on both Sylvan Lake and the Atlantic. Professional Irishman Marty Mulligan was smitten by the near-perfect location, so he bought the inn in 1986 and named it the Gaelic word for "house by the sea."

From the background music to a stained-glass window of a harp, reminders of Ireland are everywhere, as are views of lake or ocean. All units face one or the other, though third-floor rooms with cute window seats tucked under dormers have more limited views. A recent top-to-bottom renovation revamped rooms, created a glassed-in breakfast area with private tables, and added twin antiques-filled parlors in warm red. The formal air is softened by cheerful innkeeper Mary Wiernasz and dog Cody—surprisingly, not an Irish setter but rather the friendly resident retriever.

The most unusual addition to Cashelmara is a Victorian theater. Here you can spend an evening or rainy afternoon on velvet-covered antiques beneath a tin ceiling watching turn-of-a-different-century movies on a big-screen TV with surround sound. Popcorn is included.

⊞ *12 double rooms with baths, 1 suite. Air-conditioning, cable TV in 7 units and satellite TV in theater, gas fireplaces in 6 units, dining room, foyer, and parlor, minirefrigerator in suite and full refrigerator in breakfast room, whirlpool in suite, beach tags and towels, on-site parking, transportation to and from train and bus. $95–$250; full breakfast. AE, D, MC, V. Smoking on porch only, no pets, 2-night minimum on weekends Labor Day–June, 3-night minimum on weekends and 4-night minimum on holiday weekends July–Labor Day.*

The Chateau

500 Warren Ave., Spring Lake, NJ 07762, tel. 732/974–2000, fax 732/974–0007

Five blocks from the beach, a short walk from the business district and train station, and across from two parks and Spring Lake itself, this small family-owned and -operated hotel has a prime location. The original section was built in 1888, but over the years new rooms, a gazebo, two sundecks, the breakfast room, and an adjacent building have been added to create a rambling complex.

The emphasis is not on period decor; there are white walls, some tin ceilings, carpeting, Waverly fabrics, contemporary and wicker furnishings, and a wealth of modern amenities. All rooms have cable TV with VCRs, radios, two phones, in-room safes, small refrigerators, and marble baths, while luxury units add wet bars, wood-burning or gas fireplaces, hair dryers, and oversize soaking or whirlpool tubs. Some have full kitchens and private balconies overlooking the park.

Management prides itself on providing good values: deep off-season discounts, reduced rates for solo guests, and a family plan enabling up to two children to stay free with their parents. Seasonal extras include beach and trolley passes in summer, a midweek Continental breakfast in winter, and movies during the shoulder seasons.

▥ *30 double rooms with baths, 6 suites, 2 housekeeping units. Air-conditioning, gas fireplace in foyer, bicycle rentals, beach tags, reduced-rate fitness club passes, on- and off-site parking. $125–$225; Continental breakfast extra except winter weekdays. AE, D, DC, MC, V. No pets, 2-night minimum on weekends Sept.–June, 3-night minimum on weekends July–Aug., 2-, 3-, or 4-night minimum on holiday weekends.*

Conover's Bay Head Inn

646 Main Ave., Bay Head, NJ 08742, tel. 732/892–4664 or 800/956–9099, fax 732/892–8748

Ocean County's best-known bed-and-breakfast is a weathered-shingle house on busy Route 35. Beverly and Carl Conover bought it in 1970 and began their B&B, inadvertently becoming leaders in the movement.

Though built as a summer cottage in 1905, the building was redesigned as an inn in 1912. A tidy parlor with a white cut-stone fireplace introduces guests to the small hotel's professional grace. Beverly likes to change some of the downstairs decor with the season, and furniture coverings might be plain or plaid or flowered chintz.

Bedrooms are outfitted with antiques, English-country-style reproductions, and small vases filled with whatever is pretty and in season from the inn's English garden. Stenciling here and there continues the floral motif, often picking up wallpaper patterns. Three rooms have tiny trapezoidal windows punched into the front wall to furnish a view of the

ocean over a block of houses. For the most part, though, the windows are more beguiling for the look they impart to the rooms than for the look they provide to the sea. Six guest rooms have ocean views, and two have views of the bay. One room has an ocean-view porch.

▥ *12 double rooms with baths, housekeeping cottage. Air-conditioning and phones in rooms, gas fireplace in 1 room, refrigerator in garage, beach tags, towels, and chairs, on-site parking, transportation to and from train and bus. $120–$210; full breakfast, afternoon tea. AE, MC, V. No smoking indoors, no pets, 2-night minimum on weekends mid-Sept.–mid-June, 3-night minimum on weekends and 3- or 4-night minimum on holiday weekends mid-June–mid-Sept.*

The Green Gables Inn

212 Centre St., Beach Haven, NJ 08008, tel. 609/492–3553 or 800/492–0492, fax 609/492–2507

Like other Beach Haven inns, this 1880 green clapboard house with purple and yellow trim offers a romantic Victorian getaway a shell's throw from the beach. On the second and third stories, modest antiques are tucked into cozy rooms with old wide-plank floors, flowered wallpapers, and cheery paint, but what people really come here for is the exciting cuisine of the ground-floor restaurant.

You can sit in one of the comfortable Victorian dining salons or on the lattice-enclosed garden-side porch. There your dinner choices end. Owner-chef Adolfo DeMartino—who, along with lovely wife, Rita, hails from Italy by way of Manhattan—plans one five-course menu daily based on what's fresh at the market (be sure to mention any allergies or dislikes when you make your mandatory reservation). The less adventurous can take lunch or tea, though Green Gables's scrumptious tea pastries are an adventure in themselves. On Sunday, Russian gypsy card and tea-leaf readings are available.

Dinner/room packages enable guests to indulge in the culinary experience, collapse satisfied in a room upstairs, and awaken to home-baked goodies before a day at the beach.

🏠 *2 double rooms with baths, 4 doubles share 2 baths. Beach tags. $90–$130; Continental breakfast. AE, D, DC, MC, V. Smoking on porch only, no pets, 2-night minimum on weekends and 3-night minimum on holiday weekends mid-May–Sept.*

The Henry Ludlam Inn

1336 Rte. 47, Dennisville, NJ 08270, tel. 609/861–5847

Built by Henry Ludlam, founder of New Jersey's first public school, this 1740 Federal-style house and its "new" 1804 addition are now owned by Chuck and Pat DeArros. He works for the Cape May–Lewes ferry; she's the full-time innkeeper.

The charms of age—the cozy parlor's low-beamed ceiling, wood floors, and stairs that sag and creak—are enhanced by country touches and old-style pampering. In the hall, a wagon load of teddy bears sits on a floor painted with an apple tree. Two spruce-clad rooms under the eaves are decked with rockers and brightened by painted flowers—morning glories in one, sunflowers in the other. Trays with complimentary wine and chocolates nestle atop feather beds. The only drawback is some noise from Route 47.

Though the inn is close to but not on the shore (Stone Harbor is 20 minutes away), there's plenty to do besides beaching. Leaming's Run Gardens are just to the east, the spectacular spring spawning of the horseshoe crabs is to the west on Delaware Bay, and good bird-watching and antiques-hunting can be had in any number of locales nearby. Those more interested in staying put can enjoy 55-acre Ludlam's Pond, just across the shell driveway. Guests are encouraged to explore it in the inn's canoe, borrow rods and reels for great bass fishing, or just admire it from the gazebo or swing.

🏠 *5 double rooms with baths. Air-conditioning in rooms, cable TV in parlor, fireplaces in 3 rooms and dining room, minirefrigerator in hall, on-site parking. $95–$125; full breakfast. MC, V. No smoking, no pets, 2-night minimum on weekends May–Oct., 3-night minimum on holiday weekends.*

Hollycroft

506 North Blvd. (Box 448, Spring Lake, NJ 07762), tel. 732/681–2254 or 800/679–2254, fax 732/280–8145

One of the people who built this summer house in 1908 wanted a place at the shore; the other wanted a mountain retreat. The resulting compromise is this Adirondack-style lodge nestled among the trees on a bluff above Lake Como, at the northern edge of Spring Lake. It's a little out of the way, but it's worth the effort.

Architect Mark Fessler and his wife, Linda, who loves crafts and collecting, bought Hollycroft in 1985 and maintained its North Country mood throughout. The house was constructed of white cedar and ironstone with a half-timbered stucco-and-stone exterior. Inside, exposed log-and-stone walls peek out here and there among the knotty pine, while beamed ceilings add a sturdy exclamation point. In the living room, a 16-foot ironstone fireplace between two staircases faces a sunken, brick-floored area, where guests can sip sherry while looking out a wall of windows at Lake Como. The breakfast buffet is set out in the adjacent dining area or in the glassed-in breakfast room. In warm weather, guests eat on the patio.

If the common areas haven't completely won you over, the guest rooms will. They are individually decorated and all but one has a view of the lake. Most have iron and brass beds, though some are made of wood. Stenciling is everywhere, as is evidence of the Fesslers' artful collecting.

Pick up the phone.
Pick up the miles.

Is this a great time, or what? :-)

Now when you sign up with MCI you can receive up to 8,000 bonus frequent flyer miles on one of seven major airlines.

Then earn another 5 miles for every dollar you spend on a variety of MCI services, including MCI Card® calls from virtually anywhere in the world.*

You're going to use these services anyway. Why not rack up the miles while you're doing it?

Urban planning.

CITYPACKS

The ultimate guide to the city—a complete pocket guide plus a full-size color map.

www.fodors.com

The Pomeroy Room, in cool white and green, is like a garden. A side table is built of twigs, and the bed is made under a blanket of leaves. Upstairs, where Linda and Mark added warm mahogany floors, are five units. Grassmere has a striking custom-made, cast-iron canopy bed and a gas fireplace with tile surround (one of four in dining and guest rooms, in addition to two wood-burning fireplaces that suffuse the house with smells of a real fire). Next door, Somerset has a dark-wood four-poster bed and horse brasses, lending a masculine English-country air that's softened by a birdhouse and miniature furniture hanging in a corner. The vine-twined iron canopy bed of the luxurious 650-square-foot honeymoon suite sits beneath a cathedral ceiling with exposed log beams, under a tapestry of Lake Como (the Italian one), and across from a big stone fireplace with raised hearth. Lake views can be had from the bedroom, a screened porch, or the bathroom's soaking tub.

The inn is four blocks from the beach, and its proximity to Lake Como attracts anglers and bird-watchers. In the cooler months the Fesslers host mystery weekends.

▥ *7 double rooms with baths, 1 suite. Air-conditioning in rooms, cable TV/VCR in suite, minirefrigerator in suite and dining room, bicycles, beach tags, towels, and chairs, on-site parking, transportation to and from train and bus. $125–$275; full breakfast. AE. No smoking indoors, no pets, 2-night minimum on weekends, 3-night minimum on holiday weekends May–Oct.*

La Maison

404 Jersey Ave., Spring Lake, NJ 07762, tel. 732/449–0969 or 800/276–2088, fax 732/449–4860

Unlike Spring Lake's other, mostly American- or British-inspired Victorian B&Bs, this 1870 inn has a French flair, and a visit here will have you exclaiming "Vive la différence!" Engaging Fran-cophile Barbara Furdyna bought the mansard-roofed structure in 1982, when she worked for IBM, but she is now the full-time innkeeper. She has renovated and redecorated the sparkling rooms in country French style, transformed hall walls into a gallery of works (mostly watercolors) by La Maison's staff and larger "family," and imbued the house with easy European hospitality.

Mornings start with a decidedly un-Continental breakfast—perhaps crème brûlée French toast or a Provençal omelet with chèvre and herbes de Provence, always accompanied by baguettes, artfully arranged fresh fruit, fresh-squeezed orange juice or mimosas, and cappuccino or espresso on request. Return at happy hour for wine and cheese in front of the parlor's gas fireplace, and at night melt beneath fluffy duvets in the soft sheets of a sleigh bed. To dissolve further, take the room with a skylit whirlpool for two. Not surprisingly, the inn is a favorite of visitors from Europe and those who wish they were there.

▥ *5 double rooms with baths, 2 suites, housekeeping cottage. Air-conditioning, cable TV in rooms, VCR in 1 room, outbound-only phones in rooms, minirefrigerators in dining room and hall, bicycles, outdoor shower, beach and saltwater-pool tags, beach chairs, fitness club passes, on- and off-site parking, transportation to and from train and bus. $145–$250; full breakfast, afternoon refreshments. AE, D, DC, MC, V. Smoking on porch only, small pets in cottage only, 2-night minimum on weekends Sept.–June and on weekdays July–Aug., 3-night minimum on weekends July–Aug. and on other summer holiday weekends, closed Jan.*

Normandy Inn

21 Tuttle Ave., Spring Lake, NJ 07762, tel. 732/449–7172 or 800/449–1888, fax 732/449–1070

On the National Register of Historic Places, this huge Italianate villa with

Queen Anne touches was built for the Audenreid family of Philadelphia around 1888 and became a guest house in 1909. It still had the feel of a guest house in 1982, when Michael and Susan Ingino, who had had an ice-cream business in nearby Toms River, bought the inn and began to transform it into a textbook of museum-quality high-Victorian furnishings. Deliberately undercutting the formal atmosphere, the Inginos urge guests to relax. "To see a guest curl up on a sofa with a book is just what I want," Mike explains.

With the exception of rattan furniture in the casual enclosed side porch and a few necessities, such as a sleep sofa, there are no reproductions or modern pieces. Everything is genuine American Victorian. On the first floor are gasoliers, a wood-burning fireplace, and a Renaissance Revival parlor set with women's faces carved on the arms. Renaissance Revival predominates in the guest rooms, in addition to Rococo Revival and Eastlake.

Rooms are individually decorated down to the wallpaper and carpeting. Two are particularly spectacular, but for very different reasons. The drama in Room 102 is provided by 11-foot ceilings, rich green walls, and a very impressive four-piece burled-wood bedroom set. The less-formal, rose-color Tower Room has windows on four sides. Though its bathroom is down the stairs and down the hall (robes are provided), it's only a minor inconvenience when you consider the bright sunlight, cool breezes, and views over the rooftops to the ocean.

For families (well-behaved children are always welcome), there are two suites, one of which, above a 1930s garage, has a full kitchen and green marble bath with whirlpool for two. Period needle craft lends a country flair, but the suite is still dotted with turn-of-the-century antiques.

The newest rooms include one whose marble bath has a whirlpool tub and stained glass and whose gas fireplace is rimmed by an Eastlake mantel, typical of the period wood and marble mantels

surrounding the five gas fireplaces in guest rooms. But though change is continual at the Normandy, four-course hot breakfasts remain a constant, enabling guests to skip lunch and spend the day at the beach, a two-minute walk away.

🏨 *16 double rooms and 1 single with baths, 2 suites. Air-conditioning, cable TV on side porch and in rooms (on request), phones in rooms, bicycles, beach towels and chairs, on-site parking for 9 rooms, transportation to and from train and bus. $128–$300; full breakfast. AE, D, DC, MC, V. Smoking on porches only, no pets, 2-night minimum on weekdays July–Aug. and on weekends Mar.–Nov., 3-night minimum on weekends July–Aug. and on holiday weekends.*

Pierrót by the Sea

101 Centre St., Beach Haven, NJ 08008, tel. 609/492-4424

Innkeepers Jane Loehwing and daughter Jennifer were living in North Jersey when, in 1994, in search of peace and quiet and to take on the challenge of running a business, they bought this ivory-colored B&B on Long Beach Island.

The restoration of the 1865 inn is accurate to the high-Victorian era, with the exception of a 12-foot-tall mahogany reproduction of a bedroom set that a previous owner, a professional Victorian restorer, made to see how closely he could match the style. (He matched it perfectly.) There are intricately carved walnut bedroom sets, Oriental rugs, and multiple wallpapers in the bedrooms—but oh, the stained glass.

A handful of original stained-glass windows remain, but the showstoppers all over the house were made by the previous owner. The front door has a beautiful palette of vibrant colors, the dining room has a stained-glass tree, and bedroom windows blend with each color scheme. One in a front bedroom glows at daybreak, and even the outside shower has its own stained glass.

Looking beyond the windows, you can see (and hear) the ocean from most rooms. (The inn is just a half block from the dune-backed beach.) Unfortunately, the modern motels across the street generate noise on Saturday nights in summer that, according to Jane, makes it seem like "42nd Street in a bathing suit." Air conditioners mask the sound.

A multicourse breakfast is served in the dining room in winter, while in warmer months guests and lighter fare move out to the wraparound veranda, where two rooms have private entrances. Other activities on your not-so-busy agenda might include walking, cycling, rollerblading, or taking the brick path to the gazebo for some serious seaside relaxation.

🏠 *6 double rooms with baths, 3 doubles share bath. Air-conditioning in 4 rooms, fireplace in parlor, minirefrigerator in dining room, bicycles, beach tags. $100–$175; Continental breakfast Mon.–Sat. and full breakfast Sun. Memorial Day–Labor Day, full breakfast Labor Day–Memorial Day. No credit cards. No smoking indoors, no pets, 2-night minimum on weekends late June–Oct., 3-night minimum on holiday weekends Memorial Day–Labor Day.*

Sea Crest by the Sea

19 Tuttle Ave., Spring Lake, NJ 07762, tel. 732/449–9031 or 800/803–9031, fax 732/974–0403

This Queen Anne–style B&B strives to be a romantic fantasy getaway, a goal only slightly undercut by items for sale in the foyer. The friendly owners, John and Carol Kirby, opened the three-story inn in 1990 and furnished it with French and English Victorian antiques.

Rooms are inspired by characters and themes from history, literature, and such exotic realms as Casablanca and New Orleans. Favorites are the first-floor Queen Victoria suite, with four-poster bed, wicker sitting room, and whirlpool; romance-inspiring Victorian Rose, which

boasts a carved walnut bed and Victorian fainting couch; whimsical Pussy Willow, festooned with felines; and the eclectic Teddy Roosevelt suite, which has both Roosevelt memorabilia and an array of teddy bears, not to mention a tub for two in the attached soaking room. For added romance, gas fireplaces are now found in eight units as well as the parlor.

🏠 *10 double rooms with baths, 2 suites. Air-conditioning, cable TV/VCR and phones in rooms, wood-burning stove in back dining room, minirefrigerators in 3 units and full refrigerator in hall, beach tags, towels, and chairs, bicycles, croquet, on-site parking. $159–$259; full breakfast, afternoon tea. AE, MC, V. Smoking on porch only, no pets, 2-night minimum on weekends Oct.–May and on weekdays June–Sept., 3-night minimum on weekends June–Sept. and on holiday weekends.*

The Seaflower

110 9th Ave., Belmar, NJ 07719, tel. 732/681–6006

This 1907 Dutch colonial with a turret is about half a block from the beach and boardwalk, in a sleepy residential area away from the commercial district. It is decked out in a mix of antiques, newer furnishings, and seashore bric-a-brac that creates a relaxing homey feel. The suite, for example, has a queen canopy in one room and a bay with an overgrown window seat used as a bed in the other. The "window bed" is wrapped by a spread and curtains of pansies. A window seat in the living room is filled with board games.

Innkeeper Pat O'Keefe is a microbiologist, and her partner Knute Iwaszko, now retired, is a serious runner who can plan courses of any length (the shortest is about 20 feet—just far enough to collapse on the porch). Runners of all levels, from slow joggers to such world-class competitors as Greta Waitz, stay at the Seaflower, run in the local races, and celebrate afterward with Pat and Knute.

Other popular special events are Valentine's Day and mystery weekends.

🏠 *5 double rooms with baths, 1 suite. TV/VCR in parlor, minirefrigerator in hall, beach tags, bicycles, on-site parking, transportation to and from train. $80–$140; full breakfast. AE. Smoking on porch only, no pets, 2-night minimum on weekends and 3-night minimum on holiday weekends Memorial Day–Labor Day.*

SeaScape Manor

3 Grand Tour, Highlands, NJ 07732, tel. 732/291–8467, fax 732/872–7932

This oak-sheltered home, built circa-1889 with a 1928 wing, is located in the town of Highlands, an area unlike the flat scrubby coast farther south. In fact, the inn's 230-foot elevation enables guests having breakfast or drinks on the deck to gaze down on the southern end of Sandy Hook, the mouth of New York Harbor, and, on a clear day, the New York skyline.

Ocean views are found in all but one of the bedrooms, of which the loveliest are light and airy Precious Moments, which has a private deck and a soaking tub under a picture window, and the large, plant-filled, beam-ceilinged Garden Room, whose wall of windows yields the same panorama as the deck above.

When guests are not contemplating the ocean, they're often visiting it or traveling over it. Sandy Hook's Gateway National Recreation Area, which has a natural beach, lighthouse, and ranger-led programs, is a popular destination, as is New York City, just a ferry ride away. Sisters Sherry Ruby and Gloria Miller, proprietors along with Sherry's husband, Robert Adamec, also enjoy directing guests to antiquing in Red Bank and to walks to nearby Hartshorne Woods or Twin Lights, another local lighthouse.

🏠 *4 double rooms with baths. Air-conditioning in rooms, cable TV/VCR in 1 room and sitting room, fireplace in sitting room, minirefrigerator in sitting room or, in summer, on deck, bicycles, lawn games, barbecue, beach towels and chairs, recreation area passes, on-site parking, transportation to and from train, bus, and ferry. $90–$115; full breakfast. AE, MC, V. Smoking on decks only, well-behaved pets only, 2-night minimum on holiday weekends.*

The Studio

102 Cedar Ave., Island Heights, NJ 08732-0306, tel. 732/270–6058

The 1889 home of artist John F. Peto, now owned by his chatty granddaughter, Joy Peto Smiley, is on the National Register of Historic Places. It's near Barnegat Bay, Barnegat Peninsula beach resorts, and Island Beach State Park. Visitors can walk to bay-shore beaches, rent a sailboat nearby, or sit in rocking chairs on the screened porch, looking out on Toms River.

The large wainscoted room, known as the studio, dominates the first floor. On its walls are a multitude of objects—glasses and lanterns, a spinning wheel, and swords—alongside Peto's paintings, many of them dark still lifes that seem to have frozen the knickknacks in time.

Upstairs, one bedroom has a gabled wall and green beams that hover above a double bed, while a larger room, good for guests with children, has four twins, two on a raised platform behind latticework. In fact, though most visitors are couples getting away from the city, a number of features make this a good place for families. There's the simple second-floor guest kitchen (great for packing lunch for the beach), and then there's Joy's friendly husky, Yuri, who is so loved by kids he gets fan mail.

🏠 *4 double rooms share 2 baths. Air-conditioning in rooms, cable TV in sunroom, fireplaces in studio and library, bay and river beach tags, towels, and chairs, bicycles, transportation to and from bus. $85; full breakfast. AE. No cats.*

Cape May

Cape May, the southernmost resort town on the New Jersey shore, sits at the end of the Garden State Parkway, 40 minutes south of Atlantic City. Its location at the tip of the peninsula that separates Delaware Bay from the Atlantic Ocean makes for a remarkably moderate climate and enables visitors to watch the sun both rise and set over water.

Believed to be the oldest ocean resort in New Jersey, Cape May was first sighted in 1620 by the Dutch explorer Captain Cornelius Mey, who modestly named the entire peninsula after himself. Following the example of the Lenape tribe, who summered in the area for the good fishing, vacationers have been coming here for centuries. As early as the 1760s, guest houses began to appear, and in the 19th century, large numbers of southern gentry, followed by industrialists from New York, Philadelphia, and Wilmington, made Cape May the "Queen of the Seaside Resorts." They built elaborate Victorian hotels, mansions, and "cottages" (large, rambling summer places) in a variety of styles, from Gothic to Queen Anne.

In the 20th century Cape May lost most of its business to Atlantic City and the barrier-island resorts to the north, more easily reached by car or train. A catastrophic 1962 storm forced residents to take stock of what they had. America's first Urban Development Action Grant was used to create an outdoor pedestrian street, the Washington Mall, which inspired the renovation of the Victorian buildings. Today many of these structures, carefully researched and beautifully restored, live on in the city's 2-square-mile historic district.

At about the same time, Cape May attracted a group of restaurateurs, most from Philadelphia, who found the combination of fresh seafood, locally grown vegetables, and low rents an incentive to try their luck in a town that was still too far down the parkway for most tourists. Now Cape May has many eclectic restaurants, and the genteel blend of architecture and cuisine is the small town's prime attraction.

Swimming, bicycling, boating, and fishing are also popular, however, as is bird-watching in the nearby state park, site of a restored lighthouse. During spring and fall migrations, birds and birders alike flock to this strategic spot on the Eastern Flyway. Victorian Week, in early October, combines whimsy with serious lectures on Victorian history and restoration, and Christmastime brings even more tours of inns decked out in Victorian finery. Sprinkled throughout the year are festivals honoring everything from music to tulips to kites, arts and crafts to food and wine. Though summer brings the biggest crowds (and generally minimum-stay requirements of several nights), shoulder seasons still see plenty of visitors. Only from January to March does the town truly sleep.

Places to Go, Sights to See

(Also see the section on the Jersey Shore, for attractions near Cape May.)

Cape May–Lewes Ferry (north side of canal on the bay, tel. 609/886–1725, 302/426–1155, or 800/643–3779). Cars, pedestrians, and bicycles can take the 70-minute trip to or from the small town of Lewes, Delaware.

Cape May Point State Park (Lighthouse Ave., tel. 609/884–2159). An eight-minute drive from the historic district and a pleasant destination for an afternoon bike ride, this 153-acre wildlife preserve has nature trails, a small museum, and a lighthouse with 199 steps leading to a spectacular view. Swimming is discouraged from the beach because of rough tides. Offshore is a World War II bunker, which was inland when built, showing how far the shoreline has receded. The real spectacle, though, is the hawk-watch platform, where at certain times of year, throngs of bird-watchers stand, binoculars poised, to watch birds fly over. Stop by the nearby *Cape May Bird Observatory* (707 E. Lake Dr., tel. 609/884–2736 or 609/861–0466 for bird hot line) to learn what birds have been seen lately.

Historic Cold Spring Village (720 U.S. 9, tel. 609/898–2300). Interpreters in period costume re-create rural 19th-century life and crafts.

Nature cruises. Companies running marine mammal–sighting tours include *Cape May Whale Watch & Research Center* (1286 Wilson Dr., tel. 609/898–0055 or 609/898–1122) and *Cape May Whale Watcher* (2nd Ave. and Wilson Dr., tel. 609/ 884–5445 or 800/786–5445). *Tideland Tours* (1401 Harbor La., tel. 609/884–4663) and *Wildlife Unlimited* (2nd Ave. and Wilson Dr., tel. 609/884–3100) explore coastal salt marshes and their history, ecology, and plant and animal life.

Nightlife. *Carney's* (411 Beach Dr., tel. 609/884–4424), a restaurant, is the closest Cape May comes to a loud rock-and-roll bar. *The Shire* (315 Washington Mall, tel. 609/884–4700) is a genuine jazz-improv club, where styles of music also stray to reggae and rock. *The Top of the Marq* (Marquis de Lafayette Hotel, 501 Beach Dr., tel. 609/884–3500) is the place for old-style dinner and dancing.

Sunset Beach (Sunset Blvd.). As its name implies, this is a popular place to watch the sun set over Delaware Bay and is also the site of the sunken remains of the concrete ship *Atlantis*. Ocean-polished lumps of quartz, called Cape May Diamonds, can be found along the tide line.

Tours. The best way to see Cape May is to take a walking or trolley tour run by the *Mid-Atlantic Center for the Arts* (tel. 609/884–5404). *The Cape May Carriage Company* (tel. 609/884–4466) provides tours by horse and carriage.

Restaurants

Though prices are beginning to approach those in big cities, Cape May restaurants (many BYOB) still provide must-eat experiences. Most B&Bs have a stock of menus and a book of guest comments to help you decide where to go, and innkeepers can give advice and point out spots known just to locals. **Union Park** (Macomber Hotel, 727 Beach Dr., tel. 609/884–8811) and **Washington Inn** (801 Washington St., tel. 609/884–5697) offer refined dining. Superb progressive American and Continental fare in more casual settings can be had at **Freda's Cafe** (210 Ocean St., tel. 609/884–7887), **The Mad Batter** (19 Jackson St., tel. 609/ 884–5970), **Peaches at Sunset** (1 Sunset Blvd., tel. 609/898–0100), **Tisha's** (714 Beach Dr., tel. 609/884–9119), and **Waters Edge** (Beach Dr. and Pittsburgh Ave., tel. 609/884–1717). Even more informal are **Van Scoy's Bistro** (312 Carpenters' La., tel. 609/898–9898) and the **Four Seasons** (600 Park Blvd., West Cape May, tel. 609/884–7660), especially good for carryout. For seafood try the **Lobster**

House (Fisherman's Wharf, tel. 609/884–8296) or **Axelsson's Blue Claw** (Ocean Dr., tel. 609/884–5878), on the way to Wildwood Crest. Both get most of their fish right off the boats. Another good value for fresh seafood is **Menz Restaurant** (Rte. 47 and Fulling Mill Rd., Rio Grande, tel. 609/886–9500), where there is a two-headed stuffed calf and other eclectic oddities on the walls and in cases.

Tourist Information

Chamber of Commerce of Greater Cape May (Box 556, Cape May 08204, tel. 609/884–5508). **Welcome Center** (Bank and Lafayette Sts., Cape May 08204, tel. 609/884–9562 in season).

Reservation Services

Amanda's Bed & Breakfast Reservation Service (21 S. Woodland Ave., East Brunswick 08816, tel. 732/249–4944, fax 732/246–1961). **Bed & Breakfast Adventures** (2310 Central Ave., Suite 132, North Wildwood 08260, tel. 609/522–4000 or 800/992–2632 for reservations, fax 609/522–6125). **Cape May Reservation Service** (1382 Lafayette St., Cape May 08204, tel. 609/884–9396 or 800/729–7778).

The Abbey

34 Gurney St. at Columbia Ave., Cape May, NJ 08204, tel. 609/884–4506, fax 609/884–2379

Built in 1869 as a summer home for Philadelphia coal baron John B. McCreary, the Abbey was named by current owners Jay and Marianne Schatz, who thought the Gothic Revival architecture resembled a house of worship.

Actually, the Abbey comprises two buildings. Jay and Marianne, both chemists before their love of old houses and antiques brought them to Cape May, opened the main house, the Villa, in 1979. In 1986 they renovated the adjacent 1873 Second Empire house, called the Cottage. Though each house has two parlors and bedrooms named for cities with Victorian architecture (many containing something from that city), the buildings have their own styles. The Villa, with its impressive 65-foot tower, is formal and dramatic, though some of its period antiques look a bit worn. The Newport Room's tower bath makes it an unusual guest quarter. In contrast, the Cottage, its parlor furnished in wicker, feels like a summer house.

Many B&Bs have a rack with vintage hats, but the very loquacious Jay, who admits he suffers from "achapeauphobia" (the fear of being hatless) doesn't stop there. He stashes a huge assortment of hats at the Abbey, but there's no sign of a cowl or wimple.

🏠 *12 double rooms with baths, 2 suites. Air-conditioning in 10 rooms, minirefrigerators in all rooms, beach tags and chairs, croquet, on- and off-site parking. $90–$200; full breakfast, afternoon refreshments. D, MC, V. Smoking on veranda only, no pets, 2-, 3-, or 4-night minimum on weekends, closed Jan.–Mar.*

The Albert Stevens Inn

127 Myrtle Ave., Cape May, NJ 08204, tel. 609/884–4717 or 800/890–2287, fax 609/884–8320

Pause on the porch of this cheery yellow Queen Anne–style house with red and green trim, and you might spy a cat dozing on a wicker chair. Here on the edge of Cape May, a 10-minute walk to the Washington Mall or good beaches and a little removed from the bustle of the historic district, Curt and Diane Diviney-Rangen, both former businesspeople, have created a haven for cats and others eager to escape the rat race.

There are cats galore—not merely the requisite cat or two found in many B&Bs, but a veritable caboodle. Inside, the decor has both a feline and floral flair, while out back is the Cat's Garden. More than 30 cats stroll the fenced grounds, with gazebo, picnic tables, a fountain with goldfish, statuary, and hundreds of plants and herbs, including catnip, of course. About 15 make an appearance for the thrice-weekly in-season tea and tour, given for the benefit of Diane's feral-cat foundation.

But if cats are what set this place apart from other local inns, its period antiques, hearty Norwegian-style breakfasts, and friendly innkeepers make it fit right in to the Cape May B&B scene.

🏠 *7 double rooms with baths, 2 suites. Air-conditioning in rooms, TV in 1 suite, gas fireplaces in dining room and parlor, minirefrigerator on enclosed porch, beach tags and towels, hot tub Oct.–Apr., on-site parking. $85–$165; full breakfast, afternoon tea, dinner 3 times a wk late Feb.–Apr. AE, D, MC, V. Smoking on front porch only, no pets, 2-night minimum on weekends, 3-night minimum July–Aug. and holidays.*

Barnard-Good House

238 Perry St., Cape May, NJ 08204, tel.
609/884-5381

This lavender-trimmed Second Empire home has Victorian antiques in its formal parlor and a circa-1870 copper tub in one bathroom, but what it's famous for is its filling, fanciful, and altogether outrageous breakfasts.

Nan and Tom Hawkins, she formerly a marketing director for shopping centers and he an engineer, create a four-course extravaganza. Tom starts things off with his hand-squeezed or -extracted juices (never just orange juice), and from there Nan takes over. She serves a fruit course (often a fruit soup) followed by the main course—perhaps Norwegian ham pie with tomato sauce, Italian frittata, or one of Nan's many recipes with seafood or phyllo. This is complemented by a side dish and homemade bread and followed, believe it or not, by dessert, chocolate being the most popular. With a repertoire of more than 200 dishes, Nan bases her menu on what's fresh and caters to guests' dietary restrictions and preferences. Though she's cooking lighter these days, most guests still don't have room for lunch. "I've created a monster," she admits.

▦ *3 double rooms with baths, 2 suites. Air-conditioning in rooms, beach tags, towels, and chairs, outdoor shower, on-site parking. $90–$150; full breakfast, late-afternoon refreshments 3–4 times a week. MC, V. Smoking on porch only, no pets, 2-night minimum on weekends, 3-night minimum mid-June–mid-Sept., 4-night minimum on holiday weekends, closed Nov.–Apr.*

Captain Mey's Inn

202 Ocean St., Cape May, NJ 08204, tel.
609/884-7793 or 609/884-9637

In the center of town close to the Washington Mall and the beach, this 1890 house was built for a physician and named after

Cape May's Dutch discoverer. In keeping with its heritage, the house, which became an inn in 1979, is furnished with Victorian antiques and Dutch accents, including a collection of delft blue china. What was the doctor's office is now a two-bedroom suite, and his examining room is now its bathroom, with the original tiles and medicine cabinet. If you like your bathrooms over a century newer, you can opt for a cozy third-floor room under the eaves. Its enormous new bath, previously a guest room, has both a two-person whirlpool and shower.

Outside, the wonderful wraparound veranda, bordered by a sea of purple impatiens and outfitted with wicker furniture and Victorian wind curtains, is an inviting spot for breakfast or tea in warm weather. A small, walled courtyard with a tulip garden is perfect for reading and relaxing.

Owners George and Kathleen Blinn are avid fans of the Victorian era. Kathleen collects period clothes, some of which she displays on mannequins. She delights in dressing in costumes for tours and in showing her assortment of amusing undergarments to interested guests.

▦ *7 double rooms with baths, 1 suite. Air-conditioning in rooms, TV in 2 rooms, gas fireplace in dining room, minirefrigerators in 3 rooms and hall, beach tags, towels, and chairs, on-site parking. $99–$210; full breakfast, afternoon tea. AE, MC, V. Smoking on veranda only, no pets, 2-night minimum on weekends mid-Oct.–late May, 3-night minimum on weekends Memorial Day–mid-Oct., 4-night minimum on summer holiday weekends, closed Jan.*

Carroll Villa

19 Jackson St., Cape May, NJ 08204, tel.
609/884-9619, fax 609/884-0264

Those staying at this pleasantly restored Victorian hotel are in for a treat, because a stay includes breakfast at the owner's restaurant, the Mad Batter, one of Cape

May's best dining spots. The restaurant's name should tell you something about innkeeper Mark Kulkowitz's interests. If not, stepping inside will. While the aroma of the innovative cuisine whets your appetite, you can peruse the corner that pays homage to shortstop and announcer Phil Rizzuto. A baseball buff, Mark is especially fond of the Yankees of the '50s.

Built as a hotel, Carroll Villa feels like a hotel. It once had more and smaller bedrooms, but through the years walls have been removed to create more space. Though rooms are furnished with some Victorian-era antiques, the overwhelming feeling is crisp and new.

Guests have use of a separate living-room area; the glass-walled garden terrace, painted by children with bright flowers; a back terrace with a fountain and umbrella tables, off of which is the hotel's Secret Garden; and the cupola, from which the ocean and the varied roofs of Cape May can be seen. The hotel is a half block from the beach and a half block from the Washington Mall.

🏨 *22 double rooms with baths. Restaurant (closed 2 wks in Jan.), air-conditioning and phones in rooms, cable TV in 1 room and lobby, fireplace in restaurant, beach tags, off-site parking. $98–$160; full breakfast. AE, D, MC, V. Smoking on section of porch and terrace only, no pets, 2-night minimum on weekends and July–Aug., 3-night minimum on holiday weekends, closed 2 wks in Jan.*

Holly House

20 Jackson St., Cape May, NJ 08204, tel. 609/884-7365

This immaculate guest house is one of the Seven Sister properties, seven identical houses built in 1891 on the lot of a former hotel as summer rentals for well-to-do families. It is notable for its carefully detailed green-and-red exterior and the theatrical personality of its co-owner, Bruce Minnix, a TV director who ap-

peared in the music video *What Might Have Been* for the country group Little Texas. (Ask him to show it: There won't be a dry eye in the house.) Bruce was also mayor of Cape May and fought for the preservation and restoration of the town. He helped create its popular walking tours and produced and directed the video *Victorian Cape May*. His wife, Corinne, whom he describes as "the head honcho," runs the house and is often the person to greet visitors.

Guest rooms have high ceilings with ceiling fans, bright prints and fabrics complementing crisply painted or papered walls, and several large windows, from which you can get "ocean glimpses." Two rooms on the third floor have a connecting door, useful for families. Furniture runs the gamut—some antiques original to the house, some family pieces, and some Salvation Army treasures—but the overall impression is modern and free of clutter.

🏨 *5 double rooms share 2 baths. Fireplace in parlor, beach tags, off-site parking. $60–$75; no breakfast. MC, V. Smoking on porch only, no pets, closed Nov.–Apr.*

Inn at 22 Jackson

22 Jackson St., Cape May, NJ 08204, tel. 609/884-2226 or 800/452-8177, fax 609/884-0055

Interior designer Barbara Carmichael and her partner, Chip Masemore, a restoration contractor, took a circa-1898 unheated apartment house and turned it into a striking deep-blue B&B with purple-and-white trim. Rooms were combined to make one- and two-bedroom suites and were outfitted with queen or king beds, TVs, minirefrigerators, and microwaves. Some have access to a porch or private deck.

The inn is done in warm reds and greens and manages to blend decor from the 1860s to the 1930s with flights of fancy. Across from the barber's chair in the parlor is Minerva, the "head of housekeeping." In addition to being stuffed, she seems also to be stewed, for she sits proudly on the sofa, a wine glass in one hand and a bottle in her apron pocket. Chip's collection of turn-of-the-century toys, games, and bawdy women decorates the common areas. The higher in the building you go, the bawdier they get.

The adjacent Step Sister Cottage, which has two bedrooms, two baths, a sitting room with kitchenette, and porches that look down a drive to the ocean, is nice for families or others traveling together.

🏠 *4 suites, cottage. Air-conditioning, gas fireplaces in cottage and foyer, beach tags, towels, and chairs, bicycles, off-site parking. $175–$300; full breakfast, afternoon refreshments. AE, MC, V. Smoking on porches only, no pets, 2-night minimum on weekends.*

The John F. Craig House

609 Columbia Ave., Cape May, NJ 08204, tel. 609/884-0100, fax 609/898-1307

Warm hosts and cool breezes are in store at this 1866 Carpenter Gothic inn. The focus is on "the positive aspects and beauty of the Victorian era," explain owners Connie and Frank Felicetti. "We don't want stuffy." And stuffy it is not.

There are plenty of places to curl up with a good book and plenty of books from which to choose. The library's collection ranges from heirloom to modern, and guests delight in antique volumes of Victorian poetry. You can relax in the parlor, warmed by a gas fireplace in winter and naturally cooled by floor-to-ceiling windows on late afternoons in summer, just as it was 100 years ago. Or follow the morning or afternoon sun to one of the porches enveloping the inn, where cats Heckle and Jeckle might be lolling on a leash.

For another excuse to leave the guest rooms, furnished with Eastlake and Renaissance Revival antiques and named

for Craig family members, you can attend either of two breakfast seatings. Frank, an attorney turned avid chef, prepares varied menus that include pineapple ricotta muffins, ramekin eggs, Italian sausage with fennel, and nectarines with amaretto and orange—tasty sustenance for a relaxing day.

🏠 *7 double rooms with baths, 1 suite. Air-conditioning in rooms, minirefrigerators in 3rd-floor rooms and on porch, beach tags, towels, and chairs, on-site parking for those who won't use their car. $95–$175; full breakfast, afternoon tea. MC, V. Smoking on porch only, no pets, 2-night minimum on weekends, 3-night minimum mid-July–Labor Day, closed Jan.–mid-Feb.*

The Mainstay Inn

635 Columbia Ave., Cape May, NJ 08204, tel. 609/884-8690

An 1872 men's social club formerly called Jackson's Clubhouse, the Mainstay is one of Cape May's best bed-and-breakfasts. Many a gambler whiled away the hours under these 14-foot ceilings and on the lofty veranda, which, more than 100 years later, is the city's most ostentatious spot for doing nothing.

In 1976 the property was purchased by Tom Carroll, who came to Cape May to serve at the nearby Coast Guard Training Center, and his wife, Sue, a collector of antiques. In renovating the building, they made it a focal point in the move to revive Victorian Cape May as a resort town. Included in the magnificent restoration are the house's original chandeliers as well as most of the original furniture.

The first hint of the Carrolls' astonishing attention to detail is found in the foyer, where a 13-foot-by-7-foot rosewood-framed mirror, probably weighing 1,000 pounds (no one's ever taken it down to find out) hangs beneath a dramatic ceiling patterned with 17 different wallpapers. Guest rooms are named for famous Cape May visitors, such as the General Grant and Stonewall Jackson suites, which coexist as harmoniously as the elegant antiques, some of which are museum quality.

In addition to being active in Cape May historic preservation and the city's Victorian Week festivities, the Carrolls are enthusiastic fans of Victorian culture and games, the more whimsical the better. They socialize actively with guests, some of whom have been inspired to open B&Bs of their own, and turn breakfast and tea into friendly occasions. "We like guests to feel as if they're not just staying with us, but that they're part of the Mainstay's atmosphere," says Tom.

For more privacy than the main-house drawing room and its inviting gas fireplace, gaming table, and 1886 piano afford, you can steal up to the cupola, which has a distant ocean view. Or you may choose to stay in the Officers' Quarters, the "new" building across the street. Built to house military personnel during World War I, it contains four one- or two-bedroom suites that offer the modern amenities lacking in the carefully preserved Mainstay and adjacent Cottage. Each suite here has its own cable TV with VCR, phone, whirlpool bath, gas fireplace, private porch, and snack bar; breakfast is delivered to each unit. Despite the modern comforts, however, there are enough old touches, such as antique mantels in the sitting areas and back-lit stained glass in the bathrooms, to provide vintage Mainstay charm.

🏠 *9 double rooms with baths, 7 suites. Air-conditioning in 2 buildings, microwaves and minirefrigerators in 4 suites, on-site parking for 14 rooms. $150–$275; Continental-plus breakfast June–Sept., full breakfast Oct.–May, afternoon tea. No credit cards. Smoking on veranda only, no pets, 2-night minimum on weekends Oct.–May, 3-night minimum on weekends June–Sept.*

Manor House

612 Hughes St., Cape May, NJ 08204, tel. 609/884–4710, fax 609/898–0471

"The house is so warm and welcoming and comfortable," says Nancy McDonald, who, along with husband, Tom, bought this 1905 B&B in 1995. Admitted "corporate dropouts," Tom and Nancy had stayed at the Manor House several times. "It was our favorite," confesses Nancy, and when the opportunity to own it arose, they jumped at it.

The McDonalds hope visitors will relax and mingle with other guests in the fireplace room, stocked with puzzles; the garden, with umbrellas and Adirondack furniture; or the foyer, whose window seat is perfect for sipping port or sherry each afternoon. Up the oak and chestnut staircase and past the landing's stained-glass window are the guest rooms, "named after famous numbers." They are outfitted with brass and wood beds and, a nice touch, perfumes.

Another of Nancy's aims is to create food "that people wouldn't make for themselves." Everything is made from scratch, from the four-course breakfasts, which might include bread pudding and French toast with a custard sauce or frittatas with herbs and vegetables from the garden, to cheesy and chocolaty afternoon goodies, to the cookies that appear nightly.

🏠 *9 double rooms with baths, 1 suite. Air-conditioning in rooms, TV/VCR in 1 room, minirefrigerator on side porch, whirlpool in suite, beach tags, towels, and chairs, outdoor shower, off-site parking. $125–$190; full breakfast, afternoon refreshments. D, MC, V. Smoking on porch and in garden only, no pets, 2-night minimum on weekends, 3-night minimum July–Aug., closed Jan.*

The Queen Victoria

102 Ocean St., Cape May, NJ 08204, tel. 609/884-8702

A Union Jack flying from an inviting front porch full of rockers is the first sign of what the Queen Victoria is all about. Dane Wells and his elegant wife, Joan, who is active in the restoration and preservation of Victoriana nationwide, have created a genteel country inn in the center of the historic district. It's an homage to the queen, her family, and the period named for her.

Three restored seaside villas make up the property. The 1881 Second Empire—style Queen Victoria and Stick-style Prince Albert Hall are the two main buildings. They have similar facilities, such as outfitted guest pantries, and are open to all guests, who are encouraged to move between them freely. Breakfast is served in both elegant dining rooms, while a proper afternoon tea, with sweet and savory treats, is poured on the porch of one house in summer and in the other's parlor with fireplace in cooler months. Adorning the walls are historic wallpapers (two dotted with Victoria's imperial crown) and pictures of the ubiquitous queen. Furnishings are carefully researched period pieces.

Guest rooms are named for people in the Queen Victoria and for places in Prince Albert Hall, but all have appropriate items of decor, such as a framed scarf of Victoria and her court in the Mayfair Room. Accommodations range from small rooms to luxury suites, and furnishings include white wicker, brass and iron, and the dark woods of high Victorian. Cable TV is found in suites and a parlor, and many rooms have whirlpools. Regent's Park, a small cottage with fireplace adjacent to the Prince Albert, is accessible to guests with disabilities.

Across Ocean Street is the elaborately painted (try counting its colors) Queen Anne–style Queen's Cottage. Rented to families or others traveling together, it is not open to other guests. The two rooms, one of which has a gas-log fireplace, have whirlpools for two and TVs. (A new addition to the empire, the separate, European-style Queen's Hotel offers such modern amenities as in-room phones, coffeemakers, and heated towel bars as well as policies to conserve water and energy.)

Despite the adherence to period details, the Queen Victoria lacks the antiques-cluttered spaces and stiff formality of other Victorian inns. In the cozy Arts and Crafts–style parlor, with its brick fireplace, player piano, and mountain of scrolls, is a basket of *Madeleine* books, a signal that children are welcome. (A crib, high chair, trike, and blocks are also available.) In fact, all guests will feel comfortable and royally treated here.

▥ *17 double rooms with baths, 5 suites, cottage. Air-conditioning, minirefrigerators in rooms, beach tags, towels, and chairs, bicycles. $180–$275; full breakfast, afternoon tea. AE, MC, V. Smoking on porches only, no pets, 2-, 3-, or 4-night minimum on weekends and holidays.*

The Southern Mansion

720 Washington St., Cape May, NJ 08204, tel. 609/884-7171, fax 609/898-0492

At this 1863 Samuel Sloan–designed home with 1997 wing, *B&B* might as well stand for "big and bold." But it's the scale, not the number of rooms, that's grand: Many of the 40,000-square-foot hotel's rooms are 400 square feet, ample space for the mostly king-size beds. First-floor rooms in the original building have 15 ½-foot ceilings, accommodating massive armoires (some 11 feet tall) and huge paintings of nudes, which hang on intensely hued walls.

Reclaiming the house from decades as a boardinghouse took 1½ years and 200 dumpsters. Antiques, most original to the house, are worth millions. The authentic restoration and the construction of the new wing, built in the style of the original and flanked by a pair of dramatic Honduran mahogany and purpleheart circular stairs, was overseen by Rick Wilde and his wife, Barbara, who own the mansion. They married here, as they hope many couples will (the house has two ballrooms). For those not ready for a wedding, Rick suggests reserving the cupola for a romantic dinner and perhaps a proposal.

Next to be revamped are the 2-acre grounds, to include a pool–cum–Italian reflecting pond and a pool house with saunas and hot tubs. Modern amenities, facilities for corporate retreats, and a members/guests-only dining area are aimed at an exclusive clientele, and in time, management should gain the savvy and polish to match. Like the mansion, plans are big.

🏠 *15 double rooms with baths, 9 suites. Air-conditioning, cable TV and phones in rooms, gas fireplaces in 2 suites and ballrooms, beach tags, towels, and chairs, bicycles, on-site parking. $195–$350; Continental breakfast (full breakfast from menu for extra fee), afternoon tea. AE, MC, V. Smoking on porches only, no pets, 2-night minimum on weekends Oct.–May, 3-night minimum on weekends June–Sept., 4-night minimum on holiday weekends.*

Springside

18 Jackson St., Cape May, NJ 08204, tel. 609/884-2654

Like Holly House (*see above*), Springside is a Seven Sister property. It's been home to Meryl and Bill Nelson for almost 20 years, and home is exactly what it feels like. When their children moved away, the Nelsons felt a need for company, so they opened the house to teachers, professors, nurses, psychologists, actors, and others in search of lodgings that are reasonably priced without being anonymous. "We wanted to run a place where we'd be able to stay if we left home," explains Meryl. "Bill and I really enjoy meeting and being with people who are doing interesting things." Guests feel the same way.

Bill is the author of *Surfing: A Handbook* and is a boat builder. Meryl teaches desktop publishing. Together they have filled the house with items they would want to find when on the road: big comfy beds with heated mattress pads in winter, good reading light, and books and magazines in every room. Two cats, Therapy and Rochester, make themselves available for petting.

Furnishings are eclectic, with a lot of 1930s mahogany but scarcely a Victorian piece. Walls are covered in art, much of it Meryl's fine photos, and she has taken to creating faux stained-glass windows. The nicest bit of "decor," however, is the light that streams in to the many-windowed, high-ceilinged bedrooms.

🏠 *4 double rooms share 2 baths. Beach tags and chairs, off-site parking. $60–$75; Continental breakfast on weekends. MC, V. Smoking on porch only, no pets, 2-night minimum on weekends June–Sept., 3-night minimum on holiday weekends.*

The Victorian Rose

715 Columbia Ave., Cape May, NJ 08204, tel. 609/884-2497

This Gothic Revival house and adjacent cottage are almost engulfed by more than 100 rosebushes, and rosy colors and floral patterns are everywhere, from dishes to bed linens. Walls and woodwork in the parlor, which has a gas fireplace, are pink with a capital "P." Romantic guest rooms, which are furnished with antiques and pieces from the '30s and '40s, have flowered curtains and wallpapers. One has a Monet-style pond of lilies painted above the claw-foot tub in its bath as well as a gas-log stove.

The cottage, nicknamed the "Innlett," sleeps five and is good for families. A cot or crib can be provided. There is also a first-floor suite with its own entrance.

Innkeeper Bob Mullock, who leads town walking tours, is very involved in helping orphans worldwide. While he's gone, his wife, Linda, holds the fort. She enjoys gardening and cooking the B&B's sitdown breakfasts.

🏠 5 double rooms with baths, 2 doubles share bath, 2 housekeeping suites, cottage. Air-conditioning in 4 rooms and cottage, cable TV in suites and cottage, minirefrigerator on each floor, beach tags. $88–$145; full breakfast, afternoon refreshments. No credit cards. No pets, 2-night minimum on weekends mid-Oct.–May, 3-night minimum on weekends June–Sept., closed Dec.–Mar.

The Virginia Hotel

25 Jackson St., Cape May, NJ 08204, tel. 609/884–5700 or 800/732–4236, fax 609/884–1236

Though this small hotel was built in 1879, the interior is completely modern, thanks in part to a 1997 fire. Taking the opportunity to gut large sections of the front of the hotel, management added a lighter mood to the common areas downstairs and upgraded 10 rooms upstairs, adding bathroom phones and some whirlpool tubs and glass-enclosed showers. Otherwise, rooms, which vary in size, have the same decor and amenities. Their cherry and poplar furnishings are contemporary pieces with Victorian lines, designed by John Kennedy, a popular furniture designer.

Offering such features as turndown service, a morning newspaper, room service, privileges at local golf clubs, and a conference room with the latest equipment, the Virginia is a full-service hotel on an intimate scale, and is superb for executive retreats and weddings. Kids are welcome, and cribs and roll-away beds are available. At the Ebbit Room Restaurant, Cape May–eclectic cuisine is served—grilled seafood and meats, unusual sauces, and rich desserts (dinner is $70 for two). You can enjoy a drink and live piano music by the lobby fireplace.

🏠 24 double rooms with baths. Restaurant, bar, air-conditioning, cable TV/VCR and phones in rooms, videotape rentals, beach tags, towels, and chairs, reduced-rate fitness club passes, valeted off-site parking. $180–$295; Continental breakfast. AE, D, DC, MC, V. No smoking in restaurant, no pets, 2-night minimum on weekends off-season, 3-night minimum on weekends in season.

The Wooden Rabbit

609 Hughes St., Cape May, NJ 08204, tel. 609/884–7293, fax 609/898–0842

What? A B&B in Cape May that isn't Victorian? This 1838 Federal house on a quiet tree-lined street is decorated country-style, with braided rugs, quilted pillows, and the storybook characters of Beatrix Potter. Debbie Burow has been a Potter fan from the cradle, and rabbit figurines, dolls, and illustrations run rampant through her house. "One of our guests counted 40 rabbits in the dining room and living room, and there are others about the house," Greg Burow says. "They tend to multiply." Actually, the house is only primarily rabbit; other mammals, including several affectionate cats, call the Wooden Rabbit home. Children of all ages, and their parents, are welcome at this playful and cozy inn.

Bedrooms have brass or wood beds, lacy curtains, and pull-out sofas. The entire third floor has been turned into a two-bedroom suite. On nice days, guests take tea on the glassed-in sunporch, furnished in white wicker and cool blues. In cold weather, they can warm by the fire in either the dining or living room.

🏠 2 double rooms with baths, 2 suites. Air-conditioning and TV in rooms, beach tags and chairs, on-site parking. $160–$190; full breakfast, afternoon tea. D, MC, V. No smoking, no pets, 2-night minimum on weekends, 3- or 4-night minimum July–Aug.

Delaware

The Boulevard Bed & Breakfast, **1**

Cantwell House, **3**

Eli's Country Inn, **8**

The Inn at Canal Square, **5**

The New Devon Inn, **6**

The Pleasant Inn, **9**

Spring Garden Bed & Breakfast Inn, **10**

The Towers, **4**

Wild Swan Inn, **7**

William Penn Guest House, **2**

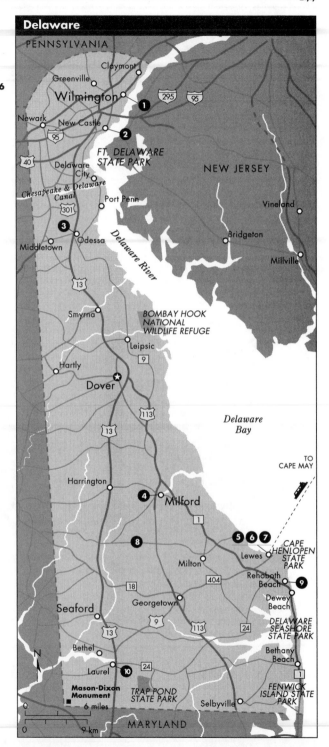

Wilmington/Northern Delaware

Delaware is all of 96 miles long and 9 to 35 miles wide, but for such a small state, it has a lot to offer. Most people know about its long chain of Atlantic beaches, but Delaware's other points of interest are seldom touted on billboards. This is especially true in the industrialized northern section of the state, where travelers zooming to Washington or New York on I–95 can easily bypass the sights worth seeing. Wilmington, the state's commercial hub, has tried to polish its cosmopolitan image by creating a downtown pedestrian mall and restoring some old buildings, including the Victorian Grand Opera House, now home of the Delaware Symphony.

It's easy to track down the extraordinary legacy of Delaware's First Family; the name du Pont is on smokestacks and street signs everywhere. The French du Ponts came to northern Delaware around 1800 and by 1920 were the wealthiest clan in the United States. They built estates, such as Winterthur, in the rolling countryside north of Wilmington, where they could show off their gunpowder fortunes. Today you'd have to travel to the Loire Valley to see such breathtaking châteaus.

To get a taste of Colonial America in the setting of a living village, head southeast from Wilmington to New Castle, on the Delaware River. The Swedes settled here around 1640; the Dutch came next, and in 1664 the British took possession. But the town's glory days came in the 18th century, when it attracted the Colonial world's rich and famous, including Washington and Lafayette. When the boundary between Delaware and Pennsylvania was surveyed, it was drawn as the arc of a circle whose center was the cupola of New Castle's courthouse. Today the cupolaed courthouse, narrow alleyways, hitching posts, mossy graveyards, and emerald town common remain much the same as they were then.

South of Wilmington are other villages redolent of the past; some, like Odessa and Delaware City, on the banks of the Chesapeake and Delaware Canal, are even quieter than New Castle. From Delaware City it's a 10-minute ferry ride aboard the Miss Kathy *to Pea Patch Island in the Delaware River, site of Fort Delaware, the largest historic fort in the country. Dating from 1823, the fort has massive ramparts from which nesting herons can be seen in the marshes below.*

Places to Go, Sights to See

Bombay Hook Wildlife Refuge (north of Leipsic on Rte. 9, tel. 302/653–6872). On these 15,978 acres of tidal marsh and timberland, muskrats, otters, white-tailed deer, and opossums make their homes, and as many as 50,000 Canada geese visit in season. The refuge offers both driving routes and walking paths.

Delaware Art Museum (2301 Kentmere Pkwy., Wilmington, tel. 302/571–9590). The English Pre-Raphaelite painters have their own gallery at this Wilmington museum, as does the illustrator Howard Pyle. In 1987 a new wing was added to accommodate sculpture, painting, ceramics, and photographs by American masters of the past 150 years, including Winslow Homer, N.C. Wyeth, and Andrew Wyeth.

Hagley Museum and Library (Greenville, tel. 302/658–2400). Here you can see how the du Ponts harnessed the waters of the Brandywine River to run a powder mill nearby. Eleutherian Mills, a modest, 12-room, white Georgian house where the first five generations of American du Ponts lived, is set on Hagley's manicured 230 acres, which feature a lovely French garden and a collection of antique autos.

Hotel du Pont (tel. 302/656–8121). At Wilmington's "company hotel," built in 1913, the du Ponts went to extremes to surround guests with the best: coffered ceilings, travertine marble walls, and a million-dollar collection of Andrew Wyeth canvasses in the Brandywine-Christina dining room. This is a place to see and be seen.

Nemours Mansion and Gardens (Rockland Rd., off Rte. 141, tel. 302/651–6912). Alfred I. du Pont's 77-room "little Versailles," situated on 300 acres, is a pink Louis XVI château. Along with gold-leaf ceilings, crystal chandeliers, and Aubusson carpets, Alfred loved gadgets, which explains the state-of-the-art 1910 bathrooms, steam cabinet, bowling alley, and spring-water-bottling generator.

Odessa. This Georgian architectural treasure trove of a town stands on the banks of the swampily atmospheric Appoquinimink River. The Brick Hotel Gallery here (tel. 302/378–4069) houses rotating exhibits of American decorative arts and furniture. The Historic District is listed on the National Register of Historic Places, and guided tours of the historic houses are the perfect way to taste the life of the 18th- and 19th-century families who inhabited them.

Wilmington and Western Railroad (tel. 302/998–1930). A steam-power iron horse leaves Greenbank Station (on Rte. 41, west of Wilmington) on Sunday (and Saturday in summer) for trips into Delaware's Red Clay Valley. Dinner trains and murder mystery trains are also available.

Winterthur Museum-Garden-Library (Rte. 52 north of Wilmington, tel. 302/888–4600 or 800/448–3883). This 200-room estate in a lush 64-acre garden sits amid nearly 1,000 acres; the museum contains one of the world's prime collections of American decorative arts (1640–1840).

Restaurants

In New Castle, the **Cellar Gourmet** (tel. 302/323–0999) in the William Janvier House is an informal spot for soup and sandwiches.

Odessa has a population of just more than 300, so your dining options are somewhat limited. Try the **Market Place Restaurant** (tel. 302/378–0688) on South Du Pont Highway, where "wing dings" are de rigueur and faded gingham triumphs. You can get a colossal 8-ounce "gourmet burger" on a kaiser bun with steak fries for $3.35.

Wilmington has a four-star restaurant in the **Green Room** (tel. 302/594–3154) at the Hotel du Pont, but reserve at Pennsylvania Avenue's **Columbus Inn** (tel. 302/571–1492) for a special night out at half the price. If you enjoy Tuscan cuisine, don't miss **Grigilia Toscana** (tel. 302/654–8001) at the Rockford Shops at 14th and Dupont streets. The northern Italian menu features meat and fish prepared on an open grill and other dishes done in a wood-burning oven.

Tourist Information

Delaware Tourism Office (99 Kings Hwy., Box 1401, Dover 19903, tel. 800/441–8846). **Greater Wilmington Convention and Visitors Bureau** (100 W. 10th St., Suite 20, Wilmington 19801–1661, tel. 302/652–4088 or 800/422–1181). **New Castle Visitors Bureau** (Box 465, New Castle 19720, tel. 302/322–8411 or 800/758–1550).

Reservation Service

Bed & Breakfast of Delaware (2701 Landon Dr., Suite 200, Wilmington 19810, tel. 302/479–9500).

The Boulevard Bed & Breakfast

1909 Baynard Blvd., Wilmington, DE 19802, tel. 302/656–9700, fax 302/656–9701

It's been more than 10 years since Charles and Judy Powell said good-bye to suburbia and moved to downtown Wilmington's fashionable Baynard Boulevard to realize their dream of opening a bed-and-breakfast. The attractive house they chose, in the Triangle section of town, is a wonderful six-bedroom dwelling with a red-tile roof, neo-Georgian elements in the facade, and eccentric, fluted columns with Doric capitals. Inside, there's a graceful "good morning" staircase (couples descend via separate routes and meet for a kiss at the landing), a window seat, large leaded windows, and more fluted columns. Equally noteworthy are the elaborate Mueller tile surrounding the library fireplace, and Judy's mammoth industrial range, where she cooks breakfast.

The Powells attract a frequently returning business clientele (they offer open meeting space for their business guests), but families do well here, too, because of the proximity of Brandywine Park and Children's Zoo, and the easy drive to the many Brandywine Valley attractions.

▥ *3 double rooms with baths, 1 double and 1 single share bath, 1 suite. Air-conditioning, cable TV, phones in rooms, fireplaces in library and parlor, whirlpool in suite, off-street parking. $60–$80; full breakfast. AE, MC, V. No smoking indoors, no pets.*

Cantwell House

107 High St., Odessa, DE 19730, tel. 302/378–4179

A narrow, sea-green Victorian built about 1840, Cantwell House is the only bed-and-breakfast in Odessa, a little-known historic village on the Appoquinimink River. Surrounded by fertile fields, the town fared well as a Colonial cosmopolitan center, but the railroad passed it by, and today it is charmingly frozen in time. The houses are lovingly maintained, and there's a branch of the Winterthur Museum here. The Corbit-Sharp House, built by a Quaker tanner in 1774; the Brick Hotel, displaying American crafts; and the Wilson-Warner House are just three of Odessa's architectural gems.

Many faithful patrons of this small, immaculately kept establishment are parents of prep-school students attending nearby St. Andrew's (where *Dead Poets Society* was filmed). The rooms, furnished with country antiques, are somewhat small, but one has a canopy bed and another has a fireplace. At press time, a new barn-style house was under construction on the property. Scheduled to open in spring of 1998, it will accommodate up to five people.

Proprietress Carole Coleman never serves any guest the same breakfast twice. She always puts out rolls, coffee, juice, and fresh fruit, and then each day she adds such items as French toast or eggs. Look to Carole also for local antiquing possibilities—she's an active auctioneer, and she knows her stuff.

▥ *2 double rooms share bath, 1 suite. Air-conditioning in suite and 2nd-floor canopy bedroom, TV in suite, fireplace in one bedroom and in living room, dining room, and kitchen. $55–$85; Continental-plus breakfast. No credit cards. No smoking, no pets.*

William Penn Guest House

206 Delaware St., New Castle, DE 19720, tel. 302/328–7736

A historic marker stands on the streets of New Castle, a block from the banks of the Delaware River: "Near here October 27, 1682, William Penn first stepped on

American soil. . . ." In the same year that Penn strode onto the shores of the New World, and on the same streets that he first trod, the William Penn Guest House appeared on the map, though perhaps not with quite the same historic significance. But Penn knew a good thing when he saw it; ask Irma Burwell, who runs the place now, and she will tell you how the founder of Pennsylvania would sometimes bed down here.

Irma will also tell you what she and her husband, Dick, charged when they started their bed-and-breakfast operation in 1956: $8 a night. Rates are still surprisingly reasonable, and they're not likely to rise in the near future, since the hosts like the sensibilities and spending habits of their longtime clientele (repeat visitors account for two-thirds of their business). The Burwells welcome an international set of diverse ages and tastes—senior ambassadors who snooze and dewy-cheeked naturalists who cycle—all of whom appreciate a quiet, civilized atmosphere that doesn't cost them an unearthly sum.

The William Penn is a handsomely restored, impressively maintained Colo-nial structure that is modest in its air and amenities. Soft, wide-board Delaware-pine floors, a claw-foot tub, and an 18th-century chandelier in the dining room take guests back to an earlier era. The bedrooms—one with king-size bed, another with one set of twins, and two with doubles—are carpeted blandly and furnished with pine antiques. If air-conditioning turns you off, there are ceiling fans to keep both second-floor units cool and ventilated in the summer.

You'll find the William Penn a perfect jumping-off point for touring Longwood Gardens, the Brandywine River Museum, Winterthur, the Hagley Museum, and Nemours Mansion. Cyclists in particular will delight in the area: The house borders Battery Park, which runs right along the river and has a 2-mile biking path and promenade, as well as benches, picnic tables, tennis courts, and play areas for children.

▦ *4 doubles with 2 baths (can be shared or private). Air-conditioning, TV in 3 rooms. $60–$85; Continental breakfast. No credit cards. No smoking indoors, no pets.*

The Beaches

As the first warm weekend in May heralds the arrival of summer, the sun-starved citizens of Washington, Baltimore, and Wilmington pack their beach umbrellas and head for Delaware's Atlantic coast—a 25-mile strip of sand and surf stretching from the hamlet of Lewes to the Maryland state line. Here they find three splendid state parks, a handful of beach towns, and opportunities aplenty for sailing, fishing, clamming, and biking.

Rehoboth Beach is the undisputed nerve center of the Delaware seashore. It sprang up as a Methodist camp–meeting ground in the 1870s (Rehoboth means "one more sinner") and was overrun by sun worshipers when the railroad reached it 10 years later. Although some vintage Victorian structures (such as the Anna Hazzard Museum and the recently restored railroad station) remain, most of Rehoboth's ocean-side motels, downtown shops, and cottages date from the 20th century. The town is beloved above all by families with children. The city's recreation department schedules concerts in the bandstand; waterfront volleyball, football, and softball games; children's arts-and-crafts programs; and teen dance parties. It's all very wholesome:

This place is stuck in the early 1960s and is not about to budge. For nightlife you'll have to head south to nearby Dewey Beach, the seashore's hot spot for singles.

Nearby Henlopen Acres, Lake Gerar, and Silver Lake attract wealthy city families who have built handsome summer homes. With its variety of upscale specialty shops and restaurants, downtown Rehoboth caters to the older, moneyed crowd that has been coming to the town for generations.

If the bustle of Rehoboth and Dewey gets to be too much, you'll find other, more peaceable sandy kingdoms at the nearby Delaware Seashore, Cape Henlopen, and Fenwick Island state parks. There you can swim, try surf fishing, or go boating. Bethany Beach, a peaceful resort where well-kept summer homes far outnumber the few shops and restaurants, lies 10 miles south of Rehoboth. Watch for Saturday-night fried-chicken and oyster dinners at the town's fire hall.

To the north is historic Lewes (pronounced lew-is), a port community at Cape Henlopen, where charter fishing is a big draw. Nowadays Lewes is well known as the Delaware terminus of the Cape May–Lewes Ferry. It was first settled by the Dutch in 1631 as a whaling colony. Unlike Rehoboth and Bethany, it is a year-round destination, so you won't barrel into locked doors at restaurants and crafts shops in the dead of winter. April heralds the Great Delaware Kite Festival at Cape Henlopen State Park; July is the month for the town's annual antiques show and sale; and the Christmas House Tour, sponsored by the Lewes Historical Society, precedes the Christmas Parade and a tree-lighting celebration in December.

Places to Go, Sights to See

Bandstands (tel. 302/227–6181). In summertime, Rehoboth and Bethany beaches hold concerts and musical events at their beachside bandstands.

Cape May–Lewes Ferry (Lewes, tel. 302/645–6346 or 800/643-3779). This fleet of five vessels cruises across Delaware Bay in a 70-minute trip connecting Colonial Lewes and Victorian Cape May.

Delaware's beach state parks. *Fenwick Island* (tel. 302/539–9060), at the south end of Route 1, is bordered by Little Assawoman Bay and the wide Atlantic; it's one of the few spots along the coast where surfing is permitted. *Delaware Seashore* (tel. 302/227–2800), on a largely undeveloped, 7-mile strip of sand between Dewey Beach and Bethany, has facilities for camping, boating, fishing, and swimming. Among the shifting sands of *Cape Henlopen* (tel. 302/645–8983) is the 80-foot Great Dune (thought to be the largest dune between Cape Cod and Cape Hatteras). The 3,320 acres of shoreline at this park contain piping plover nests and cranberry bogs.

Fenwick Island Lighthouse (tel. 302/539–2100). Built in 1859, the 1,500-pound light still shines near the strait between Assawoman and Little Assawoman bays. To the south side of the light you'll find the first marker laid in the Mason-Dixon survey of 1751.

Laurel. The historic town of Laurel, which lies across Broad Creek from Bethel on the site of a Nanticoke Indian reservation, contains 800 buildings listed on the National Register of Historic Places. The free Woodland cable ferry carries hikers over the upper Nanticoke River.

Lewes Princess (tel. 302/645–8862). Take a two-hour dinner cruise of Lewes Harbor aboard this 65-foot double-deck vessel, departing from Fisherman's Wharf. It seats about 80 for dinner.

Milton (tel. 302/684–1101). Situated on the Broadkill River, just a few miles west of Lewes, the town of Milton is well known for some of Delaware's most beautiful Victorian homes and great ice cream. Nearby, at the **Prime Hook National Wildlife Refuge,** millions of migratory birds make an annual stop. There are good trails for hiking and bird-watching, and several ponds at Prime Hook Creek provide canoeing and fishing.

Queen Anne's Railroad (730 King's Hwy., Lewes, tel. 302/644–1720). Take a one-hour excursion or a two-and-a-half-hour murder mystery train ride on the *Royal Zephyr* from March through December.

Trap Pond State Park (tel. 302/875–5153). This 965-acre park, shaded by bald cypresses and loblolly pines, features wilderness canoe trails, fishing, and a swimming area that provides "wet wheelchairs" for persons with disabilities.

Zwaanendael Museum (tel. 302/645–1148). In 1631, 32 Dutch settlers began clearing land in Lewes, only to be massacred by the Leni-Lenape tribe. That sadly terminated colony, and Lewes's Dutch heritage, are remembered at this museum, a replica of the fantastically ornamented city hall of the Dutch city Hoorn. The Zwaanendael (Valley of the Swans) was built to commemorate the 300th anniversary of Lewes. Inside, you'll find an interesting exhibit of artifacts from the British ship *DeBraak*, which sank off the Atlantic Coast in 1798.

Restaurants

In Lewes, **Gilligan's** (tel. 302/645–7866), **The Buttery** (tel. 302/645–7755, located in the New Devon Inn), and **Kupchick's** (tel. 302/645–0420) are your best bets, but prices are stiff for this region. The dark, warm, and clubby **Rose and Crown Restaurant and Pub** (tel. 302/645–2373) sells every known kind of beer. If you're a child of the '50s or '60s and you summered at any of the Delaware beach resorts, you know **Grotto's Grand Slam** (tel. 302/645–4900) like your mother knows Dr. Spock.

Rehoboth Beach is replete with fast-food franchises and boardwalk candy shops, but a decade-long culinary boom, fueled by enterprising young chefs, as well as exacting diners from Washington, D.C., Philadelphia, and Baltimore, has brought lots of first-rate eateries. Among the most chic are **Blue Moon** (tel. 302/227–6515) and **La La Land** (tel. 302/227–3887). **Sydney's Blues and Jazz** (tel. 302/227–1339) serves New Orleans–influenced American cooking along with jazz. **Dogfish Head Brewery** (tel. 302/226–2739) is Delaware's first brew pub and also offers live music. **Woody's Bar & Grill** (tel. 302/227–2561), in the Dinner Bell Inn, is casual but has an upscale air. **Nicola's Pizza** (tel. 302/226–2654) stands out from its competitors. **Pierre's Pantry** (tel. 302/227–7537) does a fast takeout business and has tables for sit-down dining. Dewey Beach touts the casual **Rusty Rudder** (tel. 302/227–3888) for crabs.

In Milford, the **Banking House Restaurant** (tel. 302/422–5708) on Front Street serves a wide selection of beef, poultry, and seafood. The plain-faced **Geyer's** (tel. 302/422–5327) offers easy-on-the-wallet prices and a child-welcoming environment.

Tourist Information

Bethany-Fenwick Chamber of Commerce (Box 1450, Bethany Beach 19930, tel. 302/539–2100 or 800/962–7873). **Delaware Tourism Office** (99 Kings Hwy., Box 1401, Dover 19903, tel. 800/441–8846). **Lewes Chamber of Commerce** (Box 1, Lewes 19958, tel. 302/645–8073). **Rehoboth Beach–Dewey Beach Chamber of Commerce** (Box 216, 501 Rehoboth Ave., Rehoboth Beach 19971, tel. 302/227–2233 or 800/441–1329). **Sussex County Convention & Tourism Commission** (Box 1273, Bethany Beach 19930, tel. 302/856–1818).

Reservation Services

Bed & Breakfast of Delaware (2701 Landon Dr., Suite 200, Wilmington 19810, tel. 302/479–9500).

Eli's Country Inn

Rte. 36 Greenwood–Milford Rd., Greenwood, DE 19950-0779, tel. 302/349–4265 or 800/594–0048, fax 302/349–9340

The seven Shrock sisters grew up on a 160-acre family farm midway between (and a half hour from) Dover and Delaware's Atlantic beaches in the Mennonite community of Greenwood. In 1992 they converted the family farmhouse into Eli's, an eight-bedroom B&B, and began farming 70 acres, planting hay meadows and corn and soybean fields. Although you're just 8 miles from the wealthy town of Milford, you can "hear the quiet" from the house's large wraparound front porch, while strolling the nature paths that surround the property, or while watching the sunsets from the garden.

The sisters can provide a country dinner (by reservation) in the informal dining room. Ask about a hot-air balloon flight after breakfast with a launch from the front lawn.

Eli's is a good place for children, because the large lawn is well suited for badminton, volleyball, and horseshoes. The inn is also one of three stops packaged in the Biking Inn to Inn Delaware (tel. 800/845–9939) program.

▥ *8 double rooms with baths. Air-conditioning, TV room. $65–$75; Continental breakfast. D, MC, V. No smoking.*

The Inn at Canal Square

122 Market St., Lewes, DE 19958, tel. 302/645–8499 or 800/222–7902, fax 302/645–7083

This decidedly upscale inn is a relatively new addition to the lodging scene in Lewes, a small, historic town that serves as both a gateway to the Atlantic beaches and a peaceful retreat for travelers along the Atlantic seaboard. This inn is special because of its waterfront location and unusual accommodation choices. Aside from 19 conventional rooms in the main building, travelers here can also opt for the *Legend of Lewes*, a houseboat with modern galley, two bedrooms, and two baths that floats peacefully at dockside (this arrangement is not recommended for families with children under 14). The inn is conveniently situated in a meandering complex of shops and a restaurant. Design purists may protest the stylistic mélange; the exterior of the inn looks like a developer's reproduction of a Nantucket village, yet the decor in the lobby resembles the interior of a typical Malibu hideaway.

In the three-story main building, the rooms are large and furnished with Federal reproductions. The honeymoon suite (Room 305) has Palladian windows and a private balcony. It is not terribly spacious, but it's cozy, enjoys the best view in the inn, and has a queen-size bed. King-size-bed advocates have their pick of three rooms on the top floor.

The simple Continental breakfast can be eaten downstairs or taken back to the bedrooms on trays. Innkeeper Lonnie Brown recommends Gilligan's, the restaurant next door, open daily in season, from 11 AM to 1 AM, or the Buttery.

Besides Lewes's Zwaanendael Museum and historic district, there are the beaches of Cape Henlopen State Park to keep you occupied; or you can try your hand at hooking a shark from a chartered fishing boat. If you're a shopper, you'll enjoy the no-sales-tax outlet stores.

▥ *17 double rooms with baths, 1 suite, 1 houseboat. Air-conditioning, cable TV and phones in bedrooms; conference room. $135–$165; Continental breakfast; houseboat $225 ($1,300 a wk). AE, D, DC, MC, V. No pets, 2-day minimum daily in houseboat, and in main building, weekends Memorial Day–Oct. and on some holiday weekends.*

The New Devon Inn

2nd and Market Sts., Box 516, Lewes, DE 19958, tel. 302/645–6466 or 800/824–8754, fax 302/645–7196

This hotel, with its striped awnings and lobby-level stores, opened in 1989 in the heart of Lewes's historic district. It has fine views of St. Peter's Episcopal Church and historic cemetery. Built in 1926, it received a complete makeover beginning in 1986 at the hands of its owners, Dale Jenkins and Bernard Nash. Little remains of its past except the lustrous heart-of-pine floors.

The guest rooms are furnished with antiques and beds swaddled in designer linens. They are relatively small but warmly appointed, immaculately clean, and quite comfortable. The corner rooms (108, for example) are the ones most requested. Room 101, with a double bed, receives buckets of early morning sunlight. There is turndown service, candy and cordials in the rooms, and morning coffee served in delicate antique cups. Silver service, crystal, and china make the Continental breakfast special.

Of late the New Devon Inn has become known as a politician's hideout—Senators Simon and Biden have both stayed here to escape media frenzy—and business travelers can rely on a highly professional staff.

🏠 *24 double rooms with baths, 2 suites. Air-conditioning, phones in bedrooms. $85–$170; Continental breakfast. AE, D, MC, V. No pets.*

The Pleasant Inn

31 Olive Ave., Rehoboth Beach, DE 19971, tel. 302/227–7311

In Rehoboth Beach, Peck Pleasanton's place is an anomaly, an inn with an adult air where you can imagine mature couples playing canasta on the porch until late and periodically ambling over to the wet bar to freshen their gin and tonics. The big, foursquare Victorian with its widow's walk was built right on the boardwalk but was moved to its present location, just one block from the ocean, following the Great Storm of 1918. It is one of Rehoboth's most coveted properties.

There are 10 double rooms in the house plus a downstairs kitchen-apartment and a studio. The guest rooms are furnished with well-worn items that may be old but are probably not antiques. All have private baths. A carriage house out back that sleeps four is rented by the week. Peck himself is a no-nonsense, slow-talking man who looks and acts as if he's seen it all. (Ask him to show you his collection of old photographs of Rehoboth.) He doesn't provide breakfast for his guests, although numerous restaurants and cafés are within easy walking distance.

🏠 *10 double rooms with baths, 2 1-bedroom apartments, 1-bedroom carriage house. Air-conditioning, limited off-street parking. $95–$150; no breakfast. No smoking, no pets, 3-day minimum on holidays.*

Spring Garden Bed & Breakfast Inn

R.D. 5, Box 283A, Delaware Ave. Extended, Laurel, DE 19956, tel. 302/875–7015

This inn reveals its character slowly and subtly. It's an abundantly lived-in place that is deeply appreciated by its owner, Gwen North. She was raised by her parents in this half-Colonial, half-Victorian farmhouse on the outskirts of Laurel before she flew the coop for New York. During that absence she came to realize that her heart lay back at home. Says Gwen, "When you stay in the same place all your life, you stop seeing what's there."

What's here is a red-shutter country house that stands beside a creek lined with daylilies in spring. As pleasant as its exterior is, the inside is even better. The Colonial section, built between 1760 and 1780 by a Captain Lewis of Bethel, remained in the Lewis family for 100 years. Its front parlor and back kitchen have wood-plank floors and the snug, slightly off-kilter feeling of a boat. Breakfast, highlighted by Scotch eggs and homegrown fruit, is served beside a wood-burning stove.

A steep, narrow staircase takes guests to the inn's two Colonial rooms; the one called Naomi (for Gwen's mother) has a fireplace, a lace-canopy double bed, and a walnut rocker. Three bedrooms in the Victorian section, added in the late 1800s, have views of the garden and are filled with a soothing collection of antique furnishings, including a Victorian spool bed and Belgian cathedral chairs.

The Atlantic beaches are about 20 miles from the inn, but Gwen is quick to point out the other diversions to be found in this landlocked region of Delaware, such as canoeing and fishing at Trap Pond State Park and exploring the historic districts of Bethel and Laurel. An antiques dealer, Gwen sells collected pieces in a barn next to the inn.

Tops among the activities here is bicycling, a pastime Gwen has encouraged by organizing the Biking Inn to Inn Delaware program (tel. 800/845–9939), a three-day tour that includes stays at Spring Garden, the New Devon Inn, and Eli's Country Inn. The route takes bikers along the flat back roads of the Eastern Shore and offers opportunities for crabbing, bird-watching, and swimming.

▥ *4 double rooms with baths, 2 doubles share bath. Air-conditioning, TV in sitting room, 3 fireplaces. $65–$85; full breakfast. No credit cards. Smoking in designated areas, no pets.*

The Towers

101 N.W. Front St., Milford, DE 19963, tel. 302/422–3814; 800/366–3814 outside DE

Edgar Allan Poe's friend and fellow poet John Lofland lived at the Towers, which was once the Milford home of Lofland's stepfather, Dr. John Wallace. Lofland was an opium addict and Poe an alcoholic, but in their wildest hallucinations neither could have dreamed up a house like the Towers, a steamboat Gothic palace adorned with 10 varieties of gingerbread painted in 12 colors. Here flamboyant Victoriana radiates from the cherry, mahogany, and walnut finishings. Inside, the music room has a coffered sycamore ceiling and an 1899 Knabe grand piano. You're likely to find a record—perhaps Gene Autry's rendition of "Rudolph the Red-Nosed Reindeer"— spinning on the Victrola. The parlor is decorated with French antiques, and the dining room provides views of the gazebo, pool deck, and rose garden in back.

The warm but unobtrusive custodians of this 200-year-old marvel (it's on the National Register of Historic Places) are Rhonda and Daniel Bond, who bought it in January 1992 and now live on the premises in the old servants' quarters. They couldn't resist the ubiquitous stained glass, the carved garlands on the fireplaces, and the gold leaf peeking from behind the plywood walls. Rhonda can tell you about the Italian architect commissioned in the 1890s to transform the structure into the Victorian extravaganza you see today; it is said that between $30,000 and $40,000 was spent on that renovation.

The Tower room on the second floor is a favorite, with a turret niche and lots of rosy stained glass. The third floor's two suites are a bit more modern in character but still whimsically wonderful. All four doubles have their own bathrooms, but guests occupying the second-floor rooms must walk through a common area to enter theirs, and the third-floor facilities have showers only.

Rhonda fortifies her guests for a day of exploring or antiquing with a full breakfast—often ricotta pancakes, served with fresh fruit or raspberry purée and ham. The inn is across the street from one of Delaware's premier eating establishments, the Banking House, which is also an 18th-century-inspired bed-and-breakfast. Dinner at the Banking House and a stay at the Towers is a perfect combination.

🏠 *4 double rooms with baths. Air-conditioning, gas-log fireplaces in music room and dining room, pool. $95–$125; full breakfast. MC, V. No smoking, no pets.*

Wild Swan Inn

525 Kings Hwy., Lewes, DE 19958, tel. and fax 302/645-8550

There's a pink Victorian house across from the library in Lewes where you can be serenaded with music from a 1912 player piano, an original 1908 Edison phonograph, or a mahogany pre–World War I Victrola. The 1900s house was built and originally occupied by Captain Arthur Hudson, who ran the Fenwick Island Lightship. Inside the classic Queen Anne Victorian-style home are high ceilings, delicately carved scroll-work, lavish wallpaper, antique furnishings, lots of eclectic collectibles, and typical Victorian detail in pattern and color.

During their five years as innkeepers, Hope and Mike Tyler have attracted lots of media attention. The recipe for their signature honey banana raisin bread has appeared in more than one cookbook. Guests are treated to even more than that: a big formal breakfast in the dining room under brass "gasolier" chandeliers. At the end of a busy day you may look forward to a cool glass of sun tea or a cordial on the porch gazebo or in the privacy of the poolside patio garden. There's plenty of fine, fun dining in Lewes, just a walk away. When you return to your room at night, you'll find it's been freshened and a plate of cookies will be waiting at your bedside.

🏠 *3 rooms with baths. Air-conditioning, bikes, gazebo, pool. $120 (mid-May–mid-Oct.), $85 (mid-Oct.–mid-May); full breakfast. No credit cards. No smoking, no pets, 2-night minimum on weekends.*

In case you want to see the world.

At American Express, we're here to make your journey a smooth one. So we have over 1,700 travel service locations in over 120 countries ready to help. What else would you expect from the world's largest travel agency?

do more ®

http://www.americanexpress.com/travel

Travel

In case you want to be welcomed there.

We're here to see that you're always welcomed at establishments everywhere. That's why millions of people carry the American Express® Card – for peace of mind, confidence, and security, around the world or just around the corner.

do more ®

Cards

In case you're running low.

We're here to help with more than 118,000 Express Cash locations around the world. In order to enroll, just call American Express before you start your vacation.

do more®

AMERICAN EXPRESS

Express Cash

Maryland

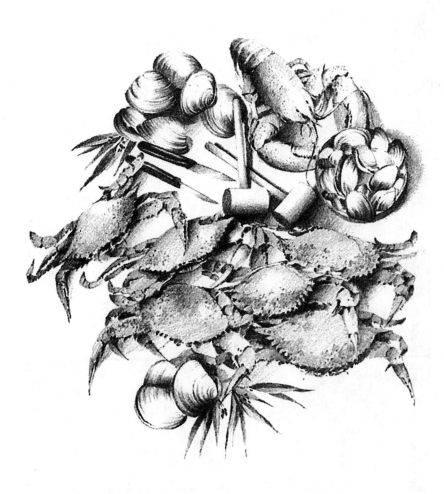

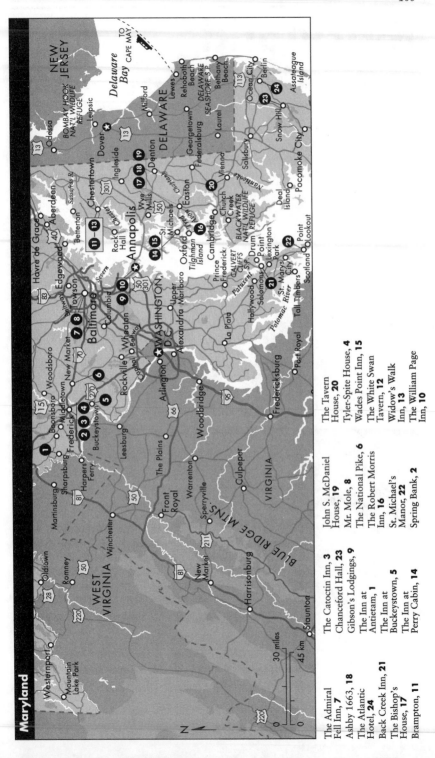

Maryland

The Admiral Fell Inn, **7**
Ashby 1663, **18**
The Atlantic Hotel, **24**
Back Creek Inn, **21**
The Bishop's House, **17**
Brampton, **11**

The Catoctin Inn, **3**
Chanceford Hall, **23**
Gibson's Lodgings, **9**
The Inn at Antietam, **1**
The Inn at Buckeystown, **5**
The Inn at Perry Cabin, **14**

John S. McDaniel House, **19**
Mr. Mole, **8**
The National Pike, **6**
The Robert Morris Inn, **16**
St. Michael's Manor, **22**
Spring Bank, **2**

The Tavern House, **20**
Tyler-Spite House, **4**
Wades Point Inn, **15**
The White Swan Tavern, **12**
Widow's Walk Inn, **13**
The William Page Inn, **10**

Oxford/Easton/Eastern Shore

In 1608 Captain John Smith called the Chesapeake "a faire bay encompassed . . . with fruitful and delightsome lande." This description was based on findings obtained while "gunkholing"—Eastern Shore jargon for frittering away your time in a boat on the tidal rivers like the Miles, the Choptank, Tred Avon, Sassafras, and Nanticoke. Gunkholing is still a favorite pastime on Maryland's Eastern Shore, where every spring fleets of boats descend on sleepy little ports that haven't seen so much action since the War of 1812—or since last spring.

You could say that Baltimore is the reason Eastern Shore towns such as St. Michael's, Oxford, Cambridge, Chestertown, Rock Hall, and Vienna have retained their small-town charm. In the 18th century these were metropoli-in-the-making, growing fat off of trade with the British. But after the discovery of Baltimore City's enviable deep-water port, the parade passed them by, and for the past 200 years these waterfront Colonial towns have changed little. It fell to the reclusive rich of this century to rediscover the Eastern Shore. The du Ponts, Houghtons, and other wealthy families quietly bought property here and moved in to get away from it all. Since their digs are set discreetly off the roads, the best way to see them is by taking a cruise from St. Michael's up the Miles River.

Besides rubbernecking and gunkholing, there are plenty of other reasons to visit the Eastern Shore. Because the terrain is flat and traversed by a network of pleasant country roads, bicyclists flock to the area, inevitably heading toward shorefront seafood restaurants and marinas. Come November, tens of thousands of waterfowl fly through on their way south, followed by hunters and bird-watchers.

Each Eastern Shore town has a character of its own. Oxford is the quintessential retirement town. In landlocked Easton you'll find the Chesapeake Bay Yacht Club, numerous quaint shops, and the November Waterfowl Festival, which features an art show, decoy displays, retriever- and bird-calling, and an auction. St. Michael's, with its renowned Maritime Museum, is all about boats, as is Tilghman Island, one of the last domains of the Chesapeake Bay watermen.

Most visitors stick to these Talbot County haunts, but there are subtler pleasures and thinner crowds in neighboring Kent and Dorchester counties. Cambridge, across the broad Choptank River (the focus of James Michener's Chesapeake), is the gateway to 700 square miles of government-protected wetlands. To the north lies Chestertown, a demure Colonial treasure whose brightest moment came in 1774, when a band of Revolutionary firebrands dumped a British brigantine's tea cargo into the Chester River—an event still celebrated every May with fife-and-drum corps, house tours, and crafts displays.

Along Delaware and Maryland's Atlantic coast, the marlin, tuna, and piping plovers roam free, but the people flock to the beaches in rigid pecking order. Well-heeled Washingtonians head to Delaware's Bethany and Fenwick beaches, while blue-collar Baltimore goes to Ocean City, a bustling resort with 10 miles of white-sand beach and a flashy 27-block boardwalk.

Places to Go, Sights to See

Assateague Island National Seashore (tel. 410/641–1441). South of Ocean City is the pristine northern portion of this sandy barrier island, one of the last great coastal wildlife refuges in the eastern United States.

Betterton Beach. At the mouth of the Sassafras River, about 12 miles north of Chestertown, the bay's only jellyfish-free beach has a bathhouse, boardwalk, picnic pavilion, and boat ramp.

Blackwater National Wildlife Refuge (tel. 410/228–2677). Occupying 17,000-plus marshy acres 12 miles south of Cambridge, this preserve is a haven for endangered DelMarVa (Delaware-Maryland-Virginia peninsula) fox squirrels, bald eagles, peregrine falcons, red-cockaded woodpeckers, and, in fall, hordes of Canada geese and ducks. For spectators there are a visitor center, a 5-mile wildlife drive, and myriad bike and walking trails.

Chesapeake Bay Maritime Museum (St. Michael's, tel. 410/745–2916). Here you'll see the bay's historic boats—including bugeyes, skipjacks, and log canoes—as well as the 100-year-old Hooper Strait Lighthouse, a working boat shop, and an assortment of other maritime displays.

Oxford-Bellevue Ferry (tel. 410/745–9023). Highway 33 will get you to St. Michael's and Tilghman Island, but the ferry linking Oxford to Bellevue and carrying up to nine cars is a much more picturesque way to go. Begun in 1683, it's the oldest privately operated ferry in the United States.

The Patriot (tel. 410/745–3100). This 65-foot cruise boat berthed in St. Michael's takes 1½-hour excursions up the Miles River.

Trimper's Amusement Park (Boardwalk and S. 1st St., Ocean City, tel. 410/289–8617). This Ocean City attraction, with a huge roller coaster and other rides, has been in operation for more than 100 years.

Trinity Church. In 1675 the Colonists built Trinity near the village of Church Creek in Dorchester County, which makes this brick building the country's oldest Episcopal church in continuous use. It's surrounded by a graveyard, where lie the remains of three Revolutionary War heroes.

Wye Mill (Rte. 662, Wye Mills, tel. 410/827–6909). The 1671 overshot gristmill is one of Maryland's oldest business enterprises: Grain was ground here for George Washington's troops in Valley Forge in 1778. Open daily from April through November, visitors can buy bags of several types of grain that have been ground here. Only about 200 yards from the mill, along Route 662, you'll see the mammoth **Wye Oak,** the state tree of Maryland. This 450-year-old tree is the largest white oak in the country. Next, along the road, you'll find the **Old Wye Episcopal Church** (tel. 410/827–8484) dating from 1721, making it one of the oldest Episcopal churches in America. It features high pew boxes and the original silver communion pieces.

Restaurants

Chestertown rolls up the sidewalks pretty early, but you'll notice clusters of cars in front of the **Ironstone Cafe** (tel. 410/778–0188) and the **Imperial Hotel** (tel. 410/778–5000).

In the Easton–Oxford–St. Michael's triangle, you'll find good food at reasonable prices at Easton's casual **Washington Street Pub and Raw Bar** (tel. 410/822–9011), as well as lots of locals and entertainment. **208 Talbot** (St. Michael's, tel. 410/745–3838) specializes in more formal dining at higher prices; the **Inn at Perry Cabin** (*see below*) is fine dining at its height, with expense to match. Try the **Latitude 38** (Oxford, tel. 410/226–5303) for an upscale menu that doesn't break your pocketbook: The seafood isn't deep-fat-fried, and the $5.95 bar dinner is surprisingly good.

Cambridge isn't renowned for its dining, but it's so gloriously prepossessing and unpretentious that you should plant yourself here anyway. **Snapper's** (tel. 410/228–0112), located on Cambridge Creek, is said to have the best jumbo lump crab cakes on the Eastern Shore.

In Ocean City, murals and carved lamps portray J.R.R. Tolkien characters at **The Hobbit** (101 81st St., tel. 410/524–8100), which has a two-angled view of Assawoman Bay. Cozy wooden booths and tables and walls decorated with photos provide the setting for **Lombardi's** (9203 Coastal Hwy., tel. 410/524–1961) thin-crust pizza, cheese steaks, and cold-cut sandwiches.

Tourist Information

Caroline County Tourism (109 Market St., Denton 21629, tel. 410/479–0660). **Cecil County Economic Development** (129 E. Main St., Elkton 21921, tel. 410/996–5300 or 800/232–4595). **Dorchester County Tourism** (203 Sunburst Hwy., Cambridge 21613, tel. 410/228–1000 or 800/522–8687. **Kent County Chamber of Commerce** (118 N. Cross St., Chestertown 21620, tel. 410/778–0416). **Queen Anne's County Visitors Service** (3100 Main St., Grasonville 21638, tel. 410/827–4810). **Somerset County Tourism** (Box 243, Princess Anne 21853, tel. 410/651–2968 or 800/521–9189). **Talbot County Conference & Visitors Bureau** (210 Marlboro St., Easton 21601, tel. 410/822–4606). **Wicomico County Convention & Visitors Bureau** (8480 Ocean Hwy., Delmar 21875, tel. 410/548–4914 or 800/332–8687). **Worcester County Tourism** (105 Pearl St., Snow Hill 21863, tel. 410/632–3617 or 800/852–0335).

Reservation Services

Amanda's Bed & Breakfast Reservation Service (1428 Park Ave., Baltimore 21217, tel. 410/225–0001 for information, 800/899–7533 for reservations, fax 410/728–8957). **Bed & Breakfast of Maryland/The Traveller in Maryland** (Box 2277, Annapolis 21404, tel. 410/269–6232, fax 410/263–4841). **Inns of the Eastern Shore** (1500 Hambrooks Blvd., Cambridge 21613, tel. 410/228–0575 for information, 888/373–7890 for reservations).

Ashby 1663

27448 Ashby Dr., Box 45, Easton, MD 21601, tel. 410/822–4235

This is a manor house *magnifico*, or a Colonial estate with Italian dressing. The original foundation was laid in 1663 for a wealthy merchant family by the name of Goldsborough, who engaged the services of some 20-odd servants. The Italian influence entered the picture in the mid-19th century, when the villalike structure arose. If the setting looks familiar to you, it's because Ashby is a star—some scenes in the movie *Silent Fall*, starring Richard Dreyfuss, were filmed here, and *Country Inn* magazine named the inn one of the top 12 in the country in 1996.

Jeanie Wagner and Cliff Meredith, both Eastern Shore natives, purchased Ashby in 1986 and transformed it from ramshackle to technologized high-gloss. Cliff, who once presided over his own contracting company, engineered all the wiring, heating, air-conditioning, and plumbing. Under his direction, small, divided spaces were demolished and opened up. No sign of the former kitchen exists, for Cliff created (from scratch) a wall-to-wall, white, custom-equipped design, which has since appeared on the cover of a popular builders' magazine.

The pièce de résistance, however, is the Goldsborough Suite on the second floor. If you've never seen a fireplace in a bathroom, now's your chance: The room is exceedingly large and sumptuous, with marble surfaces, brass railings, a bidet, a whirlpool-rigged bath, and a two-headed shower separate from the honeymooners' tub. The sleeping chamber is dominated by a four-poster canopy bed (king-size, of course) adorned with garden-print ruffles, but its best feature is its walls of glass.

The list of perks here is endless. Warm, soft-spoken Jeanie will guide you through the downstairs fitness and tanning center, outdoors around the heated pool (with a river view) and lighted tennis courts, and back in to the screen porch. Some bed-and-breakfasts claim "full" morning meals and slap an egg on your plate. Not Jeanie. Request the California eggs with salsa and sour cream, or the Belgian waffles: Both presentation and quality are superior.

🏨 *15 double rooms with baths. Air-conditioning, TV and phones in all manor house rooms, library, exercise room, tanning bed, pool table, kitchens in cottage and carriage house, pool, boat dock, paddleboat, canoe, lighted tennis court. $185–$595; full breakfast, afternoon tea, evening cocktails. AE, MC, V. No smoking indoors, no pets, 2-night minimum with Sat. reservation.*

The Atlantic Hotel

2 N. Main St., Berlin, MD 21811, tel. 410/641–3589 or 800/814–7672, fax 410/641–4928

The historic district in Berlin, Maryland, got a significant boost when a group of local investors renovated and opened the town's Victorian centerpiece, the Atlantic Hotel, built in 1895. This three-story, bracketed brick inn, just 8 miles from Assateague National Seashore and Ocean City, offers a quiet, quaint spot for a beach escape. The 16 guest rooms lining a wide central corridor are decorated with Oriental and floral-patterned rugs, tasseled draperies, Tiffany-style lamps, and antique double beds. Rooms 10 and 14, on the north and south ends, are notable for their spaciousness and Main Street views. Downstairs, at the Drummer's Cafe, there's piano entertainment on Friday and Saturday evenings and a four-star restaurant that will satisfy your sophisticated palate.

If you're looking for something else to do one evening, discover the town's most recent addition: the restored, Spanish Mission–style Old Globe movie house with live entertainment, or the interesting mix of old and new shops.

▥ *16 double rooms with baths. Restaurant, air-conditioning, phones in bedrooms. $55–$140; Continental breakfast. AE, MC, V. No smoking in rooms, no pets, 2-night minimum in summer with Sat.-night stay.*

The Bishop's House

214 Goldsborough St., Box 2217, Easton, MD 21601, tel. and fax 410/820–7290; 800/223–7290 outside MD

This handsome Victorian home (circa 1880) was built for former Maryland Governor Philip Frances Thomas and his wife. After the governor's death in 1892, the house was sold to the Episcopal Diocese and served as the Bishop's home, hence the name. Conveniently located near the heart of historic Easton, the Bishop's House features large first-floor rooms with a 14-foot ceiling and large plaster medallions. The first floor is centrally air-conditioned and offers facilities for social functions and business meetings. Second-floor guest rooms have 12-foot ceilings and are decorated in romantic 19th-century oak, walnut, and mahogany; three guest rooms have working fireplaces and two have whirlpool baths. For socializing or for people-watching there's a wonderful wraparound front porch.

Golf packages, cycling tours, and sightseeing excursions are available to guests, and since the present owners are members of Biking-Inn-to-Inn on the Eastern Shore, Inc., they can assist with arrangements for staying at other member properties. Owner Diane Laird-Ippolito is proud of the inn's hot sumptuous breakfasts and knows Easton's restaurants well. She carefully matches her guests with what will be an appropriate dining experience.

Easton is centrally located in the heart of James Michener's *Chesapeake* country. It's just 10 miles to either Oxford or St. Michael's, both popular tourist villages on Maryland's Eastern Shore. The land is flat and ideal for bicyclists, because most of the country roads offer wide shoulder lanes exclusively for bicycles. With so much water nearby, in autumn you'll hear and see large numbers of Canada and snow geese overhead and in the nearby fields.

▥ *4 rooms with baths, 2 rooms share bath. Air-conditioning in rooms, TV and VCR in common room, fireplaces in 3 bedrooms and 2 common rooms, off-street parking, bicycle storage. $65–$75 Sun.–Thurs., $85–$110 weekends and holidays; full breakfast. No credit cards. No smoking indoors, no pets, 2-night minimum on weekends and holidays.*

Brampton

25227 Chestertown Rd., Chestertown, MD 21620, tel. 410/778–1860, fax 410/778–1805

Brampton's charming character derives from both its house and its grounds. The inn is set in the fields south of Chestertown, framed by two towering, 120-year-old spruce trees at the end of a long drive. It's a three-story brick building with a white columned porch and 14 front windows, the perfect gentleman-farmer's country seat. The house is listed on the National Register of Historic Places, as are 4 of its surrounding 35 acres (the site of some famous experiments in crop rotation). Enter and pass through the airy foyer into a bookcase-lined living room, or climb the solid-walnut staircase. This front section of Brampton was built around 1860 by Henry Ward Carville as a wedding present to his wife.

Upstairs in the seven guest rooms the present owner's excellent taste becomes apparent. Michael Hanscom spent 10 years in San Francisco renovating old homes before moving here. His Swiss wife, Danielle, is responsible for the European atmosphere in the guest rooms. The bed linen and towels look and smell as if they've been dried on a line in the Alps. Every room except the suite has a working fireplace or a wood-burning stove. The ceilings on the second floor are 11 feet high. The Yellow Room at the front of the house is a favorite, a sunny paradise with an antique lace canopy above the bed. The two third-floor rooms are tucked under the sloping eaves and are decorated in country style, with locally crafted chairs and trundle beds.

The Hanscoms have operated Brampton for more than 10 years, and they've made many additions: a mammoth Vulcan commercial stove that enables them to offer guests a choice of breakfast entrées; a TV room downstairs; and the Rose Room, outfitted with a king-size bed and a large private bath (but reached by a staircase so narrow that Danielle advises no one over 6 feet to book this unit).

Danielle and Michael can suggest walks on the Brampton grounds to a pond or to the east fork of Langford Creek. There is something Old World about these unassuming hosts, both of whom are dedicated to perfecting every detail.

▥ *8 double rooms with baths, 2 suites. Air-conditioning, TV in 1 suite. $95–$155; full breakfast, afternoon tea. AE, MC, V. No smoking, no pets, 2-night minimum on weekends.*

Chanceford Hall

209 W. Federal St., Snow Hill, MD 21863, tel. 410/632–2231

What is a spruce little town like Snow Hill, Maryland, doing in among the chicken farms of the DelMarVa peninsula? For the answer, look to the narrow but deep Pocomoke River, which in the 17th and 18th centuries made Snow Hill a bustling port, frequented by tall-masted schooners sailing in from the Chesapeake. Today, you can stay at Chanceford Hall, a bed-and-breakfast inn that would have pleased any visiting Colonial dignitary. The mansion was constructed in three stages, beginning with the Georgian front section in 1759.

Some 230 years later a pair of old-house restorers, Thelma and Michael Driscoll, moved in and turned Chanceford Hall into a showplace. The Federal-style mantels, painted in cool Williamsburg greens and blues, match the moldings, and there are merino-wool mattress pads and down comforters on the lace-canopy beds. The house has seven working fireplaces and reproduction furniture crafted by Michael himself. Thelma welcomes guests with wine and hors d'oeuvres in the sitting room and will lend bikes or explain where to rent canoes for river exploring.

▥ *4 double rooms with baths, 1 suite. Air-conditioning, TV with VCR in sunroom, lap pool, bicycles. $115–$135; full breakfast, dinner on request for extra charge. No credit cards. No pets.*

The Inn at Perry Cabin

308 Watkins La., St. Michael's, MD 21663, tel. 410/745–2200 or 800/722–2949, fax 410/745–3348

This grand white frame house, much enlarged from the original farmhouse, sits serenely at the edge of the Miles River, as it has since 1810. Much of the decor of the Inn at Perry Cabin is pure Laura Ashley, which is only fitting, since this, the first Ashley Inn, is owned by Sir Bernard Ashley, husband of the late designer.

The reception rooms have been done à la English country-house hotel, and from time to time Sir Bernard and Lady Ashley would swoop down on St. Michael's, bringing new furniture and decorations (not really new, of course, but brought from their house in the Bahamas or from the antiques emporiums of the world). Every object has been chosen with care, and most of them are antique—from the Colonial American chests of drawers, highboys, and bedside tables that came with the house to the mirrors, lamps, pictures, and the Oriental rugs spread everywhere you look. All of the bedrooms are done in antiques, and all are completely Laura Ashley—fabrics, wallpapers, sprig-decorated tables, and beds with spiral posts.

The main dining room, a soaring chamber two stories high, has an open wood-burning fireplace at one end. The food is excellent, and the silent, unobtrusive service lives up to the British tone of the place. Boat owners would find it a welcome change from galley fare and marina dining. The employees run the inn impeccably. The only conceivable drawback is the unfortunately situated residential development across the harbor, but that's hardly reason for second thoughts. Service, from the moment you enter the reception hall, is exemplary. General manager Stephen Creese sees to it that mineral water, ice, a plate of fresh fruit, and homemade cookies await guests in their rooms; the rate includes a daily newspaper, full English breakfast, and afternoon tea. The addition of swimming and exercise facilities, a traditional English snooker room, and a conservatory has extended the house's pleasures, and nearby recreations are plentiful: The inn arranges outings for everything from golf, fishing, and sailing to helicopter tours and riding lessons. It's worth noting, for business travelers, that the management accommodates any and all conference and meeting requirements.

▦ *38 double rooms with baths, 3 suites. Restaurant, air-conditioning, cable TV and phones in rooms, indoor pool, steam room, sauna, exercise room, snooker room, conservatory, library, room service, croquet, short-term docking facilities, free bikes. $195–$575; full breakfast, afternoon tea. AE, DC, MC, V. No smoking in dining room, no pets.*

John S. McDaniel House

14 N. Aurora St., Easton, MD 21601, tel. 410/822-3704 or 800/787-4667

This big, turreted Queen Anne in Easton has seven guest rooms. In the turret nook, the Prentiss Ingraham Room is particularly desirable. The decor is a mixed bag of family-style collectibles: nothing fancy, but all neat as a pin. Host Dawn Rehbien will be happy to fill you in on all the local action, including the inside scoop on the best places to eat—try Legal Spirits or Jin Jin, just a few blocks away.

Spend some time unwinding on the wide McDaniel House porch, where you'll find a swing, lots of white wicker furniture, and hanging plants. If you're headed to Easton for the November Waterfowl Festival, this is an excellent, homey place to stay.

▦ *6 double rooms with baths, 2 doubles share bath. Air-conditioning. $75–$110; Continental breakfast. AE, MC, V. No smoking, no pets.*

The Robert Morris Inn

314 North Morris St., Box 70, Oxford, MD 21654, tel. 410/226-5111, fax 410/226-5744

Although the town of Oxford and its historic inn came vividly into the public eye around the time of the American bicentennial celebration, the Robert Morris has managed to avoid being spoiled by success. Built by Robert Morris, Sr., as a residence in 1710 and run as an inn since the 1940s, it was bought by Ken and Wendy Gibson in 1975 and is just what a country inn should be.

The 18th-century section of the inn is on Oxford's Morris Street, facing the ferry dock, where there's always a line of tourists waiting to board the tiny Tred Avon Ferry, which tools between Oxford and Bellevue. You might also find a line at the Robert Morris restaurant, which occupies most of the inn's first floor. Its Hitchcock chairs and murals (actually 140-year-old hand-printed wallpaper samples) make it an attractive place to eat; crab cakes and Oxford coolers head the rather predictable menu. The slate-floor tavern beyond the dining room has a working fireplace and is reputedly where James Michener wrote the outline for *Chesapeake.*

Staying at the Robert Morris may prove more difficult than simply supping here. The Gibsons begin taking reservations on January 10 of each year and won't book a room more than a year in advance. Historic-minded souls should be adamant about claiming rooms in the 1710 section, where there's a rare, enclosed Elizabethan staircase and white-pine floors fastened with hand-hewn pegs. Top choices among the four guest rooms here are 2 and 15, the latter with a step-up poster bed and hand-stenciled borders on the walls. You might also request the room occupied by Robert Morris, Jr., a signer of the Declaration of Independence, or that of his father (who met a lamentable fate when he was hit by a cannon fired in his honor).

The Gibsons know that some people are willing to dispense with history altogether in favor of luxurious quietude. To that end they've restored a roomy 1875 Victorian home, surrounded by mimosa and weeping copper-beech trees, just steps from the main house. Almost all the rooms in Sandaway feature screen porches, pine paneling, and immense claw-foot tubs (ask for 203, which has a chandelier over the bath; for 303, with its own staircase; or for one of the romantic River Rooms overlooking the Tred Avon).

🏠 *33 double rooms with baths, 2 efficiencies. Restaurant, air-conditioning, TV in 1 efficiency. $90–$240; Continental breakfast included midweek, breakfast extra other days. MC, V. No smoking, no pets.*

The Tavern House

111 Water St., Box 98, Vienna, MD 21869, tel. 410/376–3347

Vienna, Maryland, is a genuine backwater on the Nanticoke River and probably quieter now than during the Revolutionary War, when the British made a habit of raiding the town. It is home to this small inn, which has been lovingly restored by Elise and Harvey Altergott.

Ask Harvey to show you the wood-case door locks and the palm-trees-and-coconuts carving above the entryway, and take notice of the gray, green, and blue wainscoting and the gracefully curving stair. Upstairs is the River Room, the first choice because of its four-poster bed, working fireplace, Colonial wall sconces, and river views.

The bulwark of an old bridge can be seen from the inn, as can the splendid Nanticoke, bordered by marshes and cattails that shimmer in the breeze. There are osprey nests in the marshes out front, an owl in the chimney, and plenty of peace. Bicyclists exult here, and stay-at-home partners can curl up with something to read—Elise has a fine library of books and periodicals—on some of the most comfortable bedding around. How long has it been since you've met anyone who irons the sheets?

🏠 *4 double rooms share 2 baths. Air-conditioning. $65–$70; full breakfast. MC, V. No smoking in guest rooms, no pets.*

Wades Point Inn

Wade's Point Rd., Box 7, St. Michael's, MD 21663, tel. 410/745–2500, fax 410/745–3443

Aside from a chartered yacht, there's no better place from which to appreciate the blue sweep of the Chesapeake than the Wades Point Inn. Halfway between St. Michael's and Tilghman Island, this rambling bed-and-breakfast on 120 acres is surrounded on three sides by the bay.

The oldest section of the inn was built in 1819 by shipwright Thomas Kemp, whose sleek Baltimore clippers were credited with winning the War of 1812. On the land side, this glowing white Georgian house has porches on two floors and chimneys at either end; an observation nook attached to one chimney was Thomas Kemp's lookout and is reached through a trapdoor in one of three rooms in the old portion of the house.

In 1890 Kemp built an addition to the house on the bay side and opened the place as an inn. The present owners, Betsy and John Feiler, call this addition the Bay Room and have put it to use as a common area; it's large enough to hold a cotillion and is lined with windows and furnished with white wicker. Above the Bay Room is the Summer Wing, which holds six small chambers. These aren't air-conditioned, but given their proximity to the water and multitude of windows, they don't need it. There are washbasins in all of the Summer Wing rooms, as well as pastel prints and dancing white curtains that catch the rejuvenating breeze. Maybe that's why Mildred Kemp, the last of the family to occupy Wades Point, looked so hearty at age 90, when Betsy Feiler met her. "If living at Wades Point made her look like that," Betsy says, "I wanted to buy the place."

Building additions seems to be something of a tradition with the owners of Wades Point. There's a four-room summer cottage, and in 1989 Betsy and John completed a 12-room guest house about 200 yards from the main inn. These modern rooms have water views, private porches, and balconies, and the two queen-size beds and kitchenette in three of the rooms make them a good choice for families. If you're looking for bona fide old Chesapeake Bay atmosphere, however, opt for a room in the main house.

▦ *15 double rooms with baths, 9 doubles share 5 baths. Air-conditioning in new guest house, TV and fireplaces in common rooms, pond, private crabbing and fishing dock, walking and jogging trail, public boat ramp nearby. $80–$195; Continental breakfast. MC, V. Smoking on porches only, no pets, 2-day minimum on weekends, closed Jan.–Feb.*

The White Swan Tavern

231 High St., Chestertown, MD 21620, tel. 410/778-2300, fax 410/778-4543

To Horace Havemeyer, Jr., old-house restoration was a science. He brought in a team of archaeologists when he bought the Colonial White Swan Tavern to help return it to its 18th-century appearance. A dig at the rear of the brick building unearthed clay pipes and mugs and a Pennsylvania-flagstone tavern yard. Today, the room that was the original kitchen, to the right of this patio area and shaded by a giant elm, is the inn's most requested guest room. Its rough ceiling beams, brick floor, and large fireplace attest to its antiquity and make it an eminently cozy place to sleep. The chambers in the tavern's main section are more formal, with stately wing chairs, canopy beds, and paneled walls. In the years since its renovation White Swan has become a Kent County landmark, popular for its daily tea. Its enviable High Street location puts guests within walking distance of shops, an old-fashioned movie theater, the Confederate Monument on the green, a small park on the banks of the Chester River, and two good places to eat—the Ironstone Café and the fancy Hotel Imperial Restaurant.

▦ *4 double rooms with baths, 2 suites. Tearoom, air-conditioning, cable TV in sitting room. $100–$150; Continental breakfast. No credit cards. No pets.*

Widow's Walk Inn

402 High St., Chestertown, MD 21620, tel. 410/778-6455, 410/778-6864, or 888/778-6455

A journalist once wrote of Chestertown: "Norman Rockwell would have plenty to paint, and Sinclair Lewis would be busy taking notes." Once a thriving port, Chestertown today claims the distinction of a population that has not increased since 1900.

Don and Joanne Toft's highly symmetrical Victorian (circa 1877) stands in the heart of the historic district. This large cream clapboard residence, with cranberry awnings and window shutters and lively eave detail, houses spacious spic-and-span rooms furnished with antiques, dried-flower arrangements, potted plants, ceiling fans, and family treasures. Pull back the drapes and bathe in the sun: The tall, tightly clustered windows let in abundant natural light.

Widow's Walk is close to most places of interest: The historic district, the best restaurants, Washington College, and the Chester River are all in easy walking distance.

🏠 *1 double room with bath, 2 doubles share bath, 2 suites. Air-conditioning, TV in sitting room. $85–$110; Continental breakfast, refreshments on arrival. MC, V. No smoking indoors, no pets, 2-night minimum on weekends Apr. 1–Nov. 1.*

Annapolis/Western Shore/ Southern Maryland

Bounded by 7,325 miles of coastline, the Chesapeake Bay is the nation's largest estuary and Maryland's defining feature. Its Eastern and Western shores were joined in 1952 by the 4½-mile Chesapeake Bay Bridge. Since then, sun worshipers from Baltimore, Philadelphia, and Washington have had easy access to the Atlantic beaches, and the bay has become a favorite with wealthy retirees, recreational sailors, artists, and many others.

During their easterly migration along Route 50/301, the sun-and-surf crowd was quick to rediscover Annapolis, founded in 1647 near the mouth of the Severn River. John D. Rockefeller passed it over in favor of Williamsburg while looking for a Colonial capital to restore, but Annapolitans don't care. Their city, the state capital, boasts more pre-Revolutionary brick buildings than any other in America, the oldest statehouse in continuous use, the U.S. Naval Academy, a renowned harbor, a huge October boat show, and a July feast during which 20,000 blue crabs are devoured. The streets radiating from the heights around Church and State circles are a walker's paradise, but summer weekends can be crowded (and parking a challenge), so it's a good idea to steal away to Annapolis on weekdays or in the November-to-March off-season.

South of Annapolis on the Chesapeake's Western Shore lie three Maryland counties that time forgot—Calvert, St. Mary's, and Charles, where the broad Potomac and Patuxent flow gently past tobacco fields, and the mood is redolent of the Old South. Today, though Washington's suburban sprawl is beginning to encroach from the north, the three counties remain a fine frontier along which travelers can investigate 18th-century churches; manor houses such as Sotterley; the small but bustling marine center at Solomons Island; lonely land's-end lighthouses; and St. Mary's City, which predates Annapolis as a capital of Colonial Maryland.

Places to Go, Sights to See

Calvert Marine Museum (tel. 410/326–2042). This complex of buildings in the town of Solomons includes the restored J.C. Lore and Sons Oyster House and the Drum Point Lighthouse, built in 1883 to mark the entrance of the Patuxent River, and one of the last cottage-type lights remaining on the bay.

City Dock. Here's where to find the Tourist Information Booth (tel. 410/268–8687), a fleet of spiffy yachts, and sightseeing boats that cruise Annapolis Harbor and call at Eastern Shore ports. The historic Victualling Warehouse, Maritime Museum, Middleton Tavern, and seafood-laden Market House are across the square from the dock.

Eastport. Just over the Spa Creek drawbridge is Eastport, a nautical hub full of boatyards, marinas, and watering holes such as Marmaduke's (tel. 410/269–5420), a favorite with yacht crews.

Historic Homes of Annapolis. These debonair Georgian and Federal buildings include the Hammond-Harwood, Chase-Lloyd, Brice, and William Paca houses, the last a must-see for its grand Palladian design and formal gardens. Maps pinpointing their locations (all within walking distance of one another) are available at the Tourist Information Booth on City Dock (*see above*), and tours can be arranged through *Historic Annapolis, Inc.* (tel. 410/267–8149) or *Three Centuries Tours* (tel. 410/263–5401).

Maryland State House (tel. 410/974–3400). The oldest American statehouse in continuous legislative use, this Georgian brick building dates from 1772 and served as the nation's capital for nine months, in 1773 and 1774. In its chambers, which are decorated with hand-carved tobacco-leaf borders, General George Washington resigned his commission and the Treaty of Paris was signed, ending the Revolutionary War.

Point Lookout State Park (tel. 301/872–5688). Point Lookout, at the tip of the tri-counties peninsula, served as an appallingly overcrowded hospital during the Civil War. Now its character is far more benign, offering campsites as well as facilities for swimming, crabbing, and fishing.

St. Mary's City (tel. 301/862–0990 or 800/762–1634). Approximately 60 miles south of Annapolis is this restored village, the site of the fourth permanent settlement in Colonial America. Points of interest include the bucolic St. Mary's College of Maryland, the Godiah Spray Tobacco Plantation, and a working reconstruction of *The Dove*, a square-rig sailing vessel that brought settlers from England to St. Mary's in 1634. Some 800 acres here are devoted to a disarmingly vibrant re-creation of 17th-century life, and recent archaeological finds—most prominently three 300-year-old lead coffins—have made national headlines.

U.S. Naval Academy (tel. 410/293–1000). Every year, 1,000 midshipmen are commissioned at the Academy, which was founded in 1845. The body of John Paul Jones rests beneath its chapel, and the wardroom is so big the entire student body (4,500 strong) can sit down to dine together. Guided tours of the 329-acre campus leave from the information center at Ricketts Hall.

Restaurants

Courtney's (tel. 301/872–4403), near Scotland, is the outstanding place for fresh fish (especially when Julie's cooking). On Solomons Island, **Dry Dock** (tel. 410/ 326–4817), a waterside, no-smoking space that changes its menu nightly, is dependable, judiciously priced, and exceedingly cordial. The larger, less intimate **Lighthouse Inn Restaurant** (tel. 410/326–2444) will run you $12–$27 for a full meal, excluding drinks, tax, and tip.

In Annapolis, **Griffins** (tel. 410/268–2576), on the city dock, is a solid choice for steaks and fresh seafood. **McGarvey's** (tel. 410/263–5700) is a celebrated saloon and oyster bar. **Treaty of Paris** (tel. 410/263–2641) and **Piccolo Italiano Ristorante** (tel. 410/381–8866) are fancier places. If you venture to Eastport, you can count on **O'Leary's** (tel. 410/263–0884) for the best seafood dinner in the area. Finally, sooner or later everybody goes to the honky-tonk **Buddy's Crabs & Ribs** (tel. 410/626–1100) on Main Street—bet you've never seen fish-shaped french fries.

Tourist Information

Annapolis and Anne Arundel County Conference and Visitors Bureau (26 West St., Annapolis 21401, tel. 410/280–0445). **Calvert County Department of Economic Development** (Calvert County Courthouse, Prince Frederick 20678, tel. 410/535–4583). **Charles County Tourism** (Charles County Government Bldg., Box B, La Plata 20646, tel. 301/934–9305). **St. Mary's County Chamber of Commerce** (28290 Three Notch Rd., Mechanicsville 20659, tel. 301/884–5555).

Reservation Services

Amanda's Bed & Breakfast Reservation Service (1428 Park Ave., Baltimore 21217, tel. 410/225–0001). **Annapolis Association of Licensed Bed & Breakfast Owners** (Box 744, Annapolis 21404). **Bed & Breakfast of Maryland/The Traveller in Maryland** (Box 2277, Annapolis 21404, tel. 410/269–6232).

Back Creek Inn

Alexander and Calvert Sts., Solomons, MD 20688, tel. 410/326–2022, fax 410/326–2946

Seascape painters and beachcombers would do well on Solomons Island, a finger of sand connected to the mainland by a bridge, bounded on the west by the Patuxent River and on the east by Back Creek Bay. They'd do well at Carol Pennock and Lin Cochran's Back Creek Inn, too. Dating from the 1880s, the robin's-egg-blue waterman's house is unprepossessing from the front, but inside Carol has used her grandma's quilts and Lin her green thumb to brighten up the guest rooms. Lin's catering skills are evident in the homemade breakfast breads and muffins. The main house and an annex added in 1984 wrap around the heady-smelling herb garden, which in turn surrounds an outdoor whirlpool bath. From the garden and patio it's fun to watch the water traffic on Back Creek.

▥ *4 rooms with baths, 2 suites, 1 cottage. Air-conditioning, cable TV in common area and in cottage and suites, access to nearby swimming pool, bicycles, dock with 2 deep-water slips. $65–$145; both full and Continental breakfast (full breakfast served later in morning). MC, V. Smoking in common rooms only, no pets, 2-day minimum holiday weekends, closed mid-Dec.–mid-Feb.*

Gibson's Lodgings

110 Prince George St., Annapolis, MD 21401, tel. 410/268–5555

Two hundred years ago they called Annapolis Harbor's infamous dockside neighborhood Hell's Point. Well, yesterday's hell is a gentrified haven today, with narrow, brick-paved streets, shade trees, and houses with landmark plaques. Two at the bottom of Prince George Street have been converted into a rambling inn by ex-Illinoisans Cary and Ayrol Ann Gibson. The Patterson dwelling, built between 1760 and 1786, is a brick Georgian town house with dormer windows. Next door, the red stucco Berman home dates from the last century. The Gibsons combed the towns along the Intracoastal Waterway for antiques, yet the decoration of these 18th- and 19th-century neighbors is extremely simple, a little like that of a small-town hotel. There's also the Lauer House, an annex built a few years ago.

▥ *5 double rooms with baths, 13 doubles share 7 baths, 2 suites. Air-conditioning, TVs and phones in parlors and rooms with baths, conference room with kitchenette, free off-street parking. $68–$125; Continental breakfast. AE, MC, V. No smoking, no pets.*

St. Michael's Manor

5200 St. Michael's Manor Way, Scotland, MD 20687, tel. 301/872–4025

Dusk is a good time to arrive at St. Michael's Manor, when there's a pale blanket of mist hanging over owner Joe Dick's vineyards and over the creek behind the house. Once inside, guests might find Nancy Dick playing her antique organ and Joe offering his homemade wine in front of the roaring fire in the parlor hearth. The four bedrooms at the manor are furnished with quilts and seem homey rather than grand. In the morning you'll awake to find yourself on an inlet of the Chesapeake Bay, at the southern tip of Western Shore Maryland. After breakfast, you may stroll the manor's 10 acres or try the tire swing out front, then perhaps go paddling in the canoe, visit nearby St. Mary's City, or cruise to Point Lookout State Park on a bike. At the state park there are boat excursions to isolated Smith Island and swimming (before jellyfish season starts in June).

▥ *4 double rooms share 2 baths. Air-conditioning, 2 fireplaces in parlor, pool, bicycles, canoe, rowboat. $45–$70; full breakfast. No credit cards. Smoking downstairs only, no pets, 2-day minimum on holiday weekends.*

The William Page Inn

8 Martin St., Annapolis, MD 21401, tel. 410/626–1506, fax 410/263–4841

If your travels take you to Annapolis for Commissioning Week at the Naval Academy, for the December Parade of Lights, or simply to nose around the city's walkable historic district, there's rest for the weary explorer at the William Page Inn. Built in 1908, this brown-shingle Victorian is a youngster by Annapolis standards, but one with an accommodating style. Its wraparound porch offers deep Adirondack chairs, and the boxwood in the William Paca House gardens perfumes the air. Somewhere over the high white wall at the end of Martin Street you might hear Naval Academy "middies" drilling, and four blocks away, at eateries around City Dock, crabs are being devoured, but on the William Page porch such distractions seem light-years away.

The genial innkeeper is Rob Zuchelli, a designer of theatrical lighting. He took very early retirement to refurbish the inn, which had served as the First Ward Democratic Clubhouse for 50 years. He aired out the smoke-filled rooms; stripped 11 coats of paint from the mas-sive staircase, to reveal oak, mahogany, and cherry wood; and filled the inn with Queen Anne and Chippendale reproductions. He also turned the third floor into one smashing suite, with a sleigh bed, skylight, window seats, and balloon shades that lift to reveal views of the Annapolis rooftops. Guests might take the presence of a whirlpool bath in the suite in stride, but they are likely to be surprised by the one attached to the little blue room on the second floor.

There's a wet bar stocked with setups, a working fireplace in the carpeted downstairs common room, and a discreet dog named Chancellor, who is always happy to accompany guests on walks. Breakfast, served from the sideboard in the common room, consists of freshly baked muffins and breads, fruit-and-cheese trays, and perhaps an egg casserole or crepes, depending on chef Rob's mood.

🛏 *2 double rooms with baths, 2 doubles share bath, 1 suite. Air-conditioning, cable TV in suite, wet bar, 2 whirlpool baths, robes for guests using shared bath, off-street parking. $85–$175; full breakfast. AE, MC, V. No smoking, no pets, 2-day minimum during special events, 5-day minimum during Boat Show and Commissioning Week.*

Baltimore

Two decades ago, Baltimore transformed itself and its once-dormant waterfront into a bustling tourist attraction, with shopping, restaurants, and the acclaimed National Aquarium. In the process the city became a model for urban redevelopment across the country.

Now the city, which celebrated its bicentennial in 1997, finds itself in the midst of another renaissance. A new stadium is going up next to Camden Yards for the city's new NFL franchise, the aptly named Baltimore Ravens. On the other side of Inner Harbor, the Columbus Center Hall of Exploration, an entertainment complex devoted to marine life, prepares to open in 1998. And Port Discovery, a children's museum being designed by the Walt Disney Co., is also slated for a 1998 debut.

Away from its thriving harbor, Baltimore remains a city of historic neighborhoods, including Mount Vernon and Fells Point. It is a city steeped in history, too. Babe Ruth, Edgar Allan Poe, and H.L. Mencken and the "Star-Spangled Banner" are as synonymous with Baltimore as the Orioles and blue crabs.

Places to Go, Sights to See

American Visionary Art Museum (800 Key Hwy., at Covington St., tel. 410/244–1900). Housed in a former whiskey distillery near Federal Hill, this museum showcases the works of self-taught artists. Exhibits include works by farmers, housewives, those who have disabilities or are homeless, and others.

Baltimore Museum of Art (Charles and 31st Sts., tel. 410/396–7101). Works by Rodin, Matisse, Picasso, Cézanne, Renoir, and Gauguin are on display; a separate wing houses 20th-century art, including 15 Andy Warhol paintings.

B&O Railroad Museum (901 W. Pratt St., tel. 410/752–2490). One of the world's largest train museums sits on the site of the country's first railroad station. Locomotives and railroad cars are on display.

Fells Point. A short trolley or water-taxi ride from the Inner Harbor takes you to Fells Point, once a thriving shipbuilding center and now a neighborhood of cobblestone streets and historic redbrick houses, many of them antiques shops, galleries, restaurants, and taverns.

Fort McHenry (Fort Ave., off Key Hwy., tel. 410/962–4290). Built in 1803, this star-shape, brick-and-earthen fort is most famous for its role in the War of 1812, when it withstood a 25-hour bombardment by the British, subsequently immortalized in the national anthem.

Inner Harbor. One of the city's liveliest neighborhoods as well as a working port, the Inner Harbor is abuzz with shops, restaurants, and major cultural attractions.

National Aquarium in Baltimore (Pier 3, tel. 410/576–3800). More than 5,000 species of marine life, including sharks, dolphins, beluga whales, and puffins, make their home here.

Oriole Park at Camden Yards (Camden and Howard Sts., tel. 410/685–9800). This 50,000-seat stadium, which opened in 1992, has a brick facade and asymmetric playing field that evoke the big-league parks of the early 1900s.

Sherwood Gardens (Stratford Rd. and Greenway, tel. 410/366–2572). If you visit in late April or early May, this park is worth a special trip to see 80,000 peaking tulips and azaleas.

Walters Art Gallery (N. Charles and Centre Sts., tel. 410/547–2787). Some 30,000 objects from antiquity through the 19th century—Egyptology exhibits, medieval armor and artifacts, decorative arts and paintings—are housed in this Italianate palace.

Restaurants

Donna's (1 Mt. Vernon Sq., tel. 410/385–0180) is a good bet for both fresh-baked morning scones and after-theater espresso—it's open until 1 AM on Friday and

Saturday. Since its opening in 1926, **Haussner's** (3244 Eastern Ave., tel. 410/327–8365) has been one of Baltimore's favorite special-occasion spots. The walls are adorned with pieces by Gainsborough, Rembrandt, Bierstadt, Van Dyck, and Whistler. **Joy America Cafe** (American Visionary Art Museum, 800 Key Hwy., tel. 410/244–6500) offers museum goers an unconventional seasonal menu that draws on the flavors of many countries. **O'Brycki's Crab House** (1727 E. Pratt St., tel. 410/732–6399), a 50-year-old Baltimore institution east of Inner Harbor, has a homey dining room with brick archways and early 1900s city scenes. **The Prime Rib** (1101 N. Calvert St., tel. 410/539–1804) is consistently ranked among the city's best restaurants; the traditional menu is headed by sterling prime rib and an even better filet mignon.

Tourist Information

Baltimore Area Visitors Center (301 E. Pratt St., 21202, tel. 410/837–4636 or 800/282–6632). **Office of Promotion** (200 W. Lombard St., 21201, tel. 410/752–8632).

Reservation Services

Amanda's Bed & Breakfast Reservation Service (1428 Park Ave., Baltimore 21217, tel. 410/225–0001). **Bed & Breakfast of Maryland/The Traveller in Maryland** (Box 2277, Annapolis 21404, tel. 410/269–6232).

The Admiral Fell Inn

888 S. Broadway, Baltimore, MD 21231, tel. 410/522-7377 or 800/292-4667, fax 410/522-0707

Funky chic is perhaps the best way to describe Fells Point, a historic waterfront section of Baltimore where hulking warehouses cast long shadows on the narrow streets, tugs dock at the old City Pier, and the bars don't close until late. At the center of this Maryland Macao lies the Admiral Fell Inn, an assemblage of eight buildings constructed between the late 1770s and the 1920s, that once housed a vinegar-bottling plant. Rest assured that the place has since been fumigated; in fact, it's been handsomely renovated and ingeniously converted into an 80-room inn with a restaurant and pub in the cellar. The rooms, which vary in shape, are decorated with Federal-style reproductions and offer views of the erratic rooftops of Fells Point. Three suites and eight rooms have whirlpool baths, and 15 rooms have two double beds. Two rooms have balconies with harbor views. Although there are other, more quietly graceful lodgings in town, no place is more convenient to Baltimore's nightlife, and none better evokes this port city's past.

🏠 *80 double rooms with baths (55 no-smoking). 3 restaurants, air-conditioning, TV and phones in rooms, conference room, room service, parking, free van service in city 7 AM–10:30 PM. $145–$350; Continental breakfast. AE, DC, MC, V.*

Mr. Mole

1601 Bolton St., Baltimore, MD 21217, tel. 410/728-1179, fax 410/728-3379

How did such an elegant townhome in Baltimore's exclusive Bolton Hill neigh-borhood get such a name? It all goes back to the children's book *The Wind in the Willows*, where Mole exclaims "Oh My" each time he encounters exceptional hospitality and accommodations. Mr. Mole is ideally situated for guests who want the convenience of a city inn and the comfort usually associated with large suburban properties. In downtown Baltimore's Bolton Hill, a onetime suburb of the wealthy, Mr. Mole is within walking distance of Baltimore's "Cultural Corridor" (including the Lyric Opera House, Myerhoff Symphony Hall, and Howard Street's Antique Row).

Co-owners and hosts Paul Bragaw and Collin Clarke have spared no effort to make their accommodations unique and comfortable. The first floor consists of a dining room with a large, lovely bay window and two sitting rooms full of color and elegant clutter. Guests can eat at individual tables or in the adjoining rooms. Typically, the Dutch-style breakfast consists of fresh fruits, Amish cheeses and meats, homemade breads, and coffee cake.

Each of the five guest suites has a private white bath, fresh flowers, a direct-dial phone, a clock radio, and a garage. The second-floor Explorer Suite feels like a tented en-suite camp for African adventurers. Also on this floor is the Print Room, filled with prints and engravings, which is actually part of a two-bedroom suite with a marble fireplace, chairs and sofas, and loads of books on the shelves. A plant-filled sunroom on the third floor is probably the most romantic suite.

🏠 *5 rooms with baths. Air-conditioning, private-line direct dial phones and fax, fresh flowers, Caswell-Massey amenities. $97–$155; Continental-plus breakfast. AE, D, MC, V. No smoking, no pets, 2-night minimum on weekends.*

Frederick and Thereabouts

*In Frederick, about an hour's drive west of Baltimore and
Washington, D.C., Interstates 270 and 70 meet. Although the
character of these thoroughfares has changed dramatically in
the past 200 years (I–270 has become such a jungle of office
parks that it's known as the Technology Corridor), it is
historically appropriate to think of the Frederick area as a
transportation hub. America's oldest federal turnpike, the
National Road, ran through the town, which was founded in
1745 by Daniel Dulaney. Frederick grew up as a way station
on the route west. Some settlers—in particular those of
German extraction—cut their journey short, unloaded their
Conestoga wagons, and put down roots in town. To encourage
settlement here, land speculators donated property for
churches, resulting in a downtown of clustered spires. These,
as well as the immaculately kept Federal and Victorian
houses in Frederick's 34-block historic district, are well
charted in a walking-tour brochure available at the visitor
center on Church Street. In July 1864, Confederate General
Jubal Earley held the town ransom for $200,000. Since the
Civil War, Frederick has attempted, without success, to have
the money reimbursed by the Federal government.*

The land around Frederick is dotted with farms and villages such as Woodsboro, New Market, Thurmont, and Emmitsburg (the site of a shrine to America's first native-born saint, Elizabeth Ann Seton). This area is ideal for biking and back-road exploring. Everywhere, historic markers tell tales of Civil War action along the Monocacy River, atop Sugarloaf and South mountains, and outside Sharpsburg, at Antietam.

Places to Go, Sights to See

Antietam (tel. 301/432–5124). Just outside Sharpsburg, in Washington County, is the Civil War battlefield where 87,000 Union soldiers under General George B. McClellan attacked General Robert E. Lee's 41,000-man army of Northern Virginia. Twenty-three thousand lives later the North had won the day, prompting President Lincoln to deliver the Emancipation Proclamation. But Antietam is remembered not as a Union victory, but as the scene of the ugliest carnage in the history of American warfare. The visitor center shows an orientation film and provides maps.

Boonsborough Museum of History (113 N. Main St., Boonsboro, tel. 301/432–6969). Local historian Doug Bast has been collecting Civil War memorabilia in his hometown since his childhood. Local families have helped expand his museum to include Native American artifacts, historic relics, knives and weapons, glass, porcelain, and lots of curiosities. It is a most interesting spot to spend an hour or so.

Catoctin Mountain National Park and Cunningham Falls State Park (tel. 301/271–7574). Franklin Roosevelt established a presidential retreat here in the Catoctin Mountains called Shangri-la, which later came to be known as Camp David. Here you'll also find Cunningham Falls, a man-made lake, miles of hiking trails, two campgrounds, and fly-fishing on Hunting Creek.

Frederick. Visitors to this pleasant town should not be deterred by the urban sprawl that surrounds it. The city's charm lies downtown, where—from April through November—visitors will find the *Old City Hall*, built as a courthouse in 1862; the *Barbara Frietchie House* (tel. 301/698–0360), a reproduction of the Civil War heroine's home; the *Francis Scott Key Museum* (tel. 301/663–8687; tours by appointment only), built in 1799; the *Frederick Historical Society Museum* (tel. 301/663–1188), with displays of antique dolls, Native American artifacts, and Amelung glass; the *Hessian Barracks*, on the grounds of the Maryland School for the Deaf, constructed in 1777 as a prison for British prisoners of war; and the *Brunswick Rail Museum* (tel. 301/834–7100).

Frederick County covered bridges. There are three, all in the Thurmont area, all built in the mid-1800s: Loy's Bridge, on Route 77, which crosses Owens Creek; the Roddy Road Bridge, also over Owens Creek, on Route 15; and, on Utica Road a mile east of Route 15, the Utica Mills Bridge, which once spanned the Monocacy River, before being swept downstream by the Johnstown Flood of 1889.

New Market. No one knows precisely why this immensely friendly village cast its lot with the antiques trade, but today there are some 40 shops peddling aged items, in a town that is only a few streets wide. *Mealey's Restaurant* (tel. 301/ 865–5488), New Market's other attraction, occupies a Georgian brick building on Main Street and serves Maryland cuisine.

Rose Hill Manor. This Colonial estate dating from the 1790s was home to Maryland's first governor, Thomas Johnson, who nominated his close friend George Washington as commander-in-chief of the Continental Army. Today the estate's 43 acres encompass a county park and a children's museum (tel. 301/694– 1648) where youngsters explore hands-on historic displays.

South Mountain and the Washington Monument. At the summit of South Mountain, accessible by car along Alternate Route 40, lies the nation's first monument to George Washington, constructed by the citizens of Boonsboro in a single day. Nearby are the Dahlgren Chapel, built in 1882, and Old South Mountain Inn. Now a restaurant (tel. 301/432–6155), the former stagecoach stop and hostelry was seized by John Brown just before he raided the Harpers Ferry arsenal.

Restaurants

Word has it George Will took regular lunches with Nancy Reagan at the **Yellow Brick Bank** (tel. 304/876–2208 or 304/876–2604), on a cozy corner of charming Shepherdstown, West Virginia, just a few miles southwest of Sharpsburg. The menu features inventive pasta and fish entrées. Other Antietam visitors can enjoy the prime rib at the elegant, sophisticated **Old South Mountain Inn** (tel. 301/371–5400) in Boonsboro. New Market proprietors will steer you to **Mealey's** (tel. 301/865–5488) for dinner and to the **Village Tea Room** (tel. 301/865–3450) for a generous, inexpensive lunch.

As for Frederick: The Continental **Brown Pelican** (tel. 301/695–5833) rates high marks for presentation, service, and cuisine (entrées $13–$20). The less formal **Province** (tel. 301/663–1441) specializes in "creative American" food and wonderful desserts. Casual diners will enjoy the **Cozy Restaurant and Village** (tel. 301/271–4301) at nearby Thurmont. Country fare and daily buffets are reasonably priced. Within the complex, there's the Cozy Country Inn and 12 unique specialty shops. In addition, dozens of pubs, coffee houses, tearooms, and trendy hangouts line Market and Patrick streets in the historic district.

Tourist Information

Frederick Visitors Center (19 E. Church St., Frederick 21701, tel. 301/663–8687 or 800/999–3613). Ask for the brochure "Inns of the Blue Ridge." **Maryland Office of Tourism Development** (217 E. Redwood St., Baltimore 21202, tel. 410/ 767–3400 or 800/543–1036), for statewide information.

Reservation Services

Bed & Breakfast Accommodations of Frederick and Western Maryland (7945 Worman's Mill Rd., Frederick 21701, tel. 301/694–5926). **Bed & Breakfast of Maryland/The Traveller in Maryland** (Box 2277, Annapolis 21404, tel. 410/269–6232).

The Catoctin Inn

MD Rte. 85, 3613 Buckeystown Pike, Box 243, Buckeystown, MD 21717, tel. 301/874–5555 or 800/730–5550, fax 301/874–2026

Just south of Frederick, in the historic village of Buckeystown, you'll find the Catoctin Inn right on the picturesque main street. Get there before Hollywood discovers this beautifully restored stretch of 18th-century structures. You couldn't want a more central location for touring Maryland's Civil War sites and memorials, and it's within a short drive of Harpers Ferry, Antietam, the Monocacy Battlefield, Frederick, the C&O Canal, Sugarloaf Mountain, the Appalachian Trail, New Market (Maryland's antiques capital), and the world-famous Lilypons Aquatic Gardens (tel. 800/999–5459). In summer, you might enjoy a visit to Frederick to watch the Keys, a Baltimore Oriole farm team.

The inn, circa 1780, shares 4 acres with a 1890s carriage house, now used as a conference center. All guest rooms have queen- or king-size beds, cable TV, phones, and private baths; 12 rooms feature a whirlpool tub. A full hearty breakfast is served in the dining room or on the sunporch. Businesspeople will find the inn well suited for their traveling needs; the large lawn and wraparound veranda are ideal for special functions and events, and the conference center can accommodate 130 people.

🏨 *4 rooms with baths, 1 suite, 11 cottages. Air-conditioning, TV, phones, fireplaces, robes, hair dryers, business facilities, whirlpool baths in cottages. $65–$150. AE, D, MC, V. Smoking in 1 bedroom only, no pets.*

The Inn at Antietam

220 E. Main St., Box 119, Sharpsburg, MD 21782, tel. 301/432–6601, fax 301/432–5981

Anyone who's ever visited a Civil War battlefield knows how haunting the site is, how the dawns seem to echo with the sound of bugles and gunfire, how at night the voices of soldiers rise like mist from the glades. Antietam, which surrounds the dusty little town of Sharpsburg, is surely one of the most stirring of such places, for it was here in September 1862 that one of the worst battles of the Civil War claimed more than 23,000 lives in a single bloody day.

Just north of town there's a national cemetery, with a statue by Daniel Chester French (who sculpted the statue of President Lincoln at Washington's Lincoln Memorial), called "The Private Soldier," which serves as the headstone for 5,000 Union dead. Adjoining the graveyard on a hillock facing the hazy Blue Ridge is the Inn at Antietam, a 1908 Queen Anne cottage with a wraparound porch, shaded by a giant silver maple and set amid fields. Owners Cal and Betty Fairbourn have restored the place in the style of the Civil War period, filling the parlor with Rococo Revival walnut furniture, the porch with rockers, and guest rooms with Eastlake dressers and beds.

The Fairbourns, who had restored another house in the area before moving into this one in 1983, enlisted the aid of a decorator here, which resulted in beautifully finished guest rooms. The converted smokehouse at the rear has a large brick fireplace, a sitting room lined with beaded paneling, and a loft bed. The master suite, another favorite, has an 1880s four-poster bed; matching spread, curtains, and wallpaper; and Battenberg lace.

After breakfast, served in the formal dining room on Royal Copenhagen china, Cal and Betty can offer tips on how best to see the battlefield—on foot, by bicycle, or even on cross-country skis. The surrounding area is also surprisingly rich in good restaurants, such as the Yellow Brick Bank, in nearby Shepherdstown, West Virginia, and Old South Mountain Inn in Boonsboro. During the first weekend in December, the Valley Craft Network runs an annual Holiday Studio

Tour; pottery, quilts, furniture, and natural fiberwear make ideal Christmas offerings. Shutterbugs should ask Cal about local photo opportunities.

🏠 *4 suites. Air-conditioning, TV in smokehouse suite. $95–$105; full breakfast. AE. No smoking, no pets, 2-night minimum on weekends and holidays, closed Dec. 22–Feb. 1.*

The Inn at Buckeystown

3521 Buckeystown Pike (General Delivery), Buckeystown, MD 21717, tel. 301/874–5755 or 800/272–1190, fax 301/874–5479

Buckeystown, on the Monocacy River, is a lovely collection of Federal and Victorian homes and buildings, among them a mansion built in 1897 and an 1884 church that are the grandest structures in town. Both have been converted into accommodations for guests. The mansion is a white frame building with three stories (one might say layers, since it looks like a wedding cake) on a 2½-acre lawn with azaleas. Owner Dan Pelz has created a true country inn crammed with eccentric memorabilia, including an American Indian collection, vintage postcards of Harpers Ferry, and Victorian furniture. Every day of the week an evening meal is served family style, with such dishes as consommé Madrilene, London broil in port sauce, and blueberry parfait. Plan to dress for it—this is a festive place. For the traditional-inn feeling, we suggest the Winter Suite or the Love Room.

🏠 *3 double rooms with baths, 2 suites, 2 cottages. Air-conditioning; TV with VCR in Parson's Cottage, Far West Suite, and St. John's Cottage; fireplace, kitchen, outdoor hot tub, piano in St. John's Cottage; fireplace in Winter Suite. $140–$240; $200–$300 with dinner, snacks, and breakfast. AE, MC, V. No smoking, no pets, dining room closed Mon.–Tues.*

The National Pike

9–11 W. Main St., Box 299, New Market, MD 21774, tel. 301/865–5055

The National Pike is located in the historic district of New Market, "The Antiques Capital of Maryland." Built in three sections between 1796 and 1804, this Federal-style brown-brick building was topped with a tower at the turn of the 20th century. Tom and Terry Rimel are the proprietors; he's a master at slate roofing, which sparked his interest in restoring old homes. The two have done a fine job on the National Pike, whose parlor has Williamsburg-blue paneling, a fireplace, and two armchairs for watching the action on the historic turnpike out front. There is also an organ, played by their son, who became organist for the local Episcopal church at the age of 10.

The two snug guest rooms in the rear section have brass-and-oak beds and are decorated in a country style; they can also function as a suite. There's a new double room with private bath in the 1804 section of the house. The long backyard has azalea gardens, a smokehouse, and a carriage house from the 1830s.

🏠 *4 double rooms with baths, 1 suite. Air-conditioning, TV in sitting room. $85–$125; full breakfast. MC, V. No smoking, no pets, 2-night minimum during "New Market Days" (Sept.) and holiday weekends.*

Spring Bank

7945 Worman's Mill Rd., Frederick, MD 21701, tel. 301/694–0440, fax 301/694–5926 (call first)

When you ask Beverly and Ray Compton why they bought their cavernous, 100-year-old farmhouse just north of Frederick in 1980, Beverly has a disarming answer: "We bought it to live and be happy in." And indeed it seems this warm couple is happy here, though the road to inhabiting the house was paved with hard work interspersed with joyful architectural surprises. While restoring the Italianate and Gothic Revival structure, the Comptons found details that seemed too good to be true: engraved designs in the glass of the front door, random-width hardwood floors, faux-marble mantels, antique William Morris wallpaper, and a wet-plaster fresco on the ceiling of the old billiard room—now a first-floor guest room. Some of these design points had been damaged over the years, but after a thorough cleaning, they stand as witnesses to another time and lifestyle. Ray is the son of a Chadd's Ford, Pennsylvania, antiques dealer, and perhaps his penchant for restoration is in his blood; in 1990 he received an award from the Historical Society of Frederick for the work he's done here. Beverly haunts local auctions and flea markets, and during the week she commutes to a federal job in Rockville.

The brick house is built in textbook-perfect telescoping style, with porches stretching across the front and along two stories on the side. The backyard gives way to farmland; the 20th century rarely intrudes at Spring Bank, despite its proximity to Highway 15. Choose your room upon arrival; the converted billiard parlor and the Sleigh Bedroom on the second floor are favorites, both sparely decorated with Eastlake-style antiques. In keeping with the 19th-century ethos the baths have not been extensively modernized—no whirlpool tubs or French magnifying mirrors here.

For breakfast, the Comptons serve homemade breads with local jams and plenty of information on nearby auctions, held almost every day. One note of advice: If you have fears about booking a room with a shared bath, you should put them to rest. No one has to wait in line here, and if you were to pass up Spring Bank for this reason, you'd be missing out on one of the handsomest, best-run establishments in western Maryland.

🏠 *1 double room with bath, 4 doubles share 2½ baths. Air-conditioning, cable TV in parlor. $65–$95; Continental breakfast. AE, D, MC, V. No smoking, no pets, 2-night minimum on holiday weekends and weekends Apr.–mid-June and mid-Sept.–mid-Nov.*

Tyler-Spite House

112 W. Church St., Frederick, MD 21701, tel. 301/831–4455

Built in 1814 by Dr. John Tyler in Frederick's prestigious Courthouse Square, the Tyler-Spite House features eight working fireplaces (all with carved marble mantels), 14-foot ceilings, elaborate woodwork with raised paneling and intricate moldings, a majestic staircase encircling a magnificent chandelier, and six beautifully appointed bedrooms.

Hosts Bill and Andrea Myer and their daughter Annalee offer impeccable rooms, with pure cotton sheets, down comforters, spring water, sherry, turndown service, and toiletries.

A multicourse breakfast is served in the formal dining room, except when warmer weather allows service on adjacent patios, with the quietude of a beautiful walled garden. There's high tea at 4 PM served in the library or in the music room with a crackling fire in winter. In summer months, tea is served in the garden near the heated, in-ground pool. Arrangements can be made for hot-air balloon rides, theater tickets, local vineyard tours, and train excursions.

🏠 *4 rooms with shared baths, 1 suite. Air-conditioning in rooms, fireplaces in all bedrooms and 3 common rooms, heated outdoor pool. $100–$200; full breakfast, high tea weekends. AE, D, MC, V. No smoking, no pets.*

Virginia

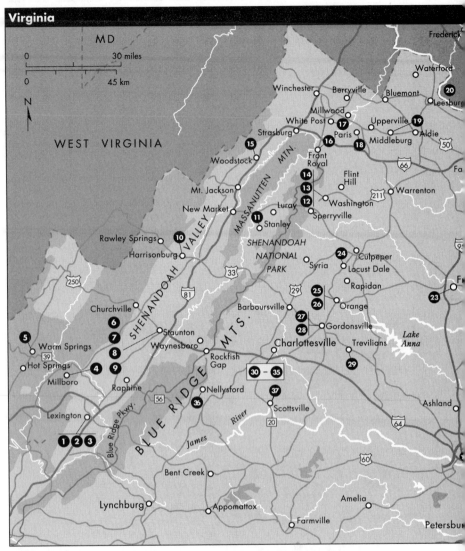

Applewood, **40**
Ashby Inn and Restaurant, **18**
Ashton Country House, **7**
The Bailiwick Inn, **21**
Belle Grae Inn, **8**
Bleu Rock Inn, **14**
Cape Charles House, **47**

The Channel Bass Inn, **53**
Chester House, **16**
Clifton, **30**
Colonial Capital, **41**
Edgewood, **38**
1817 Historic Bed & Breakfast, **34**
Fassifern, **1**
Fort Lewis Lodge, **4**

The Garden and the Sea Inn, **49**
High Meadows and Mountain Sunset, **37**
The Holladay House, **25**
The Inn at Gristmill Square, **5**
The Inn at Little Washington, **13**
The Inn at Meander Plantation, **24**

The Inn at Monticello, **31**
The Inn at Narrow Passage, **15**
The Inn at Poplar Corner and the Watson House, **51**
Island Manor House, **52**
Jordan Hollow Farm Inn, **11**

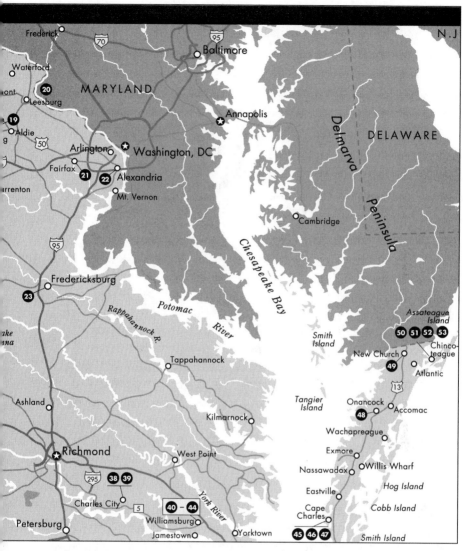

Northern Virginia

With intriguing hamlets, abundant antiques stores, top-notch inns, and some of the state's most lurid history, northern Virginia is an ideal getaway. Its rolling hills have nurtured great numbers of American revolutionaries; almost half the battles of the Civil War were waged in this countryside. Nowadays, though, refugees from Capitol Hill's partisan wars and the District's unstable city services are claiming a stake in northern Virginia. Office parks and shopping malls are encroaching. Development, the new enemy, is being tenuously held at bay.

The fast track to this Eden west of Washington, D.C., is I–66 (except on Friday and Sunday afternoons), but the well-versed opt for U.S. 50, which in an easy hour of driving puts you in Middleburg, the capital of hunt country. This subdued town breathes—and caters to—old money, with a collection of upscale galleries, antiques stores, and gun shops. Hunt season in Loudoun, Fauquier, Clarke, and Rappahannock counties begins in late October with an opening meet, peaks around Thanksgiving, and continues into March.

Frankly, most hunt-country visitors prefer to spend their time window-shopping at Middleburg real-estate offices and driving Loudoun County's back roads. (Routes 622, 626, 710, 713, and 734 are highly recommended. These back roads lead to many country pleasures. Hamlets such as Hillsboro, Hamilton, Delaplane, Aldie, Purcellville, and Millwood offer plenty of opportunities for collectibles shoppers. Wineries—including Naked Mountain, Meredyth, Linden, Piedmont, and Oasis—abound in the area. (For a map of them, contact the Virginia Wine Marketing Program, VDACS, Division of Marketing, Box 1163, Richmond, VA 23218, tel. 800/828-4637.) Many farms have seasonal tours. (For the "Farms of Loudoun Getaway Guide," contact the Loudoun County Department of Economic Development, Agricultural Development Office, 1 Harrison St. SE, 5th Floor, Leesburg, VA 22075, tel. 703/777-0426.)

Northeast of Middleburg lies Leesburg, founded about 1760, which remained in Federal hands during the Civil War and thus retains much of its Colonial architecture. Leesburg's spruced-up storefronts and row houses now function as restaurants and shops.

South and west of Leesburg, a 30-mile corridor between Flint Hill and Syria makes for peak sightseeing by auto. Here the Blue Ridge looms on the horizon as the roads wind up into the foothills. Fauquier County offers horseback riding in Shenandoah National Park; mounts can be claimed at the Marriott Ranch.

At the southern border of the area sits Fredericksburg, boyhood stomping ground of George Washington and a hotly contested site during the Civil War. Between 1862 and 1864, four major battles were fought—at Chancellorsville, Wilderness, Spotsylvania Court House, and in Fredericksburg itself—resulting in more than 17,000 casualties. Fredericksburg's 40-block national historic district has more than 350 18th- and early 19th-century buildings. Shopping for artists' wares is popular here, as is antiquing, with more than 100 dealers in a six-block area.

Established in 1749 by a group of Scottish merchants, Alexandria—a mere 10-minute drive from Washington, D.C.—has impressive historical credentials. It was an important Colonial port and a social and political center. Tobacco was shipped from here to the smoky coffeehouses of London, and dissident Scots rankled over the Act of Union with England flocked here. This may explain Alexandria's continuing fascination with things Scottish. Alexandria is considered George Washington's hometown; Light Horse Harry Lee and Robert E. Lee both lived here. Old Town has more 18th- and 19th-century architectural gems than any other city in the country. A walk along Alexandria's shady lanes takes visitors by handsome brick homes and offers peeks into labyrinthine courtyards. There's lots of shopping to be done, and the ethnic variety of the more than 100 restaurants within walking distance of the visitor center makes it difficult to choose a place to eat.

Places to Go, Sights to See

Alexandria Archaeology (105 N. Union St., Suite 327, tel. 703/838–4399). This research facility, open to the public as a museum, preserves treasures from prehistoric times through the Colonial era and the late 19th century hidden beneath the paving stones of Old Town.

Carlyle House (121 N. Fairfax St., Alexandria, tel. 703/549–2997). Built in 1752–53 by Scottish merchant John Carlyle (and still the grandest house in town), it served as headquarters for General Edward Braddock in 1755, when he summoned five Colonial governors to plot the strategy for the French and Indian War.

Christ Church (118 N. Washington St., Alexandria, tel. 703/549–1450). Its parishioners have included George Washington and Robert E. Lee.

Fredericksburg/Spotsylvania National Military Park (120 Chatham La., Fredericksburg, tel. 540/373–6122) is midway between Washington, D.C., capital of the Union, and Richmond, capital of the Confederacy. Four major Civil War battles were fought in and around Fredericksburg, a region that saw the most intense fighting of the war, with casualties exceeding 100,000.

Gadsby's Tavern Museum (134 N. Royal St., Alexandria, tel. 703/838–4242). The rooms have been restored to their 18th-century appearance; of particular note is the hanging musicians gallery in the ballroom. George Washington socialized here. Nearby *Gadsby's Tavern* (138 N. Royal St., tel. 703/548–1288) has been dispensing spirits and victuals off and on since 1792.

Gunston Hall (10709 Gunston Rd., Mason Neck, tel. 703/550–9220), 15 miles south of Alexandria, was the Georgian mansion of George Mason, author of the first Virginia constitution and the Virginia Declaration of Rights. Built around 1755, it has a Palladian parlor and a Chinese-inspired dining room.

Historic Fredericksburg. Sights in the 40-block national historic district include the *Mary Washington House* (1200 Charles St., tel. 540/373–1569), bought by a dutiful son for his retired mother; the *James Monroe Museum and Memorial Library* (908 Charles St., tel. 540/654–1043); the *Hugh Mercer Apothecary* (1020 Caroline St., tel. 540/373–3362); and *Rising Sun Tavern* (1304 Caroline St., tel. 540/371–1494). The *Fredericksburg Visitors Center* (*see* Tourist Information, *below*) has maps for several walking tours.

Kenmore (1201 Washington Ave., Fredericksburg, tel. 540/373–3381). This Colonial mansion, famous for its decorative plaster moldings, was the home of George Washington's only sister, Betty. Its dining room has been called one of the 100 most beautiful rooms in America.

Manassas National Battlefield Park (12521 Lee Hwy., tel. 703/754–1861) was the scene of the First and Second Battles of Manassas (Bull Run), during which the Confederacy lost 11,456 men and the Union 17,170.

Morven Park (17263 Southern Planter La., Leesburg, tel. 703/777–2414), a classic example of Greek Revival architecture, started out as a simple 18th-century farm residence and later was home to governors of two states: Thomas Swann, Jr., of Maryland in the 19th century and Westmoreland Davis of Virginia in the 20th century. Gardens contain an impressive collection of American boxwood, hollies, magnolias, and other flowering trees.

Mount Vernon (8 mi south of Alexandria, tel. 703/780–2000) is George Washington's home and burial place. The museum holds Jean-Antoine Houdon's bust of Washington, as well as the first president's sunglasses and sword.

Oatlands (20850 Oatlands Plantation La., near Leesburg, tel. 703/777–3174), a classical-revival mansion, was built in 1803 by George Carter, grandson of the Williamsburg planter "King" Carter. Its terraced formal gardens are considered some of the most distinguished in the state.

The Saturday Morning Market at Market Square (Alexandria), by City Hall, is the country's oldest operating farmers' market. Vendors offer baked goods, fresh produce, plants, flowers, and high-quality crafts. Come early; the market opens at 5 AM, and by 9:30 AM it's all packed up.

Torpedo Factory (105 N. Union St., Alexandria, tel. 703/838–4565). It's just that: Naval torpedo shell casings produced here were used during World War II. The waterfront building is now a complex of studios where 160 artists produce and sell their works.

Trinity Church (Rte. 50, Upperville, tel. 540/592–3343) is one of the most striking Episcopal churches in America. The style was adapted from French country stone churches of the 12th and 13th centuries.

Waterford, a village north of Leesburg, evokes rural England so dramatically that it could tug at the heart of any Anglophile. It is now a National Historic Site.

Woodlawn Plantation (9000 Richmond Hwy., Alexandria, tel. 703/780–4000) is the estate bequeathed by George Washington to his adopted daughter, Eleanor Parke Custis, and his nephew Lawrence Lewis. The impressive brick mansion was designed by Dr. William Thornton, architect of the U.S. Capitol. Also on the grounds is Frank Lloyd Wright's Pope-Leighey House.

Restaurants

Many of northern Virginia's top inns offer outstanding meals. Not to be missed are the extraordinary dinners at the Inn at Little Washington (*see below*). In Flint Hill, **Four and Twenty Blackbirds** (650 Zachary Taylor Hwy., tel. 540/675–1111) features local ingredients. Leesburg's favorites are **Lightfoot Cafe** (2 W. Market St., tel. 703/771–2233), which has a bistrolike atmosphere, and **Tuscarola Mills** (203 Harrison St., tel. 703/771–9300), known for its varied menu and fine wine list. For local color, reasonably priced sandwiches, and a fantastic selection of baked goodies, try the **Upper Crust** (2 N. Pendleton St., tel. 540/687–5666), across the street from Safeway in Middleburg. **Fiddler's Green** (Loudoun and Stuart Sts., tel. 540/253–7022) is popular in the Plains. In Fredericksburg, recommended spots are **Sammy T's** (801 Caroline St., tel. 540/371–2008) and **Merriman's** (715 Caroline St., tel. 540/371–7723) for casual dining, **Le Lafayette** (623 Caroline St., tel. 540/373–6895) for French fare, and **Ristorante Renato** (422 William St., tel. 540/371–8228) for Italian cuisine. In Alexandria, **Le Refuge** (127 N. Washington St., tel. 703/548–4661) and **Le Gaulois** (1106 King St., tel. 703/739–9494) are relaxed French bistros, **Landini Brothers** (115 King St., tel. 703/836–8404) and **Geranio Ristorante** (722 King St., tel. 703/548–0088) are the spots for fine Italian dining, and **Bilbo Baggins** (208 Queen St., tel. 703/683–0300) is a cozy café with imaginative fare. **King Street Blues** (112 N. Saint Asphah St., tel. 703/836–8800) has a funky-Southern menu in a funky setting.

Tourist Information

Alexandria Convention and Visitors Association (221 King St., Alexandria, VA 22314, tel. 703/838–4200). **Fairfax County Visitors Center** (7764 Armistead Rd., Suite 160, Lorton, VA 22079, tel. 800/732–4732). **Fredericksburg Visitors Center** (706 Caroline St., Fredericksburg, VA 22401, tel. 540/373–1776 or 800/678–4748). **Loudoun Tourism Council** (108-D S St. SE, Market Station, Leesburg, VA 20175, tel. 800/752–6118). **Virginia Tourism Corporation** (901 E. Byrd St., Richmond, VA 23219, tel. 804/786–2051 or 800/847–4882).

Reservation Services

Blue Ridge Bed & Breakfast Reservation Service (Rocks & Rills Farm, Rte. 2, Box 3895, Berryville, VA 22611, tel. 540/955–1246 or 800/296–1246). **Princely Bed & Breakfast Reservation Service** (819 Prince St., Alexandria, VA 22314, tel. 800/470–5588). For a copy of the **Bed and Breakfast Association of Virginia**'s directory, call the **Virginia Division of Tourism**'s B&B line (tel. 800/ 262–1293). The **Virginia Tourism Corporation**'s Washington, D.C., office also operates a B&B and small-inn booking service (tel. 202/659–5523; 800/934–9184 outside DC).

The Ashby Inn & Restaurant

692 Federal St., Paris, VA 20130, tel. 540/ 592–3900, fax 540/592–3781

West of Middleburg and Upperville along U.S. 50, the turnoff for minuscule Paris may surprise unwary motorists; half the travelers looking for this hamlet in a hollow below the road probably miss it completely and end up crossing Ashby Gap or the Shenandoah River. At the Ashby's restaurant, visitors are treated to some of rural Virginia's most sophisticated food, masterminded by innkeepers Roma and John Sherman. The menu changes seasonally; crab cakes, game bird potpie, and venison prepared any number of ways reign as favorites. Dinner runs about $70 for two.

Perhaps the only danger in staying at the inn is that dinners leave many guests too blissfully comatose to appreciate their rooms. There are six in the main building and four in the adjacent former schoolhouse. Those in the main building are all furnished with a spareness that is a calming contrast to the rich food. Quilts, blanket chests, rag rugs, and the occasional cannonball bed set the country tone, though in every case, the views are the chief enhancement. As morning light shines through the windows, some guests may feast anew upon the garden, Blue Ridge foothills, lowing cows, and other pastoral delights. The coveted Fan Room has four skylights and a glorious fan window opening onto a balcony.

The four expansive rooms in the former one-room schoolhouse are top-of-the-line and excellent values. Each has a private porch that opens onto those splendid countryside views. The Glascock Room has deep red walls, a canopied four-poster bed, and an antique trunk with extra towels. Oriental rugs cover the many hardwood floors, though some are carpeted, and there are two sinks in each large bathroom. Two wing chairs facing the fireplace and a window seat are inviting places for curling up with a book.

Roma and John take a tag-team approach to serving and mingling with guests during breakfast, which usually consists of eggs cooked to order and muffins. Roma, an avid equestrian, left advertising for innkeeping. John, once a House Ways and Means Committee staffer and speechwriter, now tends the garden, where he grows seasonal herbs and vegetables for the restaurant. Between stints as the inn's maître d' he even hunts some of the fowl used in the restaurant's potpies.

▥ *8 double rooms with baths, 2 doubles with sinks share 1½ baths. Restaurant (closed for dinner Sun.–Tues., open for Sun. brunch), air-conditioning, TVs, phones, and fireplaces in schoolhouse rooms. $100–$220; full breakfast. MC, V. No smoking in bedrooms, no pets, closed Jan. 1, July 4, Dec. 24–25.*

The Bailiwick Inn

4023 Chain Bridge Rd., Fairfax, VA 22030, tel. 703/691–2266 or 800/366–7666, fax 703/934–2112

As visitors to the Bailiwick, Annette and Bob Bradley fell in love with the inn, and when it went on the market they spontaneously bought it. They've given the dining room a French-American flair but retained the Bailiwick's historic theme, befitting its location on one of the nation's oldest roads, across the street from the courthouse where George Washington's will is filed.

Each room in the 19th-century house honors a famous Virginian in portraits, accessories, and biographies. The window treatment and red-and-gold scheme in the Thomas Jefferson room mimic the decor of his bedroom in Monticello. The sumptuous Antonia Ford suite, named for a Confederate spy, has dormer windows, a Chippendale sitting room, and a bath with whirlpool tub. All rooms have plump feather beds and goose-down pillows.

There are two elegant parlors for lounging by the fire or taking afternoon tea. Guests staying here can head west to the countryside or hop the Metro going into the nation's capital.

🏠 *13 double rooms with baths, 1 suite. Restaurant, air-conditioning, phones in rooms, fireplaces in parlors and 4 rooms, turndown service, whirlpool baths in 2 rooms, TV in sitting room and in guest rooms by request. $130–$299; full breakfast, afternoon tea. AE, MC, V. No smoking indoors, no pets.*

Bleu Rock Inn

12567 Lee Hwy., Washington, VA 22747, tel. 540/987–3190 or 800/537–3652, fax 540/987–3193

Set on 80 acres of the former Blue Rock Farm, the Bleu Rock Inn enjoys a bucolic setting. The Blue Ridge Mountains form the backdrop, and a pond with ducks and geese, rolling pastures, and 7½ acres of vineyards lie in the foreground. Guests can fish for bass and bluegill in the pond and pluck peaches and apples in the farm's orchards.

The guest rooms, simply furnished in pastels with light woods and lace curtains, are pleasing. A decanter of complimentary brandy and a fruit basket are left in each one. The four upstairs rooms have private balconies; nos. 2–4 overlook the serene pond and have views out to the mountains.

The food is the star here. Owners Bernard and Jean Campagne operate the successful La Bergerie Restaurant in Alexandria and may be seen around the inn on weekends. Chefs Richard and Lynn Mahan's eclectic menu features Mediterranean and Asian favorites, including lamb chops with chanterelle mashed potatoes and red wine sauce, as well as a series of delicious seasonal desserts; in the fall, expect dark chocolate and hazelnut mousse cake; in the summer, key lime cake with fresh strawberry sauce.

🏠 *5 double rooms with baths. Restaurant, air-conditioning, fireplaces in dining rooms and lounge. $109–$195; full breakfast. AE, D, DC, MC, V. No smoking, no pets, closed Mon.–Tues. and Dec. 24–25.*

The Inn at Little Washington

Middle and Main Sts., Washington, VA 22747, tel. 540/675–3800, fax 540/675–3100

In 1978, in a village of 160 people an hour and a half west of Washington, D.C., master chef Patrick O'Connell and his partner, Reinhardt Lynch, opened a restaurant that grew into a legend, attracting guests from all over the world to these eastern foothills of the Blue Ridge. From the outside, the three-story white-frame building looks like any other quiet Southern hotel; only the Chinese Chippendale balustrade on the second-floor porch suggests the decorative fantasy within. The garden, with crabapple trees, fountain, and fishpond, cries out to be used as a stage backdrop.

The rich interior of the inn is the work of British designer Joyce Conway-Evans, who has designed theatrical sets and rooms in English royal houses. The settees in the inn bear as many as 13 elegantly mismatched pillows each. One bedroom has a bed with a bold plaid spread, shaded by a floral-print half-canopy—and, amazingly, the mélange works. In the slate-floor dining room with William Morris wallpaper, a fabric-swathed ceiling makes guests feel like pashas romantically sequestered in a tent.

A room and a suite in the guest house across the street are good for two couples traveling together, but they lack the sumptuousness of the main building. At press time, the kitchen was being expanded and two junior suites were being added over it.

Chef O'Connell's food appears to cast a spell over those who sample it, as the abundant positive reviews testify. The menu, which changes nightly, makes compelling reading; the seven-course dinner costs $108 per person on Saturday, $98 Friday, and $88 Sunday and weekdays, not including wine and drinks. Some rare vintages rest in the 14,000-bottle cellar, representing more than 900 selections.

Breakfast, served overlooking the courtyard garden, is far above the usual Continental fare. Miniature pastries and muffins are tucked in a basket alongside tasty croissants; raspberries glisten in large goblets. Those not still sated from dinner can order, for $18, a full breakfast—a lobster omelet with rainbow salsa and a baked Irish oatmeal soufflé with rum-soaked currants.

Clearly the inn, with its staff of 50, is a place for indulgence, and anyone unwilling to succumb to it—both psychologically and financially—should opt for humbler digs. But the waiting list alone suggests there are plenty of hedonists out there.

🛏 *9 double rooms with baths, 5 suites. Room service, air-conditioning and phones in rooms, fireplace in entrance lobby and 1 suite, robes, turndown service, whirlpool baths and separate double showers in suites, in-room safes, bicycles. $260–$720; Continental breakfast, afternoon tea. MC, V. No smoking in dining room, no pets (kennel available), closed Dec. 25 and Tues. except in May and Oct.*

L'Auberge Provençale

Rte. 340 (Box 119), White Post, VA 22663, tel. 540/837–1375 or 800/638–1702, fax 540/837–2004

Fourth-generation chef Alain Borel and his wife, Celeste, have brought the romance, personal touches, and fine dining of a French country inn to tiny White Post, an hour and a half west of the Belt-

way. This 1753 stone house is set on 8½ acres and is surrounded by rolling pastureland. Inside are the Borels' special accents: Alain's great-grandmother's copper pots in the dining room, provincial prints in the guest rooms, whimsical carved carousel animals, painted tiles, and art by Picasso, Buffet, and Dufy.

Don't fill up on the plate of fresh fruit, chocolate, and homemade cookies that welcomes you to your room; instead, save your appetite for the five-course prix-fixe dinner ($57). The menu changes monthly to take advantage of seasonal produce. In spring, it may include La Truite Shenandoa—Shenandoah mountain trout with sesame seed batter, fresh local Blue Ridge Morel mushrooms, tomato *concasse*, and tarragon. Celeste, who handles the wine, has assembled a 250-selection list, plus the captain's list, with rare vintages for the connoisseur. Breakfast in the sunny, bay-windowed, peach-colored dining room starts with a mix of tangerine and orange juice and is followed by such delicacies as fresh fruit, rich croissants, poached egg in phyllo cups, applewood smoked bacon, and house-cured smoked salmon.

If you ask, a bit of Borel magic can accompany you in the form of a picnic basket (tablecloth, fruit, cheese, sandwiches, salads, chocolates, and wine) to be savored in some nook along Skyline Drive or at one of the local wineries. Alain's particularity extends to his gardens, where he fusses over herbs and vegetables grown from seeds imported from France or one of the 54 fruit trees, including such exotics as Asian pears, persimmons, and kiwis.

Celeste is as deft a decorator as she is a wine selector. The four rooms in the new wing are furnished with the fabrics and colors of Provence, accented by hand-painted Spanish tiles; they have fireplaces and private entrances opening onto the gardens. Room 9, the Chambre des Amis, features a canopy bed, cheery yellow and blue prints, and windows facing two directions. For lazy hours with a book or for just viewing the countryside, the large private deck off Room 7 in the main house is perfect.

🏠 *8 double rooms with baths, 3 suites. Restaurant (closed Mon.–Tues.), air-conditioning, TV in suite, phone jacks in 3 rooms, fireplaces in 6 rooms, living room, and dining room. $125–$275; full breakfast. AE, D, DC, MC, V. No pets, inn closed Jan.*

The Morrison House

116 S. Alfred St., Alexandria, VA 22314, tel. 703/838–8000 or 800/367–0800, fax 703/684–6283

Under new ownership since early 1996, this inn, led by managing partner Peter Greenberg, retains the charm instilled by its previous proprietors, whose name it still bears. Most visitors continue to assume that the handsome property, with its reddish-brown brick laid in a Flemish bond, white-pillared portico, and double-hung windows, is another of the renovated Federal structures that abound in Alexandria. But the five-story Morrison House was built in 1985, under the watchful eye of a curator from the Smithsonian.

All guest rooms are different but have the Federal look about them, with camel-back sofas, Chippendale-style chairs, swagged draperies, and a few decorative fireplaces. Still prominent, too, is the Morrisons' handiwork, which includes the customized armoires, with TVs, drawers, and room for hanging clothes. Little luxuries abound, including Italian marble bathrooms with scales and lighted, magnifying makeup mirrors, big towels, and double sinks in most rooms.

The pastel-colored Elysium, the hotel's fine dining outlet, features American cuisine. There's also seating in the more casual Elysium Grill, with its cherry-wood floors, red-leather chairs, and, on several evenings, piano entertainment.

The Morrison House is a six-block walk from the Metro station, making a jaunt

to D.C. just minutes away. Guests can ramble through the shops and galleries of Old Town Alexandria, or they can just unwind here, savoring the inn's tranquillity and polished service. (There is 24-hour room service and concierge, and a multilingual reception staff.)

🏠 *42 double rooms with baths, 3 suites. 2 restaurants, air-conditioning, cable TV and phones in rooms, fireplace in parlor, robes, turndown service. $150–$295; extra for breakfast, afternoon tea. AE, DC, MC, V. Smoking on 1 floor and in the Grill only, no pets.*

The Norris House Inn

108 Loudoun St. SW, Leesburg, VA 20175, tel. 703/777–1806 or 800/644–1806, fax 703/771–8051

Before leaving their marketing careers in California to become Virginia innkeepers, Pamela and Don McMurray spent four years looking at almost 200 B&Bs. In 1991 they finally settled on the Norris House, a Federal-style home in the center of historic Leesburg with 14-inch-thick brick walls. The McMurrays spent two years restoring the home, built in stages from 1760 to 1885, and landscaping the gardens. Two celebrated early 19th-century builders, the Norris brothers, are responsible for the portico with turned spindles, the Adam-style mantel in the parlor, and the shiny wild-cherry bookcases in the library. A four-poster bed with lace canopy can be found in the Norris Room. Across the gardens is the Stone House Tea Room, another McMurray business. Guests also have access to a self-service business center.

The McMurrays are amateur genealogists, and they offer special packages to guests sharing their interest. But since 1991 there hasn't been much time for tracing ancestors. Instead, in a gesture guests will be able to appreciate, they have devoted spare moments to tending their garden, which in 1995 was named the county's Garden of the Year.

🏠 *6 double rooms share 3 baths. Air-conditioning, phone jacks in rooms, fireplaces in 3 rooms, robes, turndown service. $75–$145; full breakfast, evening refreshments on weekends. AE, D, DC, MC, V. Smoking on veranda only, no pets, 2-night minimum weekends Apr.–Dec.*

The Red Fox Inn

2 East Washington St., Middleburg, VA 20118, tel 540/687–6301 or 800/223–1728, fax 540/687–6053

This former tavern, built by Joseph Chinn in 1728 on the estate of Lord Fairfax, became a popular frontier stopping point for westward-bound colonists and later helped Middleburg grow into its role as the center of Virginia fox-hunt country. It still holds the charm and much of the rustic appeal that attracted a young surveyor named George Washington for a stay some 250 years ago. Too bad for the nation's first president that he was unable to enjoy one of the many four-poster beds with lace canopy, air-conditioning, and other modern appointments available in every room. The original building, an impressive three-story fieldstone structure in the middle of town, has just six rooms; the rest of the inn's 24 rooms are scattered in seven additional historic buildings over a two-block area.

During the Civil War, when the Red Fox Inn (formerly a frontier tavern, built in 1728 and known as the Ordinary) was known as the Beveridge House, it saw action as a Confederate headquarters and hospital. Confederate General Jeb Stuart held strategy sessions in the guest room named in his honor. In the main building, exposed wide-plank floors slope and creak a bit—lest guests forget the stories they could tell. Homemade chocolates and two bottles of complimentary wine—one red, one white, and both from local vineyards—greet guests in every room. Those in search of a romantic hideaway will enjoy the Belmont Suite (1½ blocks from the main building) with its two walls of pane-glass windows overlooking manicured shrubs and a garden area. There's even a grand piano in the Belmont's spacious living room.

The inn serves up country breakfasts (for an extra charge; Continental breakfast is included in rate), lunches, and dinners in The Red Fox Restaurant. You can't miss the restaurant—its greeting stand doubles as the lodging's registration area.

🏠 *13 double rooms with bath and 11 suites. Air-conditioning, phones in rooms, 6 fireplaces (gas or electric), robes. $135–$245; Continental breakfast. AE, D, DC, MC, V. Smoking in designated public areas only, 3 no-smoking rooms, small pets only (with $200 advance deposit).*

The Richard Johnston Inn

711 Caroline St., Fredericksburg, VA 22401, tel. 540/899–7606

In a prime Caroline Street location, just above the Rappahannock River and across from the visitor center, is this diminutive-looking 18th-century brick row house with a third-floor dormer and a pleasant patio shaded by magnolia trees. Inside, restoration work has been top-drawer, and owner Susan Williams, married on site in September 1996, has lavished loving care on the immaculate inn.

In the common rooms downstairs, board floors are polished to a rich luster and covered with Oriental rugs. Among the traditional antique furnishings are some Chippendale pieces. Room 5 has an imposing, queen-size, 19th-century mahogany plantation bed, and Room 2 has a dormer, a king-size brass bed, and Victorian furnishings. Two commodious suites, with hand-hewn ceiling beams, wet bars, and wall-to-wall carpeting, have private entrances opening onto the patio, where Susan's two friendly dogs may show a passing interest in new arrivals before drifting back to sleep.

Susan serves her freshly baked breads and muffins in the vast dining room, set with fine china, crystal, and silver. With such amenities, it's little wonder the inn has become a major destination, especially during the Renaissance Festivals that have sprung up in town over weekends in May and June.

▥ *6 double rooms with baths, 2 suites. Air-conditioning, cable TV in 3 rooms. $95–$145; Continental breakfast. AE, MC, V. No smoking, no pets.*

Sycamore Hill

110 Menefee Mountain La., Washington, VA 22747, tel. 540/675–3046

Cameras should be poised for the serious photo opportunities available at Sycamore Hill, a ranch-style house seemingly dropped from the sky onto the crest of Menefee Mountain. Winding through the mile-long approach from town, many a visitor may doubt there could be a lodging at road's end. But eventually the forest gives way to Kerri Wagner's extensive gardens, including a vast perennial bed featuring peonies in spring and mums in fall, and the Virginia fieldstone house, wrapped by a 65-foot veranda.

The view from this spot is the raison d'être of Sycamore Hill—there's Old Rag to the right, Tiger Valley, and Red Oak Mountain. And the 52-acre lot is a certified wildlife sanctuary. With its views and gardens, this is a spot for the nature lover. The best view is from the 6-foot picture window in the master bedroom, which has a queen-size four-poster bed. Kerri Wagner is an energetic hostess who treats her guests like friends, aided by her husband, Steve, an artist whose fascinating magazine covers line the walls, and by a shaggy white mop of a dog named Molly Bean.

▥ *3 double rooms with baths. Air-conditioning, TV in living room and 1 room, fireplace in living room, turndown service. $115–$165; full breakfast, afternoon refreshments. MC, V. No smoking indoors, no pets, 2-night minimum holiday and May weekends and Oct.*

The Eastern Shore

Most people think of the long peninsula east of the Chesapeake
Bay as territory claimed by the states of Maryland and
Delaware. Indeed, the most developed and touristy parts of
DelMarVa (Delaware-Maryland-Virginia peninsula) are. Yet
those who look closely at a map may see a boundary line and
a beguiling strip of land tapering off to the south bearing the
name of Virginia. This cusp of land is the Old Dominion's
Eastern Shore, encompassing two counties—Northampton
and Accomack—with a combined population close to that of
Charlottesville. The area was settled in the 1600s by English
colonists; visited by vacationers (who made the trip by
ferryboat) in the 19th century; and surveyed by the railroad,
which reached the peninsular terminus at Cape Charles, in
about 1885. Several decades ago the peninsula was bisected by
a highway, U.S. 13, which brought some—but not many—
1950s-style motels and drive-in restaurants. Off U.S. 13,
however, the Eastern Shore lives and looks the way it did
around the turn of the century—no quaint restored villages or
tony resorts. True back-roaders will like it immensely—
providing they understand a few basic facts in advance.

Above all, Virginia's Eastern Shore is not a beach haven,
except for the stellar sandy stretches at its northeast corner
lying within the Chincoteague National Wildlife Refuge. On
the bay side, tidal creeks and marshes predominate. Seaside, a
string of barrier islands has kept beaches from forming at the
shoreline. The islands themselves are either privately owned
or, like the islands of Cobb, Smith, and Hog, provinces of the
Nature Conservancy's Virginia Coast Reserve. Reaching them
requires chartering a boat or signing up for one of the VCR's
infrequent island trips. There are spring and fall boat tours
and three-day photography weekends (tel. 757/442–3049) led by
trained naturalists.

Nor are there any cities of note on Virginia's Eastern Shore,
with the possible exceptions of Chincoteague, whose meager
population swells in peak summer months but otherwise
figures at about 3,500, and Cape Charles, which thrived
during ferry and railroad days but now has only a cranking
cement factory to keep it from succumbing to the sand.
County maps show many other towns (with colorful names
such as Temperanceville, Birds Nest, and Oyster), but these
are really only crossroads with, perhaps, a general store.
East of U.S. 13, skinny local arteries such as Routes 679 and
600 reach such villages and the architectural contradictions
that surround them. The Virginia peninsula has its own
unique building style, followed for hundreds of years:
"chain" houses made of frame, consisting, when the pattern
holds, of big house, little house, colonnade, and kitchen
linked in a row. A good example is the privately owned Holly
Brook Plantation, on the west side of U.S. 13, some 8 miles
south of Nassawadox.

The town of Chincoteague lies on 7-mile-long Chincoteague
Island (not to be confused with the island holding the wildlife
refuge, Assateague Island, to which it provides access via a
bridge) and exists almost wholly to cater to tourists, with
motels, restaurants, and shops. In atmosphere, it is more
subdued than other, more developed Atlantic beach resorts in
Maryland and Delaware; the area's low-lying, marshy location,

which brings occasional septic and mosquito problems, may in part explain the difference. Still, it has one attraction that will probably never cease drawing crowds: the legendary Pony Penning event, held in late July. The ponies swim the channel between Assateague and Chincoteague and are then corralled and auctioned off at prices averaging about $1,750 each. This roundup began in 1924, though it was made nationally famous by Marguerite Henry's Misty of Chincoteague *in 1947. Misty herself was a real pony; her descendants can be seen roaming free on Assateague throughout the year.*

Places to Go, Sights to See

Accomac. This picturesque town has enough restored Colonial architecture to rival Williamsburg, and it is one of two villages on the Eastern Shore (the other is Eastville) with an 18th-century debtors' prison. The Victorian clerk's office on the west side of the courthouse green holds records dating from 1663.

Cape Charles, a place decidedly in the slow lane, was by 1953 abandoned by the passenger railroad and ferry service that allowed the town to flourish around the turn of the century. Today most of its 136 acres are a historic district. A walking tour takes visitors past two Sears-catalog homes built in the mid-1920s, the pleasant bayside boardwalk, and a wonderful art-deco movie house. Some may argue that the industrial works to the south mar the townscape, though the process of loading freight trains onto barges for passage to Norfolk makes for interesting viewing. Yet it is just this slow, elemental way of life and the reasonably priced property that have begun to lure more and more refugees from northern metropolises to the area.

Chesapeake Bay Bridge-Tunnel (tel. 757/331–2960). This 17½-mile, $200 million engineering marvel links Virginia's Eastern Shore with Norfolk and Virginia Beach. Completed in 1964, it has brought the Eastern Shore into the Virginia fold only to a degree, largely due to the $10 toll each way—which is actually a pretty good bargain when you consider the time and expense involved in taking a ferry or driving around via Washington, D.C. To support its mammoth span, four islands were built; one has a scenic stopping place, a 625-foot fishing pier, a restaurant, and a gift shop. To accommodate Chesapeake Bay ship traffic, the two-lane bridge gives way to two 1-mile-long tunnels. The trip is either awesome, unsettling, or soporific, depending on the soundness of motorists' stomachs and nerves. Construction of an additional two-lane span is due to be completed in July 1999—widening the stretch to four lanes.

Chincoteague National Wildlife Refuge (8231 Beach Rd., tel. 757/336–6122). Despite the surfboarders and sun worshipers headed toward its long stretch of Atlantic beach, the refuge exists first and foremost for the benefit of birds, snakes, ponies, rare DelMarVa gray squirrels, and Sika deer. Many of the species preserved in this veritable Noah's Ark are visible from a 6-mile loop drive that winds through forests and marshes. There are, as well, a visitor center, lighthouse (built in 1866), crabbing ridge, and fishing area—but no restaurants, camping, or bonfires. In season the refuge sponsors a wildlife safari (tel. 757/336–6155), which takes nature lovers along back roads to observe the intimate habits of the famed Chincoteague feral ponies.

Eastern Shore of Virginia National Wildlife Refuge (5003 Hallett Circle, Cape Charles, tel. 757/331–2760). This 651-acre refuge provides good birding year-round. Each fall, migrating birds gather in large groups until favorable conditions permit an easy crossing of Chesapeake Bay.

Eyre Hall (Eyre Hall Rd., opposite Rte. 636). The peninsula's most handsome and historic plantation was built in 1735, on land granted to the owners in 1662. The privately owned house near the bay is open only during Historic Garden Week in April, but its grounds, with ancient plantings, flowering shrubs, and venerable trees, can be visited year-round.

Hare Valley (near Exmore). Constructed in the early 1700s, this is in all likelihood the peninsula's oldest house. The one-room cottage with a chimney and loft is owned by the Association for the Preservation of Virginia Antiquities (tel. 757/229–1616) and is currently unrestored. It can be seen from Route 689.

Hopkins & Bro. General Store (2 Market St., Onancock, tel. 757/787–4478). This 1842 country store–cum–restaurant at the town dock is a Virginia Historic Landmark, with a menu featuring crab cakes and seafood salad.

Kerr Place (69 Market St., Onancock, tel. 757/787–8012). This distinguished brick mansion on the outskirts of town was built in 1799. It houses the collections of the Eastern Shore of Virginia Historical Society, including costumes, portraits, and furnishings.

Kiptopeke State Park (tel. 757/331–2267). Located 3 miles north of the Bay Bridge Tunnel on Route 704, this park has a wide swimming beach and biking and hiking trails. Its Atlantic Flyway location has made it a bird-banding site for 30 years.

NASA Goddard Flight Center and Wallops Flight Facility Visitor Center (Wallops Island and areas surrounding Chincoteague, tel. 757/824–2298). The first rocket at this 6,000-acre NASA enclave was launched in 1945. The visitor center, which is the only part of the complex open to visitors, displays space suits, moon rocks, and scale models of satellites and space probes. On the first Saturday of every month NASA conducts model-rocket launches on the grounds.

Refuge Waterfowl Museum and The Oyster & Maritime Museum (7059 Maddox Blvd. and 7125 Maddox Blvd., Piney Island, tel. 757/336–5800 and 757/336–6117, respectively). These two tiny museums are neighbors on Piney Island (barely an island really, as it's only tenuously separated from Chincoteague by skinny Eel Creek). The Waterfowl Museum has a collection of handcrafted decoys, and the Oyster Museum tells the life story of the bivalve (mollusk).

Tangier Island. Made popular by the 1980s PBS television series *The Story of English*, this tiny island, stuck like a buoy in the middle of Chesapeake Bay, has had a little heavier tourist traffic in the last few years. To reach it, catch the *Captain Eulice* at Onancock harbor (tel. 757/891–2574). The boat sails Memorial Day weekend–October 15 at 10 and returns at 3. A livestock-grazing range before the Revolution, Tangier is now home to approximately 900 souls—most of them named Crockett, Parkes, Pruitt, and Shores—whose speech rings with an English West Country dialect barely changed since the first settlers moved in. (It was this linguistic insularity that secured the island its spot in the documentary.) Today, residents, who have been known to turn away from less than tactful attempts to observe their speech patterns, remain devotees of seafood harvesting and Methodism. A fixture of the island, with one main street too narrow for cars, is the *Chesapeake House* (Main St., tel. 757/891–2331), whose reputation for family-style shellfish feasts has spread far and wide. Slightly less renowned is *Double-Six* (Main St., tel. 757/891–2410), a local haunt once featured in *National Geographic* because it serves hot oyster sandwiches.

Wachapreague. This sleepy village on the Atlantic side of the peninsula once held a 30-room hotel and attracted vacationers from as far away as New York City. But the hotel burned down, leaving only the 340-odd permanent residents, along with a carnival ground that still lights up in late July. The village remains a fishing mecca, especially for those seeking flounder.

Restaurants

Virginia's Eastern Shore has two culinary stars. The first is the **Garden and the Sea** (4188 Nelson Rd., New Church, tel. 757/824–0672), where chef Tom Baker takes advantage of the fine seafood market across the street to whip up delights from a broad American Continental repertoire, including his signature dish, a shrimp, scallop, and oyster special in chardonnay sauce. The menu (entrées $16–$24) features seasonal desserts and changes every three weeks. The second is **Eastville Manor** (6058 Willow Oak Rd., Eastville, tel. 757/678–7378), where chef Bill Scalley, formerly of Washington's Four Seasons and Mayflower hotels, serves entrées ($9–$14) garnished with herbs from his and wife Melody's own garden along with crab cakes that even the locals have declared heavenly. Prospective patrons may want to call ahead to secure space at evening seatings, since Scalley's galley is fast becoming a major draw.

For casual dining, guests should not be put off by the truck-stop appearance of **Stingray's Restaurant at Cape Center** (26507 Langford Hwy., Cape Charles, tel. 757/331–2505). Locals call it "Chez Exxon" (for its proximity to the gas station) and praise the sophisticated dinner entrées and reasonable prices. Other casual options include **Ray's Shanty** (Rte. 175, Wattsville, tel. 757/824–3429), the **Village** (6576 Maddox Blvd., Chincoteague, tel. 757/336–5120), and **AJ's on the Creek** (6585 Maddox Blvd., Chincoteague, tel. 757/336–5888). In Onancock, trendy **Armando's** (10 North St., tel. 757/787–8044) has a bistro atmosphere, while **Hopkins & Bro.** (4 Market St., tel. 757/787–4478) is a pleasant setting for lunch. The casual **Formy's Pit Barbecue** (Rte. 13, Painter, tel. 757/442–2426) is the Eastern Shore's only barbecue restaurant.

Tourist Information

Chincoteague Chamber of Commerce (Box 258, Chincoteague, VA 23336, tel. 757/336–6161). **Virginia Tourism Corporation** (901 E. Byrd St., Richmond, VA 23219, tel. 804/786–2051 or 800/847–4882). **Virginia's Eastern Shore Chamber of Commerce/Tourism Commission** (Box 460, Melfa, VA 23410, tel. 757/787–2460).

Reservation Services

Amanda's Bed & Breakfast Reservation Service (1428 Park Ave., Baltimore, MD 21217, tel. 410/225–0001). **Bed & Breakfast of Tidewater Virginia Reservation Service** (Box 568, Norfolk, VA 23501, tel. 757/627–1983). For a copy of the **Bed and Breakfast Association of Virginia**'s directory, describing more than 100 establishments, call the **Virginia Division of Tourism**'s B&B line (tel. 800/262–1293). The **Virginia Tourism Corporation**'s Washington, D.C., office also operates a B&B and small-inn booking service (tel. 202/659–5523; 800/934–9184 outside DC).

Cape Charles House

*645 Tazewell Ave., Cape Charles, VA
23310, tel. 757/331–4920, fax 757/331–
4960*

This 1912 Colonial-revival frame house,
with its spacious wraparound front
porch, is one of Cape Charles's largest
and most opulent inns. Innkeepers Carol
and Bruce Evans, who renovated the inn
in 1994, quickly learned how to make
their guests feel pampered, from the soft
classical music in the parlor to gourmet
and heart-healthy breakfasts. Carol
credits a fellow innkeeper with per-
suading the Evanses to move from
Chesapeake to join the reawakening of
what she calls "this jewel of a town."

Rooms, named after prominent people in
Cape Charles's history, are furnished
with antiques, unusual collectibles, and
family items, such as furniture painted
by Carol's mother. The tiniest room is
named after Alexander Cassatt, former
vice president of the local railroad and
brother of artist Mary Cassat, whose
works are featured here. The Julia
Wilkins Room has a whirlpool and private balcony.

Carol is writing a cookbook of breakfast,
lunch, and dinner specialties; she teaches
cooking classes and serves five-course
dinners (about $100 per couple).

🅷 *5 double rooms with baths. Air-
conditioning, cable TV in parlor, ceiling fans, whirlpool tub in 1 room, beach
chairs, bicycles. $80–$105; full breakfast, afternoon refreshments. AE, D,
MC, V. Smoking on porch only, no pets.*

The Channel Bass Inn

*6228 Church St., Chincoteague, VA
23336, tel. 804/336–6148 or 800/221–5620,
fax 804/336–1342*

The Channel Bass Inn occupies one of
Chincoteague's oldest buildings, a pale-
lemon structure built in the 1880s and
added onto in the 1920s. The inn, just off

Main Street, got a facelift in 1996 and is
a more welcoming destination than ever.
It is under the command of David
Wiedenheft and his wife, Barbara, who
also manage the successful Miss Molly's
(*see below*), just a stone's throw away.

The six guest rooms, located on the second and third floors, are extremely large
and open onto airy seating areas. None
of them share a common hall, so they are
all very quiet. Rooms and halls abound
with original artwork. Ceramic tile baths
meet the expectations of formal decor
set by the inn's neat peach-and-green facade. One self-contained suite offers all
the space more privacy-conscious guests
could seek, along with its own mini-re-
frigerator. The comfortable front sitting
rooms downstairs make pleasant space
for reading.

🅷 *5 double rooms with baths, 1 suite.
Air-conditioning. $89–$175; full breakfast. No smoking, no pets, 2-night minimum weekends, 3-night minimum
during holidays, and 4-night minimum
during Pony Penning.*

The Garden
and the Sea Inn

*4188 Nelson Rd., New Church, VA
23415, tel. 757/824–0672; 800/824–0672
outside VA*

The Garden and the Sea Inn sits on a
quiet lane near Route 13, the main thoroughfare along the Eastern Shore, in
tiny New Church, just 1½ miles south of
the Maryland border and 15 minutes
from Chincoteague. The main house of
the inn is composed of the 1802-built
Bloxom's Tavern and its 1901 addition. A
few years ago New Church's oldest
farmhouse, dating from the mid-19th
century, was moved onto the property.
It's now the Garden House, with a parlor where guests can relax with sherry,
apples, and brownies; an inviting wide
porch; and three guest rooms.

In 1994 Sara and Tom Baker bought the
inn because they wanted to be in busi-

ness together. After looking at properties from Pennsylvania to Florida, the newly married couple visited this property, and Tom said, "Let's do it."

Although it has less of the feel of a little French inn than the previous owners imparted (mainly because of a more American slant on the menu), the Garden and the Sea is still a sophisticated, inviting place to stay. The decor mixes antique furnishings, French wicker, Oriental rugs, ballooning fabrics, Victorian moldings and detail, and bay windows. From the multicolored gingerbread trim on the wide front porch to the sunny, rose-hued dining room, it's exceptionally appealing. Guest rooms are spacious. In the main house, the Chantilly Room, with a wicker sleigh bed and painted dresser, and the Giverny Room, with floral prints and dark-green lacquered wrought-iron furniture, have large baths with double sinks and bidets. The large, private Champagne Room in the Garden House has a two-person whirlpool tub and shower and a wrought-iron canopy bed.

Tom, who has been the chef at top Washington hotels, creates dinners featuring produce from local farms and fresh fish from nearby waters in menus that change every three weeks. There are two fixed-price menus, as well as à la carte choices (entrées run about $18–$24). Specialties include a sea scallop, shrimp, and oyster dish and Tom's outstanding soups. The mainly self-serve buffet breakfast, a bit of a letdown after the excellent dinner, is available in the dining room or—when weather permits—in the garden patio beside the lily pond and fountain.

🏠 *6 double rooms with baths. Restaurant, air-conditioning, ceiling fans, robes, whirlpool bath in 4 rooms, sheltered outdoor area for small pets. $75–$175; Continental breakfast, afternoon refreshments. AE, D, MC, V. Smoking in parlor and on open porches only, 2-night minimum weekends, closed Dec.–Mar.*

The Inn at Poplar Corner and the Watson House

4240 Main St. (Box 905), Chincoteague, VA 23336, tel. 757/336–6115 or 800/336–6787, fax 757/336–5776

As more and more tourists discover Chincoteague, proprietors Tom and Jacque Derrickson are watching the path to the doors of their twin locations on Main Street become more well trod. Newly opened over the last six years, these structures, which sit astride the intersection with quiet Poplar Street, deceptively look as though they date from the same era. The Watson House, for architecture buffs, is the real McCoy (dating from the 1890s), but the more elaborately decorated Inn, inspired by a Victorian in Suffolk, Virginia, is of 1995 vintage. Guests at both benefit from the warm, attentive hospitality of Jacque and co-owner JoAnne Snead and the thoroughness of innkeeper Karen Mason.

The Watson House offers country Victorian furnishings and a claw-foot tub in the Bayview Room. The Inn at Poplar Corner features all Victorian decor, with oak and walnut head- and footboards and a private balcony in Room 1. Operation of the B&Bs is a shared responsibility for the Derricksons and co-owners JoAnne and husband David Snead. Tom and David are natives of the island and, over generous breakfasts and refreshments either at the long antique dining table or on the side porch, may be eager to share stories of growing up among the wild ponies.

🏠 *10 double rooms with baths. Air-conditioning, whirlpool tubs in 4 rooms, 1 room with private balcony, beach chairs and towels, bicycles. $65–$149; full breakfast, afternoon refreshment. MC, V. Smoking on veranda only, 2-night minimum weekends, 3-night minimum some weekends, closed Dec.–Mar.*

Island Manor House

*4160 Main St., Chincoteague, VA 23336,
tel. 757/336–5436 or 800/852–1505*

In this 1848 three-story, T-shape white-frame house on Main Street, Charles and Carol Kalmykow, married on site in September 1995, have created a special destination. The house is furnished in Federal style with an impressive collection of antiques. Classical music plays quietly in the impeccable, rose-color Garden Room, a serene retreat with fireplace, big windows, and French doors opening onto a brick courtyard with roses and a fountain. The large Nathaniel Smith Room has a sloped ceiling, a sitting area, and four dormer windows, each with a window seat. The premier room is the Mark Twain, which has a king-size bed.

Carol prepares lavish breakfasts with homemade bread each morning, and Charles, who has given up his job in western New York to focus on the inn, helps attend to maintenance and guests' needs. For those eager to visit nearby Assateague island but avoid the $4 park admission, ask the innkeepers about passes they may have available.

Since Miss Molly's (*see below*) is just across the street, travelers can choose from two distinct personalities—the more casual Miss Molly's or the more formal, well-appointed Island Manor House.

▥ *6 double rooms with baths, 2 doubles share 1 bath. Air-conditioning, bicycles. $70–$120; full breakfast, afternoon tea. MC, V. Smoking in courtyard only, no pets, 2-night minimum weekends, 3-night minimum holidays.*

Miss Molly's Inn

*4141 Main St., Chincoteague, VA 23336,
tel. 757/336–6686 or 800/221–5620, fax 757/336–1342*

In stark contrast to the high-priced, high-rise resorts up the coast, Chincoteague's Miss Molly's Inn instills visitors with a sense of place that for some may prove indelible. Like the small island on which it sits, whose isolation and thin soil have never caved in to the various booms that threatened to consume it, the inn reflects persistence in the face of change. It lies on the island's main drag, which is orderly and navigable even on holiday weekends, just over the causeway bridge from the wisp of the mainland. Although the island as a whole may once again be undergoing something of a rediscovery, Miss Molly's is a quiet retreat, an enclave of simple hospitality and respectful company.

A chief reason is innkeeper Barbara Wiedenheft, co-owner of this 1886 Victorian, which she recently transformed from a low, unobtrusive structure into a "painted lady" with mauve, pumice, grayish-green, and cream exterior accents. Flanked by a series of porches and sitting just off Main Street, it is named after builder J.T. Rowley's daughter, who lived here until she was 84. In a previous incarnation as a rooming house, the inn played host to Marguerite Henry, author of *Misty of Chincoteague*. Barbara will point out the second-floor room where Henry stayed while writing the book, which has helped produce a constant stream of guests since its publication in 1947. The cozy upstairs rooms have Victorian furnishings, reading lights, and copies of the text especially for insomniacs. Guests may wander onto the inn's various porches to enjoy the sea breeze or into the screened-in gazebo, which faces the channel and its fishing traffic.

Barbara, who is fluent in three languages, and her husband, David, are expatriates from the Washington, D.C., area, where she worked for the British embassy. Now she splits her time between Miss Molly's and the Channel Bass Inn (*see above*), just around the corner, which the Wiedenhefts also operate. Guests of both inns mingle here over Barbara's scrumptious scones.

⌂ *5 double rooms with baths, 2 doubles share 1 bath. Air-conditioning, clock radios, wood stove in dining room, beach equipment, bicycles. $69–$155; full breakfast, afternoon tea. D, MC, V. No smoking, no pets, 2-night minimum weekends, 3-night minimum holiday weekends, closed Jan.–Mar. 15.*

Nottingham Ridge

28184 Nottingham Ridge La., Cape Charles, VA 23310, tel. 757/331–1010

More than 10 years ago, Bonnie Nottingham opened her brick Williamsburg-style house to guests. Built in 1975, it lies 2 miles off the main road, on a long stretch of private beach on the Atlantic Flyway. The land has been in the Nottingham family since the 18th century. This is a bird-watcher's paradise, and the Birding Festival, held in October, brings an influx of visitors to the inn. The smashing Chesapeake Bay sunsets and visitations by herons and egrets enhance nature's performance.

Inside, the inn is a cheerful place with two fireplaces in common rooms, a back porch, and four bedrooms. Romantics favor a downstairs room with wrought-iron bed and a homey down comforter. An upstairs room, with a private entrance and separate sitting and sleeping room, is great for families. Bonnie is a warm, lovable host. Be sure to sample her country ham, sweet-potato biscuits, and homemade jam at breakfast. Exact directions to Nottingham's Ridge (no signs exist) are given with reservation confirmation.

⌂ *3 double rooms with baths, 1 suite. Air-conditioning, TV with VCR in den and suite, beach. $85–$130; full breakfast, afternoon refreshments. No credit cards. No smoking, no pets.*

Pickett's Harbor

28288 Nottingham Ridge La., Cape Charles, VA 23310, tel. 757/331–2212

Sara and Cooke Goffigan's beige house with brick side walls sits off an isolated country lane 4 miles north of the Chesapeake Bay Bridge-Tunnel and 2 miles west of U.S. 13. The front yard is a vast stretch of private beach frequented by deer and horseshoe crabs and, for 12 years, adventurous guests of Pickett's Harbor.

Sara's warmth and the high-ceilinged rooms furnished with antiques and family items immediately make guests feel as if they were sharing an immensely cozy home with friends. The one downstairs bedroom has a four-poster bed, easy chairs, and an exceptional water view. The upstairs rooms, with quilt-covered beds and water views, are pretty, too.

Sara serves a country breakfast that routinely features sweet-potato biscuits, Virginia ham, and popovers. Before she heads off to teach school, guests may want to ask her about her family, a clan that came to the Eastern Shore in the 1600s, not long after Captain John Smith explored the peninsula.

⌂ *3 double rooms with baths, 2 doubles share 1 bath. Air-conditioning, TV with VCR in family room, fireplaces in family and dining rooms, bicycles. $80–$130; full breakfast. No credit cards. Smoking on porch only, 2-night minimum holiday weekends.*

The Spinning Wheel Bed and Breakfast

31 North St., Onancock, VA 23417, tel. 757/787–7311, fax 757/787–8555

For five years, this 1890s Victorian home in the heart of Onancock was Karen and David Tweedie's summer home. Then in 1993, they jump-started their plans to open a B&B by converting the house, a job Karen declares was "more fun than we ever expected." Karen, a spinner, displays her collection of antique spinning wheels throughout the house. David serves elaborate morning meals in the dining room or indulges guests who request it with Continental breakfast in bed. Their huge sheepdog, Nelly, is a third host. When not at the Spinning Wheel, which is open late spring to fall, the Tweedies operate an antiques shop, art gallery, and a mail-order jewelry business, which, as Karen proudly says, features items "culled from the landscape of the Eastern Shore." They also work with the hearing impaired at Gallaudet University in Washington, D.C.

Of the guest rooms, a favorite is Room 2, decorated with oil lamps, an oak dresser, and crocheted pillow covers. In Room 1 there is a wedding-ring quilt on the brass bed. Closet space was sacrificed throughout to make room for the private baths. There are just rods or racks with hangers and little drawer space, but who needs a lot of clothes for casual Onancock?

▥ *5 double rooms with baths. Airconditioning, wood-burning stove in living room, bicycles. $75–$95; full breakfast, afternoon refreshments. MC, V. No smoking indoors, no pets, closed Thanksgiving.–Apr.*

Williamsburg and the Peninsula

"Down in Virginia there is a little old-fashioned city called Williamsburg. It stands on the ridge of the peninsula that separates the James and York rivers." So begins The City of Once Upon a Time, *a children's book written by Gilchrist Waring in 1946. That book and the* Official Guide to Colonial Williamsburg *are two of the best introductions to the legendary city, which more than a million people visit every year.*

Williamsburg was the capital of Virginia between 1699 and 1780, when the colony was immense, extending west to the Mississippi River. A planned city like Annapolis, Maryland, and a thriving commercial hub serving the farms and tobacco plantations between the rivers, it was an alluring place then and remains so to this day, even if its legislative chambers and trading floors have fallen silent. In 1926 the rector at Williamsburg's Bruton Parish Church persuaded John D. Rockefeller, Jr., to restore the town. The continuing project has resulted in a living-history museum of 173 acres, a mile long and a half-mile wide, holding 88 restored and 50 major reconstructed buildings and surrounded by a 3,000-acre "greenbelt." The restoration has become a pattern for similar endeavors nationwide. Outlying discount malls and commercial strips woo travelers to bargain emporiums like the Williamsburg Pottery Factory and Berkeley Commons. The attractive Merchants Square, adjoining the historic district, houses a movie theater, restaurants, and some 40 shops.

Having located Colonial Williamsburg proper, visitors can simply wander in and soak up the atmosphere, perhaps slaking their thirst on cups of cider, peddled streetside. Others may opt to stop at the visitor center (102 Information Center Dr., tel. 757/220–7645, daily 8:30–5), which lies off Colonial Parkway (the National Park artery that connects Jamestown, Williamsburg, and Yorktown) to view a 35-minute film and buy passes that enable entrance to buildings and quick access to shuttle bus rides linking the top sights.

Williamsburg is not the oldest continuous English settlement in the United States. That title is held by nearby Jamestown, where a sea-weary party of 104 men and boys aboard the Susan Constant, Godspeed, *and* Discovery *landed in 1607 and clung to survival, despite hostile relations with Native Americans, disease bred in nearby swamps, and chaos fueled by the fear that they'd been forgotten by suppliers across the Atlantic. Today Jamestown Island, the site of a national park, is a much more rustic place than civil Williamsburg. One singular enjoyment wrought of its earthiness, however, is the glassblowing shop.*

It is entirely understandable that visitors to the area should feel overwhelmed. Several different paths of the nation's history converge in the area. Those mindful of the roles of African and Native American people in the nation's heritage will note that Williamsburg is where the first slaves entered the colonies in 1619 and that Jamestown marks the starting point for a long, often brutal push westward of the continent's native inhabitants by English-speaking settlers. Besides Jamestown and Williamsburg, there's nearby Yorktown to explore (the scene of the last Revolutionary War battle and the surrender of General Cornwallis) and a half dozen plantations along the James River, which are formidable attractions in their own right. Charles City County, which hugs the river between Richmond and Williamsburg, is truly a place apart. The same handful of families have owned and farmed its plantations since the 17th century and have stoically kept development out, as a drive along Route 5 will reveal. The high-traffic shipping channel lying just beyond the mouth of the James was the site of the Civil War battle between the ironclads Monitor *and* Merrimack, *which made military and maritime history. More recently, the region has played a crucial role in the development of the nation's space program.*

Finally, the thing to keep in mind about Williamsburg's bed-and-breakfasts is that none of them lie within the historic district; indeed, none of them occupy a historic home, though several are exceedingly fine places to stay. Those intent on booking accommodations in a bona fide Colonial structure with a historic pedigree should contact the Williamsburg Inn (tel. 757/229–1000 or 800/447–8679). It manages 85 rooms in taverns and houses in the restored district.

Places to Go, Sights to See

Abby Aldrich Rockefeller Folk Art Center (307 S. England St., Williamsburg, tel. 757/220–7670). Some 3,000 pieces—furniture, paintings, carvings, textiles, and decorative useful wares—make this the nation's leading American folk-art center. Mrs. Rockefeller's 424-work collection forms the core.

Busch Gardens Williamsburg (off U.S. 60, Williamsburg, tel. 757/253–3350). This theme park re-creates things German, French, Italian, and English and offers rides on such curiosities as the Loch Ness Monster.

Carter's Grove (Williamsburg, tel. 757/220–7453). An 18th-century plantation 8 miles east of the historic district, Carter's Grove was built in 1750 by a grandson of the Colonial tobacco tycoon Robert "King" Carter and renovated and enlarged in 1928. It's now part of the Colonial Williamsburg Foundation, and a one-way country road wends its way back to the historic district. The *Winthrop Rockefeller Archaeology Museum*, on the grounds of Carter's Grove, explores the discovery of the Wolstenholme Towne site here. This village had fewer than 50 inhabitants; all were massacred by Native Americans in 1622.

The College of William and Mary (Williamsburg, tel. 757/221–2630). The second-oldest college in the United States (after Harvard, which dates from 1636) was founded in 1693 by charter from King William and Queen Mary of England.

Its centerpiece, the Sir Christopher Wren Building, begun in 1695, is the country's oldest academic building still in use.

Colonial Williamsburg (51 mi southeast of Richmond, tel. 800/447–8679). In the restored district, some of the most interesting historic buildings are the *Capitol*, where Patrick Henry delivered his famous speech; *Bruton Parish Church*; and the handsome *Governor's Palace*, with its stable, kitchen, exquisite gardens, and working wheelwright's shop. The *Courthouse* in *Market Square*, fronted by pillories and stocks, offers reenactments of 18th-century court trials. Along Duke of Gloucester Street are the *Printing Office*, *Shoemaker's Shop*, the *James Anderson Blacksmith Shop*, and *Golden Ball Silversmith*. Crafts shops in the historic district include *Prentis Store*, for pottery, baskets, soaps, and pipes; the *Post Office*, for books, prints, maps, stationery, and sealing wax; and *Raleigh Tavern Bake Shop*, for ginger cakes and cider.

DeWitt Wallace Decorative Arts Gallery (325 Francis St., Williamsburg, tel. 757/220–7554). This modern museum behind the Public Hospital contains 10,000 examples of English and American furniture, ceramics, textiles, prints, metals, and costumes primarily from the 17th and 18th centuries.

Hampton. This town is the birthplace of America's space program and home to the *Virginia Air & Space Center* (600 Settlers Landing Rd., tel. 757/727–0800), which houses some of the most dramatic artifacts from the U.S. space program. From the nearby visitor center, the *Miss Hampton II* (710 Settlers Landing Rd., tel. 757/727–1102) cruises Hampton Roads harbor and passes the world's largest naval base. Visit St. John's, the country's oldest continuous English-speaking parish, or ride the 1920-built Hampton Carousel.

Historic Air Tours (Williamsburg Airport, tel. 757/253–8185 or 800/822–9247). Narrated flights over Colonial Williamsburg, Yorktown, Jamestown, the James River Plantations, and Hampton Roads give an intriguing perspective on the area's history and growth.

James River Plantations. On Route 5, where descendants of Virginia's earliest families still live, work, and preserve a way of life spanning three centuries, these estates are open for tours. *Berkeley* (12602 Harrison Landing Rd., Charles City, tel. 757/829–6018)—where English settlers observed what is believed to have been the first official Thanksgiving celebration on December 4, 1619—is a perfect Georgian. Built in 1726 and later inhabited by a signer of the Declaration of Independence and two U.S. presidents, William Henry Harrison and Benjamin Harrison, it is surrounded by 10 acres of formal boxwood gardens. Guests can dine in its *Coach House Taverns* (12604 Harrison Landing Rd., Charles City, tel. 757/829–6003). *Evelynton* (6701 John Tyler Memorial Hwy., Charles City, tel. 757/829–5075 or 800/473–5075) was the site of several fierce Civil War skirmishes. Today the 2,500-acre farm is still family-owned and -occupied, and the house brims with photographs and portraits. *Sherwood Forest* (14501 John Tyler Memorial Hwy., Charles City, tel. 757/829–5377) was purchased in 1842 by John Tyler, the 10th president of the United States, who moved here when he left the

White House. The current occupants are the third generation of Tylers to live here. At 321 feet, this is the longest frame house in the country. *Shirley Plantation* (501 Shirley Plantation Rd., Charles City, tel. 757/829–5121 or 800/ 232–1613), a Georgian house, capped by a handcarved pineapple finial, has been owned by 10 generations of Hills and Carters (Anne Carter was the mother of Robert E. Lee). Shirley was founded six years after the settlers arrived in Jamestown, with the house erected in 1723. Its three-story "flying" staircase, which looks unsupported, and the Queen Anne forecourt are noteworthy. *Westover* (7000 Westover Rd., Charles City, tel. 757/829–2882), seat of the Byrd family, is one of the finest Georgian plantations in the United States. Its grounds are open daily, though the house can be seen only in late April, during Virginia's Historic Garden Week.

Jamestown Colonial National Historical Park (Colonial Pkwy., Jamestown, tel. 757/229–1733). The site is an island, which is why the colonists chose it for a settlement in 1607. It was a bad choice; in one year nine-tenths of the settlers died of starvation, violence, or disease, and the capitol burned four times before it was moved to Williamsburg. Visitors will find an information center, museum, paths leading through the ruins of "James Cittie," a scenic loop drive, and the Glasshouse, where craftspeople may pique the imaginations of those still puzzling over the logistics of ships-in-a-bottle.

Jamestown Settlement (Off Jamestown Rd., next to the National Historical Park, tel. 757/253–4838 or 888/593–4682). This state-operated museum depicts the Jamestown experience in its gallery and outdoors, with living-history re-creations of the colonial fort and Powhatan Indian village and replicas of the three English ships that arrived in 1607.

The Mariners' Museum (100 Museum Dr., Newport News, tel. 757/596–2222). Here maritime history is documented, from the Native American dugout canoe and Chesapeake workboats to modern shipbuilding efforts at Newport News.

Williamsburg Winery (5800 Wessex Hundred, tel. 757/229–0999). Tours and tastings are given. Especially noteworthy are the chardonnay and the Governor's White. A tavern serves light lunches all year.

Yorktown and Yorktown Battlefield Colonial National Historic Park (Colonial Pkwy. and Rte. 238, Yorktown, tel. 757/898–3400). Here Washington laid siege to Cornwallis's army, and in 1781 the British negotiated terms for surrender in the (restored) Moore House. English, French, and American breastworks still line the battlefield. It's a good idea to stop at the visitor center first to view the dioramas, see the 15-minute orientation film, and rent a taped tour.

Yorktown Victory Center (Rte. 1020 and Colonial Pkwy., tel. 757/887–1776). This state-operated museum chronicles America's evolution from colony to nation in gallery exhibits, living-history Continental Army encampments, and an 18th-century farmsite.

Restaurants

Visitors can choose from a host of Colonial taverns scattered around Williamsburg's historic district, among them the **King's Arms, Shields,** and **Chownings** (tel. 757/ 229–1000 or 800/447–8679 for reservations). These serve such traditional fare as prime rib, game pie, Sally Lunn (slightly sweet raised bread), and peanut soup. For expensive formal dining, there's the award-winning **Regency Room at the Williamsburg Inn** (136 E. Francis St., tel. 757/229–7978). **The Trellis** (403 Duke of Gloucester St., tel. 757/229–8610), in Merchants Square, features a changing menu of regional food and decadent desserts. **The Old Chickahominy House** (1211 Jamestown Rd., tel. 757/229–4689) is noted for its Brunswick stew; **Pierce's** (I–64 exit 238 westbound, exit 234 eastbound, tel. 757/565–2955) has good barbecue. At **Indian Fields** (Rte. 5, Charles City, tel. 804/829–5004) the menu has such Tidewater delicacies as Virginia ham in pineapple-raisin sauce for lunch and crab cakes Harrison at dinner.

Tourist Information

Colonial National Historical Park (Jamestown-Yorktown) (Superintendent, Yorktown, VA 23690, tel. 757/898–3400). **Colonial Williamsburg Foundation** (Williamsburg, VA 23187, tel. 757/229–1000 or 800/447–8679). **Hampton Visitor Center** (710 Settlers Landing Rd., Hampton, VA 23669, tel. 757/727–1102 or 800/ 800–2202). **Jamestown-Yorktown Foundation** (Box 1607, Williamsburg, VA 23187, tel. 757/253–4838 or 888/593–4682). **Virginia Division of Tourism** (901 E. Byrd St., Richmond, VA 23219, tel. 804/786–2051 or 800/847–4882). **Virginia Plantation Country** (Box 1382, Hopewell, VA 23860, tel. 804/541–2206). **Williamsburg Area Convention & Visitors Bureau** (Box 3585, Williamsburg, VA 23187-3585, tel. 757/253–0192 or 800/368–6511).

Reservation Services

Bensonhouse (2036 Monument Ave., Richmond, VA 23220, tel. 804/353–6900). For a copy of the **Bed and Breakfast Association of Virginia**'s directory, describing more than 100 establishments, call the **Virginia Division of Tourism**'s B&B line (tel. 800/262–1293). The **Virginia Tourism Corporation**'s Washington, D.C., office also operates a B&B and small-inn booking service (tel. 202/659–5523; 800/934–9184 outside DC).

Applewood

605 Richmond Rd., Williamsburg, VA 23185, tel. 757/229–0205 or 800/899–2753, fax 757/229–9405

Applewood is so named because its owner collects things with an apple theme and hails from an Indiana town named after fabled apple shooter William Tell. This spotlessly tidy bed-and-breakfast is about four blocks from the historic district. It contains ceramic apples, apple prints, and even a copy of John Cheever's *The World of Apples.* Like other houses in the area, it was built in the late 1920s by a Colonial Williamsburg restorer, who added many of the kinds of details he'd been working on in the historic area: a Flemish-bond brick exterior, a handsome 18th-century-style portal, and detail crown moldings in the interior. The trim is painted those milky blues and greens that are so common in Williamsburg.

Applewood has four bedrooms for travelers. The Colonel Vaughn suite has a canopy bed, fireplace, and private breakfast area and entrance. The Golden Pippin Room sleeps four, one in a trundle bed. Innkeeper Jan Brown provides afternoon refreshments and serves a full breakfast, including, of course, apple dishes.

▦ *3 double rooms with baths, 1 suite. Air-conditioning, cable TV and fireplace in parlor. $90–$150. AE, D, MC, V. No smoking indoors, no pets, 2-night minimum holiday and special-event weekends.*

Colonial Capital

501 Richmond Rd., Williamsburg, VA 23185, tel. 757/229–0233 or 800/776–0570, fax 757/253–7667

The Colonial Capital, a three-story frame house painted spring-mist green, is within walking distance of the historic district, Merchants Square, and the College of William and Mary. The exceedingly nice

innkeepers, Phil and Barbara Craig, are a retired stockbroker and a university administrator, respectively, who moved to Williamsburg after 25 years in North Carolina. The Colonial's five rooms are named after Tidewater-area rivers. The York has an enclosed, green-canopied bed, and the second-floor Potomac room has a new private porch. Prettiest, though, is sunny Pamlico, with window seats and a white-canopied bed. The third floor can be made into a two-bedroom suite, a plus for families. Downstairs there's a large parlor with a wood-burning fireplace and access to a screened-in porch and brick patio, where the Craigs keep games, books, and puzzles. In the rear, near the Colonial garden, is guest parking, which solves a serious problem in teeming Williamsburg.

▦ *4 double rooms with baths, 1 suite. Air-conditioning, cable TV with VCR in parlor and suite, turndown service, bicycles. $95–$145; full breakfast, welcoming drink. AE, D, MC, V. Smoking outside only, no pets, 2-night minimum during peak weekends.*

Edgewood

4800 John Tyler Memorial Hwy., Charles City, VA 23030, tel. 804/829–2962 or 800/296–3343

Says frothy innkeeper Dot Boulware in her liquid southern accent, "I have to tell you, I am a romantic." And so is Edgewood—three marriage proposals were made in one week here. But before she and her husband, Julian, bought Edgewood Plantation, on scenic Route 5 approximately half an hour from Colonial Williamsburg, in 1978, she didn't care a bit for Victoriana. Fortunately tastes change, and when she became the mistress of an 1849 Carpenter Gothic house, she began collecting Victorian antiques like a woman possessed.

Dot's eight-bedroom house, visible from Route 5, looks on the inside like Miss Havisham's dining room, minus the cobwebs. It is full to bursting with old dolls, antique corsets and lingerie, lace curtains and pillows, love seats, baby carriages, stuffed steamer trunks, mighty canopied beds, highboys, Confederate caps—the list goes on and on. At Christmastime she professionally decorates 18 trees and festoons the banister of the graceful three-story staircase with bows. Clearly, more is better at Dot Boulware's Edgewood.

In her hands, Victoriana is thoroughly feminine, even though in one chamber, the Civil War Room, she's tried to cater to the opposite sex, decorating with intimate details of men's 19th-century apparel. Large people of either sex will have a hard time moving freely in this wildly crowded bed-and-breakfast. Lizzie's Room, the favorite, has a king-size pencil-post canopy bed and a private bath with a double marble shower and claw-foot tub. The room enshrines the memory of a teenager who, Dot says, died of a broken heart when her beau failed to return from the Civil War. Prissy's Quarters, a large upstairs room in the main building, has a kitchen area.

Breakfast is served in the dining room by candlelight. The brick-walled, beam-ceilinged downstairs tavern is a cozy sitting area with a fireplace, backgammon board, TV, and popcorn machine. There are also fireplaces in the dining room, a kitchen, a tearoom, and three bedrooms. Outside there's an unrestored mill house dating from 1725, an antiques shop, gazebo, swimming pool, and formal 18th-century garden (which makes a delightful wedding setting). Edgewood is centrally located for touring the James River plantations.

🛏 *6 double rooms with baths, 2 suites. Air-conditioning, TV and VCR in rooms, satellite TV in the downstairs tavern, tearoom, turndown service, pool. $120–$188; full breakfast, light afternoon refreshments. AE, MC, V. Smoking on porch and patio only, no pets, 2-night minimum holiday weekends, William & Mary graduation, Grand Illumination.*

Liberty Rose

1022 Jamestown Rd., Williamsburg, VA 23185, tel. 757/253–1260 or 800/545–1825

Bed-and-breakfast keepers in Williamsburg are in something of a bind. Because all the historic buildings in town are owned by either the Williamsburg Foundation or the College of William and Mary, they can't offer travelers authentic Colonial accommodations. Some have Colonial-style decoration anyway, but others, like Sandi and Brad Hirz, owners of the Liberty Rose, have come up with different, imaginative solutions to the dilemma.

Sandi and Brad have a tremendously romantic story. They were just friends when Sandi decided to leave the West Coast to open a B&B in Williamsburg. Brad was helping Sandi house-hunt when they looked at a 1920s white clapboard and brick home a mile west of the restored district (on the road to Jamestown). Sandi bought it in five minutes. Then Brad started seriously courting her, but it was Sandi, and not the B&B, who inspired him. Now they run Williamsburg's most beguiling B&B, decorated à la nouvelle Victorian with turn-of-the-century touches.

Sandi, a former interior designer, has a special talent for fabrics and is responsible for the handsome tieback curtains, many-layered bed coverings, and plush canopies. The patterns are 19th-century reproductions. Brad has held up his end of the business by managing remodeling details. The bathrooms are particularly attractive: One has a floor taken from a plantation in Gloucester, a claw-foot tub, and an amazing freestanding, glass-sided shower. The sumptuous Suite Williamsburg has an elaborate carved-ball and claw-foot four-poster bed and a fireplace. (The parlor, too, has a fireplace.) Magnolia's Peach, upstairs, has a side room with a single twin featherbed all to its own. Each room has a TV with VCR and a collection of videos, and an amenities basket bulging with everything the traveler might need, from bandages to needle and thread. The furnishings are a fetching mix of 18th- and 19th-century reproductions and antiques. The latest romantic touch is two tree swings (one a two-seater) by the courtyard.

Liberty Rose sits on a densely wooded hilltop, and the lake on the William and Mary campus is within easy walking distance. A stroll at dusk may be hard to resist, since romance sets the tone here all year round.

🏠 *1 double room with bath, 3 suites. Air-conditioning, phones and TV with VCR in rooms, turndown service. $135–$205; full breakfast, afternoon refreshments. AE, MC, V. No smoking indoors, no pets.*

Newport House

710 S. Henry St., Williamsburg, VA 23185, tel. 757/229–1775

The Newport House takes the prize for the most unusual bed-and-breakfast in Williamsburg, if not all of Tidewater Virginia. It is a meticulous reproduction of a house that once stood in Newport, Rhode Island, designed by the Colonial architect Peter Harrison. The three-story, dormered structure, painted creamy yellow, stands just across the street from the William and Mary Law School on a small lot that contains an herb garden. It is furnished in period style, with English and American antiques and reproductions. Both guest rooms have canopy beds.

The owners, Cathy and John Millar, are practicing Colonial country dancers; they hold country dancing from 8 PM to 10 PM in the ballroom on Tuesday and, occasionally, Scottish country dances on Thursday. (They can also arrange for costume rentals.) Breakfast, from Colonial recipes, is accompanied by a fascinating historical lecture given by John, who also shares his video library of movies set in the 18th century with guests.

🏠 *2 double rooms with baths. Air-conditioning, TV with VCR and videos in rooms, fireplace in living room. $130; full breakfast. No credit cards, no smoking indoors, no pets, 2-night minimum weekends and holidays.*

North Bend Plantation

12200 Weyanoke Rd., Charles City, VA 23030, tel. 804/829–5176 or 800/841–1479

Routinely, a stay at this Charles City County plantation begins with a tour of the house and grounds conducted by Ridgely Copland, a farmer's wife and a nurse (once named Virginia nurse of the year). Along the way Ridgely points out Union breastworks from 1864, wild asparagus, herds of deer, a swamp, and the wide James River. This is a well-maintained working farm, and the Coplands are salt-of-the-earth people striving to keep their 850 acres intact in the face of modern agricultural dilemmas.

North Bend, on the National Register of Historic Places and also a Virginia Historic Landmark, was built for Sarah Harrison, sister of William Henry Harrison, the ninth president, who died in office having served just one month. It's a fine example of the Academic Greek Revival style, a wide white-frame structure with a black-and-green roof and a slender chimney at each corner. Built in 1819 with a classic two-over-two layout, large center hall, and Federal mantels and stair carvings, it was remodeled in 1853 according to Asher Benjamin designs. But beyond its architectural distinctions, North Bend is drenched in history. The Sheridan Room, the premier guest bedroom, represents both sides of the Civil War. It contains a walnut desk used by the Union general Philip Sheridan, complete with his labels on the pigeonholes. A copy of his map was found in one of its drawers and is now laminated for guests' viewing. The room's tester bed belonged to Edmund Ruffin, the ardent Confederate who fired the first shot of the war at Ft. Sumter. The headboard is a reproduction; a Yankee cannonball in 1864 splintered its predecessor. The Federal Room has a new iron-and-brass bed.

Above all, though, at North Bend history means family. George Copland is the great-great-nephew of Sarah Harrison and the great-great-grandson of Edmund Ruffin. Family heirlooms are everywhere, as is the amazing collection of Civil War first editions, which make fascinating bedtime reading. There's an inviting upstairs wicker-furnished sunporch and a one-of-a-kind children's area with vintage toys.

▦ *4 double rooms with baths, 1 suite. Air-conditioning, TV in rooms, fireplace in 1 room, ceiling fans, robes, pool, tandem bicycles, croquet, horseshoes, badminton, volleyball. $115–$148; full breakfast, welcoming refreshments. MC, V. Smoking on porches only, no pets, closed Thanksgiving and Dec. 25.*

War Hill Inn

4560 Longhill Rd., Williamsburg, VA 23188, tel. 757/565–0248 or 800/743–0248

The War Hill Inn is 3 miles north of town; this is a drawback or an attraction, depending on whether visitors prefer to stay overnight in the thick of Colonial things or put some space between their lodging and the crowds. Adding to the inn's feeling of remoteness are the surrounding pastures, where owner Bill Lee's prizewinning Black Angus cows munch on the grass. Bill is a retired veterinarian who built the house in 1968 to raise a family along with his wife, Shirley. Together with son Will, they run the place and keep it in excellent condition.

The inn, where each room is named after a Virginia native who became an American president, is a copy of the Anderson House in Colonial Williamsburg, and a fine one at that. Inside are architectural features that came from other places— the heart-pine floors from a schoolhouse and a staircase from a Lutheran church. The decor in the guest rooms is a mélange of Colonial reproductions and family things; the downstairs Tyler Room is notable for its size and privacy. War Hill is a good choice for families— thanks to its fenced-in grounds, a small orchard of peaches and plums, and The Washington Cottage, a two-bedroom suite that sleeps five.

▦ *4 double rooms with baths, 1 cottage. Air-conditioning, cable TV in rooms, fireplace in parlor, whirlpool bath in cottage. $75–$120; full breakfast. MC, V. No smoking, no pets, 2-night minimum weekends.*

Piedmont

Few cities in this country are so deeply devoted to—one might say, so in love with—a single man as is Virginia's Piedmont capital, Charlottesville. On a farm east of town (in the present-day hamlet of Shadwell), Thomas Jefferson, the third president of the United States, was born; and on a mountaintop overlooking a countryside Jefferson himself considered Edenic, he built his home. Even the youngest of visitors has already seen Monticello, for it appears on one side of the nickel, though its minted image hardly does it justice. The breathtaking edifice, constructed on architectural principles that would change the face of America, is a house that reveals volumes about the man who built it and lived there.

For instance, in the terraced vegetable gardens (restored according to Jefferson's garden book), he helped popularize the tomato in North American cuisine and raised 19 types of English peas, his favorite food. (Mr. Jefferson, as he is called around here, attributed his long life—he lived to be 83—to his vegetarian eating habits.) Here he built a glass-enclosed pavilion, where he went to read, write, and watch his garden grow. Most of the 20,000 letters he wrote were penned in his study in a reclining chair with revolving desk (he had

*rheumatism and worked from a semirecumbent position).
Jefferson was also a collector; the walls of the formal parlor
are lined with portraits of friends, like Washington and
Monroe, and the east entrance hall displays mastodon bones
and a buffalo head brought back from the West by Lewis and
Clark. Still, on the estate of the man acclaimed as a leading
architect of American liberty, the irony of the nearby slave
quarters will not be lost on more than a few visitors.*

*"Architecture," wrote Jefferson, "is my delight and putting up
and pulling down one of my favorite pastimes." Originally he
built Monticello in 1779 as an American Palladian villa, but
after seeing the work of Boullée and Ledoux in France, he
returned to Monticello with a head full of new ideas, above all
about its dome, and an aversion to grand staircases, which he
believed took up too much room. Today the full effect is best
seen from the flower gardens on the west side.*

*There's another reason for Charlottesville's love affair with
Jefferson—the University of Virginia. If Monticello is a taste
of Jeffersonian style, the school's rotunda and colonnade offer
up a banquet. Jefferson began designing the university
buildings at the age of 74; in 1976 the American Institute of
Architects voted them the most outstanding achievement in
American architecture. The rotunda was inspired by the
Pantheon, in Rome, but the dual colonnade that extends from
it, intended as both dwelling place and study center for
students and faculty, is all Jefferson's own. Students still
inhabit the colonnade rooms, amid fireplaces, porches, and
rocking chairs.*

*Downtown Charlottesville has been converted into a
pedestrian mall where shoppers find intriguing stores, such as
the Signet Gallery, for extraordinary crafts; and, for great
arrays of vintages, Market Street Wineshop & Grocery and
Tastings, which doubles as a café.*

*Charlottesville lies in the Blue Ridge foothills, and the driving
here is fun and scenic. Route 20, called the Constitution Route,*

takes travelers past Montpelier (James Madison's home) in Orange, 25 miles north of Charlottesville. It also takes motorists south to the village of Scottsville on the James River, once the seat of Albemarle County, rich in Revolutionary and Civil War history. It's a favorite spot for canoe and inner-tube trips. Twenty miles to the west the Blue Ridge rises, with access to the Skyline Drive or Parkway at Rockfish Gap.

Places to Go, Sights to See

Ash Lawn–Highland (James Monroe Pkwy., Charlottesville, tel. 804/293–9539). Just down the road from Monticello, this is the restored home of James Monroe; its mountaintop site (selected by Jefferson) offers views of Monticello's dome. A tour covers the original rooms and the warming kitchen. Today it's still a working 550-acre farm where sheep and peacocks roam. Summertime brings a Festival of the Arts and Plantation Days.

Barboursville Vineyards (17645 Winery Rd., Barboursville, north of Charlottesville, tel. 540/832–3824). In addition to tasting the several varieties produced here, you can explore the ruins of Governor James Barbour's plantation home. Among the other dozen or so wineries in the area are *Oakencroft* (1486 Oakencroft La., Charlottesville, tel. 804/296–4188), *Horton/Montdomaine* (6399 Spotswood Trail, Gordonsville, tel. 540/832–7440), and *Totier Creek Vineyard* (1652 Harris Creek Rd., Charlottesville, tel. 804/979–7105). (For a map of Virginia wineries, contact the Virginia Wine Marketing Program, VDACS, Division of Marketing, Box 1163, Richmond, VA 23218, tel. 800/828–4637.)

The Exchange Hotel & Civil War Museum (Rte. 15, Gordonsville, tel. 540/832–2944). Built in 1860 as a railroad hotel, this Greek Revival structure served as a military hospital during the Civil War and is now an excellent museum devoted to the military and medical history of that conflict.

Michie Tavern (683 Thomas Jefferson Pkwy., Charlottesville, tel. 804/977–1234). This tavern, dating from 1765, was moved to its present location on the road to Monticello in 1920. This is quite a commercial operation; visitors might be advised to call ahead to request a narrated (not recorded) tour. The cafeteria-style restaurant serves such historic dishes as fried chicken, black-eyed peas, and stewed tomatoes. The *Virginia Wine Museum* is within the tavern, and part of the tour.

Monticello (Rte. 53, Charlottesville, tel. 804/984–9822). Jefferson's home lies about 2 miles southeast of the intersection of I–64 and Route 20. The tour, which ascends Mr. Jefferson's "little mountain" by shuttle bus, lasts about half an hour and is extremely rewarding. Afterward visitors are free to roam the gardens, view the hidden dependencies, and make a pilgrimage to the great man's grave. Earlier arrivals make for shorter waits.

Montpelier (11407 Constitution Hwy., Montpelier Station, tel. 540/672–2728). James Madison, despite two terms as president through the War of 1812, is best known as the father of the Constitution and formulator of the Bill of Rights. Somewhat lost in Jefferson's shadow (he stood only 5'2"), Madison and his wife, Dolley, lived here from 1817 to 1836, later followed by William du Pont, Sr., who bought it in 1901. Those with rocky in-law relations will savor the tale of acrimony that festered among the Madison family members. The guided tour of the 2,700-acre estate leads visitors around the grounds and through the 77-room house. Visitors may conduct self-guided walking tours of the formal gardens and Madison's grave. Held here now, on the first Saturday in November, is the Montpelier Hunt Race.

Moormont Orchards (6530 Moormont Rd., Rapidan, tel. 540/672–2730; 800/572–2262 in VA). In season you can pick your own apples, peaches, plums, and nectarines.

Orange. The *James Madison Museum* (129 Caroline St., tel. 540/672–1776) is filled with James's and Dolley's possessions and correspondence, and local historical and agricultural exhibits. Next door, *St. Thomas' Episcopal Church* (tel. 540/672–3761) was created with Jefferson's only known (and now demolished) ecclesiastical work in mind.

Scottsville sits on the James River and is where Lafayette made a successful stand against General Cornwallis in 1781. The village holds 32 Federal-style buildings and the locks of the James River Kanawha Canal, which were a target for 10,000 bluecoats under General Sheridan during the Civil War. The nearby *James River Runners* (10082 Hatton Ferry Rd., tel. 804/286–2338) rents tubes, rafts, and canoes.

University of Virginia (Charlottesville, tel. 804/924–7969). Visitors may wander the grounds or take one of the rotunda tours conducted several times daily (except on holidays and during exams). Inside the rotunda is Alexander Galt's statue of Jefferson, which students saved from the fire of 1895.

Walton's Mountain Museum (Rockfish River Rd., Schuyler, tel. 804/831–2000). Earl Hamner, Jr., creator of the long-running TV series *The Waltons*, based the family's tales on his own experiences growing up in this small village. The simple museum re-creates the TV sets and has lots of memorabilia, videotapes, and photos of the show and cast.

Restaurants

In addition to top dining at the area's inns, there's a cosmopolitan assortment of restaurants in Charlottesville. **Metropolitan** (214 Water St., tel. 804/977–1043) serves popular nouvelle American cuisine. **Memory & Company** (213 2nd St., SW, tel. 804/296–3539) has a terrific wine list and prix-fixe dinners whose prices vary widely depending on the seasonal selections. **C & O** (515 E. Water St., tel. 804/971–7044) has a bistro downstairs and formal French dining upstairs. **Eastern Standard** (Downtown Mall, tel. 804/295–8668) has the same formal upstairs/bistro downstairs set-up. For casual dining in Charlottesville, there's **Court Square Tavern** (E. Jefferson and 5th Sts., tel. 804/296–6111), with a pub atmosphere and more than 120 imported beers, and **Southern Culture** (633 W. Main St., tel. 804/979–1990), a reasonably priced mix of Caribbean and Cajun. In Gordonsville, **Toliver House Restaurant** (209 N. Main St., tel. 540/832–3485) gets top ratings, as does the **Bavarian Chef** in Madison (Rte. 29 S, tel. 540/948–6505).

Tourist Information

Charlottesville/Albemarle Convention & Visitors Bureau (Box 161, Charlottesville, VA 22902, tel. 804/977–1783). **Orange County Visitors Bureau** (Box 133, Orange, VA 22960, tel. 540/672–1653). **Virginia Division of Tourism** (901 E. Byrd St., Richmond, VA 23219, tel. 804/786–2051 or 800/847–4882).

Reservation Services

Guesthouses Bed & Breakfast, Inc. (Box 5737, Charlottesville, VA 22905, tel. 804/979–7264) can arrange entrée to private houses that are otherwise closed to the public. For a copy of the **Bed and Breakfast Association of Virginia's** directory, describing more than 100 establishments, call the **Virginia Division of Tourism's** B&B line (tel. 800/262–1293). The **Virginia Tourism Corporation's** Washington, D.C., office also operates a B&B and small-inn booking service (tel. 202/659–5523; 800/934–9184 outside DC).

Clifton

1296 Clifton Inn Dr., Charlottesville, VA 22911, tel. 804/971–1800 or 888/971–1800, fax 804/971–7098

From the warm, paneled library and the comforter-covered beds to the sunny terrace and the languid lake, there are reasons aplenty to settle in here. One of the state's top inns, Clifton stands in quiet Shadwell, a small community in Charlottesville, near Jefferson's birthplace.

It's no wonder the inn is a National Historic Landmark: The handsome white-frame, six-columned manse was once home to Thomas Mann Randolph, governor of Virginia, member of Congress and husband of Jefferson's daughter, Martha. It's now owned by a Washington attorney but ably administered by innkeeper Craig Hartman. As chef, Craig also oversees Clifton's wonderful meals (the applewood-smoked loin of veal with Vidalia-onion marmalade has lots of takers). Midweek dinners are $48; Saturday's five-course, prix-fixe dinners ($58) include entertainment.

There are guest rooms in the manor house, the carriage house, the livery, and Randolph's former law office. All have wood-burning fireplaces and antique or canopy beds. Six rooms have recently renovated large baths with multiple showerheads that grow vertically up the wall so no part of the body gets missed. French limestone floors were installed in all bathrooms. Some rooms have French windows, some have lake views, and there are plenty of antique bed-coverings. Rooms in the dependencies have a fresh, cottagelike feel, with whitewashed walls, bright floral prints, and lots of windows. Manor House rooms are bright and airy with touches of the original woodwork and design still intact to remind guests of the history that surrounds them. Suites in the carriage house have windows, shutters, and other artifacts from the home of the explorer Meriwether Lewis.

The grounds spread through 48 acres of woods. The 20-acre lake offers good fishing (the inn provides rods and tackle boxes) and lazy floats on inner tubes. Vines and slate stonework blend the swimming pool and heated spa tub into the bucolic setting. There's a clay tennis court, as well as croquet, volleyball, horseshoes, and badminton. For pure loafing, there are wooden chairs scattered across the lawns and a small gazebo. The extensive gardens are carefully tended: The estate grows its own flowers, lettuce, and herbs, many of which find their way into Craig's epicurean creations.

With fireplaces in common areas, Clifton offers a magical combination of elegance and hominess. It is rapidly gaining national attention for superbly attentive (but not hovering) guest service. A smiling staff member is always nearby, ready to assist guests with any needs they may have. A corner of the big butcher-block island in the kitchen is for guests, who often sit and chat with Craig as he cooks. A jar of cookies is always there, and sodas are in the refrigerator. Underneath the manor house is a newly installed wine cellar, complete with 220 varieties, and a formal tasting table. The tasting room, equipped with state-of-the art audiovisual equipment, can be used for small-group meetings.

▦ *10 double rooms with baths, 4 suites. Restaurant, air-conditioning, lake, pool, spa tub, tennis court. $150–$315; full breakfast, afternoon tea. MC, V. No smoking, no pets, 2-night minimum weekends.*

1817 Historic Bed & Breakfast

1211 W. Main St., Charlottesville, VA 22903, tel. 804/979–7353 or 800/730–7443, fax 804/979–7209

The 1817 Historic Bed & Breakfast is ideal for parents and alums visiting the University of Virginia, since the campus is just a block away. The Federal-style town house, built by James Dinsmore, one of Thomas Jefferson's craftsmen, was just the historic gem that interior designer Candace DeLoach was seeking when she came to the area in 1992. Raised in Savannah, with parents in the antiques business, Candace used her background in Southern hospitality and decorating to create an eclectically furnished inn connected to her antiques shop.

Guest rooms include the room named for Miss Olive, a turn-of-the-century guest; another with a private marble bathroom and glassed-in shower; a small hall room (without windows), filled with Candace's grandmother's furniture; a white-paneled sleeping porch with two double white-metal beds; and a vast suite with yellow walls and a rose ceiling. The inn's small tearoom offers imaginative sandwiches, homemade soups, and Candace's prizewinning muffins.

🏠 *4 double rooms with baths, 1 suite. Air-conditioning, cable TV in rooms, phones in 2 rooms and suite, bicycles. $89–$199; Continental-plus breakfast, lemonade and tea on arrival. AE, MC, V. Smoking on porch and in tearoom only, no pets, 2-night minimum on UVA-event weekends, 3-night minimum at graduation.*

High Meadows and Mountain Sunset

High Meadows La. (Rte. 4, Box 6), Scottsville, VA 24590, tel. 804/286-2218 or 800/232-1832

High Meadows, which stands on 50 acres in Scottsville, is above all a bed-and-breakfast inn done by hand. The hands in question are those of Peter Shushka, a retired submariner, and his wife, Mary Jae Abbitt, a financial analyst.

In this unique B&B, Federal and late-Victorian architecture exist side by side, happily joined by a longitudinal hall. It wasn't always so. The Italianate front section was built in 1882 by C.B. Harris, who had intended to level the older house several paces behind it. But bear-

ing in mind her growing family, his wife refused to give up the old place, built in 1830, and for a time a plank between the two was the tenuous connector that kept the marriage intact. Today High Meadows is on the National Register of Historic Places.

Peter and Mary Jae have decorated the place with great originality, keeping intact the stylistic integrity of each section. They've also used fabrics on the bed hangings and windows imaginatively. Fairview, in the 1880s portion, is the quintessential bride's room, with a fireplace, flowing bed drapery, a three-window alcove, and a claw-foot tub. The Scottsville suite, upstairs in the Federal section, has stenciled walls lined with antique stuffed animals, a fireplace, and rafters across the ceiling. A two-person whirlpool sits in the middle of the Music Room.

The Carriage House, also called Glenside, is a contemporary building of cedar, glass, and slate on the site of the original; this two-room suite has a kitchen, deck, and two-person outdoor hot tub. The property also includes the Mountain Sunset (named for its view), a 1910 Queen Anne manor house with two suites, two rooms, fireplaces, decks, and plenty of privacy.

Full country breakfasts may include strada (potato, cheese, and onion cooked together and served in a small bowl); Hungarian *bonitza*; or Amish pancakes. On Saturday, a six-course dinner is included in the room rate; during the week, dinner runs $20–$30 per person and includes wine. The inn has 5 acres of vineyards, which produce pinot noir grapes for its own private-label wine.

🏠 *7 double rooms with baths, 7 suites. Air-conditioning, cable TV in 1 suite, fireplaces in 11 rooms and 4 common areas, robes, turndown service, whirlpool baths in 3 rooms. $79–$185; full breakfast, evening hors d'oeuvres and wine tasting Fri.–Sun. and some Thurs. MC, V. No smoking indoors, pets permitted in ground-level rooms by ar-*

rangement only, 2-night minimum all spring, fall, and holiday weekends, closed Dec. 24–25.

The Holladay House

155 W. Main St., Orange, VA 22960, tel. 540/672–4893 or 800/358–4422, fax 540/672–3028

The Holladay House, in the center of Orange, makes a good stop for anyone visiting Montpelier or driving the country roads in between. Pete Holladay (a former school administrator), wife Phebe, or inn-sitter Shirley Ramsey welcomes guests to the 1830 Federal-style home, where Pete's great-grandmother's crazy quilt hangs on one wall, and most of the furnishings are family pieces. According to Pete, much of the house looks just as it did when it was built despite extensive renovations.

The guest rooms are simply furnished and have modern black-and-white tiled baths. The Suite has sitting rooms and a bathroom with a vast whirlpool tub and a double-head shower. A private brick patio was recently added for each of the two ground-floor rooms, including Room 7, which has a kitchen, TV, and phone—ideal for business travelers.

Acclaimed by other innkeepers as "Virginia's best muffin maker," Pete brings breakfast to his guests' rooms.

▥ *4 double rooms with baths, 2 suites. Air-conditioning, cable TV in 2 rooms. $95–$195; full breakfast. AE, D, MC, V. No smoking, no pets, 2-night minimum weekends Oct.–Nov. and during graduations, closed Thanksgiving, Dec. 22–26.*

The Inn at Meander Plantation

U.S. Rte. 15 (Rte. 5, Box 460A), Locust Dale, VA 22948, tel. 540/672–4912 or 800/385–4936, fax 540/672–0405

Even those already versed in the treasures of the Piedmont region may be guilty of a gasp when they visit the Inn at Meander Plantation, just off Route 15 about 10 miles north of Orange. The simple sign and whitewashed brick markers give little hint of the architectural jewel that comes into view at the top of the driveway. Located on an estate settled in 1727 by Joshua Fry, a map-making partner of Thomas Jefferson's father, the inn bears faithful testament to its Colonial origins, replete with slave quarters and summer kitchen.

Innkeepers Suzanne Thomas and Suzie Blanchard—both former newspaper people who, along with Blanchard's husband, Bob, run the establishment—offer a reliably warm welcome that has kept a host of visitors coming back regularly to this historic hilltop residence.

An ample parlor and dining area, an occasional low-slung hallway, and bedrooms notable for their high, roomy beds and large windows recall the days before electric light and central air, when natural assets had to be exploited. The series of outbuildings, including a stable, recalls the role that equestrian expertise has played in the area's history, both military and economic. The owners still keep horses on the property.

Another dependency, the summer kitchen, circa 1760s, separated from the main house by a shaded brick walkway decked out with an American boxwood hedge, features a two-story suite with a claw-foot tub and shower in the sunny bathroom upstairs. Here, as in any of the other spacious rooms, visitors can revel in the immense solitude the estate affords or contemplate the nearby attractions, a list of which the hosts provide at check-in. Located far beyond the reach of city lights and sounds, the inn has a wide back porch for those who want to savor the dusk, and brick paths for others who want to take the property's name at face value and wander off to enjoy the pristine view of the constellations.

⊞ *5 double rooms with baths, 1 suite. Air-conditioning units on request, TV in library, fireplaces in 5 rooms and in living room of main building, piano, conference facilities, hiking, fishing, tubing, pony rides, stabling for horses, lawn games. $105–$195; full breakfast. No smoking.*

The Inn at Monticello

Hwy 20 South, 1188 Scottsville Rd., Charlottesville, VA 22902, tel. 804/979–3593, fax 804/296–1344

Norman and Rebecca Lindway took innkeeping courses before they purchased the Inn at Monticello in the fall of 1996. They left their jobs as education administrators in Cleveland for the land of Jefferson and this 1850s manor house, which lies south of town and just 2 miles from Jefferson's oft sought-out abode. The condos on a hill in the back hardly spoil the peacefulness for guests, who sit on the two-story front gallery soaking up the bucolic view of a brook trickling over the long front lawn.

Downstairs there's a parlor, a twin-bedded room, and a nicely furnished honeymoon room. There are three upstairs bedrooms, including a lilac and a yellow room, both with cotton balloon shades. The bed linen is downy soft and complemented by European coverlets. Mornings begin with gourmet breakfasts, which might include crisp apple pancakes, fresh fruit, blueberry French toast, scones, and quiche. The rest of the day can be spent strolling the Lindways' flower and herb gardens, snoozing in a rocker on the wide front porch, or visiting nearby Monticello.

⊞ *5 double rooms with baths. Air-conditioning, fireplaces in 2 rooms. $115–$140; full breakfast, afternoon refreshments. MC, V. No smoking, no pets, 2-night minimum some high-season weekends.*

Keswick Hall

701 Club Dr., Keswick, VA 22947, tel. 804/979–3440 or 800/274–5391, fax 804/977–4171

A visit to Keswick Hall is like spending a weekend with friends in the English countryside—that is, if those friends are very wealthy and live in a vast house with armies of antiques, plump chairs and couches, a butler to serve drinks, and a golf course in the backyard. Keswick sits on 600 acres in the wooded, rolling countryside east of Charlottesville. It's owned by Sir Bernard Ashley, who was married to the late Laura Ashley, so fabrics and furnishings from the company are used throughout. Tiny floral prints, though, do not dominate the place. Instead, fabrics, none of which are repeated, run the gamut from crisp stripes to elegant brocades. Sir Bernard's personal collection of antiques, century-old books, paintings, and silver-framed family photos gives the house the lived-in-for-generations look. An innkeeping colleague of Ashley's once said, somewhat in awe, that each interior door alone contains $1,000 worth of hardware.

Bedrooms are individually decorated in color schemes ranging from soft beige and white to crisp blues to cozy dark green. All have comfy chairs, couches, or cushioned window seats. Baths have extra touches, such as whirlpool tubs in six rooms, extralong tubs in several others, heated towel racks, hair dryers, an abundance of thick towels, terry-cloth robes, and dishes with cotton balls. Some rooms have private terraces with golf-course views, and several have decorative fireplaces.

Visitors want to loaf here, perhaps in front of a roaring fire on chilly days, lingering over coffee and the paper in the sunny morning room, having afternoon tea with delicate madeleines and scones in the yellow Crawford Lounge, or penning a letter at Sir Bernard's desk in the library. The all-red snooker room is the spot for predinner drinks and canapés and a late-night brandy, served by the friendly butler.

There's a full country breakfast with a wide range of choices in the Ashley room. Prix-fixe four- and five-course dinners are served there for $58.

Guests have access to the Keswick Club, a private facility with an Arnold Palmer–designed 18-hole golf course, fitness facilities, an indoor-outdoor pool, tennis courts, a croquet lawn, and a wood-paneled casual dining room.

▦ *45 double rooms with baths, 4 suites. Restaurants, air-conditioning, cable TV and phones in rooms, turndown service, conference facilities, tennis courts, golf course, massage, and fitness facility, bicycles, pool. $225–$595; full breakfast, afternoon tea. AE, DC, MC, V. No smoking in dining rooms, no pets.*

Prospect Hill

2887 Poindexter Rd., Trevilians, VA 23093, tel. 540/967–0844 or 800/277–0844, fax 540/967–0102

For elegance and luxury, Prospect Hill is one of Virginia's finest inns, lying just east of Charlottesville in the 14-square-mile Green Springs National Historic District. Built circa 1732, it's the oldest continuously occupied frame manor house in Virginia. But except for the obligatory dependencies and impressive boxwood hedges, Prospect Hill doesn't look like a plantation, because it was expanded in the Victorian era, when a columned facade and decorative cornices were added. The innkeepers have painted it lemony yellow.

Fresh flowers, a basket of fruit, and just-baked cookies welcome guests to their rooms. There are four nicely furnished rooms in the main house, but the big treat is the six refurbished dependencies. Sanco Pansy's cottage, 100 feet from the manor, has a sitting room and whirlpool tub for two. The carriage house, lit by four Palladian windows, offers views of ponies in the meadow nibbling the green Virginia turf. Surrounded by such *luxe, calme, et volupté*, it's strange to consider that in the last century, the dependencies were filled with hams, ice blocks, and livestock.

Dinner at the inn is a marvelous production, not so much for the cuisine (French-inspired and well above average) as for the ceremony. This begins with complimentary wine and cider a half hour before supper—outdoors in good weather. When the dinner bell rings, guests file in to hear the menu and an earnest grace recited by second-generation innkeeper Michael Sheehan, who recently took over after he and his father, Bill, had run the place together for years. Michael is also the chef and serves up excellent five-course dinners (Tues.–Sat., $45).

A hot breakfast arrives on a tray for guests wishing to stay ensconced in the dependencies. Some, however, crawl from the soothing whirlpool tub into the dining room. As splendid as the inn is, it hasn't become too smoothly professional. Even the most low-profile guest is liable to meet the gregarious innkeeper and appreciate the way his family has put its stamp on Prospect Hill.

Guests should get directions to the inn. It is several miles from Trevilians, the town where it receives mail.

▦ *5 double rooms with baths in manor, 5 doubles with baths and 3 suites in dependencies. Air-conditioning, TV with VCR in meeting room, fireplaces in rooms, whirlpools in 8 rooms, clock radios, pool. $160–$250; MAP, dinner (Tues.–Sat.) and breakfast; dinner baskets available on Mon. for $60 per couple. AE, D, MC, V. No pets, 2-night minimum with Sat. stay, closed Dec. 24–25.*

The Shadows

14291 Constitution Hwy., Orange, VA 22960, tel. 540/672-5057

Travelers will be hard-pressed to find a home more lovingly tended than the Shadows, a 1913 stone farmhouse, serenely set in a grove of old cedars on the road between Orange and Montpelier. Pat and Barbara Loffredo, refugees from New York, where Pat was a police officer, have filled their house with a cheerful collection of country Victorian antiques. Prize pieces include an intricately carved Civil War–era hunt board, an old pump organ, two claw-foot tubs, and Maxfield Parrish prints wherever the eye rests. The house is perhaps best described as Arts and Crafts style—a modified bungalow built of wood and local fieldstone. It has lustrous oak floors and windowsills around which lace curtains flutter. The four spotless guest rooms upstairs have standard Victorian trappings.

All the tangibles here are pleasant enough, but Pat and Barbara, their skills honed over a decade in the business, put the Shadows over the mark. Their joy in the home they share with guests and a friendly small dog named James Madison—in honor of the former president whose estate is just a few miles up the highway—is infectious. The Loffredos delight in coddling guests, overwhelming them with country gourmet breakfasts of French toast soufflé and poached pear with sherry cream. Guests may also appreciate the old barns and hay fields that dot the inn's 44-acre plot, especially when fall colors near their peak.

▥ *4 double rooms with baths, 2 cottage suites. Air-conditioning, gas-log fireplace in 1 cottage, turndown service. $80–$110; full breakfast, afternoon refreshments. MC, V. No smoking, no pets, 2-night minimum in May, some fall weekends, and holidays.*

The Silver Thatch Inn

3001 Hollymead Dr., Charlottesville, VA 22911, tel. 804/978-4686, fax 804/973-6156

The Silver Thatch is 7 miles north of downtown Charlottesville off U.S. 29. The oldest part of its semicircle of connected buildings is log, built by mercenary Hessian prisoners hired by the British during the Revolutionary War. Vince and Rita Scoffone became innkeepers because they wanted to spend more time together (he was a workaholic banker). The inn is decorated in a snug country-Colonial style with richly colored walls and trim. The guest rooms all have quilts, down comforters, and antiques; four have fireplaces. The four cottage rooms and the Madison Room in the main house have sparkling new bathrooms.

The restaurant menu, which changes every six to eight weeks, helps to generate a near-full house many nights; offerings have included Rock Cornish hen with a roasted-pepper walnut sauce, and pan-seared lobster with red pepper and mango marmalade. Vegetarian diners will also find a special each day. Since 1989 the wine list, featuring Vince's picks, has received an award of excellence from *Wine Spectator* magazine. Silver Thatch guests may use a pool nearby.

▥ *7 double rooms with baths. Restaurant, air-conditioning, cable TV in bar, clock radios. $115–$150; Continental breakfast. AE, DC, MC, V. No smoking, no pets, 2-night minimum weekends Apr.–mid-June and Sept.–mid-Nov., closed Dec. 24–25.*

Sleepy Hollow Farm

16280 Blue Ridge Turnpike, Gordonsville, VA 22942, tel. 540/832-5555 or 800/215-4804, fax 540/832-2515

As motorists roller-coaster past cattle farms and vineyards on Route 231, north of Charlottesville, they may pass the bright red roof of the barn at Sleepy Hollow Farm. This two-story brick house, begun in the 18th century, is surrounded by fields grazed by Black Angus and Tarentais cattle.

Sleepy Hollow is homey, eminently suited to families with children: There are rabbits in the hedgerows, and a spring-fed pond that attracts ducks and is good for fishing and swimming. The main house has three rooms, and one two-bedroom suite. The Chestnut Wood Cottage—formerly two small houses but now connected—has a fireplace, a kitchen, a deck, and a whirlpool. It can be rented as one unit or two. Sleepy Hollow's owner, Beverley Allison, came to the house as a bride, raised a family, was a news producer, served as an Episcopal missionary in Central America, then returned to open her comfortable bed-and-breakfast and tend its lush gardens. Thus, she has stories to tell, if you can persuade her; ask for the one about a ghost who frequented one of the guest rooms.

▦ *3 double rooms with baths, 1 2-bedroom suite, 1 cottage. Air-conditioning; TV in 3 rooms; kitchen, whirlpool, and fireplace in cottage; TV with VCR in sitting room; wood-burning stove in main house and 1 room; swimming pond; riding arranged. $65–$150; full breakfast, afternoon refreshments. MC, V. No smoking in dining room, 2-night minimum some weekends.*

Tivoli

9171 Tivoli Dr., Gordonsville, VA 22942, tel. 540/832–2225 or 800/840–2225, fax 540/832–3691

Sitting high on a hill outside Gordonsville, in the midst of Phil and Susie Audibert's 235-acre estate, is Tivoli, a three-story, Corinthian-columned, 24-room brick house built in 1903. Phil grew up in the house, but he and Susie now live in the farmhouse, so Tivoli stood vacant for several years. Transforming it into a stately B&B has been a major, but worthwhile, undertaking. The result, a breath-taking scene, has lately inspired a fair amount of vow-taking, too, with 16 nuptials performed here over a recent year.

The Audiberts have concentrated first on what counts most—the guest rooms. The biggest one is the Gold Room, which has an antique Venetian headboard and the original claw-foot tub. The corner Peach Room commands sweeping views of the Piedmont and the Blue Ridge Mountains. All have fireplaces. Impressive family antiques fill the house. Downstairs there's a large dining room, a living room, and a ballroom with a Steinway grand piano. These rooms still bear signs of age—watermarks, some peeling paint and paper. Complimentary beverages are always available.

▦ *4 double rooms with baths. TV with VCR in reading room, phones in rooms. $90–$125; full breakfast. D, MC, V. No smoking in bedrooms, no pets, 2-night minimum preferred on weekends.*

200 South Street

200 South St., Charlottesville, VA 22902, tel. 804/979–0200 or 800/964–7008, fax 804/979–4403

This popular small hotel in downtown Charlottesville is near three preferred eateries, Memory and Company, C&O, and Metropolitan. The complex consists of two Victorian homes built between 1850 and 1900, painted yellow, which cheers up South Street considerably. They're brimming with English and Belgian antiques, some newly reupholstered, and including spacious armoires and lace-canopied four-posters. The walls, many freshly repainted, are lined with occasional displays of local art and an interesting collection of historic Holsinger photographs. The 10 rooms and suite in no. 200 are a cut above those in the neighboring cottage, because there's a parlor there, and train tracks in back make a front room desirable. But all the rooms are inviting and immaculately renovated, and some of them contain such luxuries as whirlpool baths and fireplaces.

Youthful innkeeper Brendan Clancy fixes breakfast, and in the afternoon, tea and wine are served in the sitting room. Brendan is also happy to direct the adventurous to an indoor skating rink or the somewhat more sedentary to a six-screen movie theater, both one block away.

🏨 *17 double rooms with baths, 3 suites. Air-conditioning, cable TV in 3rd-floor lounge, phones in rooms, fireplaces in 9 rooms, turndown service, whirlpool baths in 7 rooms. $100–$210; Continental buffet breakfast, afternoon tea and wine. AE, MC, V. No smoking in public rooms, no pets, 2-night minimum weekends Apr.–May and Sept.–Oct.*

The Blue Ridge/Shenandoah Valley

The standard way to see the Blue Ridge Mountains is to pile
into a car on a weekend in October and drive south from Front
Royal along the Skyline Drive. Bumper-to-bumper traffic
may keep many a vexed motorist from covering the 105-mile
course in full. But even with a turnoff around Rockfish Gap
(just east of Waynesboro), where the drive becomes the equally
(some would claim more) splendid Blue Ridge Parkway, the
trip will hardly constitute a disappointment. Above all, the
landscape at Virginia's western border, with mountains,
forests, and waterways smudging rectilinear boundaries,
stands in marked contrast to the rest of the state's.

In geographical terms, the Blue Ridge is the eastern wall of
the wide Shenandoah Valley, which is framed at the other side
by the Allegheny Mountains. Down the middle of the valley,
bisecting it for some 50 miles, rises a mini-mountain range
called Massanutten Mountain, even though it holds a pretty
valley of its own. The Shenandoah River, which runs through
the valley, divides north of Massanutten—to confuse the issue
further—into a North and South Fork.

Basic geography aside, visitors can plot a more informed assault by crossing the ridge along such strategic and scenic routes as U.S. 211, U.S. 33, and especially Route 56, an untrammeled two-laner that's a favorite even of view-jaded locals. These paths lead into the central and southern sections of the Shenandoah Valley.

Shenandoah National Park holds the heights of the Blue Ridge in a 100-mile strip from Front Royal to Waynesboro and provides nonpareil views of the Virginia Piedmont to the east and the splendid Shenandoah Valley to the west. Anglers come to the park to catch the crafty brook trout, and hikers come to meander. Even a short stroll from a trailhead on the Skyline Drive brings visitors within viewing range of the park's abundant and varied wildlife. Spring and fall are peak seasons for nature lovers. In May the green of new foliage moves up the ridge at a rate of 100 feet a day, with clouds of wild pink azaleas providing contrast. Fall colors are at their most vivid between October 10 and 25, when migrating hawks join the human leaf-gazers to take in the display.

Even for less lingering sightseers, there are better ways to take in the countryside than by zooming along I–81. U.S. 11 parallels the superhighway in a delightfully labyrinthine fashion, providing access to big-name sights, such as the New Market Battlefield and Luray Caverns, and running through small towns, including Woodstock, Edinburg, Mt. Jackson, and Steele's Tavern, where produce stands, flea markets, and local history museums further delay many travelers' progress.

Among Shenandoah's gems, the town of Staunton, as hilly as Rome, was Woodrow Wilson's birthplace; it also boasts pretty Mary Baldwin College and the Museum of American Frontier Culture. Lexington lives and breathes for Stonewall Jackson and Robert E. Lee, who was president of Washington and Lee University after the Civil War. Nearby stands Virginia Military Institute, where Jackson taught before bedeviling Union armies as a Confederate general.

West along winding country roads from Staunton and Lexington lies a countryside often neglected by valley visitors. U.S. 33, U.S. 250, and Route 39 lead to the Appalachian plateau and West Virginia, bordered by the thick foliage of the George Washington National Forest. The roads frequently cross rocky waterways—such as that lovely trio of rivers, the Bullpasture, Cowpasture, and Calfpasture—providing excellent spots for wading and picnicking. Most of the towns in this area are no more than crossroads, with the exception of Hot Springs, site of the Homestead, a 15,000-acre resort that's a Virginia institution. The town of Hot Springs has a pleasant collection of arts-and-crafts shops, gourmet delis, and restaurants.

Places to Go, Sights to See

Belle Grove (336 Belle Grove Rd., Middletown, tel. 540/869–2028). This mansion, built of local limestone in 1794, shows the architectural influence of Thomas Jefferson. It suffered greatly in 1864, when Confederate forces launched an attack on a Union Army headquartered here.

Blue Ridge Parkway. One of the country's most breathtaking drives begins at the southern end of the Skyline Drive and follows the mountain crest south to North Carolina and Tennessee.

Luray Caverns (Hwy. 211 W, Luray, tel. 540/743–6551). They're famed for the "stalacpipe organ," which gets played on cave tours. The valley's underground world can also be surveyed at Grand, Shenandoah, Endless, Skyline, and Dixie caverns.

Massanutten (Rte. 644, McGaheysville, near Harrisonburg, tel. 540/289–9441). A four-season resort has downhill skiing on 14 slopes, golf, tennis, and indoor swimming.

Museum of American Frontier Culture (1250 Richmond Rd., Staunton, tel. 540/332–7850). In four farmsteads reminiscent of those the early settlers left behind in Europe, costumed workers show how families planted, harvested, and did chores.

Natural Bridge (Rtes. 11 and 130, Natural Bridge, tel. 540/291–2121 or 800/533–1410). As a young surveyor, George Washington carved his initials in the limestone walls. Thomas Jefferson was so impressed by this 215-foot-high, 90-foot-long rock span that he bought it in 1774. Visitors would be advised to focus on the spectacular rock formation and overlook commercial intrusions, such as the wax museum.

New Market Battlefield (8895 Collins Dr., New Market, tel. 540/740–3101). Of all Civil War memorials, this is one of the most affecting, for in 1864, 247 cadets from the Virginia Military Institute were sent here to a "baptism of fire." Though some in the battalion were just 15, the line of VMI soldiers died that day.

The Shenandoah National Park (3655 U.S. Hwy. 211 E, Luray, tel. 540/999–3500). Extending 80 miles along the Blue Ridge, the park was created to restore the scenic terrain to the condition in which the earliest settlers found it. A movie shown at the Byrd Visitors Center at Big Meadows tells the story of the park's creation. Information on trails, overlooks, facilities, and activities is available here and at the Dickey Ridge Visitors Center south of Front Royal and at Lost Mountain Information Center north of Waynesboro.

Shenandoah River Floating. The wide, lazy river offers opportunities for gentle canoe and raft rides, with a little fishing, swimming, and inner-tubing thrown in. Good outfitters include the *Downriver Canoe Company* (884 Indian Hollow Rd., Bentonville, tel. 540/635–5526 or 800/338–1963) and *Shenandoah River Outfitters* (6502 S. Page Valley Rd., Luray, tel. 540/743–4159 or 800/622–6632).

Shenandoah Valley Folk Art and Heritage Center (Bowman Rd. and High St., Dayton, tel. 540/879–2681). The museum focuses on local history, culture, and tradition. An electronic map traces the movements of troops in Stonewall Jackson's Valley Campaign.

Skyline Drive. The spectacular 105-mile route that meanders through Shenandoah National Park passes scenic overlooks, hiking trails, restaurants, and visitor centers along the way.

Statler Brothers Complex (501 Thornrose Ave., Staunton, tel. 540/885–7297). Even more than Woodrow Wilson, Staunton loves the Statlers, because the four country musicians are local boys who defied Nashville by cutting their records in their hometown. A converted elementary school showcases artifacts from their careers.

Stonewall Jackson House (8 E. Washington St., Lexington, tel. 540/463–2552). This trim, brick two-story is where Thomas Jonathan Jackson, a natural philosophy professor at VMI, lived with his second wife before he rode away to lead the men in gray. General Jackson died after the Battle of Chancellorsville at the age of 39.

Theater at Lime Kiln (Box office: 14 S. Randolph St., Lexington, tel. 540/463–3074). Set in an abandoned lime quarry, this stage for a professional company of actors has been called the most unusual theater setting in the United States. The Memorial Day–Labor Day schedule includes concerts and plays.

Virginia Horse Center (Rte. 39 W, Lexington, tel. 540/463–2194). The huge equestrian complex has 720 stalls, a 3,800-seat coliseum, regulation dressage areas, horse trails, cross-country courses, and a full calendar of shows and events.

Virginia Military Institute (Letcher Ave., Lexington, tel. 540/464–7000). Founded in 1839, VMI has made recent headlines over its ill-fated fight to remain all-male while continuing its tradition as the nation's first state-supported military school. Uniformed cadets conduct tours of the campus (an austere and blocky Gothic Revival fortress) and parade most Fridays at 4:30 PM during the school year. *VMI's Museum* (Letcher Ave., tel. 540/464–7232) highlights the institute's history and most famous graduates. A taxidermic Little Sorrel, Stonewall Jackson's warhorse, is here, as is the black raincoat that Jackson was wearing when he was shot in 1863. The *George C. Marshall Museum and Library* (Parade Ground, VMI, tel. 540/463–7103) is devoted to the general, a 1901 graduate of VMI. He is the only professional soldier awarded the Nobel Peace Prize (on display here), which he received for his plan to rebuild Europe's economy after World War II.

Washington and Lee University (Washington St., Lexington, tel. 540/463–8400). Founded in 1749, Washington and Lee was subsidized by George Washington when the institution was near bankruptcy in 1796 and presided over by Robert E. Lee in the late 1860s. More recently it has served as a backdrop in the memoir *Jeb and Dash*. An extraordinary front colonnade and the Lee Chapel and Museum, where the general is buried, are its most noteworthy sights.

Wintergreen (Rte. 664, Wintergreen, tel. 804/325–2200 or 800/325–2200). This 11,000-acre, four-season resort lies on the eastern flanks of the Blue Ridge. It has golf, skiing, horseback riding, swimming, restaurants, and an acclaimed nature program.

Woodrow Wilson Birthplace and Museum (24 N. Coalter, Staunton, tel. 540/885–0897). The imposing white Greek Revival home, in the prettiest section of town, has lots of Wilson memorabilia, including his Pierce Arrow limousine.

Restaurants

In Staunton, there's a varied menu in the formal dining rooms or casual pub at **McCormick's** (41 N. Augusta, tel. 540/885–3111) and Italian fare at **L'Italia** (23 E. Beverly St., tel. 540/885–0102). Harrisonburg's **Joshua Wilton House** (412 S. Main St., tel. 540/434–4464) and the **Osceola Mill Country Inn** (Rte. 56, tel. 540/377–6455) in Steele's Tavern get top ratings. In **Front Royal,** the ribs at **Dad's Restaurant** (10 Commerce Ave., tel. 540/622–2768) were voted best in the Valley; **Grapevine Restaurant** (915 N. Royal Ave., tel. 540/635–6615) serves seafood, steaks, and pasta. **The Springhouse** (325 S. Main St., Woodstock, tel. 540/459–4755) serves up reasonably priced food in a comfortable setting. In Lexington, **Il Palazzo** (24 N. Main St., tel. 540/464–5800) serves traditional Italian food. For casual dining there's **Harbs' Bistro** (19 W. Washington St., tel. 540/464–1900) and the **Palms** (101 W. Nelson St., tel. 540/463–7911).

Tourist Information

Front Royal Chamber of Commerce (414 E. Main St., Front Royal, VA 22630, tel. 540/635–3185 or 800/338–2576). **Harrisonburg-Rockingham Convention**

and Visitors Bureau (10 E. Gay St., Harrisonburg, VA 22801, tel. 540/434–2319). **Lexington Visitor Center** (106 E. Washington St., Lexington, VA 24450, tel. 540/463–3777). **Shenandoah Valley Travel Association** (Box 1040, New Market, VA 22844, tel. 540/740–3132). **Staunton-Augusta County Travel Information Center** (Box 810, Staunton, VA 24402, tel. 540/332–3972 or 800/332–5219). **Virginia Division of Tourism** (901 E. Byrd St., Richmond, VA 23219, tel. 804/786–2051 or 800/847–4882). **Winchester and Frederick County Visitors Center** (1360 S. Pleasant Valley Rd., Winchester, VA 22601, tel. 540/662–4135).

Reservation Services

Bed & Breakfasts of the Historic Shenandoah Valley (355 Orchard Dr., Mt. Jackson, VA 22842-9753, tel. 540/477–2400 or 800/478–8714). **Virginia's Inns of the Shenandoah Valley** (Box 1387, Staunton, VA 24401). For a copy of the **Bed and Breakfast Association of Virginia**'s directory, describing more than 100 establishments, call the **Virginia Division of Tourism**'s B&B line (tel. 800/262–1293). The **Virginia Tourism Corporation**'s Washington, D.C., office also operates a B&B and small-inn booking service (tel. 202/659–5523; 800/934–9184 outside DC).

Ashton Country House

*1205 Middlebrook Ave., Staunton, VA
24401, tel. 540/885–7819 or 800/296–7819*

Owners Dorrie and Vince DiStefano,
who bought this inn in 1994, have maintained high standards for the 1860 Greek
Revival home on the outskirts of Staunton. They refurnished the inn with antiques and reproductions—improving
upon the structure's 11-foot ceilings,
original flooring and solid brick walls.
The DiStefanos know the extras that
please guests: four plump pillows on each
bed, good mattresses, reading lights,
oversize showers, bathroom vanities
with lots of counter space, and big armoires with padded hangers.

The large master bedroom suite features
a high four-poster Charleston rice bed.
Guests are free to roam the surrounding
25 acres of pasture, a good way to walk
off one of the inn's full country breakfasts, which may include made-to-order
omelets or homemade biscuits. Lots of
books, handmade quilts, keepsakes, and
the owners' hospitality make this a very
welcoming place.

🏠 *4 double rooms with baths, 1 suite.
Air-conditioning, ceiling fans in rooms,
fireplaces in 4 guest rooms, dining and
living room. $90–$125; full breakfast, afternoon refreshments. MC, V. No smoking indoors, no pets.*

Belle Grae Inn

*515 W. Frederick St., Staunton, VA
24401, tel. 540/886–5151, fax 540/886–6641*

The Belle Grae is a classic small-town
hotel occupying an old Victorian house
and several restored buildings close to
Staunton's downtown. The Old Inn, built
circa 1870, has a wide porch offering
views of Betsy Belle and Mary Grae, two
of the town's many hillocks. Its six bedrooms have high ceilings and are decorated with amiable Victorian antiques,
and downstairs there are two restaurants—one elegant, in Staunton terms,

the other a bistro bar lined with windows.

The suites in the 1870 Jefferson House
are Belle Grae's top-of-the-line, for their
spaciousness and such amenities as fireplaces, balconies, phones, and cable TV.
Town-house rooms are oversize and contain fireplaces, cable TV, and four-poster
or canopy beds. The cottage, with Mission
oak and wicker furniture, has a kitchen,
and the Bishop's Suite, with fireplace,
kitchen, and garden, is extremely private.

🏠 *9 double rooms with baths, 5 suites,
2 cottages. 2 restaurants, air-conditioning,
cable TV and phones in 11 rooms, fireplace in 13 rooms and 3 common areas,
turndown service, nearby health club.
$85–$170; full breakfast. AE, MC, V. No
smoking, no pets.*

Chester House

*43 Chester St., Front Royal, VA 22630,
tel. 540/635–3937 or 800/621–0441 (reservations only), fax 540/636–8695*

Chester House is an architectural gem.
Built in 1905 by an international lawyer
who participated in drawing up the
Treaty of Versailles, the stately Georgian mansion has thick walls, exquisite
dentil molding, and an incredible carved
Italian-marble fireplace in the dining
room. Dogwoods, wisteria, a formal English-style boxwood garden, a goldfish
pond with fountain, and statuary grace
the 2-acre grounds. The huge Royal Oak
Suite has a queen-size poster bed, fireplace, sitting room, and 6-foot bathtub.
The Blue Ridge Room is also spacious,
with a wrought-iron king-size bed and
light floral prints. The suite in the revamped carriage house offers a kitchen
(including microwave oven and refrig-
erator/freezer stocked with beverages),
living and dining rooms, and a wood spiral staircase leading up to a loft with
skylights and a whirlpool tub.

The town of Front Royal sits at the foot
of the Blue Ridge, and the house is a
short walk from Main Street's antiques

and crafts shops and from summer concerts at the Village Common's gazebo. Hospitality is Bill Wilson's seventh career; along with his wife, Ann, he's adding it to his list of successful ventures.

🏠 *5 double rooms with baths. Air-conditioning, ceiling fans, cable TV in lounges, fireplaces in 2 rooms and public rooms, robes, clock radios. $85–$180; Continental breakfast, afternoon refreshments. AE, MC, V. Smoking in TV lounge only, no pets, 2-night minimum some weekends.*

Fassifern

Rte. 39 W (R.R. 5, Box 87), Lexington, VA 24450, tel. 540/463–1013 or 800/782–1587

There are 96,000 horses in Virginia—and counting. For anyone wanting to buy or show one of them, the place to do it is the Virginia Horse Center, just north of Lexington. Visitors staying overnight in the area can show their horse sense by picking one of the Shenandoah Valley's prettiest bed-and-breakfasts, just a trot down the road. It's Fassifern, owned by Francis Whitsel Smith and named after the Scottish ancestral home of its builder, who erected this three-story, smoky-lavender brick manor house circa 1867.

There's no particular history connected to Fassifern; it's just a lovely country place with a pond, towering maple trees, and an old spring house that's been converted into two extra guest rooms. The Colonel's Quarters, perhaps the best, has wide-plank floors and pasture views. The small Pond Room overlooks the flower-rimmed pond with fountain—and the nearby road. In the main house, three more guest rooms are furnished with Victorian armoires, Oriental rugs, and crystal chandeliers.

🏠 *5 double rooms with baths. Air-conditioning, ceiling fans, fireplace in living room. $84–$92; full breakfast. MC, V. No smoking, no pets, closed Thanksgiving, Dec. 24–25, Dec. 31.*

Fort Lewis Lodge

Rte. 625 (HCR3, Box 21A), Millboro, VA 24460, tel. 540/925–2314, fax 540/925–2352

On a 3,200-acre farm in the Allegheny foothills, 10 miles off the main road, John and Caryl Cowden raise Angus cattle, soybeans, and corn. The Cowpasture River deepens into a swimming hole nearby, and Shenandoah Mountain looms above, traversed by paths and logging roads. Below the manor house there's a dining hall in an old mill, and a lodge. Common rooms contain mounted bears, raccoons, and red fox—all Allegheny Highland species. Lodge rooms are comfortable, with locally handcrafted furniture. The Cowdens have reconstructed two historic log cabins, now cozy accommodations with fireplaces, and there's a restored stone hearth in the gathering room. Rooms in the converted silo are round. In this setting of fields, rivers, mountains, and forests, it's not surprising that Fort Lewis Lodge is blissfully outdoorsy: In addition to swimming, there's tubing down the river, fishing, hiking, biking, and terrific bird-watching. It's great for kids. And at day's end comes a return to Cowden hospitality, including Carol's homemade dinners.

🏠 *8 double rooms with baths, 3 suites, 2 cabins. TV with VCR in game room, bicycles, hot tub. $145–$195; MAP. MC, V. No smoking in bedrooms, no pets, closed mid-Oct.–Mar.*

The Inn at Gristmill Square

Rte. 619, Court House Hill Rd. (Box 359), Warm Springs, VA 24484, tel. 540/839–2231, fax 540/839–5770

Bath County in western Virginia covers 540 bumpy square miles inhabited by just 5,000 souls and nary a stoplight. Warm Springs, the county seat, boasts a post office, courthouse, and inn—and that's about all. Still, the Inn at Gristmill

Square, occupying several 19th-century buildings—a blacksmith's barn, restored mill, miller's house, and hardware store—is reason enough to visit this quintessentially peaceful spot. One of the area's best places to sup is its Waterwheel Restaurant, where one thrill is wandering down to the cool subterranean wine cellar to select a bottle. The Steel House, across the lane, has a small swimming pool, sauna, and three tennis courts. The Silo has a round living room, and the large, rustic Board Room, a favorite, is paneled with barn siding and features a claw-foot tub. Janice McWilliams and her son, Bruce, are the able proprietors, former owners of an inn in Vermont. They serve a simple breakfast and the *Richmond Times Dispatch* in a picnic basket at guests' doors.

▦ *16 double rooms with baths, 1 apartment. Restaurant, bar, air-conditioning, cable TV, phones and minirefrigerators in rooms, fireplaces in 8 rooms. $85–$100; Continental breakfast; MAP available. D, MC, V. Smoking in rooms and in the bar, no pets.*

The Inn at Narrow Passage

U.S. 11 S (Box 608), Woodstock, VA 22664, tel. 540/459–8000 or 800/459–8002, fax 540/459–8001

Guests here may want to pack their inner tubes, swimming togs, and fishing rods; they'll all prove useful at the Inn at Narrow Passage, which sits right on the North Fork of the Shenandoah River. Ed Markel, owner of the inn, will kindly put in any crew of human waterbugs about a mile south, and from there it's a 3½-hour float to reach home. The oldest section of the inn was built as a way station on the Great Wagon Road (now U.S. 11) around 1740, and the Markels meticulously restored it.

The older guest rooms evoke Colonial times with queen-size canopy beds, wood floors, and stenciling. Newer rooms, though similar, open onto porches. The

Stonewall Jackson Room, a heavily requested chamber in the older section, served as the Confederate general's headquarters during the Shenandoah Valley campaign of 1863. When the valley is blanketed in snow, the inn is a cozy place—especially the living room, with its handmade reproduction couches and big limestone fireplace (one of 10 here, seven in guest rooms). Chef Jonathan Gardner serves local fare for breakfast and at dinner Saturday nights, when his rainbow trout recipe is a favorite draw.

▦ *12 double rooms with baths. Air-conditioning, TV with VCR in sitting room, clock radios. $85–$115; full breakfast, afternoon refreshments. MC, V. No smoking indoors, no pets, 2-night minimum in spring, fall, and holiday weekends, closed Dec. 24–25.*

Jordan Hollow Farm Inn

326 Hawksbill Park Rd., Stanley, VA 22851, tel. 540/778–2285 or 888/418–7000, fax 540/778–1759

As anyone who's traveled much in rural America knows, farms aren't always the idyllic-looking places about which city folk fantasize. However, this one comes close. Jordan Hollow Farm is situated on 150 acres in the middle of the scenic Shenandoah Valley at the base of the Blue Ridge range, with great views of the Massanutten Mountains. It is a restored Colonial working horse farm that has been given new life as a cozy, beautiful, and serene country inn. At the heart of the farm, amid maple trees, sits a 200-year-old farmhouse incorporating two hand-hewn log cabins and now known as the Farmhouse Restaurant.

Two of the proprietors, Gail Kyle and Betsy Anderson run the place with a staff of 20. Guests can choose from the low-ceilinged Farmhouse Room, 16 more in the Arbor View Lodge, and four upscale rooms in the Mare Meadow Lodge, which is built of hand-hewn logs. The last are carpeted and have fireplaces, quilts, cedar furniture, and whirlpool tubs. The old carriage house and corn crib have a new life as a gathering lounge known as the Great Room, whose antique couches and chairs, game tables, and a small library put guests at ease.

Half the guests here come to ride, half to savor the tranquillity. Every day, several equestrian groups (including beginners) leave the farm to wander over the foothills; youngsters go on pony rides. Guests can even bring their own horses; a stall is $15. Great hiking trails crisscross the property, and folks at the farm can direct guests to more trails in Shenandoah National Park or George Washington National Forest. Canoeing on the Shenandoah, caving, swimming, and golf are also nearby.

The Farmhouse Restaurant has built a considerable reputation with locally grown ingredients. Chef Julia Slye, an expert at regional American recipes, also ensures that Virginia wines and local microbrews remain staples of the menu.

▦ *21 double rooms with baths. Restaurant, air-conditioning, cable TV in 8 rooms and Great Room, phones in rooms, fireplace in Great Room and 4 rooms, horseback riding. $110–$150. AE, D, DC, MC, V. No pets, except horses.*

Joshua Wilton House

412 S. Main St., Harrisonburg, VA 22801, tel. 540/434-4464 or 888/294-5866

In Harrisonburg's neighborhood of well-kept, handsome old homes, the Joshua Wilton House strikes the highest note. It's a lovingly renovated and luxuriously equipped mauve, lavender, and pink Queen Anne cottage with triple-decker bays and a turret. Throughout, owners Roberta and Craig Moore have provided a sense of polished professionalism, a put-together look of coordinated decor.

Guests enter by way of a front door surrounded by leaded glass and through a foyer with gleaming parquet floor, a chandelier, and bushy potted plants. Painted mantels and pictures displayed by the Shenandoah Valley Watercolor Association populate the first floor. The guest chambers are really attractive, particularly Room 5, with its four-poster bed and white wing chairs, and Room 4, which has a three-window alcove in the turret. The café is casual, and the restaurant offers fine dining that includes such breakfast specialties as crab-and-cheese omelets.

▦ *5 double rooms with baths. Restaurant, café, air-conditioning, phones in rooms, fireplace in 1 room, bicycles. $95–$105; full breakfast. AE, D, DC, MC, V. Smoking in café bar only, no pets, 2-night minimum some weekends, closed Dec. 24–25.*

Lavender Hill Farm

Rte. 631 (R.R. 1, Box 515), Lexington, VA 24450, tel. 540/464-5877 or 800/446-4240

Four miles west of Lexington, in a hollow across the road from a river, stands Lavender Hill, a working 20-acre farm with pet goats, sheep, dogs, and cats. Newcomers John and Sarah Burleson plunged into innkeeping full time in the fall of 1996, having stayed as guests in other inns only a couple of times previously. John graduated from VMI several years ago, worked in Northern Virginia as an engineer for a while, then returned with Sarah to the part of Virginia he found most familiar.

The central section of the main building is a 200-year-old log cabin. (One guest stayed here because his research revealed that it was his grandfather's birthplace.) The inn is not filled with antiques or laden down with quaintness. Room renovations over the years have somewhat obscured the old farmhouse charm, but John and Paula are working hard to remedy this. In keeping with the farm setting, rooms are simply furnished, the windows dressed with lace curtains that ripple in summer. John is the chef, providing four-course meals (by reservation) for $14.50; his homegrown herbs are his culinary trademark. Sarah sheers the farm's sheep and lets guests help if they show an inclination. Guests may also fish in the river, bird-watch, or—the usual favorite—lounge on the porch with a cool drink. Horseback-riding packages, outdoor theater in summer, and horse boarding are also available.

▦ *2 double rooms with baths, 1 2-bedroom suite. Air-conditioning, ceiling fans, satellite TV with VCR in living room, horse boarding. $69–$105; full breakfast. MC, V. No smoking indoors, no pets, 2-night minimum holidays and special-event weekends.*

Sampson Eagon Inn

238 E. Beverley St., Staunton, VA 24401, tel. 540/886–8200 or 800/597–9722

Beltway burnouts Frank and Laura Mattingly—he from hospital administration, she from college administration—have lovingly created an inn that is affordable, elegant, and comfortable. The Mattinglys' two-year restoration of the 1795 Federal mansion with Greek Revival, Italianate, and Victorian additions earned them the Historic Staunton Foundation's Preservation Award for 1992. Furnished with antiques, the yellow mansion perches on Gospel Hill, which, like the inn, is named to honor the home's first resident, blacksmith and preacher Sampson Eagon. It's across from the Woodrow Wilson Birthplace, a short walk to downtown.

The spacious, high-ceilinged rooms have canopied queen-size beds, down or non-allergenic pillows and comforters, sitting areas, and cable TV with VCR units. The Holt Room showcases Laura's delft tile collection, setting the theme for the soothing blue-and-white decor.

▦ *3 double rooms with baths, 2 suites. Air-conditioning, phones in rooms, fax, photocopying, turndown service. $89–*

$105; full breakfast, afternoon refreshments. AE, MC, V. No smoking indoors, no pets, 2-night minimum May, Oct., and some holiday weekends.

Seven Hills Inn

408 S. Main St., Lexington, VA 24450, tel. 540/463–4715 or 888/845–3801, fax 540/463–6526

Seven Hills Inn, a classic brick, white-columned Southern Colonial dwelling in the heart of Lexington's historic Main Street district, was built in 1928 as a fraternity house for nearby Washington and Lee University. Hence the expansive living room (with fireplace), dining room, and casual downstairs chapter room (also with a fireplace as well as TV with VCR and games). It's doubtful, though, that the house had such an impeccably fresh and inviting appearance when the college crowd occupied it. Ben Grigsby, a Washington and Lee alumnus, bought the place and restored it, removing walls between the small fraternity bedrooms to create large guest rooms. When Ben's work sent him out of the country, he asked his mother, Jane Daniel, and innkeeper Shirley Ducommun to operate the bed-and-breakfast.

The pale-yellow third-floor Holly Hill Room, with a sloping ceiling, has a bath that's bigger than the bedroom. Fruit Hill has a whirlpool tub and a four-poster queen-size bed, and it can be opened into a suite with a parlor.

▦ *6 double rooms with baths, 1 suite. Air-conditioning. $80–$125; full breakfast. AE, MC, V. No smoking in bedrooms, no pets, 2-night minimum some weekends.*

Thornrose House

531 Thornrose Ave., Staunton, VA 24401, tel. 540/885–7026 or 800/861–4338

In 1984 Suzy and Otis Huston spent the night at their first B&B. "Someday," they said, "we'll do this," and they started a portfolio of properties and ideas. After a lengthy search they bought Thornrose and moved down from Buffalo, New York, where Otis had been in management with DuPont and Suzy taught school.

Thornrose has a light, fresh appearance. Windsor (all the guest rooms bear English names) has antique twin beds pushed together, with a white down duvet and white lace-trimmed pillows, and an antique armoire and dresser. Although it's the smallest room, sunny Yorkshire is favored for its garden view and claw-foot tub. The blue-and-rose Canterbury Room overlooks bucolic Gypsy Hill Park, where there is a swimming pool, tennis courts, a golf course, and summer concerts. Guests might prefer just lingering on the wraparound veranda or in the flower-filled gardens, where an 80-year-old climbing, white hydrangea and a wisteria cover two arbors and where a stream of the area's pure water dances in a new fountain.

▥ *5 double rooms with baths. Air-conditioning, cable TV in parlor, fireplaces in dining room and parlor, turn-down service, bicycles. $60–$80; full breakfast, afternoon refreshments. No credit cards. No smoking, no pets, 2-night minimum Oct. and May weekends.*

Trillium House

Wintergreen Dr., Wintergreen (Box 280, Nellysford, VA 22958), tel. 804/325–9126 or 800/325–9126 (reservations only), fax 804/325–1099

Guests from near and far alike have to hand it to Ed and Betty Dinwiddie. For the pair, building a bed-and-breakfast on the grounds of Wintergreen resort may have seemed the most natural thing in the world; after all, their family had vacationed there for years. But to skiers, refugees from the Blue Ridge Parkway, wildflower enthusiasts, and all-round mountain devotees, the idea was a stroke of genius. The fact that Trillium House lies across the road from the gargantuan sports complex, with its indoor pool, tennis courts, ski slopes, hiking trails, and golf course, should give prospective visitors a clue as to the activities available.

From Wintergreen's gate, a roller-coasterish road brings guests 3½ miles to the doorstep of Trillium House. The beige frame building fronted by a porch and a Palladian window, surrounded by trees and stylish condominiums owned by Wintergreen residents, was built in 1983. Entrance is through the Great Room, which is two stories high, near a staircase at the side leading to a loft library. The front sitting area has a wood-burning stove, above which hang several organ pipes; by the front door, a canister holds a collection of walking sticks. Breakfast is served in the dining rooms, with views of bird feeders and the backyard gazebo, and Friday and Saturday dinners (by reservation) are cooked by chef Ellen English, who formerly worked in one of Wintergreen's restaurants. The 12 guest rooms at Trillium House lie in two wings off the Great Room. Their architectural tone is slightly motelish, but decorative touches add some personality—here a quilt or a framed picture that could only have been created by one of the Dinwiddie brood, there a writing desk from the Homestead or a bed with a lace canopy.

The odds are that guests will spend most of their stay here pursuing varieties of R&R on the resort or ensconced in the Great Room, chatting with other guests or Ed and Betty, who manage to seem amazingly relaxed despite their demanding housekeeping duties. The single disappointment is that Trillium House doesn't have mountain views; those after such scenery will have to grab a stick and walk.

▥ *10 double rooms with baths, 2 suites. Air-conditioning, TV in rooms on request, cable TV with VCR and movie collection in sitting room, phones in rooms, turndown service. $95–$160; full buffet breakfast. MC, V. No smoking in dining room, no pets, 2-night minimum weekends, 3-night minimum some holidays.*

West Virginia

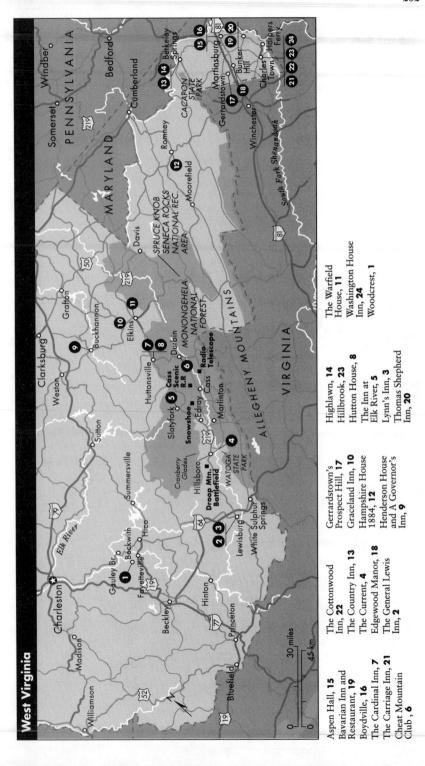

West Virginia

Aspen Hall, **15**
Bavarian Inn and
Restaurant, **19**
Boydville, **16**
The Cardinal Inn, **7**
The Carriage Inn, **21**
Cheat Mountain
Club, **6**

The Cottonwood
Inn, **22**
The Country Inn, **13**
The Current, **4**
Edgewood Manor, **18**
The General Lewis
Inn, **2**

Gerrardstown's
Prospect Hill, **17**
Graceland Inn, **10**
Hampshire House
1884, **12**
Henderson House
and A Governor's
Inn, **9**

Highlawn, **14**
Hillbrook, **23**
Hutton House, **8**
The Inn at
Elk River, **5**
Lynn's Inn, **3**
Thomas Shepherd
Inn, **20**

The Warfield
House, **11**
Washington House
Inn, **24**
Woodcrest, **1**

The Eastern Panhandle

Like so much of West Virginia, the three eastern counties that make up the panhandle region are mountainous, reaching elevations of 2,300 feet. Long a wild, uninhabitable part of the West, it was not until George Washington surveyed the area in the mid-1700s that a number of villages sprang up along the Potomac River, among them Shepherdstown, Harpers Ferry, Charles Town, and Martinsburg.

Today, the state is still relatively untamed and is a wonderland for explorers, who can drive for miles along surprisingly well-maintained highways without tripping over condo developments or fast-food restaurants. In the last few decades the state government, based in Charleston, has turned its attention to nurturing the wildest portions of the Allegheny Front and Plateau, once devastated by lumbering and strip mining, by creating a first-rate network of parks. Six-thousand-acre Cacapon State Park—with its hiking trails and Robert Trent Jones golf course—is among these, as is Berkeley Springs State Park, a funky spot equipped with tiled Roman baths, steam cabinets, and some of the best spring water in the world (beloved by George Washington, in fact).

One of West Virginia's most popular tourist attractions lies in the Eastern Panhandle—Harpers Ferry National Park. Thomas Jefferson described it best, writing: "On your right comes up the Shenandoah, having ranged along the foot of the mountains a hundred miles to seek a vent. On your left approaches the Potomac, in quest of a passage also. In the moment of their junction they rush together against the mountain, rend it asunder, and pass off to the sea . . . . This scene is worth a voyage across the Atlantic." The spot where these rivers converge so dramatically is also where, on October 16, 1859, the abolitionist zealot John Brown led his 21-man assault on the Harpers Ferry arsenal. Today, strips of Harpers Ferry national parklands line the rivers like a glove, and historic markers tell the story of John Brown's raid and of the town's tumultuous involvement in the Civil War.

Shepherdstown, sitting high above the Potomac across from Sharpsburg, Maryland, was founded in 1762 and is the oldest town in West Virginia. Visitors can browse the pleasant collection of shops along the main drag here and, since all the Panhandle's main towns are close together, can make a short trip to the Charles Town track to take in the horse races before heading back to one of the area's many fine inns.

Potomac and Shenandoah river rafting abounds, and there are numerous bicycling routes (among them Route 230 between Harpers Ferry and Shepherdstown and the Tuscarora Pike near Martinsburg) and a great variety of outlet stores in Martinsburg where you can snap up name-brand clothing and other products for a fraction of the department-store price. If you have more time to explore, head west to Berkeley Springs and Cacapon State Park, where you'll discover the real West Virginia—that of logging trucks, black bear, wild turkey, and mountains that don't let up until the Ohio River.

Places to Go, Sights to See

Berkeley Springs State Park (tel. 304/258–2711 or 800/225–5982). Located within the city limits of the town of Bath, this state park has a museum and a pool. In the bathhouse you can sample the therapeutic waters, which rush out of the springs at an unvarying temperature of 74.3°F and a volume of 2,000 gallons a minute. The bathhouse, where you can get wrinkled and revived in a Roman tub, was restored in 1996. The water's the same at other places, where the surroundings are tonier and the price tag higher. In fact, the water's the same everywhere in historic little Berkeley Springs; it comes out of every tap.

Cacapon State Park (tel. 304/258–1022 or 800/225–5982). Cacapon lies 10 miles south of Berkeley Springs, off Route 522, and encompasses a narrow strip of mountains that reaches almost to the Maryland and Virginia borders. A paved road leads to the summit of Cacapon Mountain, and the park has 27 miles of hiking trails, as well as a lodge, golf course (for which reservations are encouraged), and a man-made lake with a sandy beach.

Charles Town Races (tel. 304/725–7001). The thoroughbreds pound the turf year-round (Friday and Saturday nights and Monday, Wednesday, and Sunday afternoons), and video lottery is played daily at this track just outside Charles Town (about 5 miles southwest of Harpers Ferry).

Harpers Ferry National Historic Park (tel. 304/535–6223). This is the site of the arsenal that John Brown held for two days before it was stormed by marines under Robert E. Lee. A network of hiking routes passes through Harpers Ferry, including the Appalachian Trail.

O'Hurley's General Store (tel. 304/876–6907). This Shepherdstown emporium is crammed with "the most extensive variety of time-tested products available in this modern age," including boxes, barrels, baskets, anvils, harnesses, coffins, guns, books, and dinner bells.

Panorama Point. Follow Route 9 for 4 miles west of Berkeley Springs to the shoulder of Prospect Peak for a view of the Great Cacapon Valley, where three states—Maryland, West Virginia, and Pennsylvania—converge.

Restaurants

For German cooking and wild-game dishes, try the **Bavarian Inn** (Shepherdstown, tel. 304/876–2551), overlooking the Potomac River. The **Yellow Brick Bank** (Shepherdstown, tel. 304/876–2208) is a favorite of Washingtonians, and the Continental menu reflects those urban tastes; the food at the **Country Inn** (Berkeley Springs, tel. 304/258–2210 or 800/822–6630) is plain but good.

Tourist Information

Jefferson County Convention and Visitors Bureau (Box A, Harpers Ferry 25425, tel. 304/535–2627 or 800/848–8687). **Potomac Highlands Travel Council** (1200 Harrison Ave., Elkins 26241, tel. 304/636–8400). **Southern West Virginia Convention and Visitors Bureau** (Box 1799, Beckley 25802, tel. 304/252–2244 or 800/847–4898). **Travel Berkeley Springs** (304 Fairfax St., Berkeley Springs 25411, tel. 304/258–9147). **West Virginia Department of Commerce** (2101 Washington St. E, Charleston 24305, tel. 800/225–5982).

Aspen Hall

405 Boyd Ave., Martinsburg, WV 25401, tel. 304/263-4385

Aspen Hall, in Martinsburg, is a native-limestone Georgian manor house with a very long history. Construction was begun sometime around 1745 by a Quaker settler named Edward Beeson. It later become Fort Mendenhall, and by 1761 it was the site of a wedding attended by George Washington. Aspen Hall is at the end of Boyd Avenue in a hollow alongside Tuscarora Creek, shaded by giant locusts that were probably saplings in Washington's time. Next to it is another, smaller cottage and the 1754 blockhouse of the fort. A walk bounded by a rock wall and border of plants leads to a gazebo by the creek, complementing a shady patio.

Inside, Aspen Hall's central hall is furnished with Empire furniture and Oriental rugs. One of the front parlors has 12-foot ceilings, 19th-century antique furniture, a piano, and swag draperies. The other is a library where retired antiques dealers Gordon and LouAnne Claucherty serve daily afternoon tea to the overnight guests. Each bedroom is different. A favorite is the Gentleman's Room, with a fireplace, four-poster canopy bed, and claw-foot tub.

🏠 *5 double rooms with baths. TV in library, fireplace in breakfast room, hammock on porch. $95–$110; full breakfast. AE, MC, V. No smoking, no pets, closed Dec. 15–Feb. 10.*

Bavarian Inn and Restaurant

Shepherd Grade Rd., Rte. 480 (Rte. 1, Box 30), Shepherdstown, WV 25443, tel. 304/876-2551, fax 304/876-9355

Because of its setting high above the Potomac River in a town with one traffic light, the Bavarian Inn is "country," but it's also the last word in luxury. That won't appeal to everyone, because it

means the coat and tie go into the suitcase along with the jeans. Munich-born Erwin Asam, a former Washington restaurateur, and his British wife, Carol, have turned the 1930s mansion into a slice of Erwin's homeland, with alpine chalets overlooking the river, dining rooms with the feel of an elegant mountain lodge, and an extensive menu loaded with German specialties. Everything's here for a pampered stay, right down to the mints on the pillow. Despite big-hotel amenities, the Asams try to preserve a relaxed, personal atmosphere. Not up to the coat and tie? Slip downstairs to the wood-beamed, informal Rathskeller for dinner from the same menu, plus entertainment on weekends.

🏠 *72 double rooms with baths. Restaurant, TV and phones in rooms, 26 rooms with fireplaces and whirlpool tubs, private balconies, 3 conference rooms, pool, tennis courts, exercise room. $85–$165; breakfast extra. AE, D, DC, MC, V. No smoking in some areas and rooms, no pets, 2-night minimum on holiday weekends.*

Boydville

601 S. Queen St., Martinsburg, WV 25401, tel. 304/263-1448 or 202/626-2896

The story always told about Boydville, Martinsburg's grandest house, concerns its near destruction by Union troops during the Civil War. One often hears how some pretty Southern belle pleaded with roughshod Federals to spare her family manse, but in the case of Boydville, the tale is documented. Mary Faulkner, of the clan that has resided in Boydville for 150 years, wired Abraham Lincoln, whose decision to let Boydville stand arrived just before Northerners lit the torch.

A later Faulkner served as U.S. senator, commuting to the nation's capital by train (just as present owner La Rue Frye does today). When the six o'clock train from the District hooted over nearby Bull's Eye Bridge, the Boydville servants began crushing ice for the senator's mint julep. And when he arrived on the wide front porch and reclined in a green rocker (the very one there today), his drink was waiting.

Boydville, a limestone manor house covered with white stucco, was completed in 1812 by General Elisha Boyd, a hero of the War of 1812 and a friend of Martinsburg's founder, Adam Stephen. Obviously it's a historic place, and perhaps the northernmost outcropping of the old South. The mansion, with its ivy-covered walled patio, is surrounded by 10 parklike acres of lawn and garden. The current owner has given Boydville a new roof and repaired the water damage that had marred this historic gem. Guests are shown the case locks stamped with the imprimatur of the locksmith to King George IV, the English molding in the downstairs parlors, and English hand-painted wallpaper dating from 1812 in the foyer. The rooms are enormous, the most desirable being the Adam Stephen Room; it has hand-painted mural wallpaper imported from France in the early 1800s and the first tiled bathroom in Martinsburg.

Confederate general Stonewall Jackson retreated to Boydville for physical and emotional renewal many times during the Civil War. Thanks to La Rue and the other three working professionals who lovingly tend Boydville, the mansion still has that power to soothe.

▦ *6 double rooms with baths. Air-conditioning in bedrooms, fireplace and cable TV in common area, fireplaces in 2 bedrooms. $100–$140; full breakfast. MC, V. No smoking, no pets, 2-night minimum Memorial Day weekend and Oct. weekends. Closed Mon.–Wed., except holiday weekends; Aug.; Dec. 20–30.*

The Carriage Inn

417 E. Washington St., Charles Town, WV 25414, tel. 304/728-8003 or 800/867-9830, fax 304/725-3810

When generals Ulysses S. Grant and Philip Sheridan met at what is now the Carriage Inn to map out the Union Army's Shenandoah Valley campaign, there was a picket fence around the house and a Greek Revival portico. Otherwise, things haven't changed much at the old Rutherford place in Charles Town—anyway, guests don't mind the addition of a broad front porch and modern plumbing. The owners of this shady gray Colonial-style house are Al and Kay Standish. Al is pleased to share the house's history and suggest sightseeing activities, especially the Jefferson County Courthouse just down the street. Here's where John Brown, arrested by Col. Robert E. Lee's troops, was convicted for murder, treason, and inciting slaves to rebel against the federal arsenal in nearby Harpers Ferry. Besides hearty morning meals, the Carriage Inn offers big bedrooms (four with fireplaces), two sitting rooms, polished floors, solid brick walls, and a bookful of Civil War stories to tell—like the one about Stonewall Jackson's flag, which was buried under a fireplace hearth when the Federals came.

▦ *5 double rooms with baths. Air-conditioning, fireplaces in 4 rooms. $75–$115; 3-room carriage house, $95–$135; full breakfast. MC, V. No smoking in bedrooms, no pets.*

The Cottonwood Inn

Rte. 2, Box 61-S, Charles Town, WV 25414, tel. 800/868-1188

About 5 miles south of Charles Town along Kabletown Road, a trio of silos rises, marking the winding road to the Cottonwood Inn. This yellow brick farmhouse, just across a little wooden bridge, has occupied a hollow alongside Bullskin Run Creek for more than 150 years—as its uneven pine floors and big brick dining-room hearth attest. Joe and Barbara Sobol have dotted their pastoral inn with original quilts, a love of Barbara's. The couple produces motor-trip video guides to Europe in a downstairs studio. Guest rooms (six with queen-size and one with king-size bed) are exceptionally cozy places to rest, and Joe is glad for visitors to flip though his extensive collection of books about the Civil War or to play the grand piano. Outside, guests may stroll along Bullskin Run or peer at the stars from rocking chairs on the front porch. In 1986 the previous owners added a wing to the farmhouse with two guest rooms. These are spacious and handsomely decorated, but not as atmospheric as the rooms in the old section. The Cottonwood is close to the Blue Ridge, which beckons on the horizon. To the north lie the Charles Town Race Track and Harpers Ferry.

🏠 *7 double rooms with baths, 1 suite. Air-conditioning, TV in rooms, fireplaces in public rooms. $65–$120; full breakfast. AE, MC, V. No smoking, no pets.*

The Country Inn

207 S. Washington St., Berkeley Springs, WV 25411, tel. 304/258–2210 or 800/822–6630, fax 304/258–3986

From the outside, the Country Inn in Berkeley Springs looks a little grander than the image the name summons up; it's a four-story brick building, with a columned front porch, that was built in 1932. Then came a set of wings in 1937, and then, after former teacher Jack Barker bought the place in the early 1970s (because he disliked retirement), a conference center, motel annex, and spa out back. The additions haven't damaged the integrity of the old inn much, for its rooms are still old-timey, with mismatched quasi-antiques; a long, carpeted central corridor; and a country store downstairs. The inn is next door to Berkeley Springs State Park, but the spa facilities at the inn come with a view of the town and the ridge. The inn has two dining rooms, one a garden affair with a dance floor, where there's live music on weekends.

🏠 *66 double rooms with baths, 11 doubles share 4 baths, 5 suites. Restaurant, pub, room service, air-conditioning, cable TV in rooms, phones in annex*

rooms, spa, 2 conference rooms. $39–$136; breakfast extra. AE, D, DC, MC, V. No smoking in suites, no pets, 2-night minimum on weekends May–Oct. and major holiday weekends.

Edgewood Manor

Rte. 2, Box 329, Bunker Hill, WV 25413, tel. 304/229–9353, fax 304/229–9359

Gen. Elisha M. Boyd would not be disappointed if he returned today to the redbrick Federal house he built in 1839, especially if he arrived during one of Edgewood Manor's occasional Civil War cavalry reenactments. In the house, once temporary headquarters for Gen. Stonewall Jackson, he'd find an 1860 Austrian pianoforte, authentic Civil War paraphernalia, and a cabinet filled with American history books.

Sharon and John Feldt, she a teacher and he a lawyer, stumbled onto the vacant house while traveling to battle sites from Texas. They bought it on the spot in 1995, because it was just what Sharon and her mother, Birdie Lamkin, had envisioned for their inn. A gravel drive points to the white columned portico and house on 52 acres. Nearby, a fertile spring spews daily more than 4 million gallons of fresh water, supplying all of Berkeley County. Sharon's tasteful hand has touched each immense room, most with four-poster bed, simple lace curtains, and Oriental rugs. The Texas Room features the yellow rose, and the Gen. James Pettigrew room, like the rest of the house, carries a Civil War theme, with framed battle scenes and soldier paraphernalia.

Sharon's creative breakfasts of fresh breads, casseroles, and fruit dishes; afternoon teas; and murder mystery weekends have summoned guests both local and afar.

🏠 *6 double rooms, 2 share bath. Fireplace in 3 guest rooms. $85–$145; full breakfast. AE, MC, V. No smoking, no pets.*

Gerrardstown's Prospect Hill

Rte. 51 W, Box 135, Gerrardstown, WV 25420, tel. 304/229-3346

This handsome Georgian house, built of brick in 1804, is surrounded by a 225-acre farm that stretches to the top of North Mountain and lies along what was once the Pack Horse Trail, a main road to the West. Its old dependencies include a Flemish-bond brick slave quarters, now converted into a cottage featuring a country kitchen with fireplace, bedroom, and modern bath. Owners Charles and Hazel Hudock, who moved to Prospect Hill in 1978, restored the place and are proud of its unusual details, like the several working Franklin fireplaces dating from the 1790s and a mural depicting Prospect Hill and scenes from American life. In the spring, you may see deer grazing with their fawns on the grounds. Two ponds yield fine bass in the summer and freeze for skating in the winter. Hazel also gardens, and the fruits of her labors—homemade grape juice, fresh raspberries, and peaches—often appear on the breakfast table.

🏠 *2 double rooms with baths, 1 cottage. Air-conditioning in bedrooms, TV in apartment and living room, phones and fireplaces in rooms. $85–$95; full breakfast. No credit cards. No smoking, no pets, 2-night minimum on Oct. weekends and holidays.*

Highlawn

304 Market St., Berkeley Springs, WV 25411, tel. 304/258-5700

Algernon R. Unger built this house for his bride, Chaffie Ziler. It's a white Queen Anne cottage with a wide front porch and a tin roof that vibrates musically when it rains. The private suite has its own tin-roofed porch and hand-painted Victorian furniture. All the bedrooms have lace-curtained windows, plump pillows, and turn-of-the-century furnishings, including brass beds and rockers. Owner Sandra Kauffman and partner Tim Miller also operate two other nearby properties: Aunt Pearl's cottage, which has four Victorian rooms with private porches, and a romantic carriage house with stained glass, library nook, whirlpool bath for two, VCR, and queen-size bed in an intimate loft. On Saturday (May–October and holidays) Sandra serves a gourmet silver-service dinner (not included in price) at Highlawn. Holidays are celebrated with special meals and decorations. On the Fourth of July, guests pitch in to crank the old-fashioned ice-cream maker. Breakfasts feature herb and low-fat dishes, a vegetarian offering, and such delicacies as lemon bread with lemon butter and chocolate-chip coffee cake.

🏠 *9 double rooms with baths, 2 suites. Air-conditioning, TV in bedrooms. $83–$175; full breakfast. AE, MC, V. No pets, 2-night minimum most weekends.*

Hillbrook

Rte. 2, Box 152, Charles Town, WV 24514, tel. 304/725-4223 or 800/304-4223, fax 304/725-4455

Would Hillbrook, hidden along a country lane outside Charles Town, be such a special place without its innkeeper, Gretchen Carroll? One tends to think not, although the house itself is spectacularly eccentric, splayed in six stages along a hill, never more than one room wide or one room deep. The house has 13 sharply peaked gables, half-timbered white-stucco walls, and mullioned windows—the one in the living room has 360 panes. Ann Hathaway would feel right at home. Gretchen calls the style "Norman Tudor" and explains that during World War I a civil engineer by the name of Bamford fell in love with an inn in Normandy and determined to re-create it in the wilds of West Virginia. Erratically, he chose to start with two ancient log cabins. The logs and mortises of one of these are still apparent in the dining porch.

Gretchen was a foreign-service brat who grew up in the far corners of the world, including Turkey, Thailand, and the Ivory Coast; and Hillbrook is full of exotic curios and objets d'art. The living room holds pottery and a Senegalese fertility statue; in bedrooms you'll find Oriental rugs, an antique Vuitton steamer trunk, and a Thai spirit house. Richly patterned wallpaper, upholstery, and pillows; randomly angled ceilings; potted plants; and architectural cubbyholes complete the Hillbrook picture. The Cottage guest room, with its private entry overlooking an ancient springhouse (from which Hillbrook gets its water), has paisley-pattern wallpaper and a wood-burning stove backed with Italian tile. Locke's Nest overlooks the living room from 20 feet up and has brass double and single beds and a lavender bathtub.

The inn's seven-course dinners feature stuffed quail or grilled rosemary lamb chops; feta-cheese-and-pomegranate salad; and chocolate "decadence" cake. Breakfast specialties are sherried mushroom omelets, home-baked grilled fruitbreads, and a delightful "egg blossom" dish.

Bullskin Run Creek trickles away at the bottom of the Hillbrook lawn, the haunt of ducks, inn guests, and a cat named Princess Fuzzy Butt. There are, of course, attractions to visit in the surrounding area, but nothing that would keep one away from idyllic Hillbrook for long.

🏠 *6 double rooms with baths. Airconditioning in rooms, fireplaces in 2 rooms, tavern, high tea on Sun. Nov.–Apr. $130–$290 (MAP; lunch $20; tea $20; dinner $60 weekdays, $70 weekends). AE, D, MC, V. Dinner required with 1-night stay. No smoking in dining area, no pets.*

Thomas Shepherd Inn

300 W. German St., Box 1162, Shepherdstown, WV 25443, tel. 304/876–3715 or 888/889–8952

Shepherdstown is easily the prettiest village in Panhandle West Virginia, built in the mid-1800s and thus a showplace for late-Federal architecture. Its shoplined business district lies along German Street, where up a ways you'll find the Thomas Shepherd Inn, named for the town's founder. The inn was built in 1868 as a Lutheran parsonage and expanded in 1937. It's a gracious place that would look at home in Colonial Williamsburg, with green molding, inset shutters, and a spacious courtyard garden in the rear. Though it's been an inn since 1984, Margaret Perry, who loves to sew and cook, took over in 1989. Her breakfasts can be elaborate, featuring eggs Benedict with caviar and French toast made from brioches. All guest rooms have polished floors, Oriental rugs, and handsomely coordinated upholstery and spreads, but the favorite is Room 6 because of its garden view, claw-foot tub, and four-poster bed. The inn has become a prime way station for bikers and hikers on the C&O Canal Towpath, and for people heading for Maryland's Antietam Battlefield, 5 miles north. Harpers Ferry is 10 miles to the south.

🏠 *7 double rooms with baths. Airconditioning, TV/VCR in library, dinners and picnic lunches on request. $85–$125 (business rates available); full breakfast. AE, D, MC, V. Smoking on porch only, no pets.*

Washington House Inn

216 S. George St., Charles Town, WV 25414, tel. 304/725–7923 or 800/297–6957

Mel and Nina Vogel glided into the inn business in 1993; he was a software consultant, and she, born of restaurateur parents, an experienced flight attendant with Eastern Airlines. Pampering and personality come naturally to the duo, and they set out to transform the turreted 1899 Victorian into a plush but unpretentious spot. Nina, elected to the local city council in 1997, knows what travelers need and supplies it—from scented soaps and hard candies to tufted side chairs, Limoges china, and layers of handmade quilts. The grandnephew of the first U.S. president built the house, which is fitted with a breezy, wraparound front porch just right for lounging on its wicker chairs and flipping through the daily newspaper. Guest rooms comfort, several with fireplaces and Casablanca paddle ceiling fans, while every available public space is stuffed with knickknacks that command curiosity. Breakfast is served on the porch or in the genteel, oxblood-hued dining room. If the cinnamon French toast dripping with strawberry cream cheese won't do, then Nina might offer you a Mexican omelet, fruit cup, and array of muffins or an egg and sausage casserole.

▦ *6 double rooms with baths. Air-conditioning, fireplaces in 2 public rooms. $75–$125; full breakfast. AE, D, MC, V. No smoking, no pets.*

The Mountains

The Allegheny Mountains of West Virginia are a substantial range, reaching from Davis in the north to the Greenbrier Valley in the south. They are wide, too—it takes a hard day of driving to cross them east to west—and it's easy to sympathize with the early pioneers, who struggled over the same hills without the convenience of automobiles. Not all the settlers made it to the West, though: Some, particularly Scotch-Irish immigrants, gave up before reaching the fertile Ohio Valley and settled in this high, wild territory that would become West Virginia. They fought with the Shawnee Indians in the late 1700s, but managed to hang on to the land that would later prove a valuable source of timber and coal.

Long overlooked by the rest of the country, West Virginia has recently been rediscovered. Tourism, especially skiing, has begun to replace mining and lumbering as an Allegheny Mountain cash crop. The region's ski resorts—Canaan Valley State Park, Timberline Four Seasons Resort, and Snowshoe and Silver Creek on Cheat Mountain—have one of the longest skiing seasons in the East. Hikers, naturalists, hunters, anglers, and cyclists will also find a paradise in the Allegheny Mountains, 900,000 acres of which are part of the Monongahela

*National Forest. There are plenty of state parks, too, such as
Watoga, in addition to Cranberry Glades and the remote Dolly
Sods Wilderness. The Seneca Rocks–Spruce Knob Recreation
Area is at the top of the mountain chain, with Spruce Knob, at
4,860 feet, officially the highest point in the state.*

*As you journey south, the mountains relax into hills, sloping
down to the idyllic Greenbrier Valley and the historic town of
Lewisburg. This former frontier fort was the site of battles in
both the Revolutionary and Civil wars. Today it's a peaceful
town of fine Federal and Victorian homes. To the east, the
famed Greenbrier Hotel, a resort where the Vanderbilts and
Astors took the waters in the early part of the century, is still
as grand as ever.*

*Visitors who want to see America in all its variety and
eccentricity couldn't do better than to drive into the mountains
of West Virginia, where they can attend ramp festivals (ramps
are a mountain onion that make the eater a social outcast for
a week); go rafting on white-water rivers rated among the
wildest in the nation; bike the 75-mile Greenbrier River Trail
on an inn-to-inn odyssey; or hike the tundralike plateau of the
Dolly Sods Wilderness Area—and ponder how anyone could
ever have forgotten about West Virginia.*

Places to Go, Sights to See

Canaan Valley State Park (tel. 800/225–5982). Long known for downhill skiing,
this 21-trail park is particularly good for families because of its low prices and
great variety of activities.

Cass Scenic Railroad (tel. 304/456–4300 or 800/225–5982). Near the intersection
of routes 250 and 28, Cass is the base for the logging line that once carried
lumberjacks up Bald Knob Mountain and now carries sightseers on a four-hour
trip to the Allegheny plateau. Pack a lunch and warm clothes; you'll reach an
altitude of almost 5,000 feet.

Dolly Sods Wilderness (tel. 304/257–4488 or 304/636–1800). Near Canaan Valley
and the town of Davis, this remote refuge resembles Canada with its sphagnum
bogs, windblown spruce, heath barrens, and patches of wild onions.

Droop Mountain Battlefield State Park (tel. 304/653–4254). This restored Civil War battlefield has a small museum, observation tower, and hiking trails.

National Radio Astronomy Observatory (Green Bank, tel. 304/456–2011).This federal installation has a 300-foot movable radio telescope, the largest of its kind in the world.

New River Bridge. The world's biggest single-arch span (3,000 feet long) is situated on Route 19 between Hico and Fayetteville. On Bridge Day, the third Saturday in October, hang gliders, bungee jumpers, and assorted other daredevils are permitted to throw themselves off the bridge.

New River Gorge National River (tel. 304/465–0508). Rangers conduct guided tours of this 52-mile-long "Grand Canyon of the East." For information about river running and outfitters, tel. 800/225–5982.

Pearl Buck Home (tel. 304/653–4430). The Pulitzer- and Nobel Prize–winning author of *The Good Earth* came from Hillsboro, West Virginia, and her birthplace is now preserved as a museum.

Seneca Rocks (tel. 800/225–5982). This spine of Tuscarora sandstone rises 1,000 feet above the North Fork River; the visitor center provides telescopes for watching the precarious progress of rock climbers. Should you be tempted by the heights, contact the *Seneca Rocks Climbing School* (tel. 304/567–2600 or 800/548–0108) or *Blackwater Outdoor Center* in Davis (tel. 304/259–5117 or 800/328–4798).

Snowshoe/Silver Creek Mountain Resort (Snowshoe Ski Area, tel. 304/572–1000; Silver Creek Ski Area, tel. 304/572–4000). Snowshoe is the largest ski area in the Mid-Atlantic region, with 53 trails, full snowmaking, a sledding area, and a park for snowboarders. One lift ticket serves both areas. Snowshoe's golf course and mountain-bike trails have made the resort a year-round playground.

Watoga State Park (tel. 304/799–4087 or 800/225–5982). Seventeen miles south of Marlinton, this is West Virginia's first and largest state park. Recreational facilities, including a pool, cabins, a commissary, and a lake, are open in the summertime.

Restaurants

The **Red Fox** (tel. 304/572–1111), slopeside at Snowshoe Mountain Resort, has outstanding haute cuisine with a country touch. The restaurant at **Blackwater Falls State Park** (tel. 304/259–5216), perched on the Blackwater Canyon rim near Davis, has a limited but tasty menu. **Bright Morning B&B** (tel. 304/259–5119) in Davis serves good breakfast and dinner buffets. You can join the mountain bikers for local trout and other hearty, healthful fare next to the fireplace at the **Inn at Elk River** (tel. 304/572–3771; *see below*).

Tourist Information

Lewisburg Convention and Visitors Bureau (105 Church St., Lewisburg 24901, tel. 304/645–1000 or 800/833–2068). **Pocahontas County Tourism** (Box 275, Marlinton 24954, tel. 304/799–4636 or 800/336–7009). **Potomac Highlands Convention and Visitors Bureau** (Box 2758, Elkins 26241, tel. 304/636–8400). **West Virginia Department of Commerce** (2101 Washington St. E, Charleston 24305, tel. 800/225–5982).

The Cardinal Inn

Rte. 219 (Rte. 1, Box 1), Huttonsville, WV 26273, tel. 304/335–6149 or 800/335–6149

Eunice Kwasniewski has single-handedly worked miracles at this inn, a yellow-brick Queen Anne Victorian overlooking the Tygart River Valley. She restored this cavernous place all by herself (it took a full year and 438 gallons of stripper to remove the paint from the oak woodwork). She's also restoring a 19th-century log cabin out back, a laborious process because 20-foot-long logs have not been easy to come by. Eunice envisions the cabin as a West Virginia crafts shop. The turreted main house was built by Elihu Hutton in 1901 and is surrounded by a big white wraparound porch, providing views of the valley and the Cheat Mountain range beyond. Two of the most desirable guest rooms are the five-window Paisley Room and the rather eerie third-floor Turret Room, complete with a mounted deer head. The inn is 25 miles north of Snowshoe Mountain Resort, the Mid-Atlantic's largest downhill ski area. There's also fine cross-country skiing, and in summer, mountain biking, rafting, hiking, and golf at Snowshoe's Gary Player–designed Hawthorne Valley Golf Course.

🏨 *9 double rooms share 3 baths. TV with VCR in sitting room. $40–$55; full breakfast. AE, MC, V. No smoking, no pets.*

Cheat Mountain Club

Red Run Rd., Cheat Bridge (11 miles south of Huttonsville), Box 28, Durbin, WV 26264, tel. 304/456–4627, fax 304/456–3192

Standing 3,800 feet above sea level, on the shoulder of the colossal Cheat Mountain and surrounded by nine of West Virginia's 10 highest peaks and the 901,000-acre Monongahela National Forest, the Cheat Mountain Club has a setting that will always be enough to make it special among inns. Lovers of the outdoors are sure to appreciate the changing seasons here, whether the lodge is buried in snow, blanketed with wild rhododendrons, or enveloped in a fog so thick that no one bothers to step outside the front door. The grounds include 188 acres, across which the trout-rich Shavers Fork River flows. From it a tracery of old logging roads spirals away into the mountains—one route leading 18 miles south to Bald Knob. Five miles of trails within the club's boundaries, along which shy black bears are often spied, are groomed for hiking, mountain biking, and cross-country skiing.

Until 1988 this paradise was privately owned, used as a retreat for the executives of a logging company. Later it was sold to a group of five West Virginia families who opened it to the public. Resident manager Cynthia Loebig brings a knowledge of the outdoors and three excellent meals that are included in the club's daily rate. Fly-fishing–pro Frank Oliverio is called in to teach his delicate art to novices or share his knowledge of local streams with the more experienced.

The pine-paneled guest rooms on the lodge's second floor are functionally decorated and immaculately kept. Only one has a private bath, but the large, multiple shared bathrooms (one for women, another for men) are extremely comfortable and outfitted with tubs, showers, and piles of fresh linen; there's also a sink in each guest room. The third floor holds a dormitory-style room that can sleep extra kids. Downstairs is a large gathering hall scattered with Adirondack chairs, and a dining room with self-serve bar. There is almost always a crackling fire in both of the huge stone hearths. The room is full of topographical maps, magazines, and books and is a meeting place where guests enjoy predinner drinks.

🏨 *1 king-size room with bath; 7 doubles, 1 single, and dormitory (sleeps 6) share 2 multiple baths. Box lunches available, 2 meeting rooms, game room, fishing, mountain biking, cross-country* *skiing, canoeing, horseshoes, and snow-shoes. $80–$150 per person; full break-fast, lunch, and dinner. MC, V. No smoking in bedrooms, no pets.*

The Current

Denmar Rd., Box 135, Hillsboro, WV 24946, tel. 304/653–4722

The Current, a 1904 white frame farm-house with only a modest touch of gin-gerbread, stands along a winding country lane outside the town of Hillsboro, the birthplace of Nobel Prize–winning writer Pearl Buck and the site of the General Store, which sells everything from red Union suits and antiques to handmade butter and cheese carved from huge rolls. To reach the Current, follow signs for the Greenbrier River Trail, past fields inhabited by buffalo, peacocks, and lla-mas (part of a rich weekend farmer's pri-vate zoo) and a one-room Presbyterian Church. The bed-and-breakfast is owned by Leslee McCarty, who came to this part of her home state to work in rural com-munity development. She is now active in several local groups, including the Greenbrier River Watershed Associa-tion. In fact, most of her guests arrive on foot, bike, or by canoe from the nearby river trail and are thrilled with a soak in the hot tub and a quiet snooze on the porch. Leslee's house is full of oak wood-work, quilts, Victorian clothing, and airy white curtains. She also owns the old church and plans to convert it to addi-tional lodging to accommodate the de-mands of the cycling crowd.

🏠 *3 double rooms share 2½ baths, 1 suite. TV in sitting room, hot tub, ken-nel. $40–$75; full breakfast. MC, V. No smoking.*

The General Lewis Inn

301 E. Washington St., Lewisburg, WV 24901, tel. 304/645–2600 or 800/628–4454, fax 304/645–2600

This is a country hostel of perfect pro-portions (just 25 rooms), run by the Hock family since 1928. It lies in a shady res-idential section of Lewisburg, a National Register town with a historic academy, stone church, and Confederate cemetery. Down the street from the inn are pleas-ant shops selling West Virginia quilts, ladies' dresses, and antiques. You can see everything Lewisburg has to offer in an easy afternoon, leaving you lots of time to sit on the veranda at the General Lewis. Out front there's a restored car-riage, which used to rumble over the James River and Kanawha Turnpike (now Route 60), and in the back garden is owner Mary Hock Morgan's large old dollhouse.

Mary's parents started the General Lewis in the original house, built in the early 1800s; the architect who designed the West Virginia governor's mansion in Charleston later supervised a 1920s ad-dition to the building, which blends flaw-lessly with the older section. The Hocks were great antiques collectors, and the inn is full of their prizes, including farm-ing implements and a nickelodeon that still plays "The Man in the Moon Has His Eyes on You." The front desk came from the Sweet Chalybeate Springs Hotel and was reputedly leaned on by Patrick Henry and Thomas Jefferson. In fact, the only non-antiques you'll come across are the chairs in the dining room.

Though the inn is ably managed by Nan Morgan, granddaughter of Randolph and Mary Hock, Mary Hock Morgan is usually around to show children where to find the checkers. She lived in the General Lewis until the age of 15 and is dedicated to keeping it retrogressive. The inn has some newfangled touches, such as central heat and air-conditioning with individual room controls. But Mary balks at refinishing the furniture; she wants guests to see where generations of hands have rubbed and polished the cannonball beds.

All the rooms on the first and second floors are different, and when unoccu-pied, the doors are left open so that guests might peek inside. Because the same rate can apply to rooms of radically varying size, guests might want to ask for the largest in any given category. But even if you wind up in a cozy chamber, you won't be disappointed.

🏨 *23 double rooms with baths, 2 suites. Restaurant, room service during restaurant hrs, air-conditioning, cable TV, phones in rooms. $75–$112; breakfast extra. AE, D, MC, V. No smoking, $10 charge for pets.*

Graceland Inn

100 Campus Dr., Davis & Elkins College, Elkins, WV 26241, tel. 800/624–3157, fax 304/637–1809

When Sen. Henry Gassaway Davis built this extravagant "summer retreat" in 1893, he named it for his fifth child, Grace. Its turreted, Queen Anne architecture blends native oak, cherry, and maple timbers with Tiffany glass and a broad, imposing stairway, lending a country elegance to the rustic castle, now an inn run by Davis & Elkins College and its students. After standing empty for two decades, the National Historic Landmark underwent a $2 million restoration and reopened in 1996. With sweeping views of the town below, it has a sitting room and nine huge guest rooms (one is octagonal and measures 600 square feet), lavishly decorated with reproductions and some period pieces. Eventually, 13 rooms will be renovated. A light breakfast greets guests, but a grander repast is dinner in the Mingo Room, featuring smoked salmon pâté, veal Oscar, and grilled duck breast. Grace would be pleased at her namesake's Renaissance.

🏨 *5 double rooms with baths, 3 suites, 1 single with bath. Restaurant, TV in public room, phones in rooms, nearby conference center. $75–$175; Continental breakfast. AE, D, MC, V. No smoking, no pets.*

Hampshire House 1884

165 N. Grafton St., Romney, WV 26757, tel. 304/822–7171

Route 50, the main route across the state in the north, passes through the town of Romney at the South Branch of the Potomac River. Here you'll find Hampshire House, a perfectly kept redbrick Victorian, on a street behind the courthouse. The house and its garden are owned by Scott Simmons and his wife, Jane, who also manage the property. A substantial breakfast of whole-grain pancakes, fruit waffles, or omelets is always included in the room rate.

Scott is a collector of antique lamps, which occupy tables all over the inn. The five guest rooms are lovely, decorated almost exclusively with Victorian antiques, including Eastlake beds, Rococo Revival chairs and settees, and quilts. In addition to the formal parlor downstairs, you'll also find a big music room with a wide-screen TV, VCR, and pump organ.

Nearby is the Potomac Eagle Scenic Railroad, which hauls nature lovers on a three-hour, narrated excursion through a remote area bordered by the South Branch and home to American bald eagles. The train operates weekends from May through October.

🏨 *5 double rooms with baths. Air-conditioning, TV in all rooms, TV with VCR in music room, fireplaces in 3 rooms. $65–$85; full breakfast. AE, D, DC, MC, V. No smoking, no pets.*

Henderson House and A Governor's Inn

A Governor's Inn, 76 E. Main St.; Henderson House, 29 Sedgewick St., Buckhannon, WV 26201, tel. 304/472–2516

As a youngster growing up in Buckhannon, Jerry Henderson was intrigued by the 1910 American Four-Square house she passed on her way to school. "There was always something going on," she says, "people quilting on the front porch or making apple butter, or playing the dulcimer." In 1990, when she and her husband were looking for a potential B&B, the house of her childhood dreams was waiting for her. The six guest rooms, which share three adjoining baths, now have polished wood floors, original crystal chandeliers, brass beds, and other antiques.

A few years later, the Hendersons acquired the Queen Anne house where West Virginia's second governor lived, not far from their first inn. They spruced up the three-story brick mansion with a wraparound veranda and filled it with period furniture, knickknacks, and a vivid color.

Jerry varies the menu at both houses, switching from bread pudding with amaretto sauce one day to a cheese soufflé or French toast stuffed with cream cheese and fresh strawberries on another.

Buckhannon, home of West Virginia Wesleyan College, is a historic little town, good for browsing. It hosts the West Virginia Strawberry Festival in May, the state Square Dance Conference in August, and many activities centered around the college. At the West Virginia Wildlife Center, indigenous critters can be viewed in their natural setting.

▦ *Each house has 6 double rooms with shared baths. Air-conditioning, TV in public room, board games. $59–$79; full breakfast. AE, D, MC, V. No smoking, no pets.*

Hutton House

Box 88, Huttonsville, WV 26273, tel. 304/ 335–6701

Most of the guests at this inn overlooking the Tygart River Valley have been here before. "Regulars" have fallen in love with this Queen Anne Victorian, just as Loretta Murray and Dean Ahern did while honeymooning in the area in 1987. The couple gave up their careers and moved from Philadelphia to undertake the meticulous restoration of the house, showcasing original oak woodwork, ornate windows, arched pocket doors, a winding staircase, and a three-story turret.

Guest rooms are decorated in different styles, from the Art Deco–style Waterfall Room with its veneer furniture to the brass bed and ice-cream-parlor table of the dormered Corrine's Room. The antiques-filled and formal parlor is a quiet place to read, but the recreation room with its bumper pool table, TV, and other games sees the most use.

Breakfast is a feast of fresh fruit, crème brûlée, maple-walnut and multigrain pancakes, cheese-filled French toast, and a variety of egg dishes.

▦ *6 double rooms with baths. TV in public room, parlor, recreation room. $70–$75; full breakfast. MC, V. No smoking, no pets.*

The Inn at Elk River

Elk River Touring Center, U.S. Hwy. 219, Slatyfork, WV 26291, tel. 304/572– 3771

Also known as the Willis Farm, this lodging complex on the banks of the Elk River is an outdoor recreation center, too. Owner Gil Willis came to the area in 1977 for the downhill skiing; today he outfits Nordic skiing expeditions on a 50-kilometer trail system, conducts mountain-biking clinics, and organizes several multiday bike trips. The 100-year-old sheep farm now offers five guest rooms in the old farmhouse, two two-bedroom cottages, and a new lodge holding five more guest rooms, an equipment shop, and a restaurant (where diners feast on local trout and game, vegetarian dishes, homemade biscuits, and other stick-to-the-ribs mountain-biker fare at tables comfortably clustered around a fireplace). The lodge is best for couples, since all its rooms have private baths. But the old farmhouse, with its eclectic, many-bedded rooms, common space with wood-burning stove, and hot tub, is perfect for families and groups. You wouldn't call any of the accommodations luxurious, but at Elk River no one spends much time indoors.

🏠 *5 double rooms with baths, 5 suites share 3 baths, 2 2-bedroom cottages. Restaurant with adjacent pub, hot tub, swimming hole, Nordic ski trails. $45–$150; full breakfast. MC, V. No smoking in farmhouse, inn, or restaurant, no pets, 2-night minimum on weekends in ski season.*

Lynn's Inn

Rte. 4, Box 40, Lewisburg, WV 24901, tel. 304/645–2003 or 800/304–2003

This white-columned farmhouse, built in 1935 on 16 acres just north of the Lewisburg town line, has a long history as an inn. Owner Richard McLaughlin is no stranger to innkeeping either; his parents ran McLaughlin's Tourist Home in this house for many years while he was growing up. There are four guest rooms on the first and second floors, upstairs and downstairs sitting rooms, and a peaceful front porch from which you can see the McLaughlins' Hereford and Angus cows and watch Lynn McLaughlin gathering eggs. The guest rooms feature many pleasant touches, including locally handmade quilts, Fenton glass lamps, white wicker and golden oak furniture, walnut bedsteads that have been in the family for years, and rocking chairs, which Lynn feels are important to have in every room. Her breakfasts include those fresh eggs, homemade jellies and jams, and country ham. Often she'll whip up something special, like a hash-brown casserole or a quiche, and there's always freshly ground gourmet coffee. In the evening Lynn serves homemade refreshments in the sitting rooms.

🏠 *4 double rooms with baths. Ceiling fans in rooms, cable TV and phones in both sitting rooms. $60–$75; full breakfast. MC, V. No smoking, no pets.*

The Warfield House

318 Buffalo St., Elkins, WV 26241, tel. 304/636–4555

For five weeks every July and August the town of Elkins hosts the popular Augusta Festival, at which visitors can sign up for courses in blacksmithing, Appalachian literature, autoharp playing, weaving, herb gardening, and log-house construction, among other topics. For accommodations while visiting the festival there's no better place than the Warfield House (formerly the Wayside Inn), which sits close to the grounds of the local college, where the festival takes place. The white Queen Anne cottage was built in 1901 and is operated by Paul and Connie Garnett, a friendly couple who are restoring the property. Known as the Wayside during Elkins's boom days of coal, timber, and the railroad, the inn has a sunporch, two parlors, a library, and a formal dining room. Its glowing stained glass, intricately detailed terracotta fireplace, and grand front porch are typical of the town's turn-of-the-century architecture. One small, white-washed room, hidden above the kitchen, is especially romantic.

Across the street there's an inviting park with a playground and picnic tables. The college has tennis courts, and downtown the combined Starr Café and Augusta Books is a good idling spot. In October you can view the changing leaves or stop in on the weeklong Mountain State Forest Festival. Nearby are skiing, rock climbing, and kayaking.

🏠 *3 double rooms with baths, 2 doubles share bath. $65–$75; full breakfast. Cash or check only. No smoking, no pets.*

Woodcrest

Rte. 2, Box 520, Beckwith, WV 25840, tel. 304/574–3870

It took schoolteacher Luther Lewallen and his wife, Judy, three years to overcome legal tangles and finalize the purchase of this 100-acre gentleman's farm—and several more years to reverse the process of neglect and decay. The gray-shingled main house, built in 1928, is shipshape now and comfortably furnished with reproduction antiques (and a few real ones). All rooms have queen-size beds, and the two largest rooms also have hide-a-bed couches. Just beyond the big red barn, 300 feet from the main house, is a four-bedroom cabin with barnwood siding on the interior, a kitchen, and a large screened porch.

Woodcrest is near Fayetteville, in the heart of West Virginia's white-water rafting country. Trails for hiking and biking (rental mountain bikes are delivered to the inn) run through the property, and a Civil War cemetery on the property invites history buffs. Just a half-hour's drive away, llama lovers can try trekking with the surefooted camel cousins carrying generous gourmet lunches (contact New River Llama Trekking Co., a first in the state, at 304/574–1117).

There's a lot to be said for just hanging out on the shady back porch, down by the fishing pond, or around the swimming pool, but if you're aiming to run one of the local rivers, as most guests are, Judy's whopping, traditional breakfast served family style—eggs, bacon, sausage, pancakes, waffles, potatoes, and homemade biscuits and cinnamon rolls—will put power in your paddle. The inn is also a popular spot for weddings, with a white, horse-drawn carriage providing an especially romantic touch.

▦ *4 rooms with baths (5th room available but must share bath with another room), 4-bedroom cabin with 2 baths. Air-conditioning, TV room, library, room service, shelter by pond for picnics. $50–$70 (cabin: $100 for 4 people, $15 per additional person); full breakfast. AE, D, MC, V. No smoking, no pets, closed Nov.–Mar.*

Directory 1
Alphabetical

Directory 2
Geographical

Notes

Notes

Notes

Notes

WHEREVER YOU TRAVEL, *H*ELP IS NEVER FAR AWAY.

From planning your trip to

providing travel assistance along

the way, American Express®

Travel Service Offices are

always there to help

you do more.

American Express Travel Service
Offices are found in central locations
throughout the United States.
For the office nearest you, please call
1-800-AXP-3429.

Travel

http://www.americanexpress.com/travel